Jim Haynes was born in Sydney, the son of British migrants, and educated at Botany Public School, Sydney Boys' High School and Sydney Teachers' College. He taught writing, literature, history and drama in schools and universities from outback New South Wales to Britain and back again (attending race meetings whenever and wherever possible) and has two master's degrees in literature, from the University of New England and the University of Wales.

A professional entertainer and songwriter since 1988, Jim had several hits with novelty songs like 'Don't Call Wagga Wagga Wagga' and 'Since Cheryl Went Feral', and many albums of his songs, verse and humour were released on labels such as Festival, ABC, EMI and Sony. He still performs in variety shows and at festivals and has a weekend Australiana segment on Radio 2UE's long running *George and Paul Show*. He has also written and compiled twenty-two books.

An AJC/ATC member for many years, Jim lives at Moore Park in Sydney with his wife Robyn, collects colonial art, plays tennis three times a week and supports the Sydney Swans and London soccer club Queens Park Rangers. He can walk to Randwick racecourse in ten minutes and his favourite television channel is Thoroughbred Central.

ALSO BY JIM HAYNES

Great Australian Scams, Cons and Rorts
Australia's Most Unbelievable True Stories
The Best Gallipoli Yarns and Forgotten Stories
Australia's Best Unknown Stories
The Best Australian Yarns
The Best Australian Bush Stories
The Best Australian Sea Stories
The Best Australian Trucking Stories
Best Australian Racing Stories
The Great Australian Book of Limericks
The Big Book of Verse for Aussie Kids (editor)

THE BIG BOOK OF AUSTRALIAN RACING STORIES

GREAT TALES OF THE TURF FROM JORROCKS TO BLACK CAVIAR

JIM HAYNES

This book is dedicated to the memory and legend of J.B. 'Bart' Cummings, 1927–2015.

This edition published in 2017
First published in 2015

Allen & Unwin
83 Alexander Street
Crows Nest NSW 2065
Australia
Phone: (61 2) 8425 0100
Email: info@allenandunwin.com
Web: www.allenandunwin.com

EU Authorised Representative: Easy Access System Europe, Mustamäe tee 50, 10621 Tallinn, Estonia, gpsr.requests@easproject.com

Cataloguing-in-Publication details are available
from the National Library of Australia
www.trove.nla.gov.au

ISBN 978 1 76063 240 3

Death in the Afternoon, *The Cup is More than a Horse Race* and *Why We Came to Love Schillaci* taken from *True Grit* by Les Carlyon. Copyright © Les Carlyon 2013. Reprinted by permission of Random House Australia Pty Limited.

Set in Minion Pro by Midland Typesetters, Australia
Printed and bound in Australia by Pegasus Media & Logistics

15 14 13 12 11

The paper in this book is FSC® certified. FSC® promotes environmentally responsible, socially beneficial and economically viable management of the world's forests.

CONTENTS

PART 5 THE CUP IS MORE THAN A HORSE RACE

PART 6 A PUNT ON THE PONIES

PART 7 RACING CHARACTERS

PART 8 JUMP RACES ARE DIFFERENT

PART 9 THE GOLDEN AGE

FOREWORD

My lifetime love affair with horseracing began the first day I was dressed in my Sunday best and taken to Randwick by my dad. We probably went into the Leger enclosure, although I don't remember exactly.

If Mum was with us we always went straight into the Paddock. If it was just Dad and me we'd go into the Leger and the 'rule' was that if Dad backed a winner in either of the first two races, he paid the extra admission and we went through to the Paddock.

Although Tommy Smith and George Moore dominated Sydney racing back then, my favourite jockey was Jack Thompson, known as 'Thommo' or 'the Professor', and I always backed an old black stayer named Valerius that Thommo rode in Sir Alan Potter's all-dark-blue silks. Valerius was my favourite horse, I think because he was black and I liked his name. At school I enjoyed Ancient History and Latin, though I failed Latin, probably because I was too fond of *Turf Monthly* and not too fond of *Bembrick's Latin Grammar*.

When I say 'I backed' I mean I tried to get my father to put a bet on the horse for me, either at the track or at the local SP bookie. Dad would ride his bike up to the pub some Saturdays and put bets on and then come home and listen to the radio as he worked in the yard or in his shed.

As a kid I got to hang around the stables owned by Sid Nicholls at Mascot, because I went to school with his son. Many training families, such as the Pigginses, O'Sullivans and Nicholls, had stables in Mascot. Prior to World War II there were five racetracks in that area. As well as Randwick, there was Kensington, where the

University of New South Wales is now; Rosebery, which became a housing estate in the 1960s; Ascot, which made way for the airport; and the showpiece, Victoria Park, which is now a housing estate near Moore Park.

Some of these venues operated as 'pony tracks'—a forgotten part of our racing history. Many people today assume that thoroughbred racing is the only form of horseracing we've ever had, but 'unregistered' or 'pony racing' was huge in Sydney and Melbourne from the 1890s to the 1930s, and I am pleased to say this book has a whole section about pony racing, for which I am mostly deeply indebted to Wayne Peake, Professor of Social History at Western Sydney University.

As a kid I was fascinated by the stable atmosphere at Sid Nicholls's place, and he was kind enough to let me go to the races with the horses and even gave me an official finish photo of his good handicapper, Sea Hound, winning at Hawkesbury. That photo still hangs in my office.

Sea Hound ran second in the Villiers twice and was one of the first horses on which I ever won any real money. The 'welter' was usually the 'lucky last' on any Sydney race program and I got my dad to put my pocket money on Sea Hound at the local SP one Saturday. The gallant old gelding beat a horse called Ginnagulla in a photo finish at odds of 12 to 1. It was one of my first small steps along the rocky road of joy and pain that is the life of the punter.

One birthday I was given a collection of short stories by Jim Bendrodt. My mum was very keen to get me reading as a kid and books were always a big part of my life. But by the time I was about ten, she was trying to stop me reading all night so I'd be able to get up and go to school next morning. I had a torch hidden under my mattress and, after she turned my light out, I would read under the covers until I fell asleep or the batteries went flat. Those Jim Bendrodt stories thrilled me as a kid and I read them over and over. My favourites are in this collection, along with stories by two other well-known racing writers I admire greatly, Les Carlyon and David Hickie.

Wherever life took me I always made sure to visit the local racetracks. As a schoolteacher in the country I attended picnic and bush race meetings. When I lived in the UK for a few years I was able to get a taste of racing there and learned to love 'the jumps'. Easter visits to family in Adelaide always meant the Great Eastern Steeplechase, and business trips to Melbourne, Brisbane or Adelaide somehow always ended up including a day at Flemington, Eagle Farm or Morphettville.

Some of these stories and verses have appeared in previous collections I have done for Allen & Unwin and ABC Books. My work collecting rhymed verse kept bringing me into contact with great racing stories and yarns in the form of poetry by great horsemen and racing men such as Adam Lindsay Gordon, Will Ogilvie, Harry Morant, C.J. Dennis and Banjo Paterson.

Racing people are generally generous and helpful and I am blessed to have some friends, both old and new, who have contributed freely to this book. Bruce and Ellen Montgomerie, with whom I play tennis twice a week, introduced me to Betty Lane Holland and Peter Harris, and I met Wayne Peake through talking about his book on pony tracks on radio. Tony Kneebone, Penny Hand and Phil Purser I met via the internet, as one does these days.

Racing has given me many enjoyable moments and memories. Literature about racing has given me some great experiences as a reader. Writing, collecting and editing these stories and verses has been a labour of love and I hope there are some enjoyable moments and memories in here for you.

Part 1
RACING MEMORIES

INTRODUCTION—BEING THERE

Memories are unreliable.

The way you remember an event often differs from the reality. You find an old photo and realise you have had the wrong memory of a certain event all along.

Or you tell a great story and someone who was there says, 'No, it wasn't like that, the favourite was a bay, not a chestnut, and he didn't come along the rail, he came around the field and won easily.'

It's also true that the significant part of an event in your memory may not be the important part historically. You may remember how good the apple pie was at lunch and not remember who won the main race.

It's no good asking your wife, but you do anyway.

'Who won the Metropolitan that year we had lunch in the members with the Davidsons?'

She muses.

'That grey horse with the funny name with a Z in it ran third that year. It had green and pink silks and Emily Davidson wore that black and white empire-line dress and a red hat . . . don't know who won . . . sorry. I can't remember anything that far back, darling.'

Just how vivid a racing memory is also depends on where your money was at the time.

I have amazingly sharp memories of an old Tamworth-trained, mid-week horse named Mr Mohican winning the last race at Warwick Farm one day when I managed to get 20 to 1 in the ring from Eric Conlon and also took a box trifecta with the two favourites who dutifully finished second and third. I can see the finish of that race as clearly as I can see my desk and computer right now. I have no idea what year that was, though.

I've been lucky enough to be present to see some great horses race at some great racetracks. Here are a few random reminiscences. These memories don't include races I merely heard on the radio or watched on television; although you actually see a lot more on television than when you're on the course. This is all about being there.

I have a childhood memory of seeing Tulloch carry 63 kilos up the rise and down that Randwick straight to gallant defeat behind Sharply, carrying 48.5 kilograms, in the 1961 Sydney Cup. Handicaps can be cruel to champions, and nobody who roared for Tulloch that day at Randwick loved him any less when he failed to catch Sharply. It was a fairly sombre crowd after the race, though, I remember that, or perhaps it was just that my dad wasn't saying much.

Randwick is a track that really sorts out the champs from the pretenders down the straight. True front-runners have to be great horses to hold on up the rise, and it also takes a great horse to come from behind up the rise and pass another good one.

Which brings us to Sunline's second Doncaster in 2002. To this day I swear Shogun Lodge won that race. It was certainly a dead heat on the grounds of sheer guts and grit. They raced side by side for two entire furlongs that day. I still can't believe you could get 5 to 1 about Sunline in the ring when they jumped. And I still can't believe I didn't take it!

I should throw in Private Steer's 2004 Doncaster victory, although it was really a match race between one amazing horse and the rest of the field.

I can't even remember what I backed to beat her, but I distinctly remember being mesmerised as Glen Boss began to weave his way through the entire field like a slalom skier on horseback. They were as good as last on the turn and had no hope, not a hope in the world. Then, as they straightened, Glen Boss just picked her up and balanced her and she sidestepped her way through like a rugby winger against a tiring pack of forwards. I remember seeing the dark blue jacket with the lightning bolt move through the crowd of horses as if it was all being stage-managed by the best stunt director in Hollywood.

It was never in doubt once the dance began, she moved right through the field and put out her head and won. I was waiting for the pirouette at the end. It was beautiful to watch. It gave new meaning to the cliché 'poetry in motion'. It was enough to make a grown man cry. In fact, it did make a grown man cry. Private Steer's big burly owner, after whose grandmother she was named, cried at the presentation and I went a little teary myself; I hadn't backed her.

My own stupidity on the punt often brings tears to my eyes. Private Steer would have won the Miracle Mile at Harold Park if they'd held it that autumn and she'd started in it. I should have known that.

Flemington is the classic course for drawn-out nose-to-nose battles; the long straight there probably produces more of the 'war of attrition' type finishes than anywhere else in Australia.

My top Flemington memory is the Melbourne Cup of 1994. Vintage Crop was favourite but was under an injury cloud. The Caulfield Cup winner, Paris Lane, was also well backed and I fancied a chestnut mare by El Qahira; her name was Alcove and she had won the Oaks at Randwick in the autumn.

It was a typical Melbourne day with drizzle and grey skies for an hour or so followed by quite pleasant spring sunshine for a while. I love Melbourne but I always lose coats, scarves, pullovers and umbrellas when I'm there. You take clothes off and put them on so often in Melbourne, due to the changeable bloody weather. I tend to leave a trail of lost property in cabs and restaurants, trains and trams.

I have to admit that I am not a fan of Cup Day on the course, I like racing too much and the holiday revelry gets in the way of my enjoyment. It's one day when I am quite happy to watch the race on television. In evidence at the Cup in 1994 were the usual loonies, drunks and show-offs. I saw at least five different Elvises, a few Batmans, numerous pink tutu-clad fairies despite the cool weather, and a Phantom or two.

Having had a good look at the previous year's winner, that wonderful Irish stayer Vintage Crop, in the exercise yard, I decided the bandages looked rather ominous and plonked heavily on Alcove. As it turned out Vintage Crop could have won his second Melbourne Cup that day. The injury didn't seem to worry him and was certainly superficial; perhaps Dermot Weld was up to his usual tricks, talking down the champion's chances.

What stopped Vintage Crop winning was an eccentric ride by Michael Kinnane. Having attempted to push him across early in vain, the jockey let him race wide for the entire 2 miles and his effort to finish seventh, carrying 60 kilograms and having covered about an extra furlong, was really quite courageous.

I was standing at the rail about two furlongs out and I have a snapshot of a split-second of that race etched in my memory, a colour photograph of one exact moment.

You hear commentators talk every year about the 'wall of horses' as the Cup field swings the corner and straightens for the run home. But to experience that sight first-hand gives meaning to the cliché whenever you hear it afterwards. The leading bunch seemed to include at least half the field as they thundered past my position. The ground shook and the roar of the crowd, deafening since the jump, reached a painful intensity.

At the exact moment when that wall of horses passed my position, Alcove put her head in front of the field. I saw Paddy Payne, in the blue and white striped silks, drive her to the lead. Her eyes were wide and her nostrils flared as her chestnut head reached the front. I saw it all in incredible detail, and I can still see it clearly now in my mind's eye. I also had time, somehow, to notice that her bandages were unravelled and discoloured with blood and mud. Then the horses were gone, out of frame.

Jeune outstayed them all to defeat Paris Lane by a length and three-quarters. This came as a surprise to many, including me, who thought the imported stallion was best over a middle distance. Alcove had been galloped on in the middle stages and ran a brave race to finish fifth.

The best race I ever saw in Melbourne was at Caulfield, in the Yalumba Stakes of 2002, a match race between Sunline and Lonhro, with a few other lesser lights making up the numbers.

The huge mare was approaching the end of her career, while Lonhro was nearing his peak. I have written about the race in another story in this collection, 'They All Love Sunline', but it is worth noting that Trevor McKee, owner of Sunline, and the Ingham brothers, who owned Lonhro, rate as true enthusiasts and lovers of racing. It is to the credit of McKee that Sunline raced on as a mare to give us all so many wonderful memories. The McKee motto was always, 'We're here to race.'

The Inghams were also believers in racing horses while they were still fit and willing to compete. I will never forget Jack Ingham's answer to a question put to him after Octagonal had won his second Mercedes Classic and broken the stakes-winning record. A reporter asked Jack why he was going to risk running the champion again in the Queen Elizabeth Stakes when the horse was worth many millions as a stallion and had absolutely nothing to prove. Jack simply looked at the reporter and asked him, 'Don't *you* want to see him race again?'

The victor in the next epic from my memory bank carried the same famous all-cerise colours as Octagonal and his son Lonhro. The track was Rosehill and it was Golden Slipper Day, 2003. The great West Australian champion Northerly had never had much luck in Sydney but at weight-for-age against a depleted and pretty ordinary field, he was red-hot favourite to win the Mercedes Classic. It was a matter of 'how far' in most racegoers' minds.

The race that year was looked upon as a mere appetiser for the Golden Slipper later in the day. It would be a chance for Sydney to see the great Northerly going through the motions in a Group 1 event, a chance to salute a champion, an added attraction to the big dash-for-cash by the over-developed babies in the Slipper later in the afternoon.

The problem was that nobody had explained all that to a tough old stayer called Freemason.

Freemason was a real character. A bay gelding by Grand Lodge, he had won the Queensland Derby and the Frank Packer Plate way back in 2000. Since then he had contested most staying events in Sydney and seemed to make a habit of running a place when he started at huge odds, but running nowhere whenever he was fancied.

I made a habit of backing Freemason for a place whenever he got out past 20 to 1 in the betting; the longer the odds, the more I fancied his chances. I didn't think he would be up to a weight-for-age clash with Northerly, though. Nobody did.

I was playing host to a couple of rather beautiful showbiz friends at Rosehill that day, the wonderful Melinda Schneider and cabaret artist Nikki Bennett. Having to be civil and attentive to women at the races is never conducive to backing winners. Oddly, I also find that being at the races, or anywhere else, with beautiful women can be very distracting. Anyway, whatever the reason, I didn't check Freemason's price and I didn't have a bet. But I am wandering off topic. This is a list of memories of great races. The list that comprises my memories of lost chances on the punt is one so long that it can never be recorded.

Freemason was in the mood to race that day. In fact, he seemed so disgusted at the false pace early in the race that he took the lead as he rarely did. When Northerly came alongside in the back straight, Freemason pushed down his accelerator and decided to take the champ on, almost 1400 metres from home. It was the only time I ever witnessed a nose-to-nose, full-on, no-holds-barred, flat-out, ding-dong stoush for the entire final 1200 metres of a race.

The sheer audacity of Freemason's mad challenge when Northerly came alongside seemed to win the crowd over to support the old Sydney stayer. After all, he was a local horse and his lack of respect to the interstate hero seemed somehow courageous. Stupid, bound to end in embarrassment, a mere *beau geste* . . . but rather wonderful!

Once Northerly responded to the challenge the two horses just kept daring each other to go faster and faster. By the 1000-metre point the crowd sensed something weird and wonderful was going on; by the 400-metre mark they were in a frenzy. When would this crazy old horse realise he wasn't as good as Northerly?

The answer was . . . never.

Freemason, racing on the inside, refused to let Northerly past and there was never more than a neck between them over the final 1200 metres. They raced past the post locked together and a photo showed that Freemason had won by a short half-head in 2 minutes 26.82 seconds, a brilliant time for 2000 metres.

Punters and racegoers usually think through their pockets, but sometimes they respond with their hearts when magic occurs. Unwanted in the betting ring, Freemason was cheered again and again as he returned to scale carrying the all-cerise colours of the Ingham brothers.

I saw Black Caviar race several times and she is the best I've ever seen. She was in a class of her own: she wasn't a battler like Octagonal or a tough fighter like Makybe Diva, she was simply better than every other sprinter in the world. She was unbeatable.

The best race I ever saw, however, was the encounter of four great three-year-olds in the 1996 AJC Derby at Randwick: Nothin' Leica Dane, Saintly, Filante and Octagonal.

That race really turned the tide for racing in Sydney, and a huge crowd had flocked to the course in anticipation of the best derby for years. And they got far more than their money's worth. It seems to me that racing crowds at big meetings have been on the increase in Sydney ever since that day. It made racing more than just a form of betting in the public's mind. It made racing a spectator sport once again.

You couldn't get a seat in the stands. The atmosphere was electric. It was the biggest crowd for 30 years and the race lived up to all hype and expectations. In fact, it surpassed anything you could have imagined.

Up the famous Randwick rise and down the straight they came, racing stride for stride, the VRC Derby winner, a future Cox Plate and Melbourne Cup winner, a future Epsom and Yalumba Stakes winner, all three of them at their peak and flat out trying to stay ahead, or get ahead, of one of the toughest and bravest horses to ever race in Australia—the Big O, as he was known.

How Octagonal fought on to win that race is part of Australian racing folklore. He seemed to race quite low to the track when he let down and he just ground away, a dark brown nemesis slowly overhauling the two big chestnut horses on his inside, with his neck extended the way he always did to get his nose to the post first, as if he knew where the camera was.

I never saw a better contested finish to a race in my life and I never saw a horse with more will to win than Octagonal.

I backed him that day, too.

I took my dad to the races to see Octagonal's derby win. Dad was pretty old by then and getting a bit frail, but it was only fair. After all, my dad had taken me to see Tulloch's great attempt to win the Sydney Cup in 1961, with 63 kg on his back.

FROM POWDER PUFFS TO PIONEERS

PENNY HAND

I will never forget the day in 2005 when Kathy and Tracy O'Hara made history at Gosford, New South Wales, by being the first sisters to dead-heat in a horse race anywhere in the world. It was a sign of the future. Female jockeys were here to stay, and they were riding winners. Less than a decade later, at Orange races on Melbourne Cup Day 2014, all the jockeys in every race were female. Even more impressively, the day before Australia Day 2015, female jockeys won all eight races on the program at Mount Gambier Racecourse. Apprentice Chelsea Jokic won the first, apprentice Emily Finnegan rode three winners, and Clare Lindop and Holly McKechnie two each. The times they are a-changing!

***

In 1973, June Lossius became the first officially recognised woman jockey to win a race at a metropolitan meeting in Australia, riding Some Attraction to victory at Eagle Farm in Brisbane. Up until this point, a tradition of amateur 'ladies only' picnic races had existed in Victoria since the 1850s, as women were not permitted to compete professionally as jockeys or ride on professional racetracks.

By the start of the 1970s women were still restricted to the ladies-only events, known as the 'ladies bracelet', or colloquially as 'Powder Puff Derbies', which were held on small, non-professional racetracks.

June Lossius was a very competent rider and had challenged the restrictions facing women riders in Australia. When she was younger, June had pretended to be a boy in order to ride her own horse in an early morning training session at Flemington racetrack. She recalls, 'With my cropped hair pushed under a boy's cloth cap, scarf around my throat, wearing a roomy boy's jumper and in the dim light of dawn to confuse any suspicions, away I rode.'

Later June helped to establish the Victorian Lady Jockey's Association, which played a role in establishing The Dame Merlyn Transition Handicap at Eagle Farm in 1973. Named in honour of Victorian philanthropist Dame Margery Merlyn Baillieu Myer, the race gave Australian female riders their first chance to ride and compete on a major racecourse, with access to professional facilities and large crowds. It also brought the issue of licensing female riders as professional jockeys into the public and media spotlight. The increasing momentum of the women's liberation movement also assisted their cause.

June wasn't alone in her quest to bring female jockeys to the forefront of professional racing. Pam O'Neill was the trailblazer for female jockeys in Australia. For many years O'Neill worked as a strapper for top trainer Harry Hatten before competing in women-only races in the 1970s. She maintained a strong race record and in 1974 she won the International Jockeys race for women riders at Eagle Farm on Ropely Lad. The Queensland jockey tirelessly fought for women to be able to compete against men.

In 1979 women were given an official licence to race as professional jockeys, with Pam O'Neill and New Zealand's Linda Jones the first to be awarded licences in Australia. Like O'Neill, Linda Jones battled to obtain a licence after being rejected for many reasons: she was considered too old at 24, she was married, wasn't strong enough, and would be taking the livelihood off a male jockey.

Jones was the first female jockey to gain the right to race against men in her home country, in 1977. Apprenticed to her husband, trainer Alan Jones, Linda had her first professional ride on 12 August 1978. She then rode six winners in the first five weeks of the 1978–79 season.

She would also forge a successful racing career in Australia and become the first woman to ride a winner against male professionals at a registered meeting when she rode the tough stayer Pay The Purple to victory in the 1979 Labour Cup at Doomben, etching her name into the record books. That year, Linda would also be the first woman to ride in the Adelaide Cup, on board Northfleet trained by her husband Alan.

Continuing a long list of firsts, Linda was the first woman in the southern hemisphere to ride four winners in a day; the first woman to ride a winner at Ellerslie, and at Trentham; and the first to compete in the Auckland, Sydney and Wellington Cups. She was also the first woman in Australasia, the United Kingdom, Europe or North America to ride a derby winner—Holy Toledo in the Wellington Derby.

After she gained equality, her career was short but spectacular: in eighteen months she rode 65 winners.

Bev Buckingham was another pioneer female jockey. She grew up in Tasmania after migrating from England when she was two years old. As well as taking riding lessons, she would help her father, a racehorse trainer, in his stables and at the age of fourteen she became an apprentice jockey under his tutelage.

Bev had her first race ride in October 1980, just a fortnight after Alison Anderson had made history as the first woman to race against men in Tasmania. On arriving at the Mowbray racecourse, she found that the new facilities for jockeys had not been completed and she had to change into her race gear in a small, unlit room on the construction site.

A win on her fourth ride at Elwick in 1980, Limit Man, launched Buckingham's career. By the end of her first season's racing, she had ridden 22 winners and was ranked ninth overall on the jockey table. With a total of 63 winners in her second season, at the age of seventeen, Buckingham became the first woman in the world to win a state jockeys premiership. Over her eighteen-year career she brought home trophies for the Devonport Cup, the Launceston Cup, the Queen's Cup, and the Hobart Cup three times—in 1986, 1996 and 1998. In 1984 she became the first woman to ride in the Caulfield Cup. Bev would also become the first female in the southern hemisphere to ride 1000 winners.

Bev's riding career ended after a tragic race fall on 30 May 1998 in which she fractured two vertebrae in her neck. She spent three months in rehabilitation in Victoria, before returning to the family's Tasmanian property, Brigadoon, where she continued an intensive rehabilitation program. Told that she would never walk again, Bev has since proved doctors wrong and has forged a successful career as a horse trainer.

Pam Baker was another who blazed the trail for female jockeys. As the wife of trainer Rodney Baker, she was allowed to ride her husband's horses at trackwork, but not in races.

After a male jockey had ridden a 'shocker' on one of Rodney's horses at Terang in 1971, Pam complained bitterly that she could have done much better. Her husband agreed and said she should 'do something about it'.

Pam promptly organised a meeting with Victoria Racing Club secretary Rodney Johnson to ask why women could not ride professionally. Johnson reportedly replied that he didn't know why, except that 'no one had ever asked'.

Pam's next step was to approach then Victorian Minister for Sport, Brian Dixon. He was sympathetic to her suggestion and, in 1972, apprenticeships were made open to both sexes.

In an interview with Matt Stewart, in the *Herald Sun* in 2013, Pam remembered, 'By the time we got the technical bits out of the way, getting things organised, it took two and a half years.'

Pam helped to form the Lady Jockey's Association of Victoria and, when the first professional race for women in Victoria was held at Casterton in August 1974, the association had 45 members and the race was named the 'Pam Baker Ladies Handicap'.

In her interview with Matt Stewart, Pam recalled that the ladies had to suffer jibes and trivialising, with names such as 'jockettes' being suggested. It appears they were treated as a passing fad by the race club administrators, and the early female jockeys, such as Pam, Liz Albers, June Lossius and even later arrivals on the scene, including the Payne girls, Maree, Therese and Bernadette, had to change in a caravan. They were lucky to even have that! Franklin Caravans had come to the rescue and donated a caravan to the association, which was used for many years around the state as a mobile 'Ladies Jockeys Room'. It was well into the 1980s before the racing clubs got around to providing decent changerooms for them.

Pam, who now runs an agistment property near Geelong, told Matt Stewart in 2013, 'All I wanted was that they be given a chance to compete with the boys—no favours.'

Fast-forward and the number of female jockeys is now at its peak. Today 25 per cent of jockeys are female, while only fifteen years ago that figure was less that 5 per cent. And those numbers are set to soar with almost 50 per cent of apprenticeships being filled by young women. Female jockeys not only make up half the apprentice workforce, they are at least as successful as the boys.

Last season, four of the seven state and territory apprentice jockey titles were won by women.

In today's racing landscape, female jockeys are competing with great success across all states of Australia, and are making it known that they are not afraid to take on the boys. Jockeys such as Clare Lindop (first Australian female jockey to win a Group 1 race, on Rebel Raider in the VRC Derby, twice winner of the South Australian jockeys premiership, and the first female to ride in the Melbourne Cup), Kathy O'Hara, Linda Meech, Michelle Payne, Christine Puls, Katelyn Mallyon, Holly McKechnie, Winona Costin and Jamie Kah are just a few of the top-class female riders staking their claim on the big city tracks.

Like the female jockeys before them, they are still the pioneers in an ever-changing landscape, but the road is less rocky these days.

Penny Hand's website for all things female in racing is <www.filliesform.com>.

THE DAY THAT IS DEAD

HARRY 'THE BREAKER' MORANT

Ah, Jack! Time finds us feeble men,
And all too swift our years have flown.
The days are different now to then—
In that time when we rode ten stone.

The minstrel when his mem'ry goes
To old times, tunes a doleful lay—
Comparing modern nags with those
Which Lee once bred down Bathurst way.

The type today's a woeful weed,
Which lacks the stoutness, strength and bone
Of horses they were wont to breed
In those days—when we rode ten stone.

But all of us remorseless Fate
O'ertakes, and as the years roll on
Our saddles carry extra weight,
And old age mourns the keenness gone.

The young ones, too—'mong men, I mean—
Watch not the sires from whom they've sprung,
They nowadays are not so keen
As when we—and the world—were young.

They've neither nerve nor seat to suit
The back of Paddy Ryan's roan—
That wall-eyed, vicious, bucking brute
You rode—when you could ride ten stone.

But, Johnny, ere we 'go to grass'—
Ere angel wings are fledged to fly—
With wine we'll fill a bumper glass,
And drink to those good times gone by.

We've *had* our day—'twill not come back!
But, comrade mine, this much you'll own,
'Tis something *to have had it,* Jack—
That time when we could ride ten stone!

VALIANT LADY

JIM BENDRODT

So you go to the races? You form one of the amazing multitude who follow the Sport of Kings and deadbeats, and all the varied kinds of people in between. Perhaps the siren call of 'easy money', the thrill of a close-fought finish, the love of a satin-coated thoroughbred, the performance of a social duty, brings *you* there.

Whichever it is, there is one thing I do know, and that is that you who see the gigantic stage, set with its tens of thousands close-packed in colossal grandstands, its glorious flowers, its great green stretches where the cream of the equine world sob their hearts out in a game where only the superlative survive, know little of the work and the thoughts and the hopes and the fears of that band of men who produce the four-legged stars you come to see do battle for fame and fortune.

Well, I'll try to tell you why I go to the races. I'll tell you how I, an owner-trainer who loves a thoroughbred, feel from the time I go with a few hard-won shekels to some famous sale ring, to the moment that my colours flash into sight where the field is bunching far up the home stretch for that heart-stirring, heart-breaking run to a little white line on a little black board, and the eagle eye of a judge from whose decision there is no appeal. And if you love a thoroughbred horse, if you really love them, you can read this, and if you don't—well, read something else, because you won't be interested, and you won't understand.

They've come from the four corners of a dozen beautiful pasture lands, from the studs of men who have studied the production of the ultimate in horses for generations. Each of these soft-eyed babies could tell you that his, or her, blood lines could be traced exactly to equine horses who came from their desert homes to Merrie England, along with the fashions Charles the First made à la mode. Believe me! And some of them could speak of ancestors who cropped the grass of Devon when Henry the Eighth displayed his catholic taste in harems.

A little nervous, more than a trifle frightened, they have come from their lovely homes to this noisy, terrifying saleyard, so that you who have burned the midnight oil studying pedigrees may choose and buy a champion. If you can. Yes, indeed! If you can!

Hundreds of them, all well bred, all beautiful, or nearly all, but only a meagre handful who will ever become that miracle of speed and courage and stamina that will fling their names in flaunting banners across the sporting pages of a continent.

For days you study them. Hour after hour, you tramp from stable to stable, comparing, measuring, concentrating, and, curiously enough, it is only at night-time that you know you're weary. Then, just a few hours before the auctioneer will call the babies forth to face whatever the future may hold for them, you open the door of a box you have not yet entered and there, in a corner, stands a baby filly.

Now for weeks a colt had been in your mind. You are almost Chinese in your ironclad preference for the male of the species, but here is one little lady you feel you must really have a word with. She is too beautiful to pass by, as you have passed by so many of her sex, because you want a colt. A dark bay, this one—perfect from the points of her tiny black-tipped ears to her almost equally tiny feet. A glorious example of what hundreds of years of careful breeding can produce.

A long five minutes you study her intently, while she gazes fearlessly and just as intently back at you with her soft dark eyes. There is no fear in those eyes—just a quiet curiosity. Marvellous, you say; small, yes, but still—marvellously perfect, and she will grow—just a baby. But you want a colt, not a filly, and then, just as you turn to go, she takes a step towards you.

She is curious, or perhaps Fortune smiles, and you stop and call her softly—encouragingly. She comes and lays her muzzle in your outflung hand, and then, as she stretches her glistening neck, her lovely head comes to rest against your own hard face, and so, for a moment, for you and for her, the world stands still.

And then—well, and then believe me or, as Mr Ripley says, believe me or not, in the quiet of that stable you think you hear a tiny voice say, 'Buy me! Never mind that colt. Buy me!' And instantly you tell her, 'All right, baby, I'll buy you if I have to bust the bank-roll wide open.' And that's a promise! Weeks of study, weeks of tramping, weeks of indecision. Then finality! Just by chance—just like that!

So you go to the ring, and you wait for her, when for weeks you've thought you were going to that ring to wait for a colt, and never did lover wait for sweetheart more anxiously.

You look round those hundreds of intent faces. You study that close-packed amphitheatre. Tier on tier of keen-eyed men—prince and pauper, stable boy and lord of a million acres, cheek by jowl, shoulder to shoulder, but horsemen all, come to buy a champion if they can. Always that 'if' in racing! Will they see what you have seen? How many of them will have picked that soft-eyed filly waiting in her stall for her turn to face the play of Fortune's wheel? Where will the fall of the auctioneer's hammer send her? What sort of a master will guide her destiny?

Well, you made a promise, so you know where she'll go, if the bank-roll will stand it—if some lord of a million acres doesn't make your meagre shekels look like the change he uses for car-fare. What if they bid a figure you can't come up to? But she's very small. Oh yes, of course, that's your chance—she's *very* small.

Well then, here she comes, head held proudly like the tiny princess she is, little hoofs hardly seem to touch the velvet turf she steps upon. Eyes wide with bewilderment as she faces that crowded circle of quiet-faced men.

The auctioneer's voice drones on and on. Her father did this, her mother that, her brother did this, her sister that. The recounting of the miracles of her forebears comes to an end, and eventually the courteous question is asked, 'And now, gentlemen, what am I bid?'

And an optimist says 'One hundred guineas,' and the race is on. Once again Fortune smiles. 'Three hundred and fifty,' someone calls, and instantly you snap back, 'Three hundred and seventy-five,' and there is silence.

It's all you've got to spend on her. It isn't much, I know, but you don't own a million acres. The time will come when you'll spend ten times as much for just one horse, but you don't know that then. Quietly you pray that no one says, 'Four hundred,' and then, after what seems to you to be intolerable aeons of time, that hammer falls, and she belongs to you.

Her attendant leads her back to a stall where you are waiting to praise her and pat her, and tell her everything is OK now. And she puts her head in your arms, and rests it there, which is by way of saying, 'Thank you, master, thank you very much indeed.'

A small boy, who must lose her now, says sadly, 'I've looked after her, mister, since she was knee-high to a grasshopper. You'll take care of her?'

And you say, 'Sure, son, sure, I'll take care of her, never doubt it.'

There is so much to do from that time on. Floats, ships, attendants to take her on the ocean voyage which will bring her to the dock-side at which you wait so anxiously. There has been a cyclone. The papers tell you that the ship on which she travels, tied in a narrow stall deep in a stinking hold, is labouring in a welter of furious seas and howling gales. The Storm Gods chose an awkward time to rave and rant. Two days ago those tumbling seas were calm. Has she been hurt? You've paid a man to guard her well. Has he done the job you paid him for? Well, you'll soon know.

Out of an evil-smelling hold she comes, slung in a crate high above the ship that carried her. Winches rattle, raucous voices spill commands, the crate lands at your feet, and from it, very tired, very sick and very frightened, steps your tiny filly. Wide dark eyes seek yours in that bedlam of shouting stevedores, rattling winches, snarling motors, and your voice is very soft, and your hand is very gentle, as you tell her that she's home now, that everything at last is as it should be.

Then, after you've rattled and bumped through a great city, in a gigantic vehicle they call a float but which has precious little 'float' about it, she is 'home'. A cool, quiet stable, knee-deep in straw, water, food, and your foreman's voice: 'Sure, boss, she's beautiful, but small, strike me, very small!'

And you say, 'Sure! Her grandfather won two Ascot Gold Cups, and her grandmother won the Oaks, and she'll grow.'

Then knowing hands probe and delve as the 'stable' looks her over, and heads are shaken, and 'too small' they say, even if her grandmother won the Oaks with nineteen flaming stone.

Just for a moment you feel a tiny doubt. Perhaps a colt would have been better. There was that one from Star Sapphire, and then you look again at the weary little mite you've gone to so much trouble to get and—shrug your shoulders.

Your foreman's eyes have never left you, and he says suddenly, 'To hell with them, boss. They wouldn't know a racehorse from a Rocky Mountain goat, but me—well, I'll be looking after *her* myself.' And this, you know, is honour *in excelsis*.

'She'll grow,' you've said. Oh, yes, you've said it so many times, but she doesn't grow. And she doesn't eat, and she doesn't do any of the things you had figured on. Instead she becomes very ill. You try everything you know—uselessly. That tiny horse is very sick indeed. So you call in the vets to help you. They come, examine, question, shake their heads. No constitution—colitis, that dreaded disease—possibly had it for months—probably never race—certainly not 'early'. Still they'll do the best they can. And you know they will, even if their bills are never paid. That's racing. And you'll do your best too. Disappointing? Oh, sure!

Away in the distance a dream, something or other to do with the Gimcrack Stakes—just a dream—a long way off now—a very long way off. Horses bunched at the turn for that battle down that long home stretch. The thunder of the multitude. A name on the lips of thousands in one long roar of sound—your filly's name as she battles with the favourite at that vital furlong pole for mastery, and gains it, goes on, spread-eagles the cream of her age—flashes past that little white line against its little black board, and that judge from whose decision there is no appeal—lengths to the good!

Oh, sure! Just a dream, especially with a weary little horse, despondent and sick, asking to be petted and helped—not trained and harried about for a race a bare six months away.

Her breeder comes to Sydney. A sportsman, this. He hears the vet's report and—offers you another horse if you care to send her back. He will give you that Star Sapphire colt you liked so much in her place. You go into your filly's box to say goodbye, and you go when no one else can see you, because it isn't an easy thing to do. I mean easy to say goodbye. And then Fortune, who must take care of all horsemen, if they are ever to own a racehorse, smiles again. With that little head pressed against yours, you just can't do it, and so that night, you tell the quiet man who bred her that you'll 'carry on'.

You go to work. Day after day, week after week, month after month, the treatment continues. But that little filly is very close to those Happy Hunting Grounds to which all good horses go, before she turns the corner. You do just exactly what those clever vets have ordered—special diet, cunning medicines, warmth, care, kindness. Oh yes, lots of kindness. You feed a racehorse oats, or you feed it nitrogenous food of some sort. You have to. No alternative. But you can't feed this filly oats, or nitrogenous food of any kind. It's pure poison to her with the malady she has.

Three months go by—a coat like polished copper is beginning to glisten again. Symptoms are favourable. You try your first feed of oats. A very small feed of grain, mixed with a very large feed of hope. She eats them, and with no ill effects, praise be. No recurrence of the malady she seems to have overcome.

Well, if she can eat oats, you can train her. Gimcrack Stakes—three months away. You don't like early two-year-old racing, but that was the race you dreamed about for this little lady, because she's pitched and balanced to go like greased lightning, and she's bred to stay. Perhaps, if you're very careful, you can go far enough to let *her* tell you what to do. She'll tell you, never doubt it, if you've sense enough to know her language.

And so now it's work in earnest, but work you love. Your little horse thrives under it. Five in the morning until ten at night, your foreman watches, massages, feeds, exercises, does the thousand and one things one does when a horse is set to win a race. And in the case of this filly, two or three things that are not usually included.

And then one day, with the Gimcrack Stakes six weeks away, you decide to let her 'run down a furlong'. Ah, folks, *there* is a day for you. When, after months of preparation, you bring out the old stopwatch and prepare to learn your fate. Can she run a furlong in twelve seconds? Can she—or will she, as nine out of ten do, take longer? Can she, by some miracle, break twelve with her heavy irons on? Well, well, you'll see in the morning. And if she, as the racing argot has it, 'takes a week', there isn't anything that you can do about it—no, not a thing!

And so, when the older horses have departed, and the trainers have gone where all good trainers go at breakfast-time, when the sun had chased the frost away, you stand, timer in hand, and watch your filly canter gaily to the mark, and breaking away like a flash, run in a blur of speed to a furlong pole. You click your watch, and peek at it, and then, startled, you look again, and you say, 'Well, I'll be . . .!' and you almost went back on a promise made, in all good faith, to a little horse with black-tipped ears, and you nearly sent her home for something out of Star Sapphire.

Perhaps it's the wind that makes you shiver.

Your watch, which is a perfectly good watch, tells the story. Your filly, in working shoes, carrying 8 stone 10 pounds, and allowed to please herself, flashed over that furlong in eleven seconds and two-fifths, and that, you know, isn't galloping—that, as so many years of trying has so amply taught you, is simply flying! So who can blame you if you start to dream again?

Two weeks go by, and daily your baby horse grows stronger, bigger, faster. Did I say faster? Yes faster, because one fine morning you take her far from prying eyes, and on a track where once years ago a crack sprinter in racing shoes ran two in twenty-three and three-quarters, but on which no horse since has done so well, your filly, in working shoes, flashes over that same two furlongs in twenty-three and one-quarter, and then you know that if she runs true to pedigree, and gets an even break in the race you've set her for, she will be very hard to beat indeed. Oh, very hard!

That evening you go to a great friend who loves to make thousands grow where only one thousand was before, and you tell him, imploring secrecy, that you've got a filly big as a minute, beautiful as a sculptor's dream, faster than chain lightning, and game as an Australian bulldog ant. And he says, as a doctor will say to his patient, soothingly, quietly, 'Sure, Jim, I know. Have a drink.' But you persist, and eventually he becomes enthusiastic, and forecasts that the noble brotherhood of the Ring are due for an outsize dose of sackcloth and ashes, and a notable lack of that legendary fruit of which the resting place is that equally legendary sideboard.

Then he wants to know of her training. How many four-furlong sprints with the pressure on? And you say, 'None at all. Absolutely none at all.' And he laughs, and suggests that you talk of other things, and that's that. You speak nervously of heredity, of the values in pace work, half pace, strong three-quarter pace, of ancestry. You talk in vain. Just over your shoulder when you came into his study, Fortune beckoned him: Fortune who, in the last analysis, governs every little thing there is in racing. Fortune had gone from that room before you left.

The great day grows closer. There are barrier trials now, and daily the young ones who have been 'tried' and who have survived their early preparations thus far (so many don't) spring into flashing life from behind tapes as the starter calls.

Then one day there is a mighty gathering of babies at the official two-year-old trials, and heat after heat thunder down a lightning-fast track under racing conditions. Of the colts and the fillies, the fair sex take all honours. Two of them run four furlongs in forty-eight seconds, and that evening their names get headlines, and you know you'll have opponents worthy of your steel, which is as it should be.

At the trials, someone who knows you have a young one too, asks where your filly is, and you say, 'Having her breakfast, I suppose,' and he shakes his head.

'Great practice this, Jim,' he remarks, 'learns them race conditions.'

'Sure,' you say. 'They're fine. I know other ways.'

He grins. 'You've quaint ideas, Jim—how's dancing, or is it skating, nowadays?'

You leave it at that!

Ten days before the race, you send your own baby out 'tipped' and with her chosen horseman in silks and satins, in the saddle. And where the world doesn't see, she beats seven others similarly equipped, flying like a little bay meteor over three furlongs from the barrier, and then the crack little horseman on her back has to fight like a tiger to stop her running three furlongs more at that same terrific pace. Bred to stay? Oh sure. I told you that. Or didn't I? That dream is getting closer now!

And from then on? Well no more gallops, no more strain. Just potter about, with a bit of strong three-quarter pace work here and there. Massage, good food, kindness—oh yes, plenty of that. You say she's fit, your friends say you're crazy, your foreman grunts. So what? So someone's crazy! Maybe it's you! You have the courage of your convictions in the racing game—when you've got convictions. So often you just don't know, and neither does anyone else!

But in an education that has encompassed most things, one thing remains to be done. Have you, who watch the babies run, ever thought of their ordeal when first they see the milling thousands, hear the roar of the ring, become a part of that electric atmosphere that it is the racecourse? Stage-fright, fear, anxiety, bewilderment, leave many a baby horse half beaten long before the starter's voice sends them thundering away.

And so that she may get used to it, you take your filly to the races—to a meeting where voices bellow, and strangers come to gaze at her. Where men in red coats on white horses canter by, and all the ordered pandemonium of the Sport of Kings surrounds her.

You take your colt too. Oh yes, you have a colt, with a coat like a cloak of burnished brass, and the disposition of a Pirate King.

She takes it well. You parade them both, and your friends come in dozens to see them, and long and loud are the praises for your golden-coated colt, and long and pregnant are the silences that follow your humble suggestion that the filly is lovely too.

'Oh, yes,' they say, if they say anything at all, 'rather small though—a mite miserable—go for a couple like a scalded cat—but that colt! Now, mister, *there's* a racehorse!' And the colt, with its burnished-copper coat, and his disposition of a swaggering buccaneer, stands high in the air with his front feet pawing at a point yards above your head, and sends his shrill clear reply over ring and paddock: 'Boy, you've said a mouthful!' But what he doesn't tell them is that the little lady no one cares for could give him a stone and a start and a beating any time you like to call the tune!

And *you* don't tell them either, because you are a little sad, and a wee bit puzzled. Can't they see your lovely filly, or is it *your* eyes that cannot see her imperfections? 'Beauty is in the eye of the beholder.' Well maybe so—maybe so.

Then among the curious ones who wander past, a young 'man about town' stops long enough to remark, 'A fine colt,' and then, turning to where your little horse is standing in her scarlet silken sheet, and her spotless bandages, with the brass and leather of her head collar gleaming because proud hands have worked for hours so that her 'ensemble' may be perfect, the gentleman remarks, 'Don't think much of her,' and your foreman, fed to the teeth, and because he is a little sad too, snarls savagely, 'Mister, which end of her do you think kicks?'

Well, you take them home, and then, presently, lo and behold, the Great Day dawns. That day you dreamed about six long months ago. A dream that, before evening falls again, will have shattered into the oblivion of painful memories, or triumphed into the miracle of a *fait accompli*. That's a day, my race-going friends, that is 'just another day' to you. But for me! Oh, well, I'll try to tell you.

Coffee that morning was hot and strong, and newspapers, race papers, and tipsters' sheets made the bed covering. All that ocean of type that sums up the discoveries of that colossal espionage system that delves with the eye of an eagle, the sagacity of a fox, and the tenacity of a weasel, into the chances of the thoroughbred horse, and out of that multitude of forecasts not one gives your horse a chance! No—not even a place chance, and you think suddenly of that song you sang when you marched to war—'They're all out of step but Jim!' And then you remember that it was *Jim* who was out of step, and *your* name is Jim.

A hurried toilet, a red-and-white tie, your racing colours. She'll carry them, so you'll carry them too. Then to the stable in a car that must wonder if you think you're Malcolm Campbell. Your foreman's grunted greeting (he's 'strung up' too, though woe betide you if you say so!), the rhythmic swing of his brush massaging muscles like fluid steel beneath a satin coat, that changes in places into little pools of light as a shaft of early morning sun finds her. A velvet muzzle that spares a moment to caress your cheek, before it buries itself in sweet-smelling food. Lips that move with that curious rotary motion, jaws that grind with the even steadiness of a metronome—sweet music to the trainer's ears on race day—I'll say it is.

Dark eyes are clear, untroubled. Under those enormous hot poultice bandages, you know her legs are clean and cool and, best of all, under your inquiring fingertips, her heart beats strong and true, thirty-eight, thirty-nine, maybe forty to the minute. That marvellous muscle from which come all those things you know she's got. Well, little filly, I've done my best, and those who have helped me have done their best, and now—well, now, it's up to *you*!

The rhythmic swing of that brush goes on and on and on. How many thousand hours has he swung a brush like that? How many years has he hissed sibilantly like a disturbed snake, as is the way of all horsemen with a brush? How much of it was worthwhile? Ask him! He wouldn't know what you were talking about. It was all worthwhile from his point of view. Were they not all thoroughbred? They're born and bred that way in racing.

Hours go by, and eventually you stand with your small horse, in a big stall, with a hundred other horses in a long line of stalls on either side of you. The clamour of the racecourse envelops you, and you wish time wouldn't drag so. A famous horse is stabled next your own, and hundreds come to look him over. You step aside so that they can see your filly too. But they don't gesticulate, and they don't admire. They just walk away, and never look in your direction. After all, who are you, and who is your filly? Just one of twenty-one babies entered in an early Classic, some of whom can run half a mile in forty-eight, which is worthy of note. But what can that little one run? Well, nobody knows. Not even you know, though you *think* you do. Hardly anyone ever heard her name. Well, in a little while now, they'll fling her name in banner type across the sporting pages of a nation—well, maybe they will!

Gradually your world grows smaller until the whole of it is concentrated in just one small baby horse. The gamble of the barrier draw has given you nine marbles. Not so bad. From the nearby ring an enormous bellow calls your horse at twenty to one. A week ago, that would have seemed philanthropy—almost lese-majesty. Now, on the brink of the Great Ordeal, you're not so sure. But you know the ladies will back her—with a name like that—oh, sure they will! And you'll back her—with what you've got. She won't be friendless! Twenty to one. It's a bonny price, and they say Shylock sired the bookmaker breed. My goodness gracious! Twenty to one!

The parade is on. Twenty-one babies in their flaunting colours. Your jockey comes—smart, capable, cool. You wonder at his coolness. Thank heaven you don't have to ride her. Now you know what courage is! Look at her—calm, unflurried—and *she* knows just as well as *you* know that she's on the threshold of a hard, tough battle. *How* does she know? Bred in her, of course, and in most of those like her, over hundreds of years. How about your own courage? Well, maybe the less said about that, just now, the better. *You* don't need any; you just have to sit and watch!

A pat on a glossy neck, a last word to the jockey and your voice is hard. 'No whip, Bill, no spurs. Let her do it herself. She'll fight it out—bred that way.' And his merry, smiling answer, 'Don't worry, boss. She's home and hosed. Go put the mortgage on her.'

You don't. You couldn't, even if you had a mortgage. Curiously money doesn't seem to matter now. Only one thing matters. You flee to a spot high in a towering grandstand, as far from folk as possible, and through your glasses in the far distance you pick up a huddle of horses who wheel and dive and change in a kaleidoscope of brilliant colour.

And then your entire world narrows down to just one thing. Gone are the crowds, gone the tumult and the shouting, gone any vestige of consciousness of anything or anyone except that distant mass wheeling and diving like a flock of gulls at a five-strand barrier.

If you breathe, you don't know it, and you pray for just one thing. That she'll get away when the starter calls, and that she won't be asked to break her heart chasing a field that stole a march on her. That your dream won't go west in a split second of faulty judgement.

You can't see her colours in that shifting huddle. The day is dull, the visibility poor, but you know suddenly that they're off, and then I'll *swear* you do not breathe at all. Your glasses range forward, then backward over that flying field. You can't find her, but two horses on the rails obscure one on the outside of them. Perhaps *she's* running there outside of those you see so plainly.

Then a quarter of a mile away, they swing for home. Desperately your glasses range from the head of that flying field to the tail of it, and back again. A misty rain has blurred your vision so that the blazing colours the jockeys carry are vague and almost indistinguishable. You are conscious of a sense of unbearable urgency. You've got to find her! You've *got* to. Then suddenly you freeze into complete immobility. *That* must be her. There just outside of the chestnut on the rails, is a blood-red bay, with a great white blaze. Going like the wind. *That's* her! Then you're dreaming again.

Horses bunched at the turn for their battle down that long home stretch—the thunder of the multitude—a name on the lips of thousands in one long roar of sound. Your filly's name, as she battles with the favourite at that vital furlong pole for mastery, and gains it, goes on, spread-eagles the cream of her age—flashes past that little white line against its little black board, and that judge from whose decision there is no appeal—lengths to the good!

Then suddenly you realise it's a dream come true, and that that little filly trotting back on dainty feet, black-tipped ears pricked on lovely little head—belongs to you!

And her name, folks—oh, yes, I forgot to tell you: Gay Romance.

Owned and trained by Jim Bendrodt, Gay Romance won the Gimcrack Stakes at Randwick in 1937. She was also the dam of Gay Lover, winner of the 1956 Rosehill Guineas.

ROYAL RANDWICK

TIP KELAHER

Andrew James ('Tip') Kelaher was born in Sydney in 1914 and attended Sydney Boys' High. He enlisted in a machine gun battalion in 1940. He was killed in action at Tel El Eisa in Egypt on 14 July 1942. His commanding officer wrote, 'In the face of heavy machine gun fire, artillery and mortars he stayed by his gun and kept it in action to the last.' He wrote this poem just before his death.

***

Are the two-year-olds still racing down the Randwick mile,
Do thudding hoofs still shake the Randwick turf,
Do flower-beds and gardens still produce their springtime smile,
Does the ring-roar match the booming of the surf?

Are there still some lovely ladies to beautify the scene,
Is the band still playing marches 'neath the stand,
Is the sunshine just as brilliant and the couch grass just as green
As when we sailed to fight on foreign strand?

Is the stale cigar smell drifting, and do gripping hands denote
Glad meetings and a move towards the bar,
Is there movement, life and laughter from the 'birdcage' to the tote
As the old friends congregate from near and far?

Have you any colts like Gold Rod or Avenger or High Caste,
Or a miler like proud Ajax at his best,
Could the new lot hope to foot it with the champions of the past,
With Eurythmic, Gloaming, Poitrel and the rest?

Oh, the bay, the black, the chestnut—rippling muscles in the sun!
Close finishes! The crowd's loud, vibrant roar!
A day of keen, hard-racing, stirring contests every one,
Brings a tingle to a horseman's blood once more.

Now Randwick stands a symbol of the life we left behind,
And 'twill compensate for loss and parting pain,
When the war is safely over if I have the luck to find
I can spend a day at Randwick once again.

RACING MEMORIES

A.B. 'BANJO' PATERSON

I first butted into the racing game about 60 years ago when I was taken as a small boy to Randwick and saw two three-year-olds, Chester and Cap-a-Pie, run a dead heat in a 3-mile race and they ran the dead heat off the same afternoon.

I suppose you think that trainers ought each to have got six months for training three-year-olds like that, but races were not run from end to end those days. A Cumberland Stakes, 2 miles, in which Carbine beat Lochiel, took over five minutes to run. A trotter could pretty well do that nowadays.

I can just remember James White, a fine big man with a beard and a thorough-going Australian. He believed we could breed first-class horses here and he used Australian sires to an extent that nobody has ever approached since. His great horse Chester was by Yattendon, an Australian-bred horse, and Yattendon was by the Australian Sir Hercules.

Then Chester's son Abercorn was put to the stud, so there were four generations of Australian blood even in those early days. Mr White was like the late John Brown; he believed in breeding and racing his own horses, but he wasn't like John Brown in any other way. He stuck to the one trainer all his life, while John Brown took his whole team away from old Joe Burton simply because Joe told him that one of them was no good.

My first experience as an owner came when a country friend sent me down a polo pony, a miniature horse-giantess, thoroughbred, as long as a ship and big everywhere except in height. She could gallop like Eclipse, but was useless for polo, as she needed a 40-acre paddock in which to turn.

Obviously her game was racing, so I leased her to a pony trainer, one Jimmy Gordon, a strong silent man who was, I believe, brother-in-law to William Kelso, the crack trainer of the day. I thought that anything Jimmy didn't know, Kelso would tell him.

Then I moved in one glorious jump right up among the exclusives at the top of the business. Mainly because I was well known as a writer of racing verse I met and made personal friendships with owners like G.D. Greenwood (Gloaming), L. McDonald (Wakeful), Sol Green (Comedy King), R.R. Dangar (Peter Pan), W.A. Long (Grand Flaneur) and countless others.

Recognising that I was horse-mad, that great trainer Dick Mason used to make me welcome at his stable and take me along with him when he was saddling Gloaming and others; and here is a queer thing. In all those years I never heard one of those men say that his horse had been pulled by its rider or that he had lost a race through roguery or by interference of bookmakers.

When I first blundered into racing, Mr Henry Dangar was chairman of the Australian Jockey Club, a masterful man. He imported the great St Simon horse Positano—an animal which would never have left England only that he had a will of his own.* Mr Dangar entrusted the training of his horse to the capable hands of John Allsopp, one of the old school whose pessimistic outlook on life had earned him the nickname 'Crying Johnny'.

Positano had to go to Melbourne to race and Allsopp said that the horse would require a box to himself on the train; if other horses were put in anywhere near him he would spend the trip trying to get at them.

Mr Dangar had never heard of such a proposition, and the trainer was ordered to attend a meeting of the owner and a few of his cronies to give an explanation. 'Johnny' put up such a good 'cry' that he got his own way: nor did he resent being told that the horse's wilfulness must be his fault. Trainers are used to shouldering the blame for everything.

Another English horse which came out here under somewhat similar circumstances was Orzil. He was a really high-class performer in England in the ownership of one of the Brasseys. Mr Pat Osborne, who was later to achieve fame as the owner of Valicare, was visiting England and happened to mention to Brassey that he was looking out for a horse. He could hardly believe his ears when Brassey said that he would give him Orzil. *Give* him, mind you, when the horse was one of the best performers in England.

'He's turned unreliable,' said Brassey, 'but I can't sell him here for fear he might take it into his head to do his best and beat me in a big race. It would make me look a fool. If you take him away out to Australia and guarantee that he never comes back, you can have him for nothing.'

I have seen them all, the big punters who bestride this narrow world until one day they are missing; the small battling owners and trainers, living in hopes of finding a big punter who will 'dash it down' for them on a specially prepared horse. Here and in England it is just the same.

Taking it by and large, and expressing it in a comprehensive sort of way, the public got the idea that where there were six races in a day, there were six crimes to be detected, so stipendiary stewards were appointed to control racing.

I seem to have seen the beginnings of a lot of things in my life and among others I saw the beginnings of the stipendiary system.

One of the first men appointed was my lifelong friend, Leslie Rouse, a solicitor by profession and son of Richard Rouse, a grazier and thoroughbred breeder of Mudgee. Before long there was an outcry that Rouse was catching only the small fry and was letting the big fish escape. He said in reply that it pained him like anything to put out the small and hungry battlers, but as they did such desperate things he had no option.

As he had no legal authority to compel witnesses to appear before him, he had to get his information as best he could. 'The big races are all right,' said Rouse. 'Nobody is going to pull a horse in The Metropolitan to win a race at Menangle; but when I see a horse running three stone above his form and somebody winning a million I always wish that I could catch the man who worked it, but I very seldom can.'

A good many years ago I was asked to go along with a friend who had a commission to buy a yearling for somebody up-country. I think he took me along to share the blame if he bought a bad one.

We inspected all sorts, big and little, fat and thin, dumpy little fillies and big, awkward, angular colts.

Among the colts, one particular clumsy legs-and-wings youngster attracted our condemnation. To mark him for identification we called him The Gawk. We all agreed that if we bought The Gawk we would deserve to find ourselves in a lunatic asylum looking out, so we decided on a chunky, ready-made filly that looked like racing early.

The filly showed some early promise and then faded away into the backblocks and was never heard of again, while The Gawk, under the name of Bitalli, won the Melbourne Cup.

My friend's principal is still alive and only needs a few stimulants and he will talk for hours about the time he would have won the Melbourne Cup only to entrusting his commission to a couple of blind men.

If there is a moral to this disconnected narrative, it is that it is not as easy to buy a good yearling as one might suppose.

* *St Simon was the greatest sire of the era, but he was notoriously bad tempered and passed the trait on to his offspring, which is why the Duke of Portland purchased Carbine, who was famously placid, to stand at stud with St Simon as an outcross to St Simon mares, in order to breed controllable champion horses. It worked!*

WHAT'S IN A NAME?

JIM HAYNES

I have often been amazed and amused by the wonderful cryptic and appropriate names that owners come up with for racehorses.

Some favourites of mine over the years here in Australia include Itchy Feet, which raced in Sydney in the 1960s and was by an imported French Stallion named Le Cordonnier, which means 'the shoemaker' in French, out a mare called Ticklish.

As a kid I was amazed that race-callers didn't 'get' the name of a well-performed Sydney horse. The name was spelled C-U-R-F-T-A and race-callers always said 'Kerff-tar' but, of course, with Curfta being sired by Arrivederci, which means goodbye in Italian, the name should have been pronounced C-U-rf-ta—'See You After'.

A few of the more 'imaginative' and amusing names of recent years have been None For The Road, which was sired by Noalcoholic, out of Road To Gold; Greenie, by Naturalism out of Ozone Friendly; and Rumpus Room, by Shemozzle out of Downstairs.

Some of the most clever 'Aussie' names I can remember are Bowled Lillee, which was out of a mare named Courtmarsh; and VRC Derby winner Plastered, a West Australian colt whose mother was called Tipples.

Wakeful was out of a mare called Insomnia, while Carbine and Martini-Henry were both named for types of firearms as they were sired by Musket. Robinson Crusoe was so named because he survived a shipwreck. Archer was by William Tell, who was named after the Swiss hero who shot an apple off his son's head, and so it goes on.

Some years ago a Tamworth friend of mine, the late Sue Keating, purchased a gelding by More Than Ready from a mare named For The Moment. The horse was already named Fill Her Up and had raced a few times. The owner needed to sell and Sue was offered the horse, which was trained by Tim Martin who also trained other horses she owned. Sue hated the name but liked the horse, so a new name was needed, even though there is a racing superstition that changing a horse's registered name is unlucky.

Sue was actually at a rehearsal for a show I was involved in at the Rooty Hill RSL Club in western Sydney when she took the call confirming the purchase, and so we talked about renaming the horse. We tried several names but none were available until Sue decided on 'In Rehearsal'. *More than ready for the moment*, indeed! He went on to win the Armidale Cup and several good races in Brisbane.

Another Tamworth friend of mine is Errol Leicht, who owns the bedding retail outlet Forty Winks in Tamworth. Errol has a handy filly sired by Ready As, from a mare called Time Release who was by Switch In Time. Errol came up with a wonderfully apt name which promotes his business and acknowledges the horse's sire, dam and grandsire. The filly races as In A Wink, and won the listed race for fillies at Scone in 2015, the Denise's Joy Stakes. In A Wink's full brother, yet to race as this goes to print, is hilariously named Inner Spring!

Errol's horses are trained by Greg Bennett, who is famous for pre-training and conditioning the mighty Makybe Diva, whose name was derived by taking the first two letters from the names of the five female employees working in owner Tony Santic's office at the time: Maureen, Kylie, Belinda, Diane and Vanessa.

The winner of the 2015 Show County Quality at Group 3 level is a Clarrie Connors-trained gelding by Foreplay out of a mare called Daunting Thought—he races as Decision Time—now that is clever! Mind you, you don't have to use the horse's parents to be clever. A chestnut gelding with prominent white markings on three legs raced in Victoria a while back as Who Stole My Sock.

Some names are quite obscure and the majority of racegoers may never see the cryptic 'joke' or reference involved. Caulfield Cup winner Railings, for instance, was out of a mare called Suffragette, a daughter of Emancipation, and the name was a reference to the early suffragettes chaining themselves to the railings in Downing Street. A son of Tale of The Cat raced in Victoria a few years ago under the name of Otto Messmer. It puzzled me till I did some research and discovered that Otto Messmer was the man who drew and wrote the story lines for the *Felix the Cat* cartoons in the 1920s.

Bradbury's Luck, a brilliant sprinter of a decade ago and now a successful stallion, was foaled from a mare named Skating, just after Steven Bradbury won Australia's first ever Winter Olympic gold medal, coming from last to victory when the other four finalists all fell over in the 1000 metre speed skating final. Continuing the joke some clever owners of a filly by Bradbury's Luck named her Atishoo Atishoo – which is, of course, a phrase from the nursery rhyme where 'all fall down'.

Suzanne Philcox works at Woodlands Stud and has to find names for up to 300 foals a year. 'I try to use the dam's name,' she says. 'I also try to keep names short for the callers. Crawl is out of a mare called Traipse whose mother was Elegant Walk; another of her foals was named Swagger.'

Phar Lap is based on the Thai word for 'lightning', spelled with a 'PH' because trainer Harry Telford thought seven letters was lucky and horses with two-word names comprising seven letters won the most Melbourne Cups!

With so many opportunities to be clever with names, I often bemoan the fact that owners miss golden opportunities to be inventive, coming up with unimaginative names when some thought could have produced a real beauty. For example, let's say there's an imaginary horse by Bogtrotter out of Cakewalk, it's likely to end up being labelled with Bogwalk or Caketrotter or, even worse, Bogtrotter Lad or Cakewalk's Lass. 'Lad', 'Lass', 'Boy', 'Girl', 'Star', 'Prince', 'Lord', 'Lady', 'King' and 'Queen' are thrown onto the end of sire's and dam's names with reckless abandon to create names which, it seems to me, are harder to carry than top-weight in a welter handicap.

For me, the best and funniest racehorse name story comes from the early days of thoroughbred racing and is true—the best yarns are always the true ones!

The horse was named Potoooooooo, or Pot–Eight-Os (truly!). He was foaled in 1773, sired by the great Eclipse, and bred by a bloke with a wonderfully posh name, Willoughby Bertie, 4th Earl of Abingdon.

The horse acquired the strange spelling of his name, 'Potatoes', when a stable lad was asked to write it on a feed bin. The lad's version, Potoooooooo, was said to amuse his lordship so much that he kept it, and it appears in the English Stud Book.

Potoooooooo went on to become a well-performed racehorse who defeated some of the greatest horses of his day. He won 34 races over the span of seven years, including the Jockey Club Purse three times, and the prestigious Craven Stakes. He retired in 1783 to stand at stud and became an influential stallion himself, siring 172 winners including Champion, the first horse to win both the Derby and the St Leger (in 1800); Waxy, who won the Derby Stakes in 1793; and Tyrant, the 1799 Derby winner.

'Potatoes' was finally 'planted' when he died at Upper Hare Park in November 1800.

THE PRIZEMONEY CHEQUE

BETTY LANE HOLLAND

The welfare benefits of today were unknown during the Great Depression of the 1930s. A few people lived comfortably but there were many battlers who lived by their wits. One such was Bill.

Bill, a battling racehorse trainer, was delighted when he won his first race for three years at a northwest New South Wales race meeting in the 1930s.

In those days, country race meetings had prizemoney cheques pre-written so that as soon as correct weight was declared, all that had to be done was to write in the winning owner's name and the cheque issued. As Bill was also the owner of the horse, he lost no time in going to the secretary's office to collect his cheque.

He was walking from the office holding the cheque at eye level, looking at it with admiration, and had only gone ten paces when he heard from behind, 'Congratulations, it was a good win.'

The voice was that of the local produce merchant to whom the trainer owed money and whose patience had been stretched. Times were hard and the trainer had paid a little off the account here and there, but whenever a payment was made, it seemed the account went a little higher the following week.

Several times the produce merchant had threatened there would be no more credit but he had kept supplying as he knew the horse would be underfed if he didn't.

When the produce man said, 'Think I'd better take that cheque off what you owe me,' Bill realised he didn't have much option, so said, 'Sure, sure.' He had survived the past three years by living off his wits, so thinking quickly, added, 'But let me have twenty pounds for the phone bill. My wife's not well and we need the phone and they'll cut it off on Monday if I don't pay.'

Pleased to be getting a big slice off his long overdue account, the produce merchant plucked the cheque from Bill's fingers then pulled out his wallet, counted out twenty 1-pound notes and handed the money across to Bill.

As the produce merchant walked away, Bill with his head bent despondently, shuffled off in the opposite direction. He waited ten minutes then raised his head, stood tiptoes and scanned the area. It seemed all clear.

Back to the secretary's office with a long miserable face, he said, 'You wouldn't believe it, but I've lost that cheque. Will you cancel it and write me another one please?'

HARD LUCK

A.B. 'BANJO' PATERSON

I left the course, and by my side
There walked a ruined tout—
A hungry creature, evil-eyed,
Who poured this story out.

'You see,' he said, 'there came a swell
To Kensington today,
And, if I picked the winners well,
A crown at least he'd pay.

'I picked three winners straight, I did;
I filled his purse with pelf,
And then he gave me half a quid
To back one for myself.

'A half a quid to me he cast—
I wanted it indeed;
So help me Bob, for two days past
I haven't had a feed.

'But still I thought my luck was in,
I couldn't go astray—
I put it all on Little Min,
And lost it straightaway.

'I haven't got a bite or bed,
I'm absolutely stuck;
So keep this lesson in your head:
Don't over-trust your luck!'

The folks went homeward, near and far,
The tout, oh! Where was he?
Ask where the empty boilers are
Beside the Circular Quay.

BUSH RACES AND PICNICS

JIM HAYNES

As settlements spread out into the bush in the nineteenth century, horses became an essential part of life, and they were virtually the only means of transport. Whether it was a good saddle horse or a sulky, buggy, dray or Cobb and Co coach, horses were the only alternative to walking.

Entertainment in the bush was limited and race meetings became the most common way to let your hair down after a spell of hard work, a way to socialise after living in isolation for a while. Along with this came the love of a long weekend or a holiday, the belief that handicapping the more talented performers makes things 'more interesting', and the Australian love of gambling.

After World War II, most large inland and coastal towns in New South Wales had a registered race club which ran thoroughbred meetings under the direction of the Australian Jockey Club (AJC), and in rural Victoria thoroughbred racing was well organised and had always been popular.

Smaller towns, however, had few if any thoroughbred horses or trainers and still ran meetings more along the lines of the 'pony racing' clubs in the cities, and many race meetings outside the metropolitan areas featured non-thoroughbred horses. Until quite recently, race meetings in smaller towns, or 'bush races', were a mixture of 'pony racing' and 'grass-fed hacks', with a sprinkling of thoroughbreds.

Picnic races are a great Australian pastime and anyone who has never attended such an event is probably poorer for not having enjoyed the experience. There is still a thriving circuit of picnic races in Victoria, where you will find registered thoroughbreds racing at the same meeting as non-registered horses ridden by amateurs. There are also races especially for horses straight from the paddock, 'grass-fed hacks', whose owners are trusted to obey the convention of not feeding grain or supplements to their entries for a certain period prior to the meeting. New South Wales towns tend to have annual picnic meetings which are great social occasions. The most famous of these is the Bong Bong Picnics, featuring the Bong Bong Cup, held at Wyeera, near Bowral in the Southern Highlands.

The event began in 1886 and almost a century later, in 1985, a crowd of 37,000 behaved so badly that the AJC revoked the club's 'once a year' licence. Local MP John Fahey (later to become NSW Premier and Federal Minister for Finance) said that the rioting and public fornication at the meeting was enough to 'make a Roman orgy look like a Sunday picnic'.

The licence was reinstated in 1992 under the strict condition that the event be limited to 5000 members and guests, making it, ironically, one of the most desirable and exclusive events of the Sydney social calendar!

RIDERS IN THE STAND

A.B. 'BANJO' PATERSON

There's some that ride the Robbo style, and bump at every stride;
While others sit a long way back, to get a longer ride.
There's some that ride like sailors do, with legs and arms, and teeth;
And some ride on the horse's neck, and some ride underneath.

But all the finest horsemen out, the men to Beat the Band,
You'll find amongst the crowd that ride their races in the Stand.
They'll say, 'He had the race in hand, and lost it in the straight.'
They'll show how Godby came too soon, and Barden came too late.

They'll say Chevalley lost his nerve, and Regan lost his head;
They'll tell how one was 'livened up' and something else was 'dead'.
In fact, the race was never run on sea, or sky, or land,
But what you'd get it better done by riders in the Stand.

The rule holds good in everything in life's uncertain fight;
You'll find the winner can't go wrong, the loser can't go right.
You ride a slashing race, and lose, by one and all you're banned!
Ride like a bag of flour, and win, they'll cheer you in the Stand.

A CUNNING PLAN

JIM HAYNES

As well as his amazing record of victories, Phar Lap could probably have also easily won the Caulfield Cup of 1930. The fact that he was left in the field so long and scratched quite late was controversial at the time.

It was, indeed, part of 'a cunning plan'.

Nothing outside the rules of racing took place but some, mostly bookmakers, consider the actions of Harry Telford and fellow Sydney trainer Frank McGrath had a tinge of mischief about them, one might even say 'skulduggery'.

Most racing men say it was a stroke of genius.

I have to interrupt the narrative here to say a few things.

Firstly, I have the greatest respect for both men. Harry Telford was the astute 'genius' who had the vision to pick Phar Lap as a future champion based wholly upon his breeding, and Frank McGrath was one of the greatest trainers of stayers in our racing history. He trained Prince Foote to win the Melbourne Cup in 1909 and Peter Pan to win two more in the 1930s.

As a punter I applaud their cunning plan to empty the bookies' bags without any harm being done to man or beast and no interference with the way the races were run.

Indeed, I have it on the best authority that Frank McGrath never knowingly did anything detrimental to any of the great horses he trained. He patiently nursed Peter Pan back to health through two serious illnesses, an infection caused by running a nail through his hoof as a two-year-old, and a debilitating form of rheumatism in his shoulders which caused him to miss an entire year of racing.

In each case patience and kindness prevailed and Peter Pan won two Melbourne Cups, one after each setback.

McGrath's patience and love of the horses he trained was evident again with his stayer Denis Boy, who he nursed back to racing fitness after breaking a knee bone. McGrath kept the horse's leg in a sling until the bone healed. He then trained Denis Boy to win the 1932 AJC Metropolitan Handicap and run fourth behind Peter Pan in the Melbourne Cup.

In 1940 an attempt was made to shoot McGrath's Cup favourite, the Cox Plate and Mackinnon Stakes winner Beau Vite. The marksman managed to shoot another of McGrath's horses, El Golea, by mistake. Beau Vite ran fourth behind Old Rowley in the Cup that year, and McGrath nursed El Golea back to fitness to run third in the Mackinnon in 1941 and third in the Caulfield Cup in 1942.

Frank McGrath knew horses. He had been a good jockey and was a survivor of the infamous Caulfield Cup race fall of 1885, when sixteen horses fell in a field of 41. One jockey was killed and many injured.

As a trainer he understood how to condition a horse and how to place horses to best advantage, but more than that, he was a trainer who cared for his horses. A trainer of the old school in many ways, McGrath was also 'modern' in the sense that he always put the horse's welfare first, and his plans were always long-term. His Cups double plan was one of his best.

McGrath was astute and realistic; he knew his great stayer Amounis was unbeatable in the Caulfield Cup of 1930, if two particular horses were not there. In early markets, however, Amounis was at long odds.

The cunning plan revolved around three great horses: Amounis, Phar Lap and Nightmarch.

Nightmarch had defeated Phar Lap in the Melbourne Cup of 1929 but, the following spring, Nightmarch was defeated four times in a row by the 'Red Terror' and his owner, Mr A. Louisson, had been heard to say that if Phar Lap contested the Caulfield Cup, he would take Nightmarch back to New Zealand for the

New Zealand Cup—rather than run against the champion again in the Caulfield Cup.

In a conversation with Harry Telford, Frank McGrath suggested that his great stayer Amounis, the only horse to defeat Phar Lap twice, would win the Caulfield Cup if Nightmarch and Phar Lap didn't start. He suggested that Telford leave Phar Lap in the Caulfield Cup field until Louisson took his horse home. In that time they could get very lucrative odds about their two horses winning the Caulfield–Melbourne Cups double. Then Telford could scratch Phar Lap from the Caulfield Cup and the two trainers would make a fortune betting on the Cups double.

The plan worked perfectly.

Seeing that Phar Lap was set to contest the Caulfield Cup, Louisson took Nightmarch home—and he duly won the New Zealand Cup.

Then Harry Telford scratched Phar Lap, stating that he didn't want to over-race the champion, and Amounis duly won the Caulfield Cup.

Phar Lap, of course, famously and easily won the second leg, the Melbourne Cup, and the two trainers sent a battalion of bookies near bankrupt.

How do I know Frank McGrath was such a kind and patient trainer? Well, I play tennis twice a week with his granddaughter who assures me it's true.

She also tells me that her grandfather bought a very expensive imported motorcar . . . sometime late in 1930.

FIRECRACKER

JIM BENDRODT

I turned and looked back. Now, that is something many folk contend should not be done. But I did.

I'd sat all day at the edge of the sale ring while the thoroughbreds paraded and men paid tens of thousands for them. I'd looked with covetous eyes at horses I'd have given my very soul to own, but this was a place where hard cash talked, and I had no cash, hard or otherwise.

And so at last I had walked away because the prices were beyond me, and when I'd travelled some 50 yards towards the exit, I heard the auctioneer's derisive roar upbraiding those whose highest bid was 50 guineas.

I said I turned and looked back, and in the distance I saw a tall black horse, and once again I heard the auctioneer roar, 'What, 50 guineas? Surely, gentlemen, you haven't looked at this one!'

I started walking back, and I heard someone call 52 and a half and then, after a bit, 55, and the auctioneer shouted, 'I've got 57 and a half just over here.'

I said, 'You've got 60, mister.' And then his hammer smashed onto the rostrum.

That's how I bought Firecracker, by Cistercian out of Persian Nan. And the folk who knew Persian Nan said the mare was mad.

Well, maybe so, I didn't know his mother, so I couldn't tell you, but I do know that her son was equine dynamite. I've had so many horses but, among them all, I've never owned a horse like him.

I paid my 60 guineas at the auctioneer's desk, and I remember that the balance in my wallet wasn't much. Then I found the number of his stall, and went to see him. I found the man who cared for him and seven other yearlings. I gave him a little money, and then I said, 'Well, let's have a look at him.'

'So *you* bought the blighter, did you?' the man asked, and added, 'Well, you've got a handful.' He pulled the top and bottom bolts of the heavy door and opened it. 'You be careful,' he said, 'this coot is mad. I come from the station he was bred on, and it took five of us three days to catch him in the paddock where he's been running wild for months.'

He sidled cautiously towards the colt's near side. He had tied the horse's head to a strong ringbolt with a heavy length of rope, a thing no horseman worthy of his salt would do. 'Get over, you!' he roared, and smashed the horse in the soft underbelly with his clenched fist, and the colt struck at him with the speed of light . . . and so did I.

My right hand took his shoulder and whirled him round so that he looked at me in blank astonishment. 'Take it easy, lad,' I said, and looked at him for a little time. 'Now get out,' I ordered, 'and stay out.' He left the stall without another word, and did not come back.

We got the black colt home eventually to the humble stable that I rented for him, and began to break him in. I say 'began' because that about describes it. We couldn't break him in, and we never did, to the degree that is desirable. He was a queer horse, lean and hard and streamlined, with a lovely fine-drawn head and a remorseless wicked eye.

They are usually so gentle, so easily handled, these baby horses from the famous studs. A little touchy maybe, a trifle nervous, perhaps more difficult than a pleasant-natured dog, but not much trouble as a general rule. But Firecracker! Well, why go into it in detail? By an imported English stallion from the black mare Persian Nan, and knowing folk said Persian Nan was mad!

Well, her son was surely crazy in his first four months with us, and then he settled down and, up to a point, but not beyond it, would do as he was told, but it was always the horse that drew the line as I remember it, though we tried to.

It was in the midst of the Depression years when I bought Firecracker, and 60 guineas was a lot of money then. You may know the Palais Royal, or you may have heard of it, no doubt. The giant dance hall I owned was staggering through the lean hard times with every sail set to catch its hard-won silver pieces. We didn't get 6000 people back then, as we did in better times.

We got Firecracker ready and entered him at Menangle in a race of 5½ furlongs, just enough for Firecracker. He won at 6 furlongs eventually, but 'only just', as the horsemen put it; but that was later. At three years old he moved over 5½ furlongs like a swift machine, and then he'd stop. He wouldn't go another yard, except at a canter.

On Monday night when the show was all over, I called my Palais Royal staff together.

'Boys,' I said, and then I bowed a trifle towards the grinning girls, 'and ladies, I think the time has come to have a little talk. Now let's see, there are about 125 of you and I've been having quite a time taking care of you in this damn Depression. I think I'm right when I say most of you have been with me for years. I know you all have a faith and trust in me.'

A somewhat raucous bellow from the background interrupted me at this point. I paused and then continued, 'Well, we're going to have a gamble. Your wages for your work this week are in the bank for payment on Friday, about £600, I think. I've got the change the cashiers use, and I've hocked everything I own, which isn't much, and tomorrow I'm going to put the proceeds on a horse.

'If he wins, he'll save the Palais Royal. If he gets licked, well—that's the end of us, and I'm afraid you'll have to go to work at last. Now how about it? Two to one is the price you'll get, no matter what the price is that he starts at, and the rest is to go to keep this old show open.'

I could see Bill Swift. I could see him grin as I talked to them. Bill was the lad they'd follow in a case like this, so I talked to him, and he grinned back at me derisively, and once he interrupted with his deep rich Irish voice, 'Sure, boss, and it's a generous little soul you always were, so help me, and it's round your little finger that you'll be twisting us poor stupid goats as usual.'

'Bill,' I said, 'how well you know that, night and day, only one thought moves me, and that's your blasted welfare, else how could it be that you are my staff manager at your luscious salary, when half the world is starving?'

'Sure and it's three-quarters of my luscious salary that you've been borrowing from me to feed your crackpot horse, who would otherwise be starving like the rest of them, and now it's the lot you'll take to bet on the feckless loon tomorrow, and that'll be the end of it, so it will, or me mother's name was Rachel.'

The delighted treble of the girls' laughter fought with the rumble of the male voices when he answered me. He was a natural salesman, this Bill Swift.

He was so many other things to me. Years before I'd advertised for a fighting man. I ran a show in those days, a fine big rink in a hard tough section near the waterfront, and I needed help because respectability was its slogan, and its patrons needed guidance in the civilised amenities as ordained by me. And so I had to have a 'man of his hands' to help me in my inroads on my precious patrons' natural inclinations.

So many likely fellows came in answer to the advertisement, and when one stood before me I would say, 'And now, my lad, do you think you could whip me in a dust-up?' and, because of policy or some other reason, they all said 'No', until Bill came.

A great tall lad about my own age, from a wind-jammer in the harbour, thick in the middle even then, with a caveman's torso and lethal hands. With bright blue eyes under thick red brows, and a torrid head of hair. And when I said, 'Well, Bill, do you think you could whip me?' he said without an instant's hesitation, 'My flaming oath!'

So I took him to the rink's high roof where my small gym was, and we pulled the gloves on. He was a rough-and-tumble fighter, whose equal I knew but once before, but he was a child in the tricks of Mr Queensberry. I doubt if he'd ever seen a pair of boxing gloves. It was the rapier against the blundering broadsword, but I knew this was my man right from the start and ever since he'd been with me through tumultuous years of triumphs and disasters.

I think the things I liked best about Bill were his Irish sense of humour and his loyalty. With him, loyalty went to far extremes, and this little yarn will tell you just how far it did go.

Some years before we had rocketed out of Melbourne in my Marmon Speedster, Bill Swift, Steve and Bill Romaine, and I. We climbed the Gippsland mountains over the yellow slippery highway, and a summer cyclone kept us company. The narrow road was greasy, un-tarred, unpaved, and, at a point where the mountain was a wall on one side, my back tyres slipped, and the Marmon skidded sideways.

When she stopped, the car's rear wheels rested a bare 3 inches from the outer edge of a gentle slope that skirted the road itself, and beyond the edge of that slope where the wheels rested there was nothing. Two thousand feet below, the treetops growing in the valley looked like children's toys. The bonnet of the car thrust upwards at an angle to the road itself.

You know those old cars. You held the foot-brake on with sheer strength. The handbrake was nearly always useless. You didn't have hydraulic power in braking systems back then.

I knew I'd hold the foot-brake down for quite a long time, and I knew that when I got tired, as I must eventually, my leg would lose the power that kept the pedal level with the floor. I knew then that we'd go tumbling down to where the treetops waved so far below. I told Steve and Bill Romaine to get out quickly, but I said to do it quietly and with care. I didn't want to shake the car. Along the running-board and over the bonnet, and then onto the road. That was the way they reached safety.

And then I said to Bill Swift, 'Now, Bill, get going. I can't keep this pressure on forever.'

Bill looked at me and growled, 'No, boss.'

'But Bill, why two of us?' I asked. 'There's nothing you can do, that's obvious. You get out.' I looked at him and his heavy face was hard as granite, so I tried again in a different way: 'Please, Bill.'

'No,' he said, and nothing else.

I watched him reach for his tobacco pouch and papers. He rolled a cigarette and leaned over and put it in my mouth, then rolled another one. Above and about us the cyclone howled. He held a hooded match to my cigarette, and I said curiously, 'Why, Bill?'

He answered, 'Aw, hell, there's times a man likes company. Let's forget it.'

Then for a time there was nothing except the crazy roaring of the wind, and then Bill looked at me and his voice was gentle when he asked, 'Getting tired, boss?'

'Yes, a bit, Bill.'

Then I saw his eyes lift above my head and he said urgently, 'Take it easy, boss. Keep that foot down hard, then take a look.'

I turned my head and there, coming round the shoulder of the mountain, a hundred yards away, was a bright red Buick Phaeton.

The driver had a steel tow rope, and he said he came from Denmark, which was a queer thing because my father came from Denmark, and you wouldn't have found another Dane in all that thousand miles of mountain wilderness, especially one with a power-laden Buick Phaeton and a steel tow rope, on that tempest-ridden day.

You have to hand it to a man like that Dane. He knew as we knew, because we warned him, that when he took the strain my car might slip that bare 3 inches and, if it did, then he'd go tumbling down with us to where those treetops twisted in the gale so far below.

We thanked him a little later when the Marmon stood four-square on the road, and we drank his fiery advocaat and went on our way.

So that was Bill and that was loyalty. A handy thing. And rare. So now I beckoned Bill to bend down while my crowd of dance-hall people waited.

'Bill,' I whispered, 'it's worth the chance. They'll get their £600 in wages on Friday, then we'll have to close, and they'd get nothing else except the dole. Now, if Firecracker can make it, we'll have lots of money to carry on for weeks, and this Depression cannot last forever. How about it?'

He looked at me with his bright blue eyes alight with laughter. 'Sure, and I always said you'd talk the leg off an iron pot, but you're crazy, boss. Gold-digger will beat that long-legged loon of yours by half a mile.'

So I tried again and this time I was cunning because I didn't argue. I simply said, a little sadly, 'Quitting is a queer thing for the Irish, Bill.'

He shook his head like an angry bison, and then stood up and his great voice filled that echoing dance hall.

'Now, blast the lot of you,' he roared, 'what's all this talk about anyhow? This bonny horse the boss has got is just a certainty. Sure, and it's a fine idea and good enough for the little bit of money he wants from us. Now, get about your work. We'll get our wages Friday, and for a lot of Fridays after that. It's a grand notion, so it is.' Then *sotto voce* to me, 'May the good Lord forgive me for being Australia's greatest liar, because it'll be that chestnut rascal Gold-digger that'll be paying off tomorrow afternoon.'

By the price of him, the bookmakers agreed with Bill, because when we reached Menangle Gold-digger was at a nervous 6 to 4. We had come up in the Marmon Speedster over the dusty country roads on a lazy summer day, and there were eight of us all told in a motor built for four. They were the smartest of my big boys from the Palais Royal.

You didn't run a dance hall like that one without some headaches. Five and six thousand people in a night are a lot to care for in one big public place within four walls. They came and chattered, danced and flirted in that gaudy mausoleum, and as the night wore on the giant building shook and quivered with the thrust of stamping feet, or whispered like the wind brushing sand along a beach when the musicians played a waltz.

The smoke from cigarettes would curl up in lazy blue-grey layers to the caverns in the roof where brilliant lanterns hung in clustered thousands, and after a bit these would grow dim blood-red in colour, or hazy emerald-green, or faint old-rose. The jungle beat in the music thrust and throbbed relentlessly on the eardrums of the dancing multitude until they postured and grimaced and genuflected like a herd of mesmerised buffoons.

But you didn't succeed in a place like that because of coloured lights and mass hypnosis. You knew that among these multitudes there would be people who came to prey on lads and lasses out for fun. They didn't come to listen to the music. You had to keep the liquor out of crowds like these; I would as soon have nitro-glycerine in a place like that as sparkling wine. So you had your private army to guard your patrons from marauders, to rule your dance hall with an iron hand, and you knew you'd often have to use them in the hectic midnight hours when your famous dancing rendezvous exploded in your face.

I'd brought the best of them with me. I'd given them each one-eighth of all my money and their wages, and the funds I had borrowed on my car, my race glasses and on any other mortal thing I could get my hands on. Then, half an hour before the race, I gave each of my lads a square of bookmakers to work on. They were to commence to bet at a given signal. These bookmakers are hard to trap, especially at Menangle, but there were things that favoured me. I heard two of them talking before the race started.

'Tom, what's this Firecracker?'

'Firecracker?' Tom echoed. 'Oh, 'im. Some goat that fellow Bendrodt trains.'

'What! Trains 'im, does 'e? Well, wouldn't that rock you! What next will 'e do? 'E couldn't train a rabbit to run up a burrow.'

'Naw,' said Tom. ''E's got Cook riding 'im.'

'What!' the other fellow said in pained surprise. 'Cook! Why, 'ow did 'e get 'im to ride it, I wonder?'

'Friend of 'is, I guess,' said Tom. 'Anyway, we needn't worry about Firecracker, 'e's never had a run. Gold-digger is a certainty.'

When betting opened, Firecracker was at 10 to 1 and, when the money flowed for Gold-digger, I took my hat off and ran my fingers through my hair and, in a flash, eight good men commenced to bet as one.

In 90 seconds Firecracker was at 5 to 1 and, in 90 more, you had to fight to get the bookies to lay you 6 to 4. And no wonder. My lads were old in this game, and they had bet a lot of money—for Menangle. The vouchers they carried in their pockets would keep the Palais Royal going for a decent time to come if Firecracker won. But could he?

I legged Bill Cook up and said to him, 'Now, Bill, this is serious. So pay attention to what I tell you. This fellow's got to win, because, if he doesn't, five minutes afterwards I'll just be passing Suva going strong. No foolin', Bill, you've got to win it.'

And Bill, who rarely paid attention to anything I said, or for that matter to anything that anybody said, looked down at me and asked in consternation, 'But, boss, what's he done? He's never had a race. I can't come home without the horse, you know, it isn't done.'

'Quit fooling, Bill,' I said. 'Firecracker is a little peculiar.' Then, as alarm spread over his face and I saw him take a tighter grip on the reins, I hastened to add, 'But he's fast, Bill, very fast. He's only peculiar because his mother was Persian Nan, and she was a wee bit mad, so they tell me. You talk to him going to the post and get his confidence. Don't hit him for heaven's sake, or you'll need a parachute to bring you down. And be careful at the barrier, Bill, because that's where he really gets peculiar. He'll only go for 5½ furlongs and then he'll stop as if he's hit a wall. So hug the rails as if you loved them, and don't make him go an unnecessary yard. Out and home, Bill, that's the ticket.'

'Aw, for God's sake,' Bill replied morosely. He clucked at Firecracker and Firecracker obediently erupted through the gate onto the course and disappeared into the distance, with Bill Cook doing stunts that would have turned a Cossack green with envy.

They didn't have announcers back in the days I write about, and I couldn't see the start without my glasses. But the track was dry and sandy, so I knew when a bunch of horses travelled in a cloud of dust to a turn a quarter of a mile or more away. But I couldn't see the colours, and I didn't hear the crowd. I knew a sort of dull, sick feeling, and it seemed that every second was a year.

Then in the distance I could hear their hooves thudding on the hard dry ground as the field swung towards the furlong pole, and I could see a tall black horse skimming along the rails with a golden chestnut close behind him, and the rest 10 lengths away. And then I became a cold stone statue, and the world a place where nothing seemed to focus.

Then a smashing blow hit me between the shoulder blades, and an Irish voice roared joyously, 'By the holy saints, it's Firecracker! It's the feckless loon himself, so help me Bob!'

Part 2
THE WILD COLONIAL DAYS

INTRODUCTION—A BRIEF HISTORY OF COLONIAL RACING

No nation in the world has venerated its champion racehorses as Australia has. Every few years we seem to find a new thoroughbred to admire. It is a part of our culture to have a champion to follow as each racing year unfolds. This tradition was established quite early in colonial times.

Australians have a particular obsession with racing, which is probably due to the importance of horses in the development of the colonies in the nineteenth century. The horse was the main mode of transport until the industrial age, and without the horse this vast country could not have been settled.

Apart from the convicts, the first settlers were mostly military men and most of them owned horses—and, when given a chance and a holiday, they enjoyed racing them.

As settlements spread out into the bush, horses became even more essential. Entertainment was limited and race meetings became the most common way to socialise, relax and celebrate.

General public involvement in racing is far greater in Australia than anywhere else in the world. It is amusing to speculate that the percentage of the Australian population who actually attended Spring Carnival racing in Melbourne in the 1890s, if translated into similar figures in Britain, would have seen four million people attending the Derby meeting at Epsom!

Australian racing officially began in the colony of New South Wales in 1810, when the first three-day meeting was held at Hyde Park in Sydney. The winning post was approximately where Market

Street meets Elizabeth Street today, and the meeting established the tradition for right-handed racing in New South Wales, that being the most convenient way of going as the sun set to the west.

Both Arabian and thoroughbred horses had been imported into the colony from the time of the first European settlement, and match races had been popular prior to that first meeting in 1810.

When the 73rd Regiment was transferred to Ceylon in 1814, the colony lost its race committee and racing became uncontrolled and was banned for a time by Governor Macquarie.

The original Sydney Turf Club (STC) was formed in 1825 and began racing at Captain Piper's racecourse at Bellevue Hill under the patronage of Governor Brisbane, who had banned unofficial meetings and dangerous races around the now dilapidated course at Hyde Park.

Colonial politics and a public insult at an STC dinner led to the next governor, Governor Darling, withdrawing his patronage from the turf club in 1827. Twenty-nine members resigned in support of the governor and formed the Australian Racing and Jockey Club (ARJC).

The STC raced at Camperdown and the ARJC raced at Parramatta, and from 1832 to 1841 racing was conducted on cleared scrub land at Randwick, which was known as 'The Sandy Track'.

Racing in Sydney suffered from the poor condition of tracks until 1840, when the Australian Race Committee was formed to set up a decent racetrack at Homebush. This group then decided to form a permanent race club, and the Australian Jockey Club (AJC) was officially born in 1842. The Homebush track was used until the completion of the 'new' Randwick in 1860.

In Melbourne, racing started at Flemington in 1840. In 1848, 350 acres were officially designated to be a public racecourse, and a committee, which became the Port Phillip Racing Club, was set up to regulate racing. In the 1850s this club disbanded and two new clubs, the Victoria Turf Club (VTC) and the Victoria Jockey Club (VJC), became bitter rivals.

It was the VTC that instituted the Melbourne Cup in 1861. The third Cup, however, was a disaster: only seven horses started after all inter-colonial trainers, and many Melbourne trainers, boycotted the event when the committee refused to accept Archer's entry on technical grounds. Politics and inter-colonial rivalry threatened to ruin the event until the clearer heads of both the turf and jockey clubs came together to form the Victoria Racing Club in 1864, and Flemington and the Cup became the property of the VRC.

Australia's first popular champion racehorse was a gelding called Jorrocks, who raced in the 1840s. His story is told in this section.

Racing during Jorrocks's time was a very different affair to the racing we know today. Races were started by a man on a pony whose job it was to attempt to muster the contestants into a reasonably straight line before dropping a large white flag.

Races were most commonly run over three heats and the winner was the horse with the best overall result. There was a large pole situated on each racecourse, sometimes about a furlong from the winning post or near the turn. This was known as 'the distance' and horses that did not 'make the distance' in a heat were 'out of the running' and could not compete in the subsequent heats.

If the judges considered a finish too close to call, the heat was declared 'dead' and the horses that figured in the close finish would 'run off' over the same distance again to decide the winner. So, in those days, a 'dead heat' was not a result, but a 'non result' which required another heat to be run.

There were no saddlecloth numbers until the 1870s and official colours were not compulsory for jockeys until the AJC introduced that rule in 1842. After each race the contestants would line up in front of the judges' box. This was referred to as 'saluting the judge' and the tradition of winning jockeys saluting with their whip, holding it aloft or touching their cap as they come back to the winner's stall is a carry-over of this old tradition.

The judges then looked at each horse and rider and checked the horses' looks and jockeys' colours against the 'official entries' list, or 'race card'. The judges then announced the placegetters, who returned to scale to be weighed in.

Before the registration of names was properly controlled, different horses often raced with the same names. There were three Tim Whifflers in the Australian colonies in the 1860s: one was an imported stallion who sired the 1876 Melbourne Cup winner Briseis, and the other two Tim Whifflers both raced in the Melbourne Cup of 1867. 'Sydney Tim', trained by Etienne de Mestre, won the Cup and 'Melbourne Tim' ran fifth!

By the 1860s a new era of racing had dawned. Racing clubs had begun to regulate racing in the colonies, with the AJC taking the lead, and the famous Admiral Rous had standardised the rules of racing in Britain and established the weight-for-age system where horses of each sex carry a set weight at a certain age over certain distances. His close personal friend, Captain Standish, had left England, following a rather disastrous betting plunge in an Epsom Derby, to become Chief Commissioner of Police in the colony of Victoria.

Standish has two claims to fame in Australian history. He led the rather inept hunt for the Kelly gang and, as chairman of the Victoria Turf Club, he is credited as being the man who 'invented' the Melbourne Cup.

The Cup began in 1861, the same year that the AJC introduced the Australian Derby, and a new era of racing developed around it.

The rival clubs of Victoria put aside their differences and merged into the VRC in 1864. Meanwhile, in Sydney, the AJC, having returned to a new and improved Randwick in 1860, soon attempted to emulate the success of its Melbourne counterparts.

In 1866 the AJC introduced four new races, the Metropolitan Handicap, the first official Sydney Cup, the Champagne Stakes and the Doncaster Handicap. And along with the new races came a new champion, The Barb.

Australian racing had been through a stage of incredible growth in the 1860s, and the 1870s saw a series of unsavoury scandals involving trainers hiding horses' true abilities.

Two of the worst of these incidents involved horses from St Albans Stud near Geelong. A protest was entered the day after the 1873 Melbourne Cup over the uncertain ownership, age and identity of winner Don Juan. A tale of disguised ownership emerged, and the public image of racing suffered even more when a huge Melbourne Cup plunge on the lightly raced Savanaka occurred in 1877.

Savanaka lost the Cup to the Sydney champ Chester, but the unsavoury link between betting and training was damaging the image of racing. The tragic loss in a storm of nine Sydney horses bound for the 1876 Melbourne Spring Carnival on board the steamer *City of Melbourne* was made worse by the celebrations initiated by Melbourne's bookmakers on hearing the news.

The bookies stood to lose a fortune on early betting for the carnival on the Sydney horses and those returning to Melbourne from the Sydney Spring Carnival, particularly on the Cup where Robin Hood—the best horse Etienne de Mestre ever trained, according to the trainer himself—had been well backed. Robin Hood died in the storm along with the Cup favourite and Metropolitan winner Nemesis, and the well-backed contenders Sovereign and Burgundy.

Racing was suffering from skulduggery and shady practices throughout the 1870s. The general public had lost faith in the integrity of the sport and it was heading into very unsavoury territory and risked becoming a 'second-rate' sporting activity in the eyes of the media and the average Aussie.

This general view was not improved by the disgusting behaviour of the Melbourne bookmakers in celebrating the loss of the horses in the storm of 1876 and their unbelievably audacious and unsporting gesture of presenting a purse to the captain of the *City of Melbourne* (the hilariously named Captain Paddle), as a reward for not turning back when requested to and thus precipitating the tragic loss, and painful deaths, of nine valuable thoroughbreds.

Cheating the handicapper and nobbling horses was so rife in racing around this time that any honest trainer, owner or jockey often lived in fear of his life.

An illustration of the parlous state of racing at the time can be found in the outrageous and blatant, and ultimately successful, attempts made by bookmakers to stop the well-backed colt Newminster from winning the VRC Derby in 1876.

Newminster was a very well performed colt by The Marquis who had won the Maribyrnong Plate, Two Year Old Stakes, Sire's Produce Stakes and Ascot Vale Stakes and was thus red-hot favourite to win the AJC Derby.

It was well known that his owner Mr A. Chirnside and his trainer Frank Dakin were 'straight' racing men. This account was given in *The Australasian* newspaper not long after the near wreck of the *City of Melbourne*:

> Mr Dakin, the trainer of Newminster, had to dismiss one of his boys found talking to a bookmaker and shortly afterwards Newminster was found lying in his stable in great agony, apparently having been poisoned.

Newminster recovered from the poisoning, so the bookmakers resorted to different tactics. They paid the entry for several poorly performed horses in the derby and these also-rans caused enough interference to ensure that Newminster ran sixth.

Things improved slowly through the 1880s. The decade began with Grand Flaneur winning the Melbourne Cup and setting a record that will surely never be broken; he is the only undefeated Melbourne Cup winner in the history of the race.

The AJC had taken firm control of New South Wales racing by 1880, and the VRC established the Official Racing Calendar in 1882 and declared that all race meetings throughout Victoria had to run in accordance with the VRC rules. Horses competing on racetracks that did not comply were banned from racing at Flemington.

More importantly the VRC decided to register and license bookmakers in 1882 and the AJC quickly followed suit.

Racing was slowly building a better public image although unlicensed bookmakers still operated off course and heinous deeds were not completely wiped out.

In 1885 another of Frank Dakin's horses, the Melbourne Cup favourite and well-performed stayer Commotion, who had run third in the 1883 Cup carrying 10 st 1 lb (64 kg) and second in 1884 carrying 9 st 12 lb (62.5 kg), was found to be 'suffering from injury to the sinews of his off fore leg' according to *The Herald*, which went on to report that:

> Treatment was resorted to without avail, and the horse was scratched for all engagements. To-night's Police Gazette contains a notice offering £1000 reward for information that would lead to the conviction of the persons implicated in laming him. It is stated that a stable boy had received £200 to lame the horse by striking him with a heavy blunt instrument, probably a hammer, on the fore leg. The horse is lamed for life. The reward will not be paid for the conviction of the stable boy alone.

Nevertheless, racing was entering a golden era as the 1890s rolled around. The skulduggery and shonky practices of the 1860s and 1870s had receded to a large degree. Unregistered or 'pony racing' was growing in popularity in Sydney and Melbourne, and that form of racing would remain popular until the 1930s and perhaps provided an outlet for the 'less savoury' elements of the racing industry.

So the scene was set for the greatest champion of them all to appear and take Australia and New Zealand on the ride of a lifetime. The time was ripe for the appearance of the best racehorse that ever breathed, the mighty Carbine.

The century ended with the colonies federating to become a new nation and the 'colonial era' passing into history. This coincided with the arrival upon the racing scene of arguably the greatest mare to ever race in Australia, at least until the arrival of Makybe Diva and Black Caviar a century later. Her name was Wakeful, and her story ends this section of the book.

THE IRON GELDING

JIM HAYNES

Jorrocks, foaled in 1833, was the first horse to attain popularity and champion status in Australia. His sire, Whisker, was by the English Derby winner of the same name and had been the colony's best racehorse, winning the Governor's Cup at the very first Randwick meeting in 1833. Jorrocks's dam, Matilda, had been the colony's best race mare and the mating between the two contemporary champions produced Jorrocks. Both his parents traced their lineage back to the mighty Eclipse, and his bloodline on his dam side contained a fair dose of Arab as well as English thoroughbred.

What is odd is that, despite his excellent racing pedigree, Jorrocks didn't race until he was five. This was probably due to the sale of the property where he was bred at South Creek and his transfer to another farm near Mudgee, where Jorrocks was used as a stock horse until winning a sweepstakes at Coolah, after which he was sent to be trained at Windsor by noted trainer Joseph Brown.

His ownership changed hands many times over the years but Richard Rouse, who saw him in Joseph Brown's stables before his career had properly begun, famously bought him. The price paid by Rouse was eight heifers, valued at £40.

Jorrocks clearly had strong legs and a steely constitution and became known as the 'Iron Gelding'. He was the first racehorse in Australia to have his picture in the newspaper and poems written about him. He stood 14.2 hands—tiny by today's standards—and was a long, low animal with an amazingly deep girth and fine Arab head.

Jorrocks raced in an era when most events were decided on the best of three heats, often over 2 or 3 miles each. He probably started more than 100 times; the true figure is hard to estimate due to the three-heat system of races. We do know that he won the AJC Australian Plate five times and the Bathurst Town Plate four times. He was also victorious twice in such races as the Homebush Champion Cup, Cumberland Cup, Metropolitan Stakes, Hawkesbury Members' Purse and Town Plate.

Jorrocks began racing seriously as an eight-year-old, and at the age of seventeen he started eight times for four wins. His last hurrah came at the grand old age of nineteen.

The Australian Jockey Club had abandoned Randwick in 1842 for the Homebush course, which became Sydney's headquarters of racing until the AJC returned to the improved Randwick course in 1860. So it was at Homebush that Jorrocks won his major victories and ran his final race, finishing tailed off last in the Metropolitan Stakes of 1852.

Jorrocks was finally retired to live out his days on a farm at Richmond, about an hour northwest of Sydney. His grave is marked by a plaque and is situated on what is today the Richmond Airbase. He set the trend for champion racehorses becoming much-loved 'public figures' with the Australian press and general population.

THE BLACK DEMON

JIM HAYNES

The Barb was a small jet-black horse who became known in the press as 'The Black Demon'. Bred by the pioneering Lee family at Bathurst in 1863, he was famously stolen by bushrangers as a foal at foot.

A large group of valuable horses was taken by the bushrangers from the Lees' farm and driven south. One of the family, Henry Lee, followed the bushrangers to Monaro, where police apprehended them and all the horses except one were recovered.

The missing horse was a black colt foal that the bushrangers had left with a farmer at Caloola when it went lame and could not travel. The loss was reported in the press and the farmer returned the foal to its rightful owner a few weeks later. The foal grew up to be The Barb.

The year that the new races were introduced at Randwick, 1866, saw The Barb winning the AJC Derby. His sire, Sir Hercules, also sired the winner of the first Sydney Cup, the mighty Yattendon, and Bylong, who won the first Metropolitan Handicap.

In the true spirit of inter-colonial rivalry, the Victorian colt Fishhook was purchased for a record sum at the dispersal of Hurtle Fisher's Maribyrnong Stud by his brother, C.B. Fisher, and sent to Sydney to contest the AJC Derby.

Fishhook was from the last crop of the great English sire Fisherman, imported into Victoria to ensure that colony's superiority in the racing game. He finished a poor third to The Barb, giving the colonial-bred New South Wales champion sire, Sir Hercules, a major victory over Victoria's imported bloodlines.

Having accounted for the Victorian colt in the derby, The Barb's trainer, 'Honest' John Tait, decided to take him to Melbourne and rub salt into the wounds by winning the Melbourne Cup.

After his Cup victory as a three-year-old, The Barb went on to win sixteen of his 23 starts. These included the Sydney Cup twice, as well as the AJC St Leger, the AJC Queen's Plate and the other 'new classic' race, the AJC Metropolitan Handicap. He also took out the VRC Port Phillip Stakes and the Launceston Town Plate in Tasmania as a four-year-old. In one of his Sydney Cup wins he carried the biggest winning weight in the race's history: 10 st 8 lb (67 kg). He was virtually unbeatable at weight-for-age, and was unbeaten as a five-year-old.

In fact, one of The Barb's defeats was actually a win. He beat Etienne de Mestre's Tim Whiffler in the Queen's Plate but the jockey weighed in 2 pounds light.

When entered for the Melbourne Cup of 1868, The Barb was given the biggest weight ever allotted—11 st 7 lb (73 kg)—so John Tait decided to retire him to stud. The Barb stood at stud until his death in 1889 and produced some useful horses, but no champions.

The Barb's long and famous career only happened because those 'kind-hearted, horse-loving bushrangers' spared him as a foal and left him to recover from lameness with a farmer at Caloola. The bushrangers, incidentally, were arrested, convicted and served prison sentences.

THE SHIPWRECK HORSE

JIM HAYNES

The winner of the 1876 AJC Derby, a brown colt by Angler out of Chrysolite, was a grandson of the great imported sire Fisherman. He was owned by C.B. Fisher, who had neglected to name the horse before he won the derby.

It was not entirely unknown for horses to race unnamed in those days. The registration process was somewhat slower then and horses having their first few starts, or never racing at all, were often referred to merely by their breeding. This particular colt was known as 'the Chrysolite colt'.

Many pedigrees contain nameless unraced mares if you look back far enough. This colt would have appeared in the racebook, or race card as it was then, as 'brown colt by Angler from Chrysolite'.

It was, for some reason, fashionable to name colts in their third year back in the 1870s, no one seems to know why and it causes headaches for racing historians to this day.

Having won the derby, the colt was then sent to Melbourne for the Spring Carnival aboard the steamship *City of Melbourne*.

The *Melbourne Argus* reported, on 13 September 1876:

> An unparalleled destruction of racing stock is one of the results of the terrific gale which was experienced on the New South Wales coast during Sunday and Monday.
>
> The *City of Melbourne*, having on board 11 racehorses, the flower of the Victorian studs, left Sydney for Melbourne on Saturday. Soon after passing Cape St. George she encountered the Storm, which raged with such violence that the steamer became

> almost helpless. The decks were swept, the cabins flooded, and out of the 11 horses the following nine were speedily killed—*Robin Hood, Burgundy, Poacher, Nemesis, Etoile du Matin, Eros, Sovereign, Lecturer colt,* and *Sylvia colt*. The other two, *Chrysolite colt* and *Redwood*, were saved by the exertions of the men in charge of them, and the *City of Melbourne* having put back to Sydney, were landed yesterday in a very exhausted condition.
>
> Though no lives were lost amongst the passengers, they appear to have suffered considerably, as the cabins were completely flooded by the heavy seas by which the vessel was almost overwhelmed.

On the journey back to Sydney the 'Chrysolite colt' that had barely survived the disaster was kept alive by Joe Morrison, who had ridden him to victory in the AJC Derby. Morrison fed the horse on beer and gin and constantly massaged his cold body. There was little hope that the horse would survive the ordeal and he was so weak that he had to be carried ashore at Sydney.

Morrison had pleaded with the ship's skipper, Captain Paddle (really!), to go back to port as the horses were falling in their pens on the deck and he already had Nemesis in a sling. Paddle ignored him. Robin Hood (by Fireworks out of Sylvia), who drowned on the deck, was the winner of the VRC Derby, Royal Park Stakes, Mares Produce Stakes, AJC St Leger and AJC Plate the previous season—and high on the markets for the Melbourne Cup. The imported mare Nemesis, who also drowned, had just won the Metropolitan and was Melbourne Cup favourite. Bookmakers suspended betting on the Cup, no doubt to count their money, and presented Captain Paddle with a purse in appreciation for his role in the tragedy.

Only two horses travelling on the deck of the *City of Melbourne* survived the storm; the other nine were washed overboard or killed when thrown around the deck by the mighty waves. The captain sought shelter at Jervis Bay and luckily no human lives were lost that day, although seventeen people died when the steamship *Dandenong* was disabled in the same storm.

One of the two horses to survive was the unnamed derby-winning colt. The colt's owner, the famous racing pioneer C.B. Fisher, spared no expense in treating the horse and nursing him back to health. He miraculously recovered and went on to become not only a great champion on the racetrack, but one of the most influential sires in Australian racing history.

Although he was still often referred to in his lifetime as 'that Chrysolite colt' or 'the shipwreck horse', he is remembered in our racing history today by his registered name. After the horse survived the tragic voyage, his owner finally found a name for him—Robinson Crusoe.

THE ONLY UNDEFEATED MELBOURNE CUP WINNER

JIM HAYNES

Grand Flaneur holds a unique place in racing history—he is the only Melbourne Cup winner who was never defeated on a racetrack, starting nine times for nine wins. Added to this is the fact that he was a very successful and influential sire whose son won England's two greatest races.

Grand Flaneur was a 'Sydney Horse', owned by AJC Chairman Mr W.A. Long at a time when colonial rivalry was intense. He was by the great colonial sire Yattendon, out of an imported mare, First Lady. He won at Flemington over 5 furlongs as a two-year-old and then was rested until the Sydney Spring Carnival of 1880. He duly took out the AJC Derby and Mares Produce Stakes, and then returned to Melbourne to win the Victoria Derby, Melbourne Cup and the Victorian Mares Produce Stakes within a week, defeating the local champion, Progress, each time.

Grand Flaneur was the horse that finally gave the greatest jockey of the time, Tom Hales, his one and only Melbourne Cup win. The colt then won the 1881 VRC Champion Stakes and VRC St Leger Stakes, and ended his career by winning the 1881 VRC Town Plate.

He was taken back to Sydney for the AJC Autumn Carnival but broke down and was retired to stand at stud. Bravo, the 1889 Melbourne Cup winner, was from his first crop of foals and he also sired the 1894 Cup winner Patron and was the leading Australian sire in 1894–95.

Grand Flaneur's son Merman won the prestigious Williamstown Cup in 1896 and then went to race in Britain. Owned by the famous actress Lily Langtry, Merman won the Goodwood Cup in 1899 and the Ascot Gold Cup in 1900, the same year that his sire Grand Flaneur died, aged 22, at the Chipping Norton Stud near Liverpool, southwest of Sydney.

You might spare a thought for the good Victorian colt Progress, who ran second to Grand Flaneur five times in classic races in Melbourne. If you're from New South Wales, of course, you probably won't bother!

RACING IN AUSTRALIA

NAT GOULD

The famous English author Nat Gould lived and worked as a racing journalist in Australia for eleven years, from 1884 to 1895. His observations of Australian racing, written more than a hundred years ago, make for fascinating reading.

***

Racing, in my humble opinion, is the most absorbing and interesting of sports. In no part of the world can be found more enthusiastic followers of the turf than in Australia. To love horses is an inherent characteristic of Britishers and the bulk of the Colonial people come from good old British stock.

In England the climate is often dead against enjoying racing in the most favourable circumstances, but in Australia there is very little to complain of as regards the weather. Sunny skies in that favoured island are the rule, and it is the exception and not the rule to be let in for a drenching day's sport.

Nine months out of twelve the climate of Australia is all that can be desired, and what more can a man expect?

The racing year commences on 1st August, from which the ages of horses date, so that the three-year-olds running in the AJC Derby in the middle of September* and the VRC Derby in the first week of November, or the last week in October, are much younger than three-year-olds taking part in the English Derby.

So favourable is the climate that flat-racing is going on all year round, and there is no closed time, as in the old country.

Occasionally in the winter months it is necessary to wear a top-coat, but even then the sun is generally warm enough to make it pleasant. The lack of east winds, or frost or snow, make racing a pleasure rather than a burden.

At Christmas it is racing in sunshine to perfection, and the meeting of the AJC at Randwick on Boxing Day may be described as a few hours turned into melting moments.

Many a time, as I watched the race for the Summer Cup at Randwick, has my mind wandered to the old land, and thoughts of the snow and dull leaden sky have almost made me shiver, even with the thermometer at close upon a hundred in the shade.

Christmas in Australia is indeed a contrast to that in England. Boxing Day races in the two hemispheres are also vastly different.

In Australia we have flat-racing amidst glorious sunshine. In England races are held under the National Hunt Rules, probably with a white mantle of snow covering the earth.

There cannot be much pleasure even in backing a winner when your fingers are almost too cold to hold the money, and it must be indeed a dreary occupation to be out 'in the cold' and backing losers with the thermometer down at zero.

If Fortune be cold to us in Australia we have the consolation of knowing that Nature warms towards us.

It must be very depressing to return from a racecourse with empty pockets and a thaw setting in. Men must have strong constitutions to stand the wear and tear of English racing, season after season, and they earn the money they make.

Racing in the Australian Colonies is conducted under the most favourable atmospheric conditions as a rule, and therefore it is all the more delightful and enjoyable. I doubt if there can be found as much enthusiasm in a race crowd in any part of the globe as there is in Australia. No matter under what circumstances the racing takes place, the people enjoy it, and even the downfall of favourites has not much effect upon them.

Hundreds of men live 'on the game' and appear to do well at it. How they live is a mystery to most people. They must have money to bet with, and to pay their expenses, and they always have a pound or two to invest upon anything they fancy. These hangers-on of the turf are a nuisance to trainers, for they are constantly badgering them for tips.

Many of them are friends of the jockeys and no doubt obtain information from them; and jockeys are much more ready to talk on an Australian racecourse than they are in England.

It is a genuine cosmopolitan crowd on an Australian racecourse. The Governor of the Colony appears to forget his office for the time being and to take a delight in mingling with the people. A racing governor is bound to become popular while a governor who has no fondness for sports of any kind has no hold on the affections of the people.

Lord Carrington was one of the most popular governors New South Wales ever had, and so was Lord Hopetoun in Victoria, and both were real good sportsmen.

Class distinctions are not as marked on colonial racecourses as they are in England. There are no reserves for the Upper Ten, as at Ascot, Goodwood and other places in England. The AJC and VRC have reserves for their members, and there is far more extensive and better accommodation provided for the public in Australia. The accommodation at Flemington and Randwick is far ahead of that on principal English courses.

Racing in the sunny south is far more of a pleasure than a business. Thousands of people are not cooped up in small rings, as though they were so many sheep crowded into a pen. There is plenty of elbow-room, even on a Melbourne Cup Day there is ample room for the ladies to promenade on the spacious lawn, although there are fifty to eighty thousand people present on the course.

Ten thousand is a small crowd for a great race meeting in Australia, although it does not meet this number at suburban meetings, unless it be an exceptional day.

It is this feeling of freedom and comfort that makes turf life in the colonies so pleasant and enjoyable. There is so much geniality and goodwill about it. Although men are keen on making money, and occasionally indulge in sharp practices, most owners are not averse to the public knowing what their horses can do and what chances they have of winning.

The best part of the day, in my opinion, is the early morning, and many a pleasant hour have I spent on the training track watching the horses at work. There are no restrictions placed upon the members of the sporting press watching horses do their gallops.

Australian jockeys have a different style and appearance to the English. They are, as a rule, neat in their dress and it is an exception to see a slovenly jockey. There are some fine riders on the turf in Australia, such men as Hales, the Delaneys, the Cooks, Lewis, Kelso, Parker, Huxley, Harris and Martin Gallagher.

A good yarn is told about Martin Gallagher. At Rosehill he rode a certain horse, and he was called upon to explain its running. The chairman had a horse running in this particular race.

'You could have been much nearer to the winner,' said the chairman.

'Yes,' said Martin, 'but I could not have won.'

'Why did you not ride your horse out?' asked the chairman.

'I got jammed in,' said Martin with a smile, 'one horse kept me in all down the straight; in fact, this horse was "shepherding" me all through the race.'

'And whose horse was that?' indignantly asked the chairman.

'Yours, sir,' was the quiet but very effective reply.

Nothing came of that inquiry.

Jockeys are often accused of pulling horses when they are not at fault. I am sorry to say, however, I have seen horses deliberately stopped.

In the majority of cases the men who instruct the jockeys how to ride races are to blame. If a jockey does not carry out the instructions he receives, he does not get many mounts.

It is a pernicious practice for an owner to put a jockey up and give him orders not to win, and yet this is done by men who ought to know better.

I once asked a popular jockey why he did not decline to ride a horse when he was given orders not to win.

'If I did I should never get another mount from him,' he answered, naming a well-known owner. 'Not only that, but he would influence other owners against me.'

Accidents will happen during races, but many could be avoided if mere lads who know no more how to ride a race than they know how to fly, were not put up in the saddle. These youngsters have no fear because they are unaware of the danger.

Tom Corrigan and Martin Bourke were killed, one a few days after the other. Corrigan, about the best steeplechase rider in the colonies, was killed by his horse Waiter falling in a steeplechase at Caulfield.

Martin Bourke was killed while schooling a horse over hurdles at Flemington. Bourke was the most fearless rider, and the number of falls he had was remarkable. I think he had nearly every bone in his body broken at one time or another.

There is a vast difference in the way races are ridden in Australia to the old country. Waiting tactics are not often resorted to, and it is generally a hot pace the full distance. The severe 2 miles of the Melbourne Cup course is run at full speed, and there is not much chance of waiting on the road. This system of riding is in a great measure due to the time test. If a horse is timed to run 2 miles in say 3.29 or 3.30, then he has to do it in the race if possible.

A slow-run race is an exception. I mean, as a rule the horses go at their top, but they may not be fast enough to make good time.

It would surprise many people to see the rate at which horses go over hurdles and steeplechase fences. In a hurdle race horses very often go as fast as they do on the flat. Steeplechasers are often ridden at a breakneck pace, which says more for the pluck than the judgement of the riders.

The same superstitions exist as in the old land, and racing men are wont to regard certain signs and omens with an amount of awe not understandable to ordinary mortals. Some men invariably back the first horse they see upon entering the paddock and others back the mount of the jockey whose colours they first come across.

I was seated in a tramcar one morning when a particular friend of mine stepped in and sat down. Suddenly, without a word of warning, he jumped up and rushed out again.

I looked under the seat to see if a dog had been secreted there, and had gone for his calves, but there was nothing to cause alarm in that direction.

Much to my surprise I saw him come in at the other side of the tram and quietly sit down.

'What is the matter?' I asked. 'Too much whiskey last night?'

'No,' he replied, 'it's race day, you know, and I got in the wrong side of the tram. It's unlucky.'

* *The AJC Derby was run in Spring until 1979, when it was moved to the Autumn.*

THE CAB HORSE'S STORY

C.J. DENNIS

Now, you wouldn't imagine, to look at me,
That I was a racehorse once.
I have done my mile in—let me see—
No matter. I was no dunce.
But you'd not believe me if I told
Of gallops I did in days of old.

I was first in—ah, well! What's the good?
It hurts to recall those days
When I drew from men, as a proud horse should,
Nothing but words of praise.
Oh, the waving hats, and the cheering crowd!
How could a horse help being proud?

My owner was just as proud as I;
I was cuddled and petted and praised.
My fame was great and my price was high,
And every year 'twas raised.
Then I strained a sinew in ninety-nine,
And that's when started my swift decline.

I was turned to grass for a year or so;
Then dragged to an auction sale.
And a country sport gave me a go;
But how could I hope but fail?

'A crock,' said he. And I here began
To learn of the ways of cruel man.

A year I spent as a lady's hack—
I was growing old and spent—
But she said that the riding hurt her back;
So we parted; and I went
For a while—and it nearly broke my heart—
Dragging a greasy butcher's cart.

Then my stifle went. And I, proud horse,
Son of the nobly born,
The haughty king of a city course,
Knew even a butcher's scorn!
So down the ladder I quickly ran;
Till I came to be owned by a bottle man.

And my bed was hard and my food was poor,
And my work was harder still
Dragging a cart from door to door—
The slave of Bottle-oh Bill.
Till even he, for a few mean bob,
Sold me into this hateful job.

As I dozed and dreamed in the ranks one day,
Thinking of good days past,
I heard a voice that I knew cry, 'Hey!
Say, cabby, is this horse fast?'
And he looked at me in a way I know.
'Twas the man I'd loved in the long ago.

'Twas my dear, old master of ninety-nine,
And I waited, fair surprised.
But ne'er by a look and ne'er by sign
Did he show he recognised.

Then I heard his words ('twas my last hard knock):
'Why don't you pole-axe the poor old crock?'

And he turned aside to a low-bred mare
That was foaled on some cockie's farm,
And he drove away. What do I care?
I can come to no more harm.
In a knacker's yard I am worth at least
Some pence for a hungry lion's feast.

APPRENTICES

A.B. 'BANJO' PATERSON

Apprentice riders are supposed to be hardened little citizens, above the weakness of displaying any emotion; but, after all, they are only small boys of about 15 or so, prone to the excitability of other small boys of their age.

As Kipling says of soldiers, they are 'single men in barracks most uncommonly like you'.

The small apprentice Lightfoot, having ridden his first winner in the two-year-old race at Moorfield, burst into a storm of tears of excitement as he rode back to the weighing yard. It added a human touch to the proceedings.

It is a great thing for a small boy to ride his first winner while still at a weight at which he can get plenty of riding.

This boy Lightfoot is a son of the once well-known rider Joe Lightfoot, a jockey who weighed about as much as a box of matches, but had such wonderful 'hands' that he could hold any horse at any pace in any company. The trouble with Joe Lightfoot was that he had an incurable habit of looking round while leading in a race; in all other respects he was one of the best natural horsemen at his weight ever seen on our turf.

Without knowing anything of the circumstances of the case, one may be permitted to hope that this youngster may turn out as good a horseman as his father without suffering from the looking-round complex.

The handling of racehorses by six-stone-seven boys is one of the wonders of the world. The average grown-up man, though he may figure with distinction on a hack, could not hold a racehorse for half a minute; but these midgets can put him anywhere, and do anything with him, without exerting any physical strength at all. They are the elect out of hundreds that go into apprenticeship, only to find that 95 per cent of them will never make horsemen. It is a case of survival of the fittest, and those that do survive are entitled to all the money they make.

One of W. Kelso's apprentices, on joining the stable, borrowed a book on race riding and started to copy it out in handwriting. It is not known whether he ever finished it—it was a large book—but at any rate he copied out enough of it to make himself a very successful rider, who at the age of 20 was earning more money than most barristers of 50.

The racing business is rather overcrowded just now, but somehow there always seems to be room at the top.

ONLY A JOCKEY

A.B. 'BANJO' PATERSON

Paterson was a crusader for better treatment: better conditions, religious instruction and education for apprentice jockeys. He wrote this poem in 1887 after the Melbourne Wire Service reported: 'Richard Bennison, a jockey, aged fourteen, while riding William Tell in his training, was thrown and killed. The horse is luckily uninjured.'

***

Out in the grey cheerless chill of the morning light,
Out on the track where the night shades still lurk;
Before the first gleam of the sungod's returning light,
Round come the racehorses early at work.

Reefing and pulling and racing so readily,
Close sit the jockey-boys holding them hard,
'Steady the stallion there—canter him steadily,
Don't let him gallop so much as a yard.'

Fiercely he fights while the others run wide of him,
Reefs at the bit that would hold him in thrall,
Plunges and bucks till the boy that's astride of him
Goes to the ground with a terrible fall.

'Stop him there! Block him there! Drive him in carefully,
Lead him about till he's quiet and cool.
Sound as a bell! Though he's blown himself fearfully,
Now let us pick up this poor little fool.

'Stunned? Oh, by Jove, I'm afraid it's a case with him;
Ride for the doctor! Keep bathing his head!
Send for a cart to go down to our place with him—'
No use! One long sigh and the little chap's dead.

Only a jockey-boy, foul-mouthed and bad you see,
Ignorant, heathenish, gone to his rest.
Parson or Presbyter, Pharisee, Sadducee,
What did you do for him?—bad was the best.

Negroes and foreigners, all have a claim on you;
Yearly you send your well-advertised hoard,
But the poor jockey-boy—shame on you, shame on you,
'Feed ye, my little ones'—what said the Lord?

Him ye held less than the outer barbarian,
Left him to die in his ignorant sin;
Have you no principles, humanitarian?
Have you no precept—'go gather them in?'

Knew he God's name? In his brutal profanity,
That name was an oath—out of many but one—
What did he get from our famed Christianity?
Where has his soul—if he had any—gone?

Fourteen years old, and what was he taught of it?
What did he know of God's infinite grace?
Draw the dark curtain of shame o'er the thought of it,
Draw the shroud over the jockey-boy's face.

THE GREATEST RACEHORSE THE WORLD HAS EVER SEEN

JIM HAYNES

Carbine, always known affectionately by the racing public by his stable name of 'Old Jack', was foaled at Sylvia Park Stud near Auckland in 1885 and had multiple crosses on both sides of his pedigree back to two great eighteenth-century horses, Eclipse and Herod. His dam was the unraced imported mare Mersey, and he was the last foal of the good sire Musket, who won the Ascot Stakes and eight other races before being sent to stand at stud in New Zealand.

Musket, who died at age eighteen, was a very successful sire of stayers; his son Martini-Henry won the 1883 Melbourne Cup.

Carbine won 33 of his 43 starts and was unplaced only once, when suffering from a cracked hoof. He won fifteen races in succession, and seventeen of his last eighteen races.

After five wins in New Zealand he was sent to Melbourne for the VRC Derby in 1888. Carbine finished second; his jockey, New Zealander Bob Derrett, dropped a rein in the tight finish and Carbine was beaten by a head by Sydney-trained horse Ensign, carrying the famous blue and white colours of Mr James White and ridden brilliantly by Tom Hales.

Carbine's owner, Dan O'Brien, lost heavily on the derby and decided to sell Carbine, who had won the Flying Stakes over 7 furlongs and the Foal Stakes over 10 furlongs in the week following his narrow defeat in the derby.

At the auction at the end of the carnival, VRC committeeman Donald Wallace, who had made his fortune in the Broken Hill minerals boom, urged on by Melbourne trainer Walter

Hickenbotham, reluctantly paid 3000 guineas for Carbine, having failed to secure the horse he really wanted to buy at the sale.

Being the under-bidder on that previous lot—a now long-forgotten horse called Tradition, which sold that day for 3050 guineas—was to be the best piece of luck in Donald Wallace's life.

Walter Hickenbotham now took over training Carbine, who then ran third in the Newmarket Handicap and second in the Australian Cup to the champion Lochiel. He then went on a winning spree, taking first place seven times from his next eight starts as a three-year-old, at distances from 7 furlongs to 3 miles, including the Sydney Cup in which he carried 12 pounds (5.5 kg) over weight-for-age.

As a three-year-old Carbine won four races in four days during the Sydney Autumn Carnival in 1890, including the Sydney Cup on the second day. The next day he won the All-Aged Stakes over a mile and the Cumberland Stakes over 2 miles, and two days later he won the AJC Plate over 3 miles.

While in training for his four-year-old season Carbine cracked a heel so badly that he could not race that season without a special binding of beeswax and cloth and a modified bar shoe. This accounts for his poor start to the season: second in the Caulfield Stakes, third in the Melbourne (now the Mackinnon) Stakes, and a brave second to Bravo in the Melbourne Cup. Carrying 10 st (63.5 kg) to Bravo's 8 st 7 lb (54 kg), Carbine's hoof opened during the race and he was beaten a length by a son of Grand Flaneur.

Two days later, with his hoof repaired, he won the Flying Stakes over 7 furlongs but, two days after that, he ran last in the Canterbury Plate over 2 miles when the binding on his hoof completely fell apart. It was the only unplaced run of his career.

With a good rest and his hoof patched up again, Carbine returned to racing in March 1891 and won three of his four starts in Melbourne before heading to Sydney for the Autumn Carnival.

As a four-year-old Carbine went one better than the previous year. This time he won five races at distances from 1 mile to 3 miles in seven days: the Autumn Stakes on 5 April; the Sydney Cup, carrying 9 st 9 lb (61.5 kg), on 7 April; the All-Aged Stakes and the Cumberland Stakes on 10 April; and the AJC Plate on 12 April.

Carbine had now won seven races in succession, and would go on to win another eight before the sequence ended a year later, when he ran second in the All-Aged Stakes.

Victories in the Spring Stakes and Craven Plate came after a five-month spell; then the horse the public called 'Old Jack' travelled back to Melbourne to win the Melbourne Stakes and race into immortality in the Melbourne Cup of 1890, carrying the biggest winning weight in history, 10 st 5 lb (66.5 kg).

An account of that win by Nat Gould, 'Cup Memories', and a celebratory poem, 'Carbine's Melbourne Cup', are in the Melbourne Cup section of this collection.

Carbine raced seven more times, in the autumn of 1891, for six victories. His narrow defeat came in the All-Aged Stakes at Randwick. His hoof was so bad that day that shoes could not be fitted, so he raced without shoes and ran second to Marvel on a slippery wet track. Unperturbed, Walter Hickenbotham took Carbine back to his stall, persevered and finally managed to get shoes on the champion, who promptly went out a few races later and beat Marvel easily over 2 miles in the Cumberland Stakes.

Nat Gould, who was there that day, explained Carbine's lonely unplaced run:

> It was a wet day, and the ground was sticky. In the All Aged Stakes, a mile, Carbine ran without plates and could not obtain a hold. It was pitiable to see him floundering and not able to stretch out in his usual grand style. The same afternoon he met Marvel again in the Cumberland Stakes, two miles. This time Carbine ran in shoes. The race resolved itself into a gallop over the last mile, which was all in favour of Marvel's racing style. Carbine, however, beat him easily, and I think there is no doubt he would have won the other race had he had shoes on.

Carbine then went for a spell with the intention of being trained for the 1891 Melbourne Cup, in spite of being given 11 st (70 kg) by the VRC handicapper.

In early training Carbine injured his hoof again and suffered ligament damage, so it was decided he would stand a season at stud and perhaps return to racing in the autumn. However, the stud fee of 200 guineas was more than three times that of any other horse in Australia, and there was a stock market crash and a Depression looming; consequently Carbine served just three mares in 1891. Two foals survived to race and one of them, from a mare named Melodious, was Wallace, who would prove to be Carbine's best-performed Australian son and a huge success at stud.

It became apparent that Carbine's racing days were over and a lucrative offer—reputed to be more than £20,000—was made for him to stand at stud in America.

Donald Wallace wanted him to stay in Australia, however, and he stood four seasons at Wallace's stud near Bacchus Marsh, northwest of Melbourne, and sired the winners of 208 races, including twelve stakes winners.

His first crop included Wallace, who won the Caulfield Guineas, VRC Derby, C.B. Fisher Plate, Sydney Cup and more, before retiring to stud himself, to sire the winners of 949 races, including two Melbourne Cup winners in Kingsburgh and Patrobas, the great stayer Trafalgar and seven derby winners.

Carbine also sired Amberlite, who became, in 1897, the first horse to win the Caulfield Cup, AJC Derby and VRC Derby in the same year; and La Carabine, winner of an Australian Cup, Sydney Cup and two AJC Plates.

As the Depression hit and the drought worsened in the early 1890s, Donald Wallace's fortunes slumped drastically and he decided to sell all his horses in a dispersal sale in 1895.

The Duke of Portland, who was looking for a stallion with a quiet temperament as an outcross to mares from his brilliant but fiery champion stallion St Simon, bought Carbine for 13,000 guineas to stand at Welbeck Stud in England. Carbine was as placid as St Simon was highly strung.

Ten thousand people came to the docks to say goodbye to 'Old Jack' as the steamship *Orizaba* pulled out of Port Melbourne.

Carbine survived the trip, and an emergency stomach operation in Colombo, and was able to live in his new home, with its soft English ground, without wearing shoes. A special device was sent with the great horse to England. It was a special 'umbrella hat' to keep the rain and snow off his ears. 'Old Jack' hated rain on his ears and would run and hide from rain. Walter Hickenbotham often had to take his umbrella to the races and cover Carbine's ears as he went onto the track. He also used the umbrella to get the lethargic stallion moving towards the barrier by opening and closing it rapidly in his face until he broke into a trot.

In spite of being only 'second fiddle' sire at Welbeck, Carbine finished fourth on the list of successful sires in the UK in 1902 and 1906, and sired 138 winners and 253 second-placegetters there.

Carbine's son Spearmint won the 1906 Epsom Derby and was also a great success at stud. Spearmint's progeny won 93 races and included derby winner and great sire Spion Kop. Spearmint also sired the broodmares Catnip and Plucky Liege, which means that all horses with Nearco, Nasrullah and Northern Dancer lines trace back to Carbine, as do all progeny of Sir Gallahad III, the champion son of Plucky Liege.

Sir Gallahad III raced with great success in France and was the sire of three Kentucky Derby winners. He was the most influential stallion in the USA in the twentieth century, being leading sire in 1930, 1933, 1934 and 1940, and leading broodmare sire in North America in 1939, then from 1943 to 1952, and again in 1955.

Also out of Plucky Liege was the great Epsom Derby winner Bois Roussel, who started only three times for two wins and a third; his son, Delville Wood, was five times champion sire of Australia.

Carbine died in 1914 at the ripe old age of 29 and his skeleton is on display at the Australian Racing Museum at Caulfield. Phar Lap was Carbine's great-great-grandson and had Musket on both sides of his pedigree. Sunline had Carbine on both sides of her pedigree, and Kingston Town had multiple Carbine and St Simon bloodlines. Carbine's blood has been present in the pedigrees of more than 50 Melbourne Cup winners, including Makybe Diva.

Not bad for a horse who couldn't get his shoes on!

As far as I am concerned, and as far as Australian racing is concerned, Carbine was the greatest, and the most influential, racehorse that ever lived.

FAREWELL 'OLD JACK'

NAT GOULD

When the great racing writer and novelist Nat Gould returned to Britain in 1895, after his eleven years in Australia, he and his family travelled on the same ship as Carbine, who was on his way to stand at stud at Welbeck Abbey in England.

***

I saw Carbine win all his big races, and when he was bought by the Duke of Portland for thirteen thousand pounds, I came to London in the same vessel he was on, the Orient liner RMS *Orizaba.*

A few particulars about Carbine's voyage may be of interest.

The horse did not come on board until we reached Melbourne.

Mr Ernest Day, who had charge for him for the Duke, was naturally very anxious to get the horse shipped quietly and a notice appeared in the *Evening Herald*, on Thursday, stating Carbine would be shipped on Saturday morning.

As I happened to have a letter in my pocket stating he would come on board on Good Friday, I smiled. Evidently the paragraph had been inspired to put people off the scent. I was on board when the 'hero of a hundred fights' came to the pier. Carbine was accompanied by one of his sons, a colt out of Novelette, who had been named Lederderg by the Duke of Portland, and who was alongside of him.

'Old Jack' at first seemed inclined to remain ashore. Mr Day endeavoured to persuade him to step onto the gangway, but he declined the invitation. A handful of clover was given him, which he quietly munched, then he looked at the crowd as much as to say, 'What do you think of me?'

Cunningham, the man who had had charge of Carbine at the stud, and who came home with the horses, then went to the rescue. No sooner did Carbine see him coming along the gangway than he stretched out his neck and put one foot forward. Cunningham spoke to him, and then, quietly pulling the head-stall, Carbine followed him like a lamb.

The horse felt his footing carefully all along the gangway and crouched down when he felt the boards creak under him; but he never made the least objection to following his leader. Once in his box Carbine commenced to munch hay quietly, as though a trip to England was an everyday occurrence with him.

The colt took more trouble to get on board, but once in his box he also settled down like an old horse. Not knowing the time Carbine was to go on board, there was not a great crowd there, but on Saturday morning (13 April 1895) the people came down in hundreds to have a last peep at the champion.

When it was found Carbine had been put on board the day before, the crowd commenced to see they had been sold, but they were determined not to be done out of a sight of him. I never saw a more determined mass of people than Carbine's admirers. They crushed up the gangway and jammed up in front of his box, regardless of torn clothes and pickpockets, and there were plenty of the latter about, or what looked like them.

Hundreds of people caught a passing glimpse of Carbine as he stood quietly eating in his box. It was their last sight of 'Old Jack', and there were many present who had won money over him in that memorable Melbourne Cup.

No horse that ever ran in Australia was a greater idol with the public than Carbine, and the pier was crowded with his admirers long before the boat sailed.

When we cast off from Sandridge Pier there was a mighty burst of cheering, and cries of 'Carbine' rent the air. I was near the horse's box at the time with Mr Day, and 'Old Jack' pricked up his ears and raised his splendid head at the sound, as though he fancied there was another race to be run.

A beautiful wreath was sent on board for Carbine. It was in the shape of a horseshoe, and had Donald Wallace's colours on, and written on a card attached to it, 'For dear old Carbine; bon voyage.' Had Carbine got hold of that wreath, I am afraid he would have made short work of it.

Mr Day had several chats with me during the voyage. He is a most entertaining man, and had travelled all over the world in charge of horses. He even took a consignment of horses to India for the Ameer of Afghanistan, and safely conveyed them through the famous Khyber Pass. One morning I went with Mr Day to see Carbine have his breakfast. I pulled a few stalks of green clover out of the bundle and put them between my teeth. 'Old Jack' put his nose between the bars and took them as gently as though he had been my particular pal all his life. I never saw such a quiet, docile stallion, and throughout the voyage the horse behaved splendidly.

At Colombo Carbine had a narrow escape. He was very ill, and Mr Day had to perform an operation on him, which he did successfully, and no man could have paid more attention to the horse than he did. Cunningham held the horse's head during the operation, and Mr Day happening to look up saw blood running down his sleeve. On asking what was the matter, Cunningham said, 'Oh nothing; Old Jack had a bite at my arm.'

With two such attendants, and on board a steady boat as the *Orizaba* undoubtedly is, Carbine finally arrived safely in England.

At Welbeck, which is also home to the great St Simon, Carbine will be mated with some of the best mares in the world, and he ought to get good stock from St Simon mares. I cannot conclude from this chapter in a more fitting manner than by quoting a portion of a letter I received from Mr W. Forrester after arriving back in England. Dated Warwick Farm, 6 May. He writes:

> So you are a mate of Carbine's. Notwithstanding my thinking him the greatest racehorse the world has ever seen, I wish he had never been foaled, for as you know he cut me out of £28,400 in

the Melbourne Cup. Need I say what a surprise, as I thought I could not lose with Highborn carrying so little weight, but old Carbine, with his 10 stone 5 pounds, beat me badly.

Had I won that day I feel sure I would have cleared £50,000 over the meeting, as there were Correze and Muriel in the VRC and Free Handicaps that I looked upon as the best of good things, but I was in hobbles and, without a stake, could not have a dash.

If my mare Rosary has a colt foal by the old horse it may be a second Carbine and I am glad to tell you she is in foal to him, and should it face the starter it will be known as Fatal Bullet.

I have not the slightest doubt he will do well with the Duke of Portland's mares if they give him plenty of work and do not keep him stalled up and keep the shoes off him as much as possible. Most of a stallion's trouble in old age is with the feet, caused by being continually shod. We let them live down here without shoes on. Why not in old England?

A NICE LITTLE MARE BY TRENTON

JIM HAYNES

There was once a filly that was bred at St Albans Stud at Geelong in 1896 by Mr W. Wilson. Her sire was Trenton, a son of Musket, who was also sire of the mighty Carbine.

She was trialled as a two-year-old and showed ability before a track accident caused her to be returned to the paddock. She suffered from lameness through her two-year-old and three-year-old seasons and remained almost forgotten in the paddock at St Albans.

She would almost certainly have never raced but for the death of her owner early in 1900. At the dispersal sale after Wilson's death, she was described in the catalogue as 'a nice little mare by Trenton that should be worth a place in any Stud'. Although she was still a three-year-old filly at the time, it is obvious that all and sundry considered her only value to be as a broodmare, not on the racetrack.

Luckily, however, there was one man who knew better. Les MacDonald was a former manager of St Albans and he obviously knew a few things about the filly that others bidding at the sale didn't. He commissioned Mr Neil Campbell to make the purchase for him at 310 guineas, which was a fair amount for an unraced though well-bred filly. In hindsight it was the bargain of a lifetime.

She was to become the first female thoroughbred to achieve the position of 'Australia's most loved racehorse'. Her name was Wakeful.

It is true that two fillies, Briseis and Auraria, had won the Melbourne Cup in its first four decades and been much admired by the racing public, but neither of them achieved the true champion status and public adoration that was to be the lot of the mighty Wakeful. Indeed, the phrase 'best since Wakeful' was used by racing men all through the twentieth century to describe great racing mares and fillies. The phrase 'better than Wakeful', however, was one you would never have heard used in that time, except in jest.

Briseis and Auraria were champion three-year-old fillies whose careers were finished at four. Wakeful, on the other hand, did not race at all until her fifth year, when she won the Oakleigh Plate as a maiden at her third start.

Wakeful's story is a fascinating one, full of coincidence, good luck, victory in adversity and strange twists of fate, some of which occurred long before she was even foaled. Wakeful was cleverly named: her dam was Insomnia, who was by the champion that survived the huge storm at sea in 1876, Robinson Crusoe, a great racehorse and sire whose amazing story appears earlier in this section ('The Shipwreck Horse').

It was the hand of fate that enabled Wakeful's grandsire to survive against all odds, and it was another series of coincidences that led to the great mare having any sort of career on the track at all.

Wakeful was a powerfully built bay mare. She stood 15.2 hands, a good size for a mare in those days, and her near-perfect action was marred slightly by some awkwardness in her forelegs. She suffered from bouts of lameness all her life, which may account for the odd anomalies in consistency in her career and her occasional, uncharacteristic minor placings.

Trained at Mordialloc in Victoria by Hugh Munro, father of great jockeys Jim and Darby, Wakeful began her racing career as a four-year-old, running second over 5 furlongs at Caulfield. At her second start she raced poorly over 6 furlongs at Flemington, finishing twentieth and pulling up lame once again. She was immediately sent back to the paddock.

Four months later many things had changed. Australia had become a nation on 1 January 1901, and Wakeful had recovered from her lameness and was back at Munro's stables and running amazing times on the training track.

What occurred next must be considered one of the most amazing racing feats, not to mention betting coups, of all time. Wakeful, a maiden galloper rising five, won the Oakleigh Plate and took half a second off the race record. Not only did she win one of the nation's premier sprint races, she started at 4 to 1 favourite following a huge betting plunge by her owner Les MacDonald.

The mare was then given the maximum penalty of 10 pounds (4.5 kg) for the VRC Newmarket Handicap. Even with this penalty she carried the relatively light weight of 7 st 6 lb (47 kg) and won easily, once again backed in to start favourite at 5 to 2.

In those days the weights for the AJC Autumn Carnival were issued in January, and Wakeful, even with the maximum penalty, was thrown into the Doncaster Handicap with 7 st 10 lb (49 kg). She won the famous mile race easily and, with really no preparation as a stayer, ran a gallant third in the Sydney Cup two days later. The AJC immediately rescheduled weight declarations to prevent such a thing happening again.

In the spring Wakeful returned to racing by winning the Caulfield Stakes. She then started favourite in the Caulfield Cup. After stumbling and almost falling in the straight, she recovered to catch Hymettus and the crowd thought she had won. The judge, however, gave the race to Hymettus on the bob of the head—they had taken one and a half seconds off the race record.

Wakeful then won the first of her three consecutive Melbourne Stakes, defeating Hymettus who could only manage fourth placing. She had not been trained for the Melbourne Cup and tired to run fifth in the big race after contesting the lead in the straight with the eventual winner, her stablemate Revenue, who carried 1 stone (6.35 kg) less. MacDonald, who also owned Revenue, did not expect Wakeful to run out the 2 miles, and she started at 10 to 1.

When Wakeful returned to racing in the autumn of 1902, she had been trained and conditioned to stay, her target being the Sydney Cup. She opened her campaign by winning the 1½-mile Essendon Stakes, but on her second outing, over 3 miles, she ran second to Carbine's daughter La Carabine. In what was perhaps an attempt to toughen up the mare, two days after her second placing

Munro started her twice in one day at Flemington. She easily won the All-Aged Stakes over a mile, but could only manage third over 14 furlongs later the same day.

Munro then took the mare to Sydney where, after a three-week break, she proceeded to 'do a Carbine' by winning four major races in seven days at the Autumn Carnival. She won the Autumn Stakes over 1½ miles on the first day and, two days later, recorded what was perhaps her greatest victory. Carrying a record weight for a mare of 9 st 7 lb (60.5 kg) she won the Sydney Cup by 2 lengths, taking an amazing three seconds off the race record held by, among others, the mighty Carbine and his champion son Wallace. Three days later she won the All-Aged Stakes over a mile, and two days after that the AJC Plate over 3 miles.

As a six-year-old Wakeful started fifteen times for ten wins, four seconds and a third. Trained to stay, her wins came at distances from 9 furlongs to 3 miles and her placings, all except one at 10 furlongs, were in shorter races. The great mare bypassed the Melbourne Cup that year to concentrate on weight-for-age races. In winning her second Melbourne Stakes, however, she easily defeated The Victory, who won the Melbourne Cup at his next start.

In the twilight of her career, as a seven-year-old, Wakeful raced eight times for three wins, three seconds and a third. It is strange that, considering her amazing record and all her great wins, racing historians consider her best efforts to be two second placings. The first of these was the Caulfield Cup of 1901 when she stumbled only to recover and be unluckily placed second to Hymettus in that dubious judge's decision, which could only have been guesswork. The second, and most incredible effort of all, came in the champion mare's final race, the Melbourne Cup of 1903.

The most weight carried by a female horse to win the Cup prior to 1903 was the 7 st 4 lb (46.5 kg) carried to victory by Auraria in 1895. The most weight carried to victory by a mare in the Cup's entire history was 9 st 1 lb (58 kg), when Makybe Diva won her third Cup in 2005. Wakeful was given 10 st (63.5 kg), still the biggest weight ever allotted to the female sex in the great race's history, and it is likely to remain so for all time.

The gallant mare raced to the lead half a mile before the finish and led into the straight by 2 lengths, only to be run down by the good stayer Lord Cardigan, carrying 6 st 8 lb (42 kg)—a massive 3 st 5 lb (21.5 kg) less than Wakeful. Lord Cardigan, whose connections had successfully 'cheated' the handicapper to get the tough young stayer into the race with a featherweight, won by less than a length. Many experts considered that Wakeful could have beaten Lord Cardigan if jockey Frank Dunn had waited another furlong before going for home on the champion mare.

Wakeful was a very successful broodmare. She produced five winning sons, including Night Watch who won a Melbourne Cup, and the great sprinter Blairgour, who won an Oakleigh Plate and a Futurity Stakes. Her daughters were not successful on the track but two, San Repos and Camilla, became great broodmares, producing many good horses and passing Wakeful's genes down to later generations of good stayers like Frill Prince and Yarramba.

The year after Wakeful's gallant Cup defeat, the fairer sex had revenge when the aged mare, Acrasia, defeated Lord Cardigan by exactly the same margin as he had beaten Wakeful. The difference was that Acrasia carried 7 st 6 lb (47 kg) and Lord Cardigan carried 9 st 6 lb (60 kg), a 'turnaround' in the weights of 5 st 4 lb (33.5 kg) in favour of the mares.

Lord Cardigan was generally acknowledged as Australia's best racehorse when Wakeful retired. By the imported champion son of St Simon, Positano, out of the good Trenton mare Lady Trenton, Lord Cardigan won the Sydney Cup as well as the Melbourne Cup, but his effort in running second to Acrasia caused him to rupture and he died several days after the Cup, at the age of four. Acrasia was owned by Sydney bookmaker Humphrey Oxenham, who lost her in a card game to Lord Cardigan's owner, John Mayo, on the eve of the Caulfield Cup, but bought her back the next day for 2000 guineas.

OLD PARDON, THE SON OF REPRIEVE

A.B. 'BANJO' PATERSON

This, in my humble opinion, is the best yarn ever penned about bush racing in colonial times. Written in the days when major races were run in three heats with the winner being the best performed horse over all three, it includes that wonderful description of a heavenly racebook entry, 'Angel Harrison's black gelding Pardon, blue halo, white body and wings'.

***

You never heard tell of the story?
Well, now, I can hardly believe!
Never heard of the honour and glory
Of Pardon, the son of Reprieve?
But maybe you're only a Johnnie
And don't know a horse from a hoe?
Well, well, don't get angry, my sonny,
But, really, a young 'un should know.

They bred him out back on the 'Never',
His mother was Mameluke breed.
To the front—and then stay there—was ever
The root of the Mameluke creed.
He seemed to inherit their wiry
Strong frames—and their pluck to receive—
As hard as a flint and as fiery
Was Pardon, the son of Reprieve.

We ran him at many a meeting
At crossing and gully and town,
And nothing could give him a beating—
At least when our money was down.
For weight wouldn't stop him, nor distance,
Nor odds, though the others were fast,
He'd race with a dogged persistence,
And wear them all down at the last.

At the Turon the Yattendon filly
Led by lengths at the mile and a half,
And we all began to look silly,
While her crowd were starting to laugh;
But the old horse came faster and faster,
His pluck told its tale, and his strength,
He gained on her, caught her, and passed her,
And won it, hands-down, by a length.

And then we swooped down on Menindie
To run for the President's Cup—
Oh! that's a sweet township—a shindy
To them is board, lodging, and sup.
Eye-openers they are, and their system
Is never to suffer defeat;
It's 'win, tie, or wrangle'—to best 'em
You must lose 'em, or else it's 'dead heat'.

We strolled down the township and found 'em
At drinking and gaming and play;
If sorrows they had, why they drowned 'em,
And betting was soon under way.
Their horses were good 'uns and fit 'uns,
There was plenty of cash in the town;
They backed their own horses like Britons,
And, Lord! How *we* rattled it down!

With gladness we thought of the morrow,
We counted our wagers with glee,
A simile homely to borrow—
'There was plenty of milk in our tea.'
You see we were green; and we never
Had even a thought of foul play,
Though we well might have known that the clever
Division would 'put us away'.

Experience *docet*, they tell us,
At least so I've frequently heard,
But, 'dosing' or 'stuffing', those fellows
Were up to each move on the board:
They got to his stall—it is sinful
To think what such villains would do—
And they gave him a regular skinful
Of barley—green barley—to chew.

He munched it all night, and we found him
Next morning as full as a hog—
The girths wouldn't nearly meet round him;
He looked like an overfed frog.
We saw we were done like a dinner—
The odds were a thousand to one
Against Pardon turning up winner,
'Twas cruel to ask him to run.

We got to the course with our troubles,
A crestfallen couple were we;
And we heard the 'books' calling the doubles—
A roar like the surf of the sea;
And over the tumult and louder
Rang 'Any price Pardon, I lay!'
Says Jimmy, 'The children of Judah
Are out on the warpath today.'

Three miles in three heats—ah, my sonny,
The horses in those days were stout,
They had to run well to win money;
I don't see such horses about.
Your six-furlong vermin that scamper
Half a mile with their feather-weight up;
They wouldn't earn much of their damper
In a race like the President's Cup.

The first heat was soon set a-going;
The Dancer went off to the front;
The Don on his quarters was showing,
With Pardon right out of the hunt.
He rolled and he weltered and wallowed—
You'd kick your hat faster, I'll bet;
They finished all bunched, and he followed
All lathered and dripping with sweat.

But troubles came thicker upon us,
For while we were rubbing him dry
The stewards came over to warn us:
'We hear you are running a bye!
If Pardon don't spiel like tarnation
And win the next heat—if he can—
He'll earn a disqualification;
Just think over *that*, now, my man!'

Our money all gone and our credit,
Our horse couldn't gallop a yard;
And then people thought that *we* did it!
It really was terribly hard.
We were objects of mirth and derision
To folk in the lawn and the stand,
And the yells of the clever division
Of 'Any price Pardon!' were grand.

We still had a chance for the money,
Two heats still remained to be run;
If both fell to us—why, my sonny,
The clever division were done.
And Pardon was better, we reckoned,
His sickness was passing away,
So he went to the post for the second
And principal heat of the day.

They're off and away with a rattle,
Like dogs from the leashes let slip,
And right at the back of the battle
He followed them under the whip.
They gained ten good lengths on him quickly
He dropped right away from the pack;
I tell you it made me feel sickly
To see the blue jacket fall back.

Our very last hope had departed—
We thought the old fellow was done,
When all of a sudden he started
To go like a shot from a gun.
His chances seemed slight to embolden
Our hearts; but, with teeth firmly set,
We thought, 'Now or never! The old 'un
May reckon with some of 'em yet.'

Then loud rose the war-cry for Pardon;
He swept like the wind down the dip,
And over the rise by the garden,
The jockey was done with the whip
The field were at sixes and sevens—
The pace at the first had been fast—
And hope seemed to drop from the heavens,
For Pardon was coming at last.

And how he did come! It was splendid;
He gained on them yards every bound,
Stretching out like a greyhound extended,
His girth laid right down on the ground.
A shimmer of silk in the cedars
As into the running they wheeled,
And out flashed the whips on the leaders,
For Pardon had collared the field.

Then right through the ruck he came sailing—
I knew that the battle was won—
The son of Haphazard was failing,
The Yattendon filly was done;
He cut down the Don and the Dancer,
He raced clean away from the mare—
He's in front! Catch him now if you can, sir!
And up went my hat in the air!

Then loud from the lawn and the garden
Rose offers of 'Ten to one *on*!'
'Who'll bet on the field? I back Pardon!'
No use; all the money was gone.
He came for the third heat light-hearted,
A-jumping and dancing about;
The others were done ere they started
Crestfallen, and tired, and worn out.

He won it, and ran it much faster
Than even the first, I believe;
Oh, he was the daddy, the master,
Was Pardon, the son of Reprieve.
He showed 'em the method to travel—
The boy sat as still as a stone—
They never could see him for gravel;
He came in hard-held, and alone.

***

But he's old—and his eyes are grown hollow;
Like me, with my thatch of the snow;
When he dies, then I hope I may follow,
And go where the racehorses go.
I don't want no harping nor singing—
Such things with my style don't agree;
Where the hoofs of the horses are ringing
There's music sufficient for me.

And surely the thoroughbred horses
Will rise up again and begin
Fresh races on far-away courses,
And p'raps they might let me slip in.
It would look rather well the race-card on
'Mongst Cherubs and Seraphs and things,
'Angel Harrison's black gelding Pardon,
Blue halo, white body and wings.'

And if they have racing hereafter,
(And who is to say they will not?)
When the cheers and the shouting and laughter
Proclaim that the battle grows hot;
As they come down the racecourse a-steering,
He'll rush to the front, I believe;
And you'll hear the great multitude cheering
For Pardon, the son of Reprieve.

Part 3
BLOND BOMBSHELL TO BLACK CAVIAR

INTRODUCTION—CHAMPIONS AND FAVOURITES

Here is a random selection of stories about champions and favourite horses from the modern era, that is, 'since Phar Lap', as they say in racing.

There is, unfortunately, only so much space in a book like this to tell the great stories of the legends and the lovable favourites of more recent times. To leave out champions like Flight, Rising Fast, Vain, Gunsynd, Manikato, Dulcify, Might and Power, and crowd-pleasers such as Wenona Girl, Tails and Apache Cat, breaks my racing tragic's heart; but that's the way it is, I'm afraid.

How good were our top-class international racing ambassadors such as Choisir, Takeover Target and Miss Andretti in the UK, Elvstroem in Dubai, Sailor's Guide in the USA, and Karasi in Japan? Those stories, however, must wait for another time.

This section contains a handful of stories about some of the many great and wonderful horses we have loved over the past few generations. Other champions of this era, such as Mosstrooper, Crisp, Light Fingers and Makybe Diva, have their stories told in other sections of this collection.

HERE'S A STAYER

JIM HAYNES

'Here's a stayer!'

These were the words Frank McGrath said to his stable foreman when he first set eyes on the flashy Peter Pan.

It was a summer's day in 1932 when the colt arrived at McGrath's stables near Randwick racetrack, and the leggy chestnut with the silver mane and tail was already well into his two-year-old season.

McGrath was renowned as a trainer of stayers. He had trained Prince Foote to win the Melbourne Cup in 1909 and Peter Pan's owner, Rodney Dangar, thought the astute and patient trainer would be just the man to get the best out of his beautiful colt.

Dangar was a patient man himself. He had left Peter Pan to gallop and grow in the paddock at his family property near Singleton, New South Wales, well past the time when most promising thoroughbreds would be shipped off to training stables. He was happy to send his staying prospect to a trainer of the old school, a man who had won his only Melbourne Cup more than two decades before.

Peter Pan was the result of one of those 'happy chance' matings, a friendly gesture that was actually a last-minute afterthought on the part of Dangar's neighbour Percy Brown.

Brown had booked five mares to go to the imported stallion Pantheon. Pantheon had been brought out from Britain to race in Australia and was a very good stayer. His eight wins included the Rosehill Cup, the C.B. Fisher Plate and two AJC Randwick Plates over 2 miles. He started favourite, at 9 to 4, in the 1926 Melbourne Cup and finished third, ridden by the famous Jim Pike. He was placed a further eighteen times, giving him a good record for a stayer of 27 wins and placings from 34 starts.

Percy Brown had negotiated a good discount deal to send five mares to Pantheon in his first season at stud. However, when the time came to despatch the mares, he only had four available, so he crossed the road and asked his neighbour if he had a mare to make up the number.

Dangar had an unraced mare named Alwina, whose sire St Alwyne had also sired Melbourne Cup winners Poitrel and Night Watch. He'd bought the mare from the famous Arrowfield Stud for £210 and had no immediate plans for her when Percy Brown called in. He pointed to her in the paddock and said, 'Take that one.'

So, without any real planning, two great staying bloodlines converged to produce a horse that many believe was certainly the prettiest horse to ever win a Melbourne Cup.

Frank McGrath was impressed by the colt's good looks, too, but he was more impressed by his solid proportions and strong, clean-cut stayer's legs. He began training him as a stayer and didn't even start him in a race until four months later, in May 1932. The fact that the chestnut was unplaced in a two-year-old handicap at Randwick didn't seem to bother McGrath one bit. He immediately sent him for a spell, and that was Peter Pan's entire two-year-old campaign—one race, unplaced.

The horse managed to run a nail through a hoof and McGrath had to help him overcome an infection and nurse him back to fitness before he could return to training in the spring. This delayed plans a little but didn't stop Peter Pan being the well-backed favourite at 5 to 2 in only his second start in a race, first-up, over a mile in a novice handicap at Warwick Farm.

It was stable money that brought the price in to 5 to 2; the colt had run sensational times at trackwork and Frank McGrath said he thought he had 'the best thing ever on a racetrack'.

What the usually astute trainer had not factored into the equation was that Peter Pan had only ever raced once in a field of horses and once in front of a crowd. This almost brought the well-laid plan undone, as the colt stopped racing whenever the other horses got close around him. In desperation, jockey Andy Knox took him to the outside, only to have the inquisitive colt turn and stare at the yelling crowd.

Knox eventually managed to straighten the flashy youngster and he raced home to dead-heat for first with the runaway leader, Babili. This, at least, saved the stable from embarrassment, not to mention the trainer's bank balance.

It is remarkable to realise that Peter Pan's next start in a race, his third in the Rosehill Stakes over a mile, saw the raw young colt pitted against the Melbourne Cup winner Nightmarch, the Sydney Cup winner Johnny Jason, and Veilmond, the winner of the AJC and VRC St Legers.

Peter Pan may have been a raw young colt, but he was good enough to defeat the Melbourne Cup winner by half a length, with the Sydney Cup winner behind them in third place.

Two weeks later, in only his fourth start in a race, Peter Pan contested the AJC Derby. Ridden for the first time by Jim Pike, who had ridden his father into third place in the Melbourne Cup six years earlier, Peter Pan won, easing down, by a length and a half. Behind him were such good horses as the Chelmsford Stakes winner, and famed stayer in later life, Gaine Carrington, the AJC and VRC Sires' Produce winner Kuvera, and Oro, who would later win a Metropolitan Handicap.

By now Frank McGrath was not the only one looking at the pretty horse and thinking, 'Here's a stayer.' Peter Pan was backed in at 7 to 2 to win the Caulfield Cup at his fifth start.

Andy Knox was back in the saddle at Caulfield, as Jim Pike could not ride at the three-year-old's handicap weight of 7 st 4 lb (46.5 kg). It was to be Knox's last ride on Peter Pan.

The golden horse with the silver mane and tail was still 'a big baby' in racing parlance and, displaying his often-wayward behaviour once again, he missed the start badly. Andy Knox then raced him wide down the straight the first time round in order to catch the field and find a position, but the early sprint unsettled the horse and he pulled throughout the race and ran out of steam to finish fourth behind Rogilla, on raw talent, despite a dreadful run and a less than memorable ride.

It was a poor enough ride for Frank McGrath to sack Andy Knox and engage lightweight Melbourne jockey Bill Duncan to ride the horse in the Melbourne Stakes over 10 furlongs (2000 metres) on Derby Day.

Peter Pan had not been entered for the VRC Derby, so the Melbourne Stakes (now Mackinnon Stakes) was more or less a consolation prize for McGrath. Missing the derby was a regrettable oversight, but defeating Caulfield Cup winner Rogilla by a length to win the Melbourne Stakes race against all ages was certainly some consolation for losing the Caulfield Cup a few weeks earlier.

It may have been a consolation, but it was also an impressive enough win for the betting public to send the Sydney colt out as 4 to 1 favourite for the Melbourne Cup, at his sixth start in a race.

But it wasn't only the racing crowd who were impressed by the horse. The flashy three-year-old chestnut was all the rage. He had captured the public imagination and was a popular favourite for the Cup. In fact, his popularity rivalled that of Phar Lap, who had been favourite for the Cup for each of the previous three years, and it was as if the sporting public needed another hero to worship after Phar Lap's tragic demise in April that year. Australia was still in the grip of the Depression and people needed dreams and distractions; the golden colt with the film star looks and the silver mane was something to talk about, an equine Prince Charming with talent to match his looks.

The public may have had faith in Peter Pan, but his Melbourne Cup victory as a three-year-old was as dramatic and fraught with possible disaster as any before or since.

At around the 5-furlong mark, the colt was 'pole-axed' when crowding on the outside led to a chain reaction, which caused him to stumble and fall. As he fell he was again hit as a second wave of interference swept through the field. This caused his stablemate, Denis Boy, to barrel into Peter Pan and, strange as it seems, this second impact pushed him back onto his feet and certainly prevented a bad fall.

Frank McGrath was so certain his horse had fallen that he lowered his field glasses in disgust. He later said, 'I saw his head go down and then there was a blank space where Peter Pan had been racing.' It wasn't until he heard the course broadcaster call his name in the straight that the trainer realised Peter Pan was still running.

Denis Boy's rider, Harold Jones, told journalists: 'Just as the gap closed when Yarramba left the rails Peter Pan received a terrible bump and was whirled around until his head faced the rails. He was lucky to keep his feet as he started to fall.'

By the time Duncan got Peter Pan balanced again, the colt was at the rear of the field. How the green three-year-old managed to go on and win a Melbourne Cup and equal the race record was miraculous. Peter Pan stormed home to beat Yarramba by a neck. He returned to the mounting yard with his face covered in grass stains. The perennial old Cup campaigner Shadow King was third and Denis Boy ran fourth.

The outpouring of joy from the crowd was incredible: hats flew into the air, men cheered and women shrieked. Everyone loved the happy ending to the Melbourne Cup—won by the people's horse with the fairytale name and the movie star looks.

It was the sheer determination and patient care of two great men of the turf that won the day for Peter Pan in reality. Many good judges believe that no other jockey except the under-rated Bill Duncan could have kept the big colt on his feet that day; Duncan was a quiet man and a great jockey in an era of great jockeys.

Frank McGrath had not only nursed Peter Pan through a serious hoof infection, he had also shown patience and good judgement to get the horse to win a Melbourne Cup at his sixth race start. It is an indication of McGrath's patience and love of the horses in his care that Denis Boy, his other runner that day and the horse that helped keep Peter Pan upright, had actually been nursed back to racing fitness by McGrath after breaking a knee bone. McGrath persevered and had the horse's leg in a sling until the bone healed. He then trained Denis Boy to win the 1932 AJC Metropolitan Handicap and run fourth behind his more illustrious stablemate in the Melbourne Cup. This would be an outstanding achievement with today's technology, let alone in McGrath's era.

A trainer of the old school in many ways, Frank McGrath was 'modern' in the sense that he always put the horse's welfare first, and his plans were always long-term plans.

The Melbourne Cup victory earned Peter Pan a four-month holiday in the spelling paddock. McGrath wanted him primed for the autumn racing in Sydney. He then came out and won first-up at a mile at Randwick, once again defeating Rogilla.

At his next start his reputation for clumsiness and getting into trouble in races was given a boost—he became tangled in the starting tapes when 3 to 1 favourite for the Rawson Stakes at Rosehill, and tailed the field home.

Peter Pan was the big drawcard at the Sydney Autumn Carnival of 1933 and he took out three races in eight days: the St Leger, Cumberland Stakes and AJC Plate. The three-year-old was then handicapped at 9 stone (57 kg), 12 pounds (5.4 kg) over weight-for-age, in the Sydney Cup—the same weight Carbine had carried, as a three-year-old, in 1889.

Frank McGrath told the handicapper that times had changed since 1889 and no horse should be given such a weight at three years of age over 2 miles. He then protested in the most effective way possible by simply scratching his horse from the Sydney Cup and putting him aside to prepare for the Melbourne Cup of 1933.

Sadly, however, Peter Pan was to be absent from racetracks for twelve months. He had been handicapped at 9 st 7 lb (60.5 kg) for the Melbourne Cup of 1933 and McGrath thought that this was fair, being 7 pounds (3.2 kg) over weight-for-age for a four-year-old. However, when he returned from the spelling paddock he was found to be suffering from rheumatism in his shoulders. He was treated and left to recover naturally in the paddock, but he missed an entire year of racing—the bulk of his four-year-old season, normally a career 'prime time' for racehorses.

The golden horse of the previous Sydney Autumn Carnival resumed racing in March 1934 and took a while to get back to his peak. Unplaced over a mile at Randwick on 3 March, he improved to run a good second to old rival Rogilla two weeks later at Rosehill, but was unplaced a week later behind the mighty

New Zealand mare Silver Scorn in the Chipping Norton Stakes at Warwick Farm.

Silver Scorn had won twelve races from thirteen starts as a three-year-old and was hot favourite for the AJC Autumn Plate a week after her Chipping Norton victory.

It seemed that Peter Pan had turned the corner, however, and was finding his old form under McGrath's patient training. He trounced Silver Scorn by 2½ lengths in the Autumn Plate and followed up that win with another in the 2-mile Cumberland Plate only four days later.

Just three days after that, Peter Pan was again the punter's favourite as Jim Pike took him out onto the track to run against a classy field, including his old foe Rogilla, in the 1½-mile (2400-metre) Kings Cup.

Once again the big chestnut had another of his 'blond moments'. Nicknamed the 'Blond Bombshell', after sultry movie star Jean Harlow, Peter Pan, with his gold coat and silver mane and tail, was possibly the most beautiful horse that ever became a champion in Australia, but at times it was almost as if he had a touch of Three Stooges mayhem in his make-up.

Racing neck and neck with Rogilla, Peter Pan suddenly seemed to resent his old rival's persistence. Travelling flat-out, Peter Pan turned his head to bite Rogilla as they neared the winning post, and the terrified Rogilla stuck out his head to avoid the stallion's attack, and won the race by a head!

It certainly appeared that the great stayer had recovered from his crippling rheumatism, even if his manners had not been improved by the lengthy spell. That autumn campaign was his worst ever—six starts for two wins, two seconds and two unplaced runs—but Frank McGrath was satisfied that the horse was back to his old self, and promptly spelled him to await the spring carnivals.

Perhaps the 'Blond Bombshell' knew the score between himself and his rival when he delivered the 'lovebite' to Rogilla. The tactic certainly cost Peter Pan victory in the Kings Cup and it didn't scare off Rogilla effectively either; Peter Pan finished second to him again when he resumed racing in the Chelmsford Stakes in the spring of 1934. So, unfortunately for our chestnut hero, it was not a case of 'once bitten, twice shy'.

Frank McGrath then made a tactical move that confounded the critics. He entered Peter Pan in a 7-furlong sprint race, against the mighty Chatham, at the Victoria Park racetrack. Victoria Park is now a housing estate beside busy Southern Cross Drive near Moore Park, but it was once a beautiful showpiece proprietary racecourse owned by racing entrepreneur Sir James Joynton Smith, and rivalled Randwick as Sydney's premier racetrack in its heyday.

A huge crowd flocked to see the 'Blond Bombshell' race against Chatham, who was the sprint and middle-distance champion of his era and started at 4 to 1 favourite.

But the canny McGrath had evidently seen something in his horse's behaviour that made him believe he could go against all racing common sense and bring a stayer back from 9 furlongs to 7 at his second start in a campaign. As usual Frank McGrath's intuition was spot on—Peter Pan defeated the mighty sprinter and set a course record for 7 furlongs at Victoria Park.

Ten days later, Peter Pan was sent out favourite at odds-on in the AJC Spring Stakes at a mile and a half, only to be beaten by a head by his old nemesis Rogilla. This time Rogilla won fair and square, without the aid of a bite from his rival. That made it four times in a row that Peter Pan had finished second to Rogilla; perhaps the record-breaking sprint at Victoria Park had taken the edge off him.

Rogilla and Peter Pan had now clashed ten times, with Rogilla winning on six occasions. Rogilla was a champion himself, a horse who won 26 races including the Caulfield and Sydney Cups. He was never able to beat Peter Pan again, however, losing every one of his final seven clashes against the champion chestnut.

The Craven Plate over 10 furlongs looked like another match race between Peter Pan and Rogilla. But this time it was Chatham's time to turn the tables on them both. As Peter Pan, at 10 to 9, and Rogilla, at 6 to 4, engaged in their usual head-to-head struggle down the straight, Chatham, at 8 to 1, swept past them to win by a length.

The three clashed again, with Melbourne Cup winner of 1933, Hall Mark, in the Melbourne Stakes on the first day of the Spring Carnival at Flemington. Peter Pan carried 9 st 2 lb (58.5 kg) and ran his classy rivals off their legs to win easily.

Peter Pan had been allotted 9 st 10 lb (61.5 kg) for the Melbourne Cup, certainly a champion's weight. However, his win on the Saturday had convinced McGrath that the mighty horse was ready for another Cup win and the public were behind him also, making him equal early favourite at 5 to 1 despite his big weight. Then the weather conspired against the great horse.

The day before the Cup was run, Melbourne turned on one of its worst rainstorms: it poured and poured all day and Cup Day saw grey skies and more rain on its way. The track was a swamp, all form was 'out the window' and Peter Pan, still suffering from his perennial rheumatism which always worsened in wet weather, and carrying almost 10 stone, looked like a dead duck. Even the mug punters deserted the champion. He drifted alarmingly in the betting, out to 14 to 1.

With Jim Pike suspended, McGrath engaged Darby Munro to ride his champion in Melbourne. 'Demon' Darby was usually Rogilla's regular rider, but he had ridden Peter Pan before and won on him in Sydney and in the Melbourne Stakes.

The Cup field was as good as you could imagine that year. It included the previous year's winner Hall Mark, Rogilla, dual derby winner Theo, the great staying mare Sarcherie, and the winners of the Moonee Valley, Australian and Sydney Cups. The rain had made the surface a swamp and the result would surely be no more than a lottery of luck.

It was a gloomy scene in the saddling paddock, literally and metaphorically, as Frank McGrath legged Darby Munro onto the rheumatic five-year-old's back. All the trainer could think to say to the crack jockey as they looked at the bog track, made worse than ever by a day's racing, was, 'Don't worry, they all have to go through it.' They both knew the truth, however—they all didn't have to carry 9 stone 10! Perhaps the Blond Bombshell was truly a 'dead duck'.

As it transpired, however, Peter Pan turned out to be what racing people call 'a real duck'.

In what was a daring decision, Munro decided it was better for the champion stayer to run further on firmer ground than plough through puddles with the huge weight. He kept Peter Pan out wide all the way down the straight the first time and all around the course in the 2-mile marathon. At the turn he took the lead and raced away, still well off the fence, to defeat Sarcherie by 3 lengths slowing down, with LaTrobe third.

Munro's daring ride had managed to keep Rodney Dangar's orange and green-hooped silks cleaner than most, and he now had £5200 in prizemoney to help pay the cleaning bills.

Had Munro's bold move failed, he would no doubt have copped a lot of criticism. As it turned out, the tactic paid off and Peter Pan did the rest, running as some said 'an extra furlong or two'. He was going so well in the running that Munro later told McGrath and others, 'I was sure we would win with half a mile to go.'

So Peter Pan went into the record books as only the second horse to win two Melbourne Cups, after Archer in 1861 and 1862.

As he seemed quite well after his marathon run in the mud on the Tuesday, Frank McGrath sent him around again on the Saturday, in the 14-furlong Duke of Gloucester Cup. Ridden again by Darby Munro, and carrying top-weight of 9 st 7 lb (60.5 kg), he easily defeated Sydney Cup winner Broad Arrow.

All Sydney was waiting to see their glamorous history-making champion, so the horse was rushed back to Sydney to run in the Duke of Gloucester Plate twelve days later. He finished a tired sixth behind Oro and was sent for another of those therapeutic long spells his trainer was so keen on. No horse ever deserved a holiday more.

It is part of Cup mythology that horses that win the great race often achieve little else. This is true to an extent, more so in the modern era when horses are more likely to be trained for one result only. It is also true that many horses that win the Cup are not true stayers, and the effort and training that goes into a Cup win leaves them with little left to win with again.

Peter Pan, however, makes a mockery of the myth.

His autumn campaign of 1935 saw the great horse, with Jim Pike back in the saddle, win five races from five starts. And they were not just any old races.

Conditioned and trained to perfection by the ever-astute Frank McGrath, Peter Pan won the Randwick Stakes, Rawson Stakes, Autumn Plate, All-Aged Stakes and Jubilee Cup in succession, between late March and early May.

Spelled again, he returned in the spring, as a six-year-old stallion, to take out another three from three: the Hill Stakes, Spring Stakes and Craven Plate. In the last two races his old foe Rogilla, unbitten and now a light of former days, finished third and fourth, respectively.

Peter Pan, too, was looking like a horse nearing the end of his career. In spite of being undefeated in his past eight starts, the chestnut warrior was suffering constantly from rheumatism and only McGrath's special care, patience and knowledge of the horse was keeping him fit. No trainer ever placed a horse to better advantage than Frank McGrath did with Peter Pan as a six-year-old.

The trainer suggested to Rodney Dangar that another Melbourne Cup campaign was beyond the champion. There were even rumours about the horse's health and McGrath, a trainer who always placed his horses' welfare above all else, had to suffer the ignominy of having the RSPCA visit his stables to inspect the popular hero. They found him to be in excellent condition, fit and happy, and extremely well cared for.

What more was there for the champion to achieve? He was the best stayer ever to race in the modern era, he was as popular as Phar Lap had been, and he had done something no stayer had managed to do since 1862. He was the glamour horse with the quirky personality and the film star looks and he brightened up the mood of a nation during the Great Depression.

Dangar, however, was loath to scratch the horse from the Cup, as many people had invested money on the popular champion. In a compromise decision McGrath trained him for just two runs in Melbourne: the Melbourne Stakes and the Melbourne Cup.

Public sentiment saw the great stayer sent out an odds-on favourite in the Melbourne Stakes, but he finished unplaced and three days later, carrying a crippling 10 st 6 lb (66 kg), he ran in the Cup at 8 to 1, with many people backing him out of sentiment and respect, rather than common sense.

Peter Pan finished a creditable fourteenth behind Marabou in the 1935 Cup. He possibly could have finished closer if ridden out hard in the straight but Jim Pike, who loved the horse as much as anyone, eased him down when he realised he had no chance of winning.

After a summer spell the champion looked as good as ever and it was decided to try one more campaign in the autumn of 1936. After an unplaced first-up run in the Randwick Stakes, the old Peter Pan emerged briefly and he ran a good second in the Rawson Stakes, and a creditable third to Sarcherie in the Autumn Plate at Randwick.

Frank McGrath knew the horse well enough to tell Rodney Dangar that enough was enough, and Peter Pan retired in April 1936 to prepare for a stud career.

He proved a reasonably successful sire, with Peter, from his first crop, winning the Williamstown Cup and Eclipse Stakes, and a later son, Precept, winning the Victoria Derby.

Always his own worst enemy, the great stallion was prone to fits of madcap behaviour and coltish frolicking. In March 1941 he slipped over during one of these displays of hijinks and broke a leg so badly that he had to be confined in an attempt to heal the break. Sadly his high-spirited temperament was not amenable to confinement and the break was so bad that, after all efforts to save him had failed, he was put down.

Before Randwick was remodelled in 2013, there was a large photograph of Peter Pan, entering the birdcage after one of his famous Randwick victories in 1934, located in the walkway between the Members' Stand and the betting ring, and you passed it as you made your way back to the ring after each race.

We don't have many real staying races these days; it's all about what Banjo Paterson called 'your six-furlong vermin that scamper half-a-mile with a feather-weight up'. Staying these days is an art left mostly to dour old has-beens and overseas imports.

Often, after I'd backed some poor excuse for a stayer in some weak mid-week staying race, I'd walk back to the ring despondent and pause in front of the photo of the beautiful chestnut.

To anyone unlucky enough to be with me at the races that day, I'd say, 'Hey, come here a minute and look at this horse in the photo—here's a stayer.'

HOW WE BACKED THE FAVOURITE

C.J. DENNIS

Peter Pan was so popular that C.J. Dennis wrote a poem about the public's unerring faith in his ability to win the Cup. It was a parody of Adam Lindsay Gordon's famous verse 'How We Beat the Favourite', written in the same style and rhyme scheme. While Gordon's poem is a heroic tale of a titanic struggle, which celebrates the nobility and bravery of the racehorse, Dennis's poem is about the confidence shown by the everyday 'one shilling' punters in the Cup favourite.

Having been told that Peter Pan will win, the poet goes to see the horse and make up his own mind. Now, Peter Pan was arguably the most beautiful horse to ever win the Cup. C.J. Dennis sums up the horse with the mundane phrase 'there was little he lacked'. You can't get more Aussie than that!

***

'Sure thing,' said the grocer, 'as far as I know, sir,
This horse, Peter Pan, is the safest of certs.'
'I see by the paper,' commended the draper,
'He's tipped and he carries my whole weight of shirts.'

The butcher said, 'Well, now, it's easy to tell now
There's nothing else in it except Peter Pan.'
And so too the baker, the barman, bookmaker,
The old lady char and the saveloy man.

'You stick to my tip, man,' admonished the grip-man,
'Play up Peter Pan; he's a stayer with speed.'
And the newspaper vendor, the ancient road mender,
And even the cop at the corner agreed.

The barber said, 'Win it? There's nothing else in it.
I backed Peter Pan with the last that I had.'
'Too right,' said the liftman. 'The horse is a gift, man.'
The old jobbing gardener said, 'Peter Pan, lad!'

I know nought of racing. The task I was facing,
It filled me with pain and unreasoning dread.
They all seemed so certain, and yet a dark curtain
Of doubt dulled my mind . . . But I must keep my head!

I went to the races, and I watched all their faces.
I saw Peter Pan's; there was little he lacked.
And as he seemed willing, I plancked on my shilling
And triumphed! And that's how the favourite was backed.

Jorrocks the 'Iron Gelding', our first popular champion racehorse. (DIANNA CORCORAN/AJC)

Carbine at age four with trainer Walter Hickenbotham and VRC Chairman R.G. Casey. (ARM)

The mighty Wakeful posing for the camera for an early newspaper poster.

Bernborough leads out the field at Flemington before carrying 63 kg to victory in the Newmarket Handicap on 2 March 1946 (ERN MCQUILLAN/AJC)

The heyday of racing—Randwick racecourse in the 1950s. (AJC)

Reserved seating at the Wallabadah Races, c.1950. (PETER JENKINS)

Part of the Randwick racecourse betting ring in the 1950s, before the advent of legal off-course betting. (AJC)

The Paddock betting ring at Randwick after the last race, c.1960. (AJC)

Tommy Smith with Tulloch at the Queen Elizabeth Stakes, c.1960. (AJC)

Dalby Ladies Improver Handicap 1974. Pam O'Neill is third from the left in the back row. (QUEENSLAND RACING LIMITED)

The Hobartville Stakes at Warwick Far, 1962. (AJC)

Randwick racecourse c.1965 showing four enclosures—Flat, Leger, Paddock and Members. (AJC)

Racing in the bush.

Racing in the city. (AJC)

Octagonal wins the 1996 AJC Derby from Saintly Filante and Nothin' Leica Dane. (STEVE HART PHOTOGRAPHICS)

Lonhro with Darren Beadman wins the Caulfield Stakes from the great Sunline with Greg Childs on 12 October 2002. (STEVE HART PHOTOGRAPHICS)

THE BERNBOROUGH STORY

DAVID HICKIE

Bernborough was foaled in 1939 at Harry Winten's Rosalie Plains Stud, in the Dalby district on Queensland's Darling Downs, near Toowoomba.

His dam was the 18-year-old mare Bern Maid and his sire was supposed to be by the imported sire Emborough, a horse that had won the Manchester Cup in the UK, but there is some doubt about this and his sire may have been Monish Vella.

Bernborough, racing under the nomination of a Mr Albert E. Hadwen of Brisbane, was unplaced at his first Toowoomba start on 26 January 1942 and then ran in a maiden event for two-year-olds. Bernborough finished second to a scrubber called Dunfor, but a protest was successful. Bernborough then won four more two-year-old races at Toowoomba.

As a three-year-old he raced three times for three wins and as a four-year-old he had two starts, once coming third and once unplaced. He had eight runs, all at Toowoomba, as a five-year-old for three wins, one second and was four times unplaced.

His Toowoomba record therefore stood at 11 wins from 19 starts—impressive, but not sensational, and certainly not the sort of credentials upon which many turf experts would later base their judgement that Bernborough, of all Australian thoroughbreds, was the greatest.

In later years many people closely associated with the Bernborough camp, which won a lot of money knowing when to back the 'one day on—one day off' champ, revealed details which give reason to believe Bernborough could have won all those Toowoomba races in a canter.

Part 1 The Daylate-Brulad 'ring-in' scandal

The background to Bernborough's restricted early racing went back to Queensland's infamous Daylate–Brulad 'ring-in' scandal, when the Queensland Turf Club's investigation led to the life disqualification of Oakey farmer Fred Bach.

In December 1938 a horse named Brulad, owned by Bach and trained by Con Doyle, flashed home at double-figure odds to run third behind Tollbar in the QTC Champagne Stakes at Eagle Farm. A week later the bay gelding, by Brutus out of Lady Chillington, was heavily backed at 3 to 1 and won the 5-furlong Oxley Handicap at Eagle Farm, despite badly missing the start. The time, 61.5 seconds, was the fastest registered by a two-year-old for the season.

Brulad was sent for a spell, returning in February 1939 for three disappointing unplaced runs. Then the horse began to show form. He ran third at Eagle Farm, before being well supported and defeating the odds-on favourite, top colt Brisbane River, in the 6-furlong Juvenile Handicap at Eagle Farm in April. After that win, Fred Bach was offered £1000 for Brulad but refused to sell.

Brulad was beaten in his last three starts of that season and then, as a three-year-old, failed to show any form and was beaten in six successive starts. The horse was now in the stable of Clive Morgan, who sent the horse back to Bach in February 1940, suggesting he needed a long spell. Morgan never saw the horse again and Fred Bach told the trainer that Brulad had died. The same year a four-year-old brown gelding, Daylate, by Listowel out of Ferniehurst, was registered in the ownership of a certain J. Jackson.

Daylate's first start resulted in a second place in a Hack Handicap at Warwick, in October 1940. A month later he won easily at Bundamba. Fred Bach was at the course and backed the horse for a small fortune. 'If I had one win a year like I had at

Bundamba,' Bach later boasted, 'I would be thoroughly satisfied.' Daylate then ran third at Bundamba and fourth in a Trial Handicap at Eagle Farm.

On 4 January 1941, Daylate ran in another Trial Handicap at Eagle Farm. Leading jockey Russell Maddock was engaged and the horse was heavily backed in the betting ring. A mysterious 'Lady in Black' was reputed to have collected more than £1000 in winnings from bookmakers in the on-course betting ring alone. In 1941 that was enough to buy a couple of modest suburban homes in Brisbane.

The horse raced with the leaders until the 2-furlong mark and then dashed clear to win easily, beating a horse called Bullmar who was ridden by a youthful George Moore. Years later Maddock revealed, 'I was asked only the night before the race to ride Daylate by the owner.'

No hint emerged that day of any behind-the-scenes drama, but the following Saturday QTC chief steward J.J. Lynch, accompanied by two racecourse detectives, arrived unannounced at the Doomben stables of Daylate's trainer J.H. McIlwrick. The news spread like wildfire that authorities had made a thorough examination of Daylate.

A reporter tracked down Lynch and asked him why he had inspected Daylate. 'I cannot discuss that with you,' came the stern reply. It was also reported that two unnamed trainers, later identified as Con Doyle and Clive Morgan, who had previously trained Brulad, had also been asked to examine Daylate.

Neither trainer would make any comment but the rumour spread that Daylate bore a remarkable resemblance to Brulad, which Fred Bach had officially certified to the QTC office as being dead. Then Daylate suddenly disappeared from McIlwrick's stables.

What had happened was that a country steward named Steve Bowen, enjoying an off-duty day at Eagle Farm, had raised initial doubts about Daylate's identity and declared the winner was in fact Brulad. Similarly trainer Morgan told racecourse detective Charles Prentice that Daylate was Brulad. Prentice was at first dubious, but Bowen maintained he was certain because Brulad had a particularly unusual mane, which hung in three sections across his neck whenever the horse tossed his head—Daylate's mane fell in the same distinct pattern.

So Prentice and stewards Lynch and Williams set off in search of the mysterious owner of Daylate, 'J. Jackson', who had a postal address at a cattle station near Bowenville. When Prentice asked to speak to Jackson, the station mistress told him that all correspondence for J. Jackson was in fact handed to a Mrs F. Bacon, who was Fred Bach's daughter.

Meanwhile a policeman turned up at Bach's property near Oakey one night but was mysteriously shot at and wounded. Fred's son Jack was later tried for the crime, but acquitted—he had an alibi to prove he wasn't at the farm that evening.

When Prentice and his companions went to Bach's farm, Fred Bach wasn't there, but his son Jack told them Brulad's body had been burned after the horse had died. Prentice later officially reported, 'It was learned that the horse called Brulad had returned from Brisbane in a sick condition and subsequently died on Mister Frank Bach's property at Blaxland. Mister Jack Bach said he saw Brulad when the horse was dead and assisted his brother to burn the carcass.'

When Prentice went to see Frank Bach, however, Frank said he knew nothing about Brulad and had not helped Jack burn the carcass of any horse. It was when Prentice returned to Brisbane that Daylate suddenly disappeared from McIlwrick's stable.

Prentice, one jump ahead, had decided to 'stake out' the stables and caught Fred Bach absconding with Daylate. At about 10 p.m. he saw Fred Bach enter the yard. At 10:15 p.m. he heard 'knocking and hammering' and a few minutes later Bach led Daylate from the property. When he'd gone about 50 yards Prentice intercepted him and said, 'Good night'.

When Prentice asked his name Bach replied 'Jackson', but Prentice retorted, 'You are Fred Bach.'

Bach then said, 'You are Mister Prentice, how are you?' and shook hands.

When Prentice asked, 'Why are you mixing yourself up in this sort of thing?' Bach appeared 'flurried' and said Jackson was down the road. Prentice saw two cars further down the street and in one were two men who refused to give their names.

Eventually Bach confessed, 'Now you've got me. There's nobody else in this. There is only me. I am Jackson. I suppose I'll get life. I'll take full responsibility for everything.'

At a subsequent QTC inquiry Fred Bach denied he had admitted being Jackson and refused to answer most questions. A CIB handwriting expert testified that the same person who had signed nomination forms for Daylate in the name of Jackson had also signed nomination forms for Brulad in the name of Bach.

On 20 January 1941, QTC stewards disqualified Fred Bach for life. The ban also applied to his son, Jack.

Part 2 Bernborough's mysterious ownership history

Fred Bach had two sons, John (known as Jack) and Frank. In 1940, some months before the Daylate–Brulad controversy, Jack had purchased the old mare Bern Maid, with a foal at foot, at the Rosalie Plains Stud dispersal, for 150 guineas.

Bach subsequently claimed to have sold the foal to A.E. Hadwen but, when the horse was entered for a two-year-old event in Brisbane in 1942, QTC stewards rejected the nomination. An official reason was never given but it was generally accepted that it was because of the colt's connection with the Bach family. Officials believed that the real owner was still Jack Bach.

The horse was then sent to Sydney, ostensibly by Hadwen, and trialled at Rosehill, but the AJC affirmed the Brisbane ban and refused any nomination for the colt. So Bernborough was banned from racing on any of the major tracks across Australia.

Only the Queensland country course at Toowoomba accepted the bona fide of Bernborough's sale. This they did after an inquiry, allegedly conducted by Darling Downs steward George Kirk, into the authenticity of a receipt signed by J.R. Bach for the sale of Bernborough to Hadwen for 140 guineas.

Hadwen said he bought the horse on 22 June 1940, after asking Bach to find him a good horse. Bernborough was then purportedly leased to trainer J. Roberts and raced solely in Toowoomba for four seasons, winning 11 races under often-enormous weights.

Finally, in October 1945, the champion was sent to Sydney as a six-year-old, to be sold at public auction. Flamboyant restaurant and nightclub owner Azzalin Romano duly purchased him for Harry Plant to train at Randwick.

Romano had been told to purchase the horse by Plant and paid 2600 guineas for him. After the sale to Romano the QTC lifted its ban on Bernborough. Hence the champ raced on city tracks only in his sixth and seventh years—winning 15 of his 18 races in Sydney, Melbourne and Brisbane, at distances from 6 furlongs to one and a half miles.

Bernborough was a six-year-old bay stallion, then, when jockey Athol George Mulley first rode him. Mulley later recalled, 'Bailey Payten, to whom I was apprenticed, told me there was a very good horse from Queensland to come up for auction. He said he would like to buy him. He was prepared to pay up to £10,000 or, being conservative, at least £5000.'

Payten told Mulley, 'I could afford to buy him, but it wouldn't matter how much money I've got he can't be bought, so I won't worry.'

Years later Mulley explained this cryptic comment by hinting that Romano was not the sole owner of Bernborough and told of an argument he overheard between the two men concerned late one night when trainer Harry Plant was not present.

'My old boss, Bailey Payten, always maintained that there was no chance of anyone else ever buying Bernborough when he was put up for auction in Sydney,' Mulley said. 'He said that too many influential men of the day were involved and suggested that a certain bill of sale would have made interesting reading.'

Author Frank Hardy later wrote that Mulley told him, 'There was a mystery about the sale. Over the years, at parties, listening to various conversations, I gathered that certain important people in Sydney had arranged the sale and that apparently the original Queensland owner still retained a half-interest in the horse.'

Whatever the secret manoeuvrings away from public view, Bernborough was sold at public auction in October 1945 for 2600 guineas and duly arrived at the Randwick stables of trainer Harry Plant, a former Queensland buckjump champion and one-time professional horse-breaker. Bernborough had previously raced on only one track—Clifford Park, Toowoomba.

Part 3 A true champion

At his first Sydney start, in a Flying at Canterbury on 8 December 1945, Bernborough met severe interference and finished on the heels of the placegetters. Plant, who'd trialled the horse in secret and knew he had a champion, had told Romano to plunge heavily. Romano backed the horse to win a proverbial fortune, lost the lot, and insisted Plant replace jockey Noel McGrowdie.

Then followed Bernborough's legendary sequence of 15 straight wins under huge weights, ridden by Athol George Mulley. The sequence began with a Sydney treble in the Villiers Stakes with 9 st 2 lb (58 kg) by 5 lengths; the Carrington Stakes, with 9 st 6 lb (60 kg); and the Australia Day Handicap, with 9 st 5 lb (59.5 kg).

Mulley was 21 when he first rode Bernborough to victory in the Villiers at Randwick on 22 December 1945. He had begun riding less than four years before, at age 17.

'I was approached to ride Bernborough just for the one race and I took the ride only for one simple reason—I didn't have a riding engagement for the Villiers,' Mulley later recalled. 'I didn't know I was taking the ride on a champion. I rode him in trackwork at the old Victoria Park course before the Villiers and he was a big strong horse. He had beautiful shoulders. He measured 17 hands and 1 inch, the same height as Phar Lap, but he was better balanced than Phar Lap. Bernborough's conformation was perfect.

'I found out afterwards that he measured 67 inches from his ears to the top of his withers, and exactly the same from the top of his withers to his tail; that is a perfectly balanced measurement.' Later Bernborough's full galloping stride was measured at 27 feet (8.2 metres), 2 feet longer than Phar Lap's stride.

'That first day at the track I noticed how well balanced he was and that as a walker he was terrific,' Mulley said, 'and he had a marvellous temperament for a stallion. But if I told you I knew how good he was, I'd be telling a lie. Nobody knew then.

'I obtained my first feeling that Bernborough was a champion when I won on him in the Villiers. There were no starting stalls in those days, it was a stand-up start. He was second last on settling down and about eighth at the turn and, when I called on him, that's when I first noticed how he dropped his off-front shoulder. I pulled the whip, but I didn't use it, just waved it at him, and a furlong out he leapt straight to the lead and won by 5 lengths. And I knew I had ridden a champion racehorse.'

Mulley was given the mount again for the Carrington Stakes, over 6 furlongs, which Bernborough won carrying 9 st 6 lb (60 kg) in 1 minute 10.25 seconds.

And so it went on, 15 consecutive times, until Bernborough and Mulley were household names throughout Australia.

After his three Sydney wins Bernborough headed for Melbourne and the big autumn races. He won the Futurity Stakes by 5 lengths carrying 10 st 2 lb (64.5 kg) and the Newmarket Handicap with 9 st 13 lb (63 kg). Mulley later told how he was offered £5000, a fortune in those days, to 'pull' Bernborough in the Newmarket.

After the Futurity triumph Romano rushed up to the 21-year-old Mulley and declared, 'Georgie, my boy, I am proud of you. Name anything you like and I'll get it for you. I will even let you marry my daughter!'

Twenty-five years later Mulley told Frank Hardy, 'Bernborough's greatest performance, in my opinion, was his Newmarket win at Flemington. He had had a very hard race in the Futurity a week or so before and he carried 9 st 13 lb (63 kg) in the Newmarket and beat a field of class sprinters, including Versailles ridden by Scobie Breasley. Coming back from the 7 furlongs of the Futurity to the 6 furlongs of the Newmarket was Bernborough's greatest feat. Ordinary horses can increase their distance from 6 to 7 furlongs, 7 to a mile and so on, but only great horses can come back in their distances in top-class company.'

Mulley had ridden Bernborough in three races in Sydney, but the Futurity at Caulfield in February 1946 was the jockey's first ride ever in Melbourne.

'In the Villiers at Randwick,' Mulley recalled, 'I had to make up some ground on the turn into the straight and, coming into the turn he dipped his off-front shoulder. I'd say, without exaggerating, it was at about a 45-degree angle. I'll never forget it: in all my experience I never rode a horse with that peculiarity before or since. He dropped his shoulder and he got tremendous speed once he did that and could continue his run right to the post. He had a run of 2 to 2¼ furlongs. You had to judge it and he liked to begin it in the middle of his turn or near the end of his turn.'

There was no turn, of course, in the Newmarket, which is run down the 'straight six' at Flemington.

'There was more than one horse in that race whose jockey's job was to down Bernborough,' recalled Mulley. 'I know that because to pull Bernborough in the Newmarket I was offered £5000. I refused, of course, and a man pushed his way into my hotel room and threatened me, and he told me Bernborough wouldn't win anyway, because there were jockeys scouting for him.'

The record shows that Bernborough was cannoned into by two horses as soon as the barrier went up; and after travelling 2 furlongs he received another bad check.

'I pulled Bernborough to the centre of the track about 2¼ furlongs from home,' explained Mulley. 'He dropped his shoulder and unwound his famous cyclonic run . . . and then the "accident" happened. A horse veered out and came at us but luckily Bernborough was such a great horse and so strong that he just hit him on the shoulder and knocked him away and he never even lost his stride.'

Bernborough continued his mighty finish and got up in the last stride to collar the good sprinter Four Freedoms, ridden by Bill Cook and carrying 2 stone less in weight, right on the line.

'It turned out that Bernborough had run the last furlong in ten seconds,' Mulley later recalled, 'and won by half a head. It was his greatest win.'

To that point Bernborough had strung together five sensational wins on the trot in major races and Romano revealed that he'd already been inundated with hundreds of letters from all over Australia. He responded by sending out 300 photographs of the horse to the fans.

Back in Sydney in April 1946, Bernborough won the Rawson Stakes, Chipping Norton Stakes (beating Flight and Russia) and the All-Aged Stakes.

Bernborough then headed north to the Brisbane Winter Carnival where, on successive June Saturdays, he added to his record with wins in the Doomben Ten Thousand, carrying 10 st 5 lb (65.5 kg), and the Doomben Cup with an incredible 10 st 11 lb (68.5 kg). Romano and stable followers collected £40,000 from winning wagers on the two races and through the feature doubles.

Although Mulley named Newmarket as Bernborough's greatest race, many turf aficionados rated his Doomben Cup win superior. Bernborough began slowly, as usual, and was 14 lengths from the lead at the mile post. He eventually caught the leaders right on the finishing line; having humped 10 st 11 lb (68.5 kg) to victory in a top feature race and carrying 28 lb (12 kg) in dead weight.

'That was Bernborough's secret,' Mulley explained years later. 'I always felt he could race as fast with 10 stone as he could with 7 stone—weight made no difference to him. That's what made him a champion, his ability to carry big weights.'

Veteran Brisbane race-caller Keith Noud claimed: 'Bernborough's Doomben double in 1946, a feat yet to be duplicated, were the two great performances above all others used to underline the argument that he was the greatest horse, up to 2000 metres, yet to race in this country. The full force of that opinion is based on the massive weights he carried in those races.'

After the sensational Brisbane triumphs Romano, who had a photo of Bernborough that he always carried with him and described as his 'lucky mascot', presented Bernborough's silks to Mulley at a special function.

Now a seven-year-old, Bernborough won his next five starts, all at weight-for-age. They were the Warwick Stakes, Chelmsford

Stakes and Hill Stakes in Sydney, and the Melbourne Stakes and Caulfield Stakes in Melbourne. As a result he was allotted an incredible 10 st 10 lb (68 kg) for the 1946 Caulfield Cup and 10 st 9 lb (67.5 kg) in the Melbourne Cup.

What made those huge handicaps all the more remarkable was that eight months before the weights for the Cup were issued, very few racegoers in Australia had even heard of Bernborough. Moreover the horse was now at an age when most thoroughbreds are considered past their prime. At that time the weight-carrying record for the Caulfield Cup stood to the credit of Amounis, who had won with 9 st 8 lb (61 kg) in 1930.

'His weight-for-age wins were never as impressive as his handicap wins,' Mulley later said. 'But Bernborough should have been reserved for weight-for-age races in the spring of 1946. He'd had a lot of hard racing and his legs were bound to give out under handicap weights in big fields. He should never have run in the Caulfield Cup. But they wanted him to run in everything. They would have run him in the Stawell Gift, only it had been cancelled during World War II.'

A sport-loving, hero-worshipping nation just out of war needed an idol. And the massive, heart-stopping Bernborough filled the role precisely. He was indifferent to distance, and no weight the handicapper gave him seemed to dull his strength. Most importantly, he always won with a blistering finish that brought crowds roaring to their feet. No matter how far back he was at the furlong, everyone knew Bernborough would mow down his rivals.

'There was something special about the horse,' Frank Hardy wrote, 'the balance, the giant strides, the will to win. And about the way Mulley rode him, allowing him time to settle down and timing his paralysing finishing run to the split second.'

Bernborough became the greatest drawcard racing had ever known. That's why 107,167 patrons streamed to Caulfield racecourse for the 1946 Caulfield Cup. The press made great play of the fact that one woman, a mysterious 'woman in black' who turned out to be an Estonian woman, Miss Joanna Taks, had bet her winnings 'all-up' 15 times in a row on the champion and intended to do so once again.

The day after the race the *Melbourne Truth* newspaper reported:

> Taks, who took Melbourne by storm with her huge bets on Bernborough in the Melbourne Stakes and Caulfield Stakes, risked her money once too often yesterday and lost £6000. Miss Taks said last night that she would not back Bernborough again. 'I'm going straight back to Sydney and will retire as a punter,' she said. 'I backed Bernie because he looked so lovely, but he lost, and now I have the big headache.' Had Bernborough won, Miss Taks would have collected £13,250 from four bookmakers.

Romano himself was reported to have amassed about £110,000 in winning bets from Bernborough's phenomenal run, as well as the considerable stake money. On the eve of the Caulfield Cup he told the press, 'If only he can win, I shall be the happiest man in the world.'

Bernborough started 2 to 1 favourite after a wild betting spree and bookies gambled heavily against him. The race has since been repeatedly tagged 'the most controversial race ever run in this country'.

His winning streak finally came to an end when he finished fifth behind Royal Charm. Bernborough missed the start slightly and, after severe interference, flashed home from an impossible position in the straight. Carey shifted sharply from close to the rails as Bernborough came flashing down the run home, and the flying favourite cannoned into his rump.

Bernborough was stopped in his tracks, lost his momentum and staggered. Mulley balanced him quickly but the others were too far ahead and the post too close. Across the line it was Royal Charm, Columnist, Two Grand, Carey, and Bernborough fifth, still coming strong at the finish.

The race report noted that 'Bernborough was gathering the opposition in swiftly as they passed the post.'

Romano and Plant were so upset at Bernborough being such a long way back during the run that they replaced Mulley with 'Bustling' Billy Briscoe for the horse's next start in the

LKS Mackinnon Stakes. Plant and Mulley never spoke to each other again.

After the Caulfield Cup defeat Romano received 200 letters imploring him to scratch Bernborough from the Melbourne Cup. This was not only because of the champion's huge weight, but also because Romano had stated, as far back as the previous March after his sensational Newmarket victory, that Bernborough would have 'only a few more handicap races' and then be reserved for weight-for-age events.

'He belongs to the public now,' Romano had declared then. 'I've got back what I paid for him and we are not going to ruin him by racing him under fantastic weights in handicaps.'

The Mulley–Romano–Plant rift after the Caulfield Cup became one of the most notorious aftermaths to any major race in Australian turf history.

Almost 40 years later Mulley told Bert Lillye of *The Sydney Morning Herald*:

> I am the only one still alive to tell. Owner Romano, trainer Plant and stable foreman Ned Cullen have all gone . . . I will tell you something that I have not revealed before. There was always a meeting between Romano, Plant and myself to plan Bernborough's race programme. Mister Romano and I were both against starting Bernborough in the Caulfield Cup but we were overruled by Plant. I argued that no horse could win with that weight and that Bernborough should be restricted to weight-for-age races. Romano agreed with me.

But then the hint that Romano was not the sole owner of Bernborough came into play. And there the mystery remains.

Mulley married a few weeks after the Caulfield Cup. Despite the success of their association through Bernborough's magic succession of wins, Romano sent no wedding present, nor was he invited to the ceremony.

For many years Mulley had to suffer the rumours and allegations that he 'pulled up' Bernborough in the Caulfield Cup.

After examining the evidence years later, Pat Farrell wrote in the Sydney *Daily Mirror*, 'To say that Mulley pulled Bernborough up is the most profoundly ridiculous assertion ever known in a sport where ridiculous assertions abound.'

In any event Bernborough, with replacement hoop Briscoe aboard, tackled the fateful Mackinnon Stakes four days before the Melbourne Cup of 1946 and broke down with an injured sesamoid bone. Romano and Plant raced from the stands to their stricken champion, hobbling in pain at the top of the straight, and the distressed Romano could not speak for an hour after the race, which was won by the great mare Flight.

Bernborough was saved by veterinary surgeons and in December 1946, he was sold to Louis B. Mayer, head of Metro-Goldwyn-Mayer pictures, to stand at stud in the USA. The price was reported to be £93,000 at the time, but was later claimed to be less. (Mayer's annual salary of an equivalent to £312,675 was top of the published income lists in the USA at the time.)

Mayer subsequently sold Bernborough to a syndicate of Kentucky breeders.

Many Australians, who regarded Bernborough as their own, were horrified by the whole affair and an uproar followed the sale. Romano remained unpopular with the general public for a long time.

However, after one visit to the USA, Romano reported that his former champion was 'living like a prince'. He even had a thermometer in his palatial stall to ensure a comfortable temperature.

In the USA Bernborough sired the winners of more than $4 million in prizemoney. His progeny included many stakes winners, most notably Bernwood, who ran a mile in 1 minute 33.8 seconds to set a new national record.

BOBBY AND SAM

JIM HAYNES

Tommy Smith had an eye for a horse.

He came to Sydney with his first horse, Bragger, in 1941. He had bought the reject out of the paddock in Wagga Wagga in spite of the owner telling him the colt was mad and would never make a racehorse.

Tommy and Bragger lived side by side in two boxes at Kensington racetrack until Tommy and the horse had proved his previous owner wrong. It was touch and go for a while, though; Bragger bolted at his first barrier trial at the old Victoria Park track, threw the jockey, hurdled a fence and ended up on the beach at Botany Bay before Tommy managed to catch him.

Bragger went on to win thirteen races, including the Rosehill Cup, and set Tommy on the path to success as a trainer.

Tommy's eye rarely let him down. He famously bought Playboy for Sydney owner E.R. Williams, who later raced good horses such as Pride of Egypt and dual Cox Plate winner Hydrogen, and was annoyed when Williams said he didn't like the horse.

Williams later decided to take Playboy, but Tommy's nose was well out of joint and he refused to sell him, raced him in his own colours, and won the AJC Derby with him in 1949, along with the AJC St Leger, Craven Plate and C.B. Fisher Plate.

Tommy Smith was well established when Tulloch came along, but it is perhaps true to say that Tulloch stamped him as a great trainer and Kingston Town capped off his career.

The two champions had much in common, as well as some obvious differences. Tulloch and Kingston Town were both brilliant middle-distance horses that could stay, but they inherited that ability in different ways.

Tulloch was bred at the famous Trelawney Stud in New Zealand. He was from the handy staying mare Florida by King George VI's galloper Khorassan, who was bred by the Aga Khan and had bloodlines back to Nearco (and thus Carbine). Tulloch was bred to be dour, but was also born with brilliance aplenty.

Kingston Town, on the other hand, was bred to be brilliant and go over distance when required. His sire was Bletchingly, a son of Biscay and a grandson of Star Kingdom, and his dam, Ada Hunter, was a granddaughter of Italian legend Ribot, who had multiple St Simon blood and was unbeatable over a mile and a half, literally. In fact, Ribot was never beaten at any distance, winning all sixteen of his race starts, from 1000 to 3000 metres and including the Prix de l'Arc de Triomphe twice.

There was one thing Tulloch and Kingston Town had in common—they were both rejects.

Tulloch 'took Tommy's eye' at the New Zealand sales and he bought him, in spite of his 'sway-back', thinking he would easily find an owner for him. T.J. Smith was by then a top trainer and owners lined up to buy horses he chose.

However, no one wanted a sway-backed racehorse and Tommy was resigned to racing the colt himself when a chance meeting with Mr Evelyn Angus ('Lyn') Haley changed everything. It seems Tommy had completely forgotten a conversation in which Haley had asked him to look for a yearling in New Zealand. Lyn Haley bought the horse and named him Tulloch after his mother's hometown in Scotland.

Kingston Town was bred by wealthy owner David Hains at his property on the Mornington Peninsula. Like Tulloch, he was an unimpressive yearling, being spindly and awkward where Tulloch was small and sway-backed. Hains decided to sell the colt but the best offer was $5000, well below the $8000 reserve price. Hains was annoyed but unwilling to accept the paltry offer. He reluctantly decided to keep the horse and sent him up to Sydney to see if the great T.J. Smith could make anything of him.

Tulloch and Kingston Town were both bad-tempered and hard to handle.

Tulloch, whose stable name was the prosaic 'Bobby', was a biter and kicker who would lash out when annoyed and nip anyone he could. His strapper, Neville Johnson, was usually wearing a bandage somewhere when 'Bobby' was in the stable.

Kingston Town, known as 'Sam' in the stable, was also a biter and was so badly behaved as a two-year-old that he was gelded. At his first start at Canterbury he refused to race when the gates opened, then tried to throw Malcolm Johnson and finally tailed the field to the post, finishing last.

At two years of age Kingston Town won at his only two other starts after being gelded, whereas Tulloch started thirteen times aged two for six wins and seven seconds. He won the Sire's Produce Stakes in Victoria, New South Wales and Queensland, and defeated the champion two-year-old Todman easily when winning the AJC version of the race.

As three-year-olds the two horses both became true champions. Tulloch started sixteen times for fourteen wins and two placings, while Kingston Town's record was fifteen starts for twelve wins, a second, a third and a fourth.

In Tulloch's case T.J. Smith himself admitted the two placings, in the St George Stakes and Queen Elizabeth Stakes in the autumn of 1958, were a result of him not having the horse fit enough when he resumed after a three-month spell. It was a different matter with Kingston Town; his second in the VRC Derby was due to him tearing a lump off his hoof when he lost a plate. His third in the Caulfield Guineas and fourth in the Caulfield Cup were a result of the horse getting on his wrong foot around the Caulfield track.

Kingston Town always preferred to race clockwise. His record in Melbourne was four wins from fourteen starts. In Sydney he won 22 from 25 starts, and in Brisbane it was two from two.

Both horses won the AJC and QTC Derbies among their many classic wins at three. Tulloch added the VRC Derby; Kingston Town won the Sydney Cup.

Each horse had 'one that got away' in their stellar three-year-old seasons, races they never started in but would probably have won easily. For Tulloch it was the Melbourne Cup, and for Kingston Town the Cox Plate.

The fuss over Tulloch running or not running in the Cup has been well documented. It is true he was given a record weight for a three-year-old, but it is hard to see how he could have lost the Cup at the height of his powers, even with 52.5 kilograms, after his spectacular and effortless victory in the Caulfield Cup. Nevertheless, Haley decided to scratch him and 'Haley's Comet' was not given the chance to blaze a path to glory in the Cup.

In the case of Kingston Town it is a little more complex. He did not seem to handle the Melbourne way of going and T.J., on the strength of the colt's inability to handle Caulfield, decided the VRC Derby on Flemington's roomier track would suit him better than the Cox Plate on the tight Moonee Valley track.

In hindsight this seems a tragic assumption. Kingstown Town started three times at Moonee Valley for three wins, in three Cox Plates. As it was, at three he raced at Flemington instead, damaged a hoof, changed legs all down the straight and missed winning the derby by half a head. We can only imagine what would have happened had he won his first Cox Plate at three, instead of four.

Tulloch missed almost two years of racing with a life-threatening scouring illness and returned triumphantly to win five races from five starts at age five; he then took the Cox Plate, Craven Plate, Mackinnon Stakes, C.B. Fisher Plate, AJC Queen Elizabeth Stakes and Autumn Stakes at six, and just missed winning the Sydney Cup with 63 kilograms after being boxed in until the last furlong. He lumped 64 kilograms in the only unplaced run of his career in the 1960 Melbourne Cup and went out in a blaze of glory by winning the Brisbane Cup over 3200 metres, carrying 62.5 kilograms.

Kingston Town won four from six at four, including the Cox Plate; seven from nine at five, including the Cox Plate; and five from eight at six, including the Cox Plate. He was narrowly defeated in the Melbourne Cup of 1982, carrying 59 kilograms, but his effort to win his third Cox Plate, after legendary race-caller Bill Collins had famously broadcast 'Kingston Town can't win', will live forever in the memory of everyone who heard the call or saw the race.

Tulloch failed dismally at stud and Kingston Town retired to David Hains's property at Mornington, where he was bred.

Kingston Town was euthanised, aged fourteen, after a kick from another horse damaged a knee, which failed to heal. Tulloch died relatively young also, at fifteen. An autopsy revealed that Tulloch's heart weighed more than 6 kilograms, almost the equal of Phar Lap's, which weighed 6.3 kilograms. The average racehorse has a heart weighing about 3 kilograms.

'Bobby' and 'Sam' are long gone, but they are immortals in the rich history of Australian racing, as is Tommy Smith, who sure had an eye for a horse.

OH, PADDY BOY

TONY KNEEBONE

This is the story of how an Australian racing dynasty began. It is the story of the horse that brought the Payne family to Australia. Pat Payne's family of ten kids produced eight professional jockeys, including the six pioneering sisters Brigid, Therese, Maree, Bernadette, Catherine and Michelle, and jockeys now turned successful trainers Paddy and Andrew.

***

In 1978 Pat Payne struck equine gold, although he wasn't to know the precise value of the booty until two and half years later. With son Paddy, a rising three-year-old, for company, Pat made the four-hour trip to Hamilton for the Waikato weanling sales.

Any stock related to the grandsire Hermes demanded Pat's attention. He reckoned they made good jumpers. Pat had noted in the catalogue that a five-month-old son old Blarney Kiss out of a Hermes mare was to go under the hammer.

Blarney Kiss was a tough American galloper who had won two derbies in the United States before going to stud and producing several stakes-winning horses in that country. He was sent to New Zealand in 1974 and was yet to make an impression in the southern hemisphere but surely, Pat thought, he would pass on some staying power.

The weanling's mother, Grecian Jade, a daughter of Hermes, was the key attraction to Pat. He made up his mind to bid for the colt the moment he caught sight of him in his stall before the sale began. A punt would have to be taken that Blarney Kiss would complement the obvious strength on the maternal side to produce a useful jumper. He was further encouraged after a brief chat with fellow trainer Snowy Lupton during the sale. Lupton told Pat in passing that his luck had been out recently. His best young horse, by Blarney Kiss, broke his leg in a track gallop before getting the chance to show his ability.

Pat secured his young colt for just $1300. Toddler Paddy was more excited than anyone about the family's latest acquisition. Any visitor to the Payne property in the ensuing weeks was physically tackled by the young boy and ordered to 'Come and look at my new horse.'

Pat was highly amused by Paddy's fervent behaviour and when the time came for naming the colt the obvious leapt straight to mind. He was by Blarney Kiss so the Irish connotation could link perfectly with Paddy's enthusiastic involvement. Pat submitted the name Paddy Boy to the New Zealand racing conference and it was approved. He sold a half share in the horse, for $650, to a fellow Kiwi and former schoolmate Peter Moran.

It didn't take Pat long to see that his potential jumper was very special. Paddy Boy thrived in the Payne paddocks and, as he approached his two-year-old season, it was apparent this colt would be going to the races much earlier than originally intended. Pat could feel the youngster, with such a magnificent action and handling his workload with ease, was above average.

In December 1979, Paddy Boy was sufficiently educated and fit enough to have his first race. Pat decided to give him his debut run at nearby Awapuni racecourse over 1000 metres. At such a short distance Paddy Boy wasn't expected to win, as he had clearly shown in his early development that he had inherited the family's good staying genes. Pat was more than satisfied when the colt, after getting a long way back in the field early, ran home strongly to finish second.

The training program had to be halted after just one run, however, for Paddy Boy was suffering from shin-soreness, a common complaint in young racehorses. The remedy was four weeks in a paddock. He resumed with an encouraging effort at Trentham. Although unplaced he made up good ground in the home straight and the performance was duly noted by many onlookers.

They sent him out a warm favourite when he lined up for his third outing, over 1600 metres at Waverly, situated close to Taranaki in the Wanganui district. Paddy Boy didn't disappoint his army of supporters, winning by 3½ lengths.

Pat was excited, but certainly not getting carried away yet. He was aware the field at Waverly contained a moderate bunch of horses and he fully expected Paddy Boy to win as easily as he did.

Pat's plan next was to run the colt in a slightly tougher event at Tauherenikau, a place near Masterton, not far from Wellington and best known for the informality of its race meetings. It would be akin to a picnic program in Australia. The idea had to be scrubbed, though, when Mary Payne, who was in charge of all administrative duties, made a rare oversight and forgot to nominate Paddy Boy for the intended race.

However, the Auckland Racing Club was calling for entries for its Group 3 Champagne Stakes, over 1200 metres, to be run a day later at Ellerslie, a six-hour drive from Taranaki. The race distance was perfect, Pat thought, and even though he would be the subject of ridicule for nominating a maiden winner for such a feature, there was prizemoney allocated for fifth placegetter and the race looked like attracting a very small field.

Pat phoned up-and-coming rider Greg Childs, who agreed to take the mount. On race day the trainer hadn't gained much confidence. The field had held up in numbers and was very strong, with Gold Hope, a subsequent AJC Doncaster Handicap winner, claiming favouritism. He had won his only two previous starts.

Pat told Childs he thought his colt could run fourth or fifth, providing he was allowed to settle well back early and grind home late.

The young jockey followed those instructions, permitting his horse to drop out to the tail of the field. Approaching the home turn Paddy Boy was travelling far better than any other runner in the elite field. In the long run home he easily overpowered his rivals and treated them to a galloping lesson.

Childs had the cheek to ease down the colt 100 metres before the winning post in a Group 3 race. The official winning margin was identical to his maiden win—3½ lengths—and the New Zealand racing media trumpeted the arrival of a potential champion.

The authoritative manner in which Paddy Boy scored had his trainer scanning the racing calendar in search of greater targets and better prizemoney. The Auckland Racing Club's Sires' Produce Stakes, a Group 1 race over 1400 metres and the most coveted two-year-old event in the country, was ideal. A small late entry fee was required for Paddy Boy to compete because he was not among the original nominations.

Pat and his co-owner, Peter Moran, took little convincing that the horse had earned his place in the field. They despatched the necessary payment and Paddy Boy didn't let them down. He reproduced the same finishing power that was seen in the Champagne Stakes, but on this occasion the company was stronger and the brilliant galloper Yir Tiz refused to let him past.

The pair drew clear of the rest to fight out a mighty finish and on the line they couldn't be separated. A dead heat, and the result Pat declares is his greatest thrill in racing, outside of seeing his children ride winners.

It was time to look abroad. Prizemoney in Australia was most enticing and coming up in the Brisbane winter was a suitable race, the $40,000 dollar Marlboro Stakes over 1600 metres.

Paddy Boy had established himself as the smartest two-year-old in New Zealand. He had earned the right to challenge the best in Australia. Importantly, he had also earned his own $2500 airline ticket across the Tasman.

In the process of confirming arrangements for the Brisbane mission, Pat and Mary discussed the idea of leaving New Zealand and setting up a future in Australia. Both were quite keen on the possibility, but rather than rush into a decision they agreed to turn the Paddy Boy trip into their first family holiday and stay a few months to assess the viability of a permanent move. The couple had seven children at this time and the oldest, Brigid, was heavily involved in helping out with the horses. She and her dad shared the trackwork riding duties. Pat had another handy horse, Gentle Joker, to complete the team for the Aussie adventure.

Peter Moran, the co-owner of Paddy Boy, was living in Melbourne and working as an accountant. It was Moran's job to organise the purchase of a horse float and vehicle, and to tee up an overnight stop-off stable so the family could be on their way to Brisbane as soon as they landed.

To his horror on arrival in Sydney, Pat found neither a float nor a car waiting for him and, after a heated exchange with his partner, he also learned that no accommodation had been organised.

This disaster was the beginning of the end for the two mates and never again after Paddy Boy would they race a horse in partnership. Pat found himself behind schedule by the time he reached Brisbane. Because of the change in itinerary, the horse missed a vital track gallop.

In the week leading up to the big event, the visiting party was subjected to intense media coverage and Pat warned the public that, although certain Paddy Boy would put up a mighty fight, he was worried that the colt was a little behind in his preparation. Pat knew his horse, as usual, would give all he had.

And so he did, but it was not quite enough to snare the major purse in the Marlboro Stakes. Unfortunately for the visiting Kiwi clan, Paddy Boy, now renamed Our Paddy Boy for Australian racing, had to settle for a close second behind Royal Paree. Still the family was ecstatic that its champion had proved he could mix it with the finest in Australia and, after a short break, he could be prepared for the big spring races in Melbourne.

The Payne holiday plan, after a brief spell in the Queensland sun, involved a journey to Victoria where they hoped to establish a base. After the spring the family was to return to New Zealand.

Pat warmed to the idea of setting up camp in Ballarat, 100 kilometres from Melbourne. During his time in Brisbane he struck up a friendship with Robert Smerdon, who convinced the visiting Kiwis that Ballarat was the ideal location for them. It was similar in size to Taranaki with a population of 73,000 and the reports of its training facilities were glowing.

Smerdon may have been a little biased. He was from a racing family famous in the area. The stables he managed were passed on to him from his father, Bob, and before that his uncle, Arthur, ran the show. He convinced Pat and Mary Payne that the country town was the spot for them and even threw in a generous offer to accommodate the entire visiting contingent, horses included. They accepted gratefully.

The trip from Queensland was an uncomfortable one and not without its problems. The car Pat and Mary had hastily purchased in Sydney could only accommodate its nine occupants with a tight squeeze and after a few hundred kilometres of travel it began to protest about having to haul the two equine passengers at the back. With tyres almost flattened under the weight and the engine crying out for respite, it was a crawl to Victoria. At one point, on a fairly steep hill near Melbourne, the task was too great for the vehicle and the children were forced to jump out and help push it to the top.

Our Paddy Boy must have felt he was entitled to more luxurious travel! In fact, there was an occasion on the three-day trip when he did indicate he'd like to go his own way.

During a roadside stop at Berrigan, the colt was allowed a pick of grass and he managed to break free from Brigid, who was leading him. Panic followed as the family watched helplessly while their priceless steed disappeared into unfamiliar bushland.

A search party was quickly assembled but after two hours no one could report a positive sighting. As the concerned bunch met up at the car to consider their next move, Our Paddy Boy casually wandered out of the scrub and back to his family. His brief show of independence was not appreciated.

The Payne horses settled well in the new environment at Robert Smerdon's complex and it didn't take long for them to find the next commission for Our Paddy Boy. It involved more travel but, by this time, the horse took this task in his stride. It was August 1980, and the $10,000 Adelaide Guineas, run under set weights over 1600 metres at Victoria Park, was beckoning. With a home straight of 637 metres, the longest in Australia, Victoria Park was a highly suitable venue for the colt's racing style.

Clearly, Our Paddy Boy was the best credentialled runner. In fact, a month earlier he was officially recognised as the number one two-year-old on the Australasian Free Handicap, racing's equivalent to tennis or golf rankings.

He looked a certainty in the Guineas, and won like one should. All was in readiness for the lucrative spring carnival, culminating, they hoped, in the $150,000 Victoria Derby at the end of October.

The next step was the Mooney Valley Stakes, a Group 3 race run over 1600 metres in September. As Pat was preparing his colt for the event he received a couple of extremely tempting offers. Epsom trainer Ian Saunders had a client who was prepared to pay $200,000 to buy the horse and Perth millionaire Robert Holmes à Court offered a similar sum.

Pat discussed at length the tantalising propositions with Peter Moran but eventually they agreed the colt was worth more than $200,000.

A week after they knocked back the substantial offer, Our Paddy Boy took his place in the Mooney Valley Stakes. Mick Mallyon, a rider for the powerful Hayes stable, took the mount but, after being stuck for room on the fence and then running into the back of other horses as he tried to force his way clear, Our Paddy Boy finished a luckless sixth.

Even though it was a case of misfortune, the result was disappointing. It blemished the horse's record, and gave Pat plenty of time to agonise over whether or not he had done the right thing in knocking back that $200,000.

Well, obviously Mick Mallyon thought he had. The horse had caught the attention of trainer Peter Hayes, who confronted the jockey after the Mooney Valley Stakes for his opinion. Mallyon's response was positive and Hayes immediately set about procuring the colt for his biggest client, Robert Sangster.

He asked long-time friend and former Wright Stevenson bloodstock manager Bill Stutt to look after negotiations. Stutt was a committeeman and later Chairman of Mooney Valley Racing Club and a man Hayes knew he could trust to handle such a task competently. Three weeks after his failure in the Mooney Valley Stakes, Pat received a remarkable offer of $300,000 for Our Paddy Boy.

There was no need for long discussion between the owners this time. Much as they were sad to lose the champ, the proposal was too good to decline. Pat and Mary were to receive $150,000 for a horse which cost $1300 ($650 for their half), and this cash windfall arrived after the colt had won nearly $50,000 in prizemoney, paid for the holiday and had given them their one and only Group 1 trophy. It was a dream finish to a tremendous success story for them.

For Our Paddy Boy, though, hard work lay ahead under the guidance of his new boss. Hayes grew extremely concerned when Our Paddy Boy immediately started becoming unruly in his new environment. For three consecutive mornings at training, his main race rider, Brent Thomson, was tossed from the colt, who wanted nothing to do with him, or his new home for that matter.

Hayes couldn't understand the newcomer's problem. He was confused about why the country's premier jockey could not control the horse when an eleven-year-old girl (Brigid) had been completing the same task with ease and enjoyment. Hayes's first decision was to replace riders, swapping Thompson for Mick Mallyon in the hope that a different rider would please Our Paddy Boy. That worked, but the colt was still acting unsociably and getting himself into such a bad state that he was not going to save his best for race days.

In desperation Hayes consulted Pat Payne for advice. He was on to the problem immediately. Our Paddy Boy was missing his mate, Gentle Joker. They had been together a long time.

Gentle Joker was a handy horse at best, and his quality didn't come up to the rigid standards maintained by the Hayes operation. But there was little choice. Obviously, a place had to be found for him or Our Paddy Boy would continue to fret.

Pat Payne informed Hayes that he could take Gentle Joker for $12,000. Hayes accepted, knowing it would be up to Our Paddy Boy to recover that cost.

To his credit, though, Gentle Joker tried hard and did manage to win one race and collect a couple of city placings. More importantly, his presence at the new stable had an immediate calming influence on the good horse and Robert Sangster didn't have to wait long to start recovering his money.

Our Paddy Boy's first major assignment was the W.S. Cox Plate, in which he would be tested over his longest journey to date, 2040 metres. Competing against the very best of all ages, he turned in a mighty performance to claim third prizemoney behind Kingston Town and Prince Ruling. The minor placing, worth $39,300 to connections, confirmed the general feeling that this three-year-old would make an even greater impression on the racing scene the following autumn, allowing for natural improvement through maturity. And that's how it unfolded.

After the Cox Plate, Our Paddy Boy backed up a week later in the 2500-metre Victoria Derby and, although giving an indication that he was due for a spell, he showed his usual determination to finish third behind Sovereign Red and Real Force. The bold performance was enough to convince his trainer that distances beyond 2000 metres would be the target through 1981. He sent the horse straight to a spelling paddock in South Australia after the derby and then prepared him for the Sydney Autumn Carnival.

It was a wise and profitable move. Our Paddy Boy stole the show in Sydney. He capped a sensational campaign with dual Group 1 victories, both coming within a week. First was the AJC Derby, in which he defeated Ring The Bell and Deck The Halls, and then, with the lightweight of just 51.5 kilograms, he took on and beat the older horses in the 3200-metre Sydney Cup. My Blue Denim, a New Zealander who had finished runner-up in the previous year's Melbourne Cup, chased him home, but was no match for the three-year-old.

Hayes's attention turned to the upcoming Melbourne Cup after a spell but Our Paddy Boy developed minor leg problems and struggled through his spring campaign, although he did manage to win the Group 3 Coongy Handicap over 2000 metres at Caulfield. He made it to the start for the Cup and, while it was obvious he was not the same gifted horse because of leg woes, Hayes remained hopeful, because the horse gave so much, he could still, perhaps, pull off a fantastic victory.

It was not to be but as usual he was brave in defeat, finishing fourth to Just A Dash.

Worsening leg problems forced Hayes to retire the grand stayer and he went to stud in Queensland with total prizemoney earnings of $396,000. He failed to reach the same great heights as a stallion, siring moderately performed animals over many years.

Incidentally, his dad, Blarney Kiss, an unknown quantity in the southern hemisphere before the arrival of Our Paddy Boy, had one more burst of fame in Australia, in 1983, when another of his sons, Kiwi, produced an astonishing last-to-first run to take the Melbourne Cup. He was trained by Snowy Lupton.

WHY WE CAME TO LOVE SCHILLACI

LES CARLYON

I am waiting for the bus after the last race at Sha Tin when the urger glides up on a rumour and a prayer. In the sultry heat of late-afternoon Hong Kong, he thinks he is Peter Lorre. Dragging on a fag, he first looks around for hidden cameras, then leans forward and intones: 'I think I've got a really good horse back home.'

Yep, it is the big one. And me thinking it would merely be some tittle-tattle about Macau acquiring a nuclear arsenal.

He looks again and takes another drag. Before I can suggest we use the shoe phone, he goes on.

'They say he could be something special.'

Why do they always say these things?

Still, rituals must be followed. As with the other thousand times I have been told this fairytale, I affect deep interest and do a little Peter Lorre stuff myself. After all, the inference is that one loose word could see me being placed in quicklime by certain parties who do not wish me well.

This, remember, is racing. Idiots will tell you it's an 'industry'. Well, it may be, but before that it's a romantic comedy with a subtext of intrigue. Damon Runyon and Lewis Carroll write the scripts.

Most of these 'really good horses' are last seen at Manangatang wearing pacifiers and toupées, and attended by chiropractors and remedial farriers.

Anyway, this beast I hear about in Hong Kong has won but two races, a Kyneton maiden, worth $2925, and a mid-week at Sandown.

All this happened in 1991. The horse was Schillaci, the big grey who ended up a folk hero and now will never race again, which means we are all losers.

They were Lee Freedman, Schillaci's trainer, and his brothers Richard, Anthony, and Michael.

The 'urger' was Schillaci's co-owner, David Christensen, a company director and accountant, a committeeman at Flemington and Caulfield, and a very upright gent. Only as an owner does he take on his Peter Lorre persona, although this has paled now that he has given up smoking.

As it turned out, he had something better than a 'really good horse', and this had nothing to do with Schillaci winning eight group ones and two million bucks. Plenty of horses have won more races and more money.

Jeune is a really good horse. So is Danewin. But these and others merely inspire admiration. Schillaci belongs to another order, the guild that takes in Vo Rogue, Kingston Town, Manikato and Old Super. No, I'm not lining these five up on ability; what links them is more mysterious than that.

All could inspire affection. They came to be loved rather than admired. Because of the way they did things, they made people feel good and the sport seem grander than it is.

Schillaci was a great sprinting three-year-old, up there close behind Ajax, Vain and Manikato. He won fancy races and rewrote time records and humped big weights. This isn't why he came to be loved.

What endeared was the way he kept walking up, so honest, season after season. And the way, like Manikato, he stared down pain. In the end, his grey coat had faded to near-white, his galloping action had lost its fluency, and his walk had become a shuffle. Yet he tried as hard, ran as fast, and won as many good races as in his carefree youth. When he was entitled to cheat, he didn't.

As a six-year-old, Schillaci had punters standing around mounting yards clapping until their hands ached. When he won his last race, the Futurity at Caulfield last Autumn, Lee Freedman briefly turned away from the media scrum and said aloud but entirely to himself: 'What a magnificent horse.'

Rebecca Newman, Schillaci's strapper, took the gelding to one corner of the yard and they clapped him there. She took him to the opposite corner and they clapped him there. This went on for ten minutes. And the glory of his win was grander than most of the crowd knew.

Some of us had seen Schillaci at trackwork the day before. Hurting everywhere, he was. As he shuffled out of the stripping shed for two easy laps on the sand, one word exploded in your mind. Lame.

Schillaci stumbled, lurched, slouched, and several times stood stock still, a ghostly statue, grand but worn. Lesser beasts, full of oats and bravado, pranced and danced; Schillaci just looked tired. When he came off the track, they lifted his forelegs into tubs of ice. As Rebecca Newman recalled: 'You could almost hear him say: Here I go again.' At the races next day, a famous trainer told Christensen: 'I saw your horse this morning and he's bloody near a cripple.'

Some cripple. Near the finishing post in the Futurity, Schillaci laid his long ears back, much like a heeler about to nip a bullock, and beat Jeune and Mahogany.

A few weeks ago, Schillaci was back at Flemington for another campaign. 'He was going really well,' Michael Freedman says. 'He looked great.'

In the dark, with Damien Oliver up and going only a little faster than even time, the grey hurdled a white bandage lying on the wood-fibre track near the 600-metre mark, landed awkwardly, and in less than a second, blew away a large part of his off tendon and all of his career.

'At first, I didn't notice much wrong with him,' says Oliver. 'But coming off the track, I knew he was lame. I felt sick.'

Rebecca Newman was waiting for them. 'Damien said, "I don't think Schillaci's very well." I looked down at his leg and thought, "Oh . . . oh, dear."'

John Van Veenendaal, the veterinarian who treated Schillaci, says the grey wrecked about 40 per cent of the tendon. The irony was that Schillaci had never had tendon problems. His trouble for two years was degenerative arthritis in the coffin bones of both front hoofs. Spurs had formed on the bones near the top of the hoof line. The gelding was also plagued by corns. Schillaci had grown into a massive horse, weighing 560 kilos, maybe more, and in the end his hoofs were just too small for his body.

Early morning at Brackley Park, the Freedman property at Avenel, north of Seymour. The sky is a cloudless blue dome and the new grass sags under the dew. You feel cold and old Schillaci is warm to touch. He crunches on lucerne hay and flicks his ears to the slightest sound, be it a tractor or swallows nesting in the stables. He nuzzles you, looking for a carrot, then lays his ears back in disdain when you come up empty handed.

Schillaci will live the rest of his life here because the Freedmans asked to keep him. Christensen was touched. 'I'm delighted that Lee and his family think so much of the horse they want to give him a happy home. Knowing that makes me even more proud of him.'

Dave Hitchin, the farm manager, leaves a filly to remove Schillaci's rug. The grey nuzzles Hitchin's pullover, smells the filly on it, and squeals like the stallion he isn't. Kylie Baines takes him out to have his photo taken. At first, he is tender on his bad leg. Then he sees the colts in the day yards and starts to swagger. He wants to plunge and rear and let them know he's better than they'll ever be. As on race days, all pain is forgotten. Schillaci is some character.

And, even, with that leg swaddled in bandages, some sight: tall, better than 16.2 hands, and long, incredibly long. He is power without coarseness, refinement without prettiness. A big eye: kind, intelligent and dark. A great sweep of shoulder and a length of rein to match. Bulging forearms and, behind, swelling bunches of muscles from hip to hock, the rear end of a quarter horse on the legs of a thoroughbred.

That powerful body is half the reason Alan Bell, a Rosehill veterinarian and trainer, bought him for $70,000 as a yearling; the other half is Schillaci's blood. He descends from mares bred by the legendary Stanley Wootton, who imported Star Kingdom and, with that one stallion, changed the pattern of Australian breeding. Bell figured he was buying generations of Wootton's genius. He offered Christensen a piece of the horse a few months later.

Christensen recalls Bell said something like: 'I think this horse could be exceptional.'

Schillaci didn't race at two. He was gelded and given time to grow up. Early on, he was with Richard Freedman at Epsom. Richard, as is his way, tended to undersell the horse. But brother Anthony says, 'He'd declared him a champion before he'd even raced.' Schillaci had been sitting eight-wide in trials—and winning. Which may explain why he was odds-on for that first start at Kyneton.

At his fourth start, he won the Lightning Stakes. At his next two, he won the other legs of sprinting's triple crown: the Oakleigh Plate at Caulfield, in track record time, and the Newmarket at Flemington. Then, in perhaps the best win of his career, he took the Galaxy at Randwick, his fourth group one for the season. He was young; he could fly, and he didn't hurt anywhere.

After the grey's first win in the Lightning, Lee Freedman told the mounting-yard throng: 'This horse is another Manikato.' At trackwork last week, Freedman recalled the reaction. 'They all said to me, "Well, you've just gone straight off your head. You've gone stone mad."'

Some madness. After his three-year-old season, and despite aching hoofs, Schillaci won another four group ones, including two Futuritys. When he won a sprint on Caulfield Cup Day last year, he received a longer and rowdier ovation than Paris Lane, the Cup winner.

Lee Freedman isn't given to mushy sentimentality. Asked how he saw Schillaci, he thought long before replying.

'You get lovely racehorses,' he said softly. 'You know, they win good races for you, but this one . . .?' He sighs and his voice rises. 'Ah, he was something more: he was a lovely animal. There was no enigma with him: what you saw was what you got.'

After the accident, Freedman was drinking with friends at a Toorak hotel. The friends began toasting Schillaci and Freedman began to feel teary. He left and went shopping.

Rebecca Newman, tiny and vivacious, is sipping iced coffee and walking back to the Freedman stables at Flemington after trackwork. It doesn't seem right: Schillaci, the carrot addict, doesn't live there anymore.

'I've lost my best friend,' she says. 'There'll never be another like him. Such a character: you'd just stand there feeding him carrots and he'd do anything.

'He was so kind. On the track, you'd have to hunt him up all through his work. But when you turned him to come home, he'd turn on like an electric light and want to canter all the way home.

'Oh, he'd do things wrong. Going out sometimes, he'd stand as still as a statue, refusing to move. Occasionally, he'd whip around and dump you. Then he'd stop and stare down, as if to say: What are you doing down there?

'To strap him at the races . . . well, that was just indescribable. The crowd would follow you everywhere. People would ask me for one of his shoes. When he was retired we got fan mail. A father wrote on behalf of his son. He wanted to thank us for the pleasure the horse gave his boy.'

Long before the grey ruined his tendon, Rebecca had become proprietorial. Schillaci would annoy her when he did his 'statue act'. What she resented much more, however, were well-meaning people getting behind the grey to hunt him forward. She could scold him, but not outsiders.

'I'm going to miss him terribly,' she says.

Aren't we all.

6 October 1995

O FOR OCTAGONAL

JIM HAYNES

You hear blokes talk of champions, you see 'em come and go,
A real champ maybe comes along each twenty years or so.
I've read of Phar Lap and Carbine, those legends of the past,
And I saw Tulloch and Gunsynd and they were tough and fast,
Kingston Town was brilliant, so strong the mare Sunline,
But for true fighting spirit there was just one champ for mine!
No champion that ever strode the turf could make me feel
The way I felt about that gallant brown son of Zabeel.
O for Octagonal to be racing once again,
O for Octagonal, on him you could depend,
He never gave up trying, he'd stick right to the end,
O for Octagonal, he was the punter's friend.
Derby Day in '96 you should have heard the cheers,
From the biggest crowd the Randwick track had seen for
thirty years.
With Saintly, Nothing Leica Dane, Filante down the straight,
I won't see another race like that, however long I wait.
It was true grit and courage that wore the others down,
His will to win that drove him on to take the Triple Crown.
His stamina unparalleled, his action was sublime,
Oh what I'd give to see old 'Ocky' race just one more time!
O for Octagonal to be racing once again,
O for Octagonal, on him you could depend,
He never gave up trying, he'd stick right to the end,
O for Octagonal, he was the punter's friend.

THEY ALL LOVE SUNLINE

JIM HAYNES

'They all love Sunline.'

It was the bloke standing beside me in the TAB. The place was abuzz with comments, the usual ill-informed, well-informed and half-informed opinions that you get in any TAB when it is more than likely that a protest will be lodged. Blokes talking to anyone who will listen, or to no one in particular, or to no one at all.

But this was different.

It was not only the Cox Plate; the horses involved were the best three horses racing at the time!

It was 27 October 2001.

I'd backed Viscount, the Inghams' immaculately bred and trained three-year-old. I thought he was a classy conveyance and well suited at weight-for-age against the two champs, Sunline and Northerly. I still think the same. He should have won.

Sunline had led into the straight with Viscount behind her, waiting to start his winning run, and Northerly had been working home down the outside.

In his efforts to lift Northerly and reach the mighty mare, Damien Oliver had ridden the Western Australian champion out vigorously. Northerly had strained every sinew to the limit until the effort was too much. Then he ducked in under pressure, just as Sunline rolled out slightly for the same reason.

Viscount was the meat in the sandwich; he was crunched in between the two older horses, lost all momentum and was lucky to stay on his feet. Sunline's head went way up in the air as she, too, lost momentum, and Northerly, the main offender and the only horse of the trio to keep his momentum, pulled ahead to win by half a length.

The booing started as the horses returned to the birdcage.

That's when I commented through my pocket to the bloke beside me, 'No wonder they're booing,' I said, 'Viscount was robbed!'

He looked at me in that sad way older racing addicts have when confronted by ignorance. Then he said, 'They're not worried about the Inghams' horse, mate, they're booing 'cos Sunline didn't win—they all love Sunline.'

Maybe he was a Kiwi, but he was right anyway. They all *did* love Sunline.

Certainly all New Zealand loved her; when she died there was a news special on national television.

And why wouldn't they love her? Not only was she undefeated in her home country, she travelled to Australia and beat our best, and then went to Hong Kong and beat the mighty Fairy King Prawn over a mile in a world-class international event. She was the best middle-distance horse of her era and certainly the best mare to ever race over middle distances in Australasian turf history. Her record proves it.

When the protests came that day there were three of them: Sunline against Northerly, and Viscount against the other two, so second against first, and third against first and second.

In a travesty of justice, all were dismissed.

I still maintain that Viscount should have won. And all fair-minded racing fans consider that Sunline's record against Northerly should show one victory and two losses, instead of three losses.

I still maintain it should have been Viscount first, Sunline second and Northerly third.

In any case, we all agree the mighty mare should have been put ahead of Northerly—a champion in his own right—just once in her career!

'But Northerly won by half a length,' I hear the voice of reason saying, 'and that was why the stewards gave him the race.'

'Yes,' I answer in my imagination, with more than a hint of frustration, 'and he won by that far because the interference was *so bad*!'

Punters have long and bitter memories of racing injustices.

While I was writing this story, it was announced that Sunline had lost her long battle with laminitis and had been put down. That sad news made me think back to how I'd seen her in victory and defeat, in the flesh, not on the TAB television screens.

I have two vivid memories of Sunline. I saw her race maybe half a dozen times, but two memories are unforgettably clear. Because they were the most memorable two-horse-wars I ever saw.

Randwick is a track that really sorts out the champs from the pretenders down the straight. Sunline started there twelve times, usually carrying big weights, for six wins and four placings.

I saw her win her second Doncaster in 2002, defeating Shogun Lodge after they raced side by side for two entire furlongs. That was the best nose-to-nose tussle I ever saw at Randwick.

The crowd was in a frenzy; it was too close to call at the end. I thought she'd been beaten, but the photo showed her courage had paid off by a nose. The pundits thought she had too much weight that day to possibly win over the toughest mile course in the world.

I still can't believe you could get odds of 5 to 1 about Sunline in the ring when they jumped. And I still can't believe I didn't take it!

Strangely enough, the mighty mare also featured in the best battle down the straight I ever saw in Melbourne, at Caulfield, in the Caulfield Stakes in 2002.

It was a match race between Sunline, when she was approaching the end of her career, and Lonhro, who was nearing the peak of his career. There were some pretty handy horses in the supporting cast of the drama that day, but they were really only there for the crowd scenes, just making up the numbers.

Trevor McKee and his son, Stephen, owners of Sunline, and the Ingham brothers, who owned Lonhro, rate as true enthusiasts and lovers of racing. It is credit to the McKees that Sunline, who could have been quickly retired to stud, raced on as a mare to give us all so many wonderful memories. The McKee motto was always, 'We're here to race.'

Mind you, Sunline was an awesome force on any racetrack at any age, even at seven. She was strong and robust and towered over most of her male counterparts. She never looked frail, weak or delicate of disposition, attributes which many consider to be feminine. In fact, Greg Childs, who rode her for 32 of her 48 starts, described her as 'a freak of nature' and attributed her amazing ability to what he called her 'masculine qualities'.

She was feminine enough, however, to leave behind two sons and two daughters when she passed away prematurely at the age of just thirteen.

As usual the crowd at Caulfield that day mostly supported Sunline. Not many Victorian racegoers were fans of the New South Wales horse in the cerise colours, although they would come to admire him—and his progeny—in seasons to follow.

It was a mighty struggle between the young stallion and the seven-year-old mare, all the way down the straight, but neither horse shirked the task. Lonhro won by a head, with the rest of the field fighting out third place 6 lengths behind.

But Sunline will be remembered for the races she won, not those she barely lost.

Her two Cox Plate wins are enough to place her among the immortals. In the first she defeated Redoute's Choice, Commands, Testa Rossa, Tie The Knot and Sky Heights—an impressive line-up of legendary horses! And she won the second by a record 7 lengths, defeating Caulfield Cup winner Diatribe along with Referral, Show A Heart and Shogun Lodge, as well as Testa Rossa, Tie The Knot and Sky Heights yet again.

Add to those two Cox Plate wins her other Group 1 victories, two Doncaster Handicaps, two All-Aged Stakes, two Waikato Sprints, two Coolmore Classics (carrying 60 kg each time), a Flight Stakes, a Manikato Stakes, her controversial second to Northerly in a third Cox Plate, and her international victory in Hong Kong, and you have a record unbeaten in Australasian racing history.

From her Group 3 victory in the Moonee Valley Oaks as a three-year-old filly, until the end of her career at age seven, Sunline only ever competed in races at Group 1 or Group 2 level.

Her win rate was 68 per cent and her place rate 94 per cent, and she raced at least two seasons beyond what most consider to be the correct age for racing mares to retire. She was the top stakes-winning horse in Australasian history in her day, and the top stakes-winning mare in the world. She is the only horse ever voted Australian Horse of the Year three times.

How does her record compare to other great mares?

Well, given that comparisons from different eras are rather silly to begin with, the only racing mares who even come close to Sunline are Wakeful, Desert Gold, Tranquil Star, Flight, Emancipation and Makybe Diva.

Wakeful had a win rate of 58 per cent, well below Sunline's a century later. Her place rate, at 41 from 44 starts, is amazingly close (at 93.3 per cent) to Sunline's 45 from 48 (94 per cent). Each mare was unplaced only three times.

Wakeful was more versatile than Sunline, winning from 5 furlongs to 3 miles and carrying 10 st (63.5 kg) to run second in the Melbourne Cup, less than a length behind Lord Cardigan, carrying more than 3 stone less at 6 st 8 lb (42 kg). Wakeful comes very close to giving Sunline a run for her money, but where she won ten races that would now be considered Group 1 level, Sunline won thirteen.

Desert Gold was a New Zealander like Sunline. Her amazing run of nineteen wins in a row easily eclipses Sunline's best run of eight consecutive wins. Desert Gold, however, did most of her racing in New Zealand at a very different level to Sunline and, although she won a number of classic New Zealand races and had a great five-year-old season in Australia, winning quite a few weight-for-age events, her record at the very top level does not match Sunline's.

Desert Gold raced through the dark days of World War I for an overall record of 36 wins, thirteen seconds and four thirds from 59 starts, very close to Sunline's record. Her place rate is a very respectable 90 per cent, 4 per cent less than Sunline's. Her win rate, at 61 per cent, again comes close to Sunline's 69 per cent, but not close enough.

Tranquil Star had an iron constitution. She started 111 times for 23 wins. That was her main claim to fame, her amazing stamina.

She would have been a match for the great masculine mare, Sunline, as far as stamina went, and, like our heroine, she raced until she was past the age when most mares retired; in fact, Tranquil Star raced a season more than Sunline, well into her eighth year. Unfortunately, she doesn't really measure up in other ways.

In her three-year-old season Tranquil Star became only the second female to win the St Leger. In her fourth year, however, Tranquil Star raced 21 times for only two wins and eight placings. Her Caulfield Cup win was commendable and, like Sunline, she won the Cox Plate twice in a row.

Also, despite breaking her jaw in a bad fall at Moonee Valley, Tranquil Star went on, with a wired jaw, to win the Memsie Stakes, William Reid Stakes and the Mackinnon Stakes for the third time!

Tranquil Star was, however, a beaten favourite on a record eighteen occasions! The racegoers who had time to go on the punt during World War II must have been far more tolerant than they were in Sunline's day!

Within months of Tranquil Star's retirement, a new heroine emerged to excite the wartime and post-war crowds. Flight, famously bought for 60 guineas by Brian Crowley, would go on to race 65 times for 24 wins, nineteen seconds and nine thirds.

While her statistics don't measure up to Sunline's, we are often told that Flight had to race against one of the greatest horses of all time in Bernborough, who she only managed to beat the day he broke down in the Mackinnon Stakes in 1946. She did, however, race into her sixth year and managed to emulate Sunline with two wins in the Cox Plate, in 1945 and 1946. She also won two Craven Plates, and the Mackinnon, C.F. Orr, Adrian Knox and Colin Stephen Stakes.

Like Sunline, Flight produced only four foals before passing away. The only filly foal was Flight's Daughter, who became the mother of champion Golden Slipper winners, Skyline and Sky High. Sky High stood at stud in the USA and sired Autobiography, the best handicapper in the USA in 1972.

Flight won only six Group 1 races, less than half of Sunline's total. Her claim to fame is based as much on her impact as a broodmare as it is on her two Cox Plate wins. So any real comparison to Sunline may take years to assess.

Emancipation had many characteristics in common with Sunline. She was a great middle-distance mare and won many of the same races Sunline won: the Doncaster, All-Aged Stakes and George Main Stakes among them. In her three-year-old season she won ten from thirteen starts and her record overall was nine from fifteen; and as a four-year-old, her Group 1 tally was seven.

Emancipation failed when she travelled away from Sydney and she also failed to run out 2000 metres. She was unplaced behind Strawberry Road in the Cox Plate.

As a broodmare Emancipation, like Flight and Wakeful, made her mark. Her son Royal Pardon was placed in the AJC Derby and won good races; her daughters, Suffragette and Virage, produced champions in Railings and Virage De Fortune.

We may have to wait a generation or two before we see if Sunline's blood will resurface into champions, as did the blood of Flight, Wakeful and Emancipation. With only four living foals before her untimely death, it may be hard for Sunline to match the broodmare record of her predecessors. However, with the miraculous Sunline, who knows?

It is a strange fact that the brilliance of great race mares appears to skip a generation and reappear in the foals of their daughters, and sons to a lesser extent.

There is ample proof, as we have seen, of the daughters of great race mares being poor performers but great producers. There are also examples of sons and grandsons being great sires. Wakeful's son Baverstock only managed to win one race, but became a hugely successful sire, as did Flight's grandson Sky High.

We will have to wait to see what influence Sunline has on future generations. And that is also true of one other great mare to whom she is often compared.

Nine days before Sunline scored her last race win in the Group 2 Mudgeway Stakes at Hasting in New Zealand, a mare having her second race start and bred to northern hemisphere seasons won her maiden at Wangaratta. The mighty staying mare Makybe Diva had arrived.

There is an account of her career and place in racing history later in this collection, 'Queens of the Cup', so I will make her comparison to Sunline quite brief.

We are possibly comparing the greatest middle-distance mare that ever lived to the greatest staying mare Australia has ever seen. However, we can go through the process of comparing records, just for the sake of it.

As a stayer, Makybe Diva obviously ran in more 'lead-up' races towards her major goals, so her record of fifteen wins, four seconds and three thirds from 36 starts looks quite poor against Sunline's 33 wins, nine seconds and three thirds from 48.

The figures give Makybe Diva a win rate of 42 per cent and a place rate of 61 per cent, well below Sunline's remarkable 69 per cent and 94 per cent. But we are doing no more with such statistics than comparing oranges to apples.

Group 1 wins? Well, it's no contest. Sunline won almost twice as many times at the elite Group 1 level, with thirteen victories to Makybe Diva's seven. And when we look at overall wins at group level, it's ten to Makybe Diva and 27 to Sunline.

It's tempting to do what many have done, including the Melbourne *Herald Sun* in an article comparing contemporary champions in December 2009, and say 'Sunline was simply a one-off freak'.

That's hardly good enough, though—you can't dismiss a champion because he or she was 'freakishly talented'. After all, that's what being a champion often amounts to!

When Sunline died, her regular jockey Greg Childs, who had taken his family to visit her after her retirement, described her as 'a freak of nature' who took all New Zealand on a great journey.

'She was a big influence on my life,' Childs said. 'She lifted my profile and my bank balance. . . she helped pay for the house we are living in.

'It's not only the jockey, it is the family as well, my wife and my kids,' said Childs, 'they all love Sunline.'

DO THEY KNOW?

A.B. 'BANJO' PATERSON

Do they know? At the turn to the straight
Where the favourites fail,
And every last atom of weight
Is telling its tale;
As some grim old stayer hard-pressed
Runs true to his breed,
And with head just in front of the rest
Fights on in the lead;
When the jockeys are out with the whips,
With a furlong to go,
And the backers grow white to the lips—
Do you think *they* don't know?

Do they know? As they come back to weigh
In a whirlwind of cheers,
Though the spurs have left marks of the fray,
Though the sweat on the ears
Gathers cold, and they sob with distress
As they roll up the track,
They know just as well their success
As the man on their back.
As they walk through a dense human lane
That sways to and fro,
And cheers them again and again,
Do you think *they* don't know?

LONHRO NEVER LIKED MOONEE VALLEY

JIM HAYNES

'And Lonhro stands motionless, gazing off into the distance as he so often does before a race . . . he'll be the last to be loaded.'

It was April 19, 2004.

As the course commentator's voice echoed across from the stands, Lonhro gazed towards the traffic moving endlessly along Alison Road, then turned his head for a last long look across the wide expanses of Royal Randwick towards the University of New South Wales buildings to the south.

On nine of the eleven occasions Lonhro had raced here at Randwick he'd been victorious. Today was to be different, but somehow it hardly mattered.

It was Queen Elizabeth Stakes Day, last day of the Autumn Carnival, and the feature race was to be Lonhro's swan song, the final curtain call in a magnificent and well-orchestrated racing career. It was a race in which he had nothing left to prove, but it was an opportunity for the AJC to bring much-needed media attention to racing. It was also a chance for those who had watched and loved the horse for four glorious racing seasons to say farewell.

It was, in fact, uncannily similar to his father's farewell day at Randwick seven years earlier. There was to be a real sense of déjà vu.

Both he and his famous sire, Octagonal, finished their racing careers in the Queen Elizabeth Stakes. On both occasions the AJC made the day into a carnival and promoted it as a chance to farewell a champion. On both occasions the party was spoiled and the fairytale ending denied when the retiring champion was defeated, finishing second in the feature event.

Yet, in both cases, it hardly mattered—the race itself was simply a coda to a great career.

Octagonal had nothing left to prove when the AJC put on a party for his farewell in 1997. Having passed his target of winning an Australasian record of more than $6 million in prizemoney several weeks before, the 'Big O' could have simply headed off to stud. There was really no reason to risk running the champion again in the Queen Elizabeth Stakes when he had nothing left to prove and was worth many, many millions as a stallion.

Indeed, a reporter asked Jack Ingham that very question after Octagonal won the Tancred Cup at Rosehill: 'Why risk the horse now, when he has achieved his goal and everything you ever expected of him?'

With typical Inghamesque logic, Jack simply looked the reporter in the eye and asked, 'Don't *you* want to see him race again?'

As an AJC committee member Jack was also no doubt aware that he was giving the club a chance to attract much-needed support and media attention—he was a gracious man, Jack Ingham.

Octagonal was defeated in his farewell race by a useful stayer called Intergaze, who would go on to win an Australian Cup.

And then here we were, seven years later, watching his illustrious son stand at the 2000-metre start, gazing off into the distance before taking his position in the barrier, only to be defeated by Gai Waterhouse's good horse Grand Armee, who had also defeated Lonhro in a Doncaster Handicap.

Grand Armee's cause was helped to an extent by an atypical poorly judged ride by Darren Beadman, who allowed the winner to get away with a slow pace and an easy lead, giving Lonhro no real chance of running him down in the straight.

Unlike his father Octagonal, who crept up on the racing world through his two-year-old season, Lonhro had lived his entire life in the spotlight. Being the first foal of Octagonal's first crop, he entered the world in a blaze of publicity. His mother, Shadea, had won the Group 3 Sweet Embrace Stakes and had been placed in both the AJC Sires Produce and Champagne Stakes.

As soon as he was born at the Inghams' Woodlands Stud, his anxious owners asked for a first-hand report and were told that the foal was 'small but perfectly formed'.

This report gave Suzanne Philcox, who had the task of naming all the Woodlands foals, a good pointer towards an appropriate cryptic name for the foal. His name is a deliberate misspelling of the stock exchange code for the London Rhodesian Mining and Land Company, LONRHO. The CEO of this company was the controversial Roland 'Tiny' Rowlands, who was always sarcastically referred to as 'small but perfectly formed' by the satirical magazine *Private Eye*, which exposed some of his perfidious activities in the 1980s and 1990s. The misspelling was to avoid possible legal difficulties and enable the thoroughbred registrar to accept the name.

Lonhro finished second at his first start in November 2000 and was then spelled before winning easily over 1100 metres at Rosehill. A trip to Melbourne followed, resulting in an impressive win in the Blue Diamond Prelude and a close fourth, behind True Jewels, in the Blue Diamond itself.

The Inghams and trainer John Hawkes saw Lonhro as a potential weight-for-age horse and took their time with him. He was spelled until July and then contested the Missile Stakes as a two-year-old, finishing third. This was the last time in his entire racing career that Lonhro would lose two consecutive races.

Woodlands' other champion two-year-old of that year, Viscount, won the AJC Sires Produce and Champagne Stakes while Lonhro was in the spelling paddock.

When he returned to racing, the first son of Octagonal had developed into an impressive big, almost black horse who was to be unbeaten at three. He took out the weight-for-age Warwick Stakes, the Ming Dynasty Quality, the Heritage Stakes and the Stan Fox Stakes, one after the other, all at Group or Listed Race level. He was then sent to Melbourne to race against a class field, including stablemate Viscount, in the Caulfield Guineas. He won running away by 1½ lengths.

A minor injury saw Lonhro spelled again, leaving stablemate Viscount to wear the famous all-cerise colours in the 2001 Cox Plate.

Sandwiched between Northerly laying in and Sunline shifting out, Viscount was robbed of a Cox Plate victory in a controversial decision that saw the 'past the post' placings upheld after multiple protests.

Lonhro and another Woodlands horse, Freemason, would later avenge to a degree the 'unfair' defeat of their courageous stablemate at weight-for-age. Lonhro famously defeated Sunline in the Caulfield Stakes of 2002, and the dour old stayer Freemason handed Northerly an unexpected defeat at weight-for-age in the Tancred Cup at Rosehill on Golden Slipper Day in 2003.

Lonhro returned to racing in February 2002 to win the Royal Sovereign Stakes and the Hobartville Stakes, both at Group 2, before a virus saw him put away again until the spring. Amazingly, the Royal Sovereign Stakes was the first of 25 consecutive races in his career that saw him start favourite.

Lonhro came back in the spring, once again in the Missile Stakes over 1100 metres. Ridden for the first time by Darren Beadman, he won effortlessly by 4 lengths. Previously he had mostly been ridden in Sydney by Rod Quinn, though Digger McLellan and Jim Cassidy had also won on him. In Melbourne it had been Darren Gauci and Brett Prebble. But from the start of his four-year-old season until he retired, Lonhro was ridden by Darren Beadman and no one else.

The imposing sleek dark horse they were now starting to call 'the Black Flash', although he was never 'officially' black, was sent out red-hot favourite at his next start in the Warwick Stakes, over 1400 metres.

Perhaps he was a little flat second-up after a long spell, or perhaps the step up from 1100 to 1400 was too much, for he failed by half a head to run down Guy Walter's good horse Defier.

Lonhro was to finish behind Defier four times in his career, twice in the Cox Plate, although the gelding was easily defeated three times by Lonhro at Group 1 level in Lonhro's five-year-old season.

Defier was a gallant and unlucky horse who finished second in the Cox Plate twice, in 2002 and 2003. Lonhro finished sixth in 2002, his worst-ever result in a race, and third in 2003.

After the 2003 race Defier's trainer Guy Walter cheekily quipped, 'Finished behind us again,' to John Hawkes in the birdcage at Moonee Valley.

Hawkes famously replied, 'Yes, but ours still has his undercarriage.'

Lonhro was never at home at Moonee Valley and his two Cox Plate runs were probably the most disappointing in his stellar career. The man who knew the horse best, trainer John Hawkes, thought Lonhro never liked Moonee Valley for some reason—perhaps the StrathAyr surface didn't feel right to the big stallion. Perhaps he disliked the closed-in cauldron-like atmosphere. He didn't stand and stare for long before entering the barriers in his two runs at Moonee Valley.

Although he was never to run to his best in the Cox Plate, he went on as a four- and five-year-old to win seventeen of his 23 starts, all at Group level, at distances ranging from 1100 to 2000 metres.

There are those who claim Lonhro was a false champion who had many 'easy kills' in Group races, never won a derby or a Cox Plate, and failed to prove himself as a handicapper in the Doncaster of 2003.

There is no doubt that John Hawkes had the luxury of being able to pick the champion's races. Woodlands had other great horses, notably Viscount, racing at the time and could plan complementary campaigns for their horses.

It is also true that Lonhro was never at home at Moonee Valley. It was the only track on which he started and never won a race. His two efforts there were arguably among the four worst performances of his career—although a sixth and third in the Cox Plate are not bad for 'worst' performances.

He carried the top-weight of 57.5 kilograms to finish fourth in the Doncaster behind Grand Armee, carrying 6 kilos less, on a wet track and, as a sprinter/middle-distance horse, he was never going to run in derbies or the Melbourne Cup.

Those who question the horse's bravery and stamina, who doubt that he inherited his father's bulldog determination, should have been at Caulfield on Yalumba Caulfield Stakes Day 2002.

I travelled out to Caulfield that day to see Lonhro run against Sunline. The Caulfield Stakes that day was basically a match race between Sunline and Lonhro, with a few other pretty good horses like Republic Lass, Prized Gem, Distinctly Secret and Tully Thunder making up the numbers.

It was a rematch in a sense. Two weeks earlier in Sydney, Lonhro had finished fourth, one place behind the mighty mare, in the George Main Stakes won by Defier. It was one of those races in which a small field produces an odd tempo and tactics. Defier, Excellerator and Shogun Lodge managed to keep Lonhro pocketed until it was too late to get out and chase effectively.

Sunline was a freak; at seven she was as strong and robust a horse as I ever saw. She towered over most of her male counterparts and was fit and at her peak for the spring carnivals.

Not many of the crowd seemed to be supporting Lonhro, just the Ingham family and a few others who had strayed south of the border for the spring racing.

Lonhro proved that day that he had inherited his sire's incredible will to win.

Beadman moved Lonhro up onto the outside of Sunline as they rounded the big home bend at Caulfield and he was a half-length behind her when they straightened.

The famously religious jockey appeared to have faith in his colt's ability to run a metre faster per furlong than the mare at weight-for-age. He rode Lonhro out steadily and made ground on Sunline centimetre by centimetre. It was a two-horse war with the rest of the field forgotten, a true test of stamina, strength and courage between two champions, with neither horse giving in at any point and each stretched to the extreme. At the post it was a clear victory to the big black horse carrying the famous cerise colours.

Perhaps Lonhro's greatest victory was to come eighteen months later at what was his Melbourne farewell, the Australian Cup at Flemington.

The sporting Melbourne crowd cheered him again and again that day as he came back to the winner's stall having won a miraculous and memorable victory over the three horses Melbourne racegoers loved best at that time—Mummify, Elvstroem and Makybe Diva.

After having his momentum stopped dead twice in the straight and being turned almost completely sideways, the 'Black Flash' pushed out, started up his big engine again, and made up impossible lengths in a hundred metres to run down a good three-year-old in Delzao at weight-for-age. In doing so, he also defeated that season's VRC Derby winner, Elvstroem, the Caulfield Cup winner Mummify, and the Melbourne Cup winner Makybe Diva.

Those who wish to find fault with his record of 26 wins from 35 starts might like to consider that his Group 1 winning strike rate of 64 per cent is the best ever recorded since the system began. His overall winning strike rate of 74 per cent is far better than that of Tulloch, Kingston Town and Phar Lap. Indeed it is second only to Carbine, arguably the greatest racehorse that ever breathed, and a horse who raced a century before Lonhro was born.

It is true that Lonhro's campaigns were well planned and orchestrated to get the best results. However, it is also true that he raced in an era of great racehorses, and he didn't exactly avoid them!

Lonhro raced against and defeated Sunline, Viking Ruler, Dash For Cash, Viscount, Shogun Lodge, Tie the Knot, Universal Prince, Magic Albert, Republic Lass, Freemason, Platinum Scissors, Grand Armee, Private Steer, Clangalang, Belle Du Jour, Elvstroem, Mummify and the great Makybe Diva.

His progeny have already sold individually for more than $1 million and Denman, from his second crop, was the most exciting colt to be seen in Australia for years, before being sent to race in Dubai and Europe.

Denman is named after the town in the Hunter Valley near Woodlands Stud, where Lonhro now stands as a stallion. In between his stud duties, the beautiful near-black horse often stands motionless, gazing off into the distance.

Apparently Lonhro enjoys looking out across the upper reaches of the Hunter Valley. It's a long way from Moonee Valley. Lonhro never liked Moonee Valley.

CAVIAR TO THE GENERAL

JIM HAYNES

'She's amazing, but I'm sick of looking at her bum!'

That's what Glyn Schofield said in response to being asked his opinion of Black Caviar, just after he had ridden the great sprinter Hay List to finish second to her, for the fourth time, at Group 1 level.

It was the day the great mare equalled the record for successive race wins in Australia, in the Lightning Stakes of 2012.

Hay List was a champion, fifteen times a winner from 28 starts, as good a sprinter as you would see in a decade and the best horse Glyn Schofield ever rode according to the jockey himself. But luck and timing can be cruel things in racing and Hay List will be forever remembered as the horse who wasn't as good as Black Caviar. Still, that puts him in some pretty good company—because no horse was as good as Black Caviar. She was so good, in fact, that we didn't really understand *how* good she was.

We 'ooohed and aaahed' as she demolished fields made up of great sprinters such as Hay List, Buffering, Star Witness, Hot Danish, Crystal Lily, Karuta Queen, Epaulette and others, but few of us at the time realised what we were witnessing. There was nothing to compare her to, she was beyond the understanding of modern racegoers because she was so much better than any horse we had ever seen race.

There is a scene in Hamlet where the troubled prince talks to an actor about a play he once saw the actor's company perform. The play was wonderful, Hamlet remembers, but the general public didn't realise how good it was. Hamlet says it was, 'caviar to the general', meaning far too good for the general public to realise its worth. That was Black Caviar, she was beyond superlatives and the phrases we used to describe champion racehorses before her were simply insufficient to describe her.

She was, of course, undefeated in 25 starts, rated the world-champion sprinter four years in a row, the highest Timeform rated filly or mare in history. She broke Kingston Town's Australian record by winning fifteen races at Group 1 level and smashed the long-standing Australasian record of nineteen successive wins, held jointly by Gloaming and Desert Gold. She also won several of her races with torn muscles and she recovered from a torn suspensory ligament injury sustained in her three-year-old season to win twenty more races at the ages of four, five and six.

She also won most of her races being eased down and she won her 25 races by an average distance of 3 lengths.

A cursory glance at the great mare's pedigree reveals the mighty sprinter Vain on both sides, and no less than four generations back, along with the great Northern Dancer–Nijinski–Royal Academy male line leading to her father, the 'rather handy' sprinter Bel Esprit. Through her female side Black Caviar was a cousin to the mighty Sunline, so it's no wonder that Peter Moody happily paid a respectable $210,000 for her at the Melbourne Premier Yearling sale in 2008.

Having been syndicated to a group of eight owners, mostly comprising members of the Wilkie family, the future champ appeared on a racetrack for the first time as a two-year-old filly in the autumn of 2009 and won a restricted handicap for her age at Flemington by 5 lengths. That seemed promising, so she was entered for the much tougher Blue Sapphire Stakes—and promptly won that by 6 lengths.

After that result she was 'put away' to await the spring.

As a three-year-old in the spring of 2009, with Luke Nolan replacing Jarrad Noske as her regular rider, she won three times over 1200 metres, including the Group 2 Danehill Stakes at Flemington and the Australia Stakes at Moonee Valley.

Luke Nolan would go on to ride Black Caviar in every one of her races from that point, except the 2010 Patinack Classic when Nolan was serving a suspension and Ben Melham had the privilege of sitting on her broad back as she passed the winning post.

Her three-year-old season was terminated early by a serious suspensory ligament injury, enough to send many a good filly with her breeding and record straight to the breeding barn. The Black Caviar syndicate were there to race, however; they had not designed their new salmon and black racing colours to hang in some display case with a photograph of a handy unbeaten filly.

Produced as a four-year-old in the spring of 2010, she was no longer a 'promising filly' but a well-muscled mature mare standing 16.2 hands and ready to sprint against all-comers. After two warm-up wins at Group 2 level in the Schillaci Stakes at Caulfield and Schweppes Stakes at Moonee Valley, Black Caviar took out six Group 1 races in succession at racetracks from Flemington and Moonee Valley in the south to Randwick and Doomben further north. By the end of her four-year-old season the legend had been born, thirteen wins in succession and undefeated. We were all starting to count now.

Having won in all eastern mainland states at four, she was kept in Melbourne as a five-year-old until April 2012 and won six times, three at Group 1 level and three at Group 2. Peter Moody kept her schedule pretty much the same as the previous year with the Schillaci, Schweppes and Patinack Classic but, in January 2012, she also took out her second Australia Stakes at Moonee Valley, a race she had previously won at three. From that point on she would never again race below Group 1 level.

Black Caviar was extended beyond 1200 metres for the only time in her life to win the C.F. Orr Stakes over 1400 metres at Caulfield in February 2012.

In April 2012, she made the long journey to South Australia to win the Robert Sangster Stakes and the Goodwood Handicap. In winning the first of those races, she broke the Australasian record for the most wins in succession, which had stood since the 1920s.

But a much longer journey was just around the corner for the highest-rated sprinter in the world. Royal Ascot was calling.

The drama, hoop-la and media frenzy of that 'trip away' has been well documented and she took us all on a mighty ride of which not one moment was missed by television and newspapers in Australia. The specially designed thermal suit, the training gallops, the owners enjoying themselves in funny, old-fashioned hats, and Peter Moody's nervous cigarettes and good-natured interviews were offset by the horrible possibility that she might not win.

If the build-up to the Diamond Jubilee Stakes was agonising, the race itself was torture.

It was obvious to those of us who knew her that she wasn't at her best during the running of the race. Luke Nolan certainly knew it and felt there was 'something wrong'.

There *was* something wrong, she had torn two muscles during the race but won anyway. X-rays showed an 8-centimetre muscle tear, a grade-four tear in her quadriceps and a grade-two tear of the sacroiliac.

In trying not to hurt her, Luke Nolan eased down near the line and was almost beaten by the French-trained mare Moonlight Cloud. The margin was a head.

Nolan admitted that over-confidence and worry had led to his poor ride. 'It was an error that every apprentice is taught not to do,' he said at the time, 'and I got away with it today.'

Peter Moody admitted that the mare had not coped with the 11,000-mile journey as well as expected and said she was 'tired and worn out' after the Diamond Jubilee Stakes, as well as injured.

(Incidentally, we should take nothing away from Moonlight Cloud. She was no slouch; she won six times at Group 1 level, including the Prix de Maurice Gheest three years running!)

There was talk at the time that the great mare would retire and go to the breeding barn in the UK, perhaps even be mated to the other undefeated wonder horse of the age, the mighty Frankel, but it was just talk. Black Caviar wanted to go home and it was an obvious decision to miss the second race she was entered for, the July Cup, and bring her home.

I think many of us thought that her racing days were over, 22 races undefeated and a win at Ascot was good enough for most of us to remember. But we were to be blessed with three more wonderful races and three more victories and I, for one, am forever grateful to her connections for making that decision to go on, because I got to see her race again in her final performance, and what a day it was!

I was there, part of a sell-out crowd at Randwick, with thousands more lining the fence outside the track along Alison Road, to see Black Caviar win her last race, the T.J. Smith Stakes, on 13 April 2013. It's the only time I ever saw a standing ovation as a horse went onto the track, which was followed by an even bigger standing ovation after she cruised up the rise to her 25th win, and eternal glory. Thousands of fans bet a dollar on her just to keep the betting slip as a souvenir.

I have seen many great horses race, but I have never seen a horse accelerate and outclass the opposition like she could.

We were all given little salmon-pink flags with black spots that day and the racetrack was a sea of waving flags as she returned to scale. I've still got mine on my office bookshelf.

In spite of Glyn Schofield getting sick of seeing her bum, the rest of us never got sick of seeing her win.

Part 4
RACETRACK HUMOUR

INTRODUCTION—FUN, FACT AND FANTASY

The racetrack is a rich source of great yarns and there is something very 'Australian' about the yarns that come from the racing game. I guess they often emphasise the stoic, deadpan nature of Aussie humour, that dry self-deprecating style we seem to enjoy—laughing at ourselves.

The racing industry is so full of colourful true stories that there seems to be no reason for exaggeration or make-believe, but Aussies being what we are, there are plenty of tall tales told about the races.

So this section mixes totally factual yarns about racing with fantasy, tall stories and often-told anecdotes and jokes. You can guess which is which!

Banjo's memories of racetrack skulduggery in the 'old days' are wonderful glimpses into a time gone by, and yet they also remind us that little has changed as far as racetrack characters go. His anecdote about Breaker Morant is a favourite of mine.

The final story in the section is from Wayne Peake's collection of stories called *The Gambler's Ghost*, published by Ascot Press.

NOT BAD

JIM HAYNES

Stoicism is a common element in racetrack humour. One of my favourite stories concerns the old battling punter who heads off to the races with $20 in his pocket.

The old battler, let's call him Jim, backs the first winner at 10 to 1 and then goes all-up on the next three favourites, who duly salute the judge, giving him a bank of $500 when the fifth race comes around.

Now, Jim has done the form carefully on this race and has a 'special' which opens at 6 to 1 and drifts out to 8 to 1. Unperturbed, Jim steps in, backs his 'special' and watches it win with his hands in his pockets and no emotion on his face.

Two more all-up bets on successful favourites take Jim's bank to almost $20,000 before the final race on the card.

This race features Jim's second 'good thing' for the day, a track specialist named Wire Knot, third-up from a spell over his pet distance.

Jim extracts a $50 note from his wad, tucks it into his back pocket and puts the rest on his second 'special', Wire Knot, on the nose at 3 to 1.

Wire Knot misses the kick, flies down the outside late and it's a photo finish. The judge calls for a second print before awarding the race to the rank outsider, Mitre Guest. Wire Knot misses by a nose.

On his way to the bus stop Jim meets a mate who says, 'Hello Jim, how'd you go today?'

'Not bad,' says Jim, deadpan, 'I won $30.'

VICTOR SECOND

A.B. 'BANJO' PATERSON

We were training two horses for the Buckatowndown races—an old grey warrior called Tricolor—better known to the station boys as The Trickler—and a mare for the hack race. Station horses don't get trained quite like Carbine; some days we had no time to give them gallops at all, so they had to gallop twice as far the next day to make up.

One day the boy we had looking after The Trickler fell in with a mob of sharps who told him we didn't know anything about training horses, and that what the horse really wanted was 'a twicer'—that is to say, a gallop twice round the course. So the boy gave him 'a twicer' on his own responsibility.

When we found out about it we gave the boy a twicer with the strap, and he left and took out a summons against us. But somehow or other we managed to get the old horse pretty fit, tried him against hacks of different descriptions, and persuaded ourselves that we had the biggest certainty ever known on a racecourse.

When the horses were galloping in the morning the kangaroo-dog, Victor, nearly always went down to the course to run round with them. It amused him, apparently, and didn't hurt anyone, so we used to let him race; in fact, we rather encouraged him, because it kept him in good trim to hunt kangaroo.

When we were starting for the meeting, someone said we had better tie up Victor or he would be getting stolen at the races. We called and whistled, but he had made himself scarce, so we started and forgot all about him.

Buckatowndown Races. Red-hot day, everything dusty, everybody drunk and blasphemous. All the betting at Buckatowndown was double-event—you had to win the money first, and fight the man for it afterwards.

The start for our race, the Town Plate, was delayed for a quarter of an hour because the starter flatly refused to leave a fight of which he was an interested spectator. Every horse, as he did his preliminary gallop, had a string of dogs after him, and the clerk of the course came full cry after the dogs with a whip.

By and by the horses strung across to the start at the far side of the course. They fiddled about for a bit; then down went the flag and they came sweeping along all bunched up together, one holding a nice position on the inside. All of a sudden we heard a wild chorus of imprecations—'Look at that dog!' Victor had chipped in with the racehorses, and was running right in front of the field. It looked a guinea to a gooseberry that some of them would fall on him.

The owners danced and swore. What did we mean by bringing a something mongrel there to trip up and kill horses that were worth a paddockful of all the horses we had ever owned, or would ever breed or own, even if we lived to be a thousand. We were fairly in it and no mistake.

As the field came past the stand the first time we could hear the riders swearing at our dog, and a wild yell of execration arose from the public. He had got right among the ruck by this time, and was racing alongside his friend The Trickler, thoroughly enjoying himself. After passing the stand the pace became very merry; the dog stretched out all he knew; when they began to make it too hot for him, he cut off corners, and joined at odd intervals, and every time he made a fresh appearance the people in the stand lifted up their voices and 'swore cruel'.

The horses were all at the whip as they turned into the straight, and then The Trickler and the publican's mare singled out. We could hear the 'chop, chop!' of the whips as they came along together, but the mare could not suffer it as long as the old fellow, and she swerved off while he struggled home a winner by a length or so.

Just as they settled down to finish Victor dashed up on the inside, and passed the post at old Trickler's girths. The populace immediately went for him with stones, bottles, and other missiles, and he had to scratch gravel to save his life. But imagine the amazement of the other owners when the judge placed Trickler first, Victor second, and the publican's mare third!

The publican tried to argue it out with him. He said you couldn't place a kangaroo-dog second in a horserace.

The judge said it was *his* (hiccough) business what he placed, and that those who (hiccough) interfered with him would be sorry for it. Also he expressed a (garnished) opinion that the publican's mare was no rotten good, and that she was the right sort of mare for a poor man to own, because she would keep him poor.

Then the publican called the judge a cow. The judge was willing; a rip, tear, and chew fight ensued, which lasted some time. The judge won.

Fifteen protests were lodged against our win, but we didn't worry about that—we had laid the stewards a bit to nothing. Every second man we met wanted to run us a mile for one hundred pounds a side; and a drunken shearer, spoiling for a fight, said he had heard we were 'brimming over with bally science,' and had ridden forty miles to find out.

We didn't wait for the hack race. We folded our tents like the Arab and stole away. But it remains on the annals of Buckatowndown how a kangaroo-dog ran second for the Town Plate.

LUNCH FOR DIPSO DAN

JIM HAYNES

Here is a yarn I heard years ago and turned into a poem. It's one of the funniest stories I ever heard based on horses' names. The central idea of a drunk confusing a horse's name with the advertised lunchtime in a pub was how the 'joke' worked when I heard it. I added a few twists and turns and it took me a while to think up the final tagline. Then I put the whole thing into rhyme so I could copyright it! You can't copyright a joke, but you can copyright a poem.

Dipso Dan is the town drunk in my 'perfect country town', Weelabarabak.

***

Dipso Dan is a man who can strike any time,
You rarely get any warning,
He's thrown out of the pub as the minister passes
Late one Saturday morning.
'G'day there Reverend,' says Dipso Dan,
'Got any good tips today?'
'Well Dan,' says His Reverence, 'Lunch might be
A good thing for you I'd say.'

'Thanks for that Reverend, Good on ya,' says Dan,
'I never forget what I'm told.'
To himself he mutters, 'Never heard of Lunch,
It must be a two-year-old.'
Back in the pub goes Dipso Dan,

The drinking day is still young.
And the first thing he sees is a sign that says,
'Lunch is 12 to 1'.

'Look at the odds!' says Dipso Dan,
'That's gotta be worth a chance!'
But a firm hand grips his collar
And another the seat of his pants.
He's back on the street, but now he's obsessed,
'That Lunch might be a goer.
I'll go down the Royal and back it,' says Dan,
'Before the odds get any lower'.

So Dan staggers off to the other pub,
At the other end of the shops.
Halfway down there's the Chinese restaurant—
That's exactly where Dan stops.
And he stares at the sign in the window.
It says, 'Lunch is 11 to 2'.
'They're backing the thing for a fortune,' says Dan,
'That minister musta knew!'

'Fancy missin' out on 12s,
That's just the thing to spoil
Me afternoon, I'll hurry up,
I'll back it at the Royal.'
Dan staggers on and he's almost there
When he stops with a strangled yell.
'Lunch 1 to 2', says the blackboard sign
At the door of the Royal Hotel.

'Bloody odds-on, I've missed it,' says Dan,
'Me chance of a fortune is wrecked!'
Then he slides down the wall of the Royal Hotel,
Booze and exercise take their effect.
He sleeps through the paddy-wagon ride

But he wakes when they lock the cell.
He hears them walking away with the keys
And he knows he'll have to yell.

'I wanna know about Lunch,' yells Dan,
'And I've got a terrible thirst.'
'Bad luck about lunch,' the sergeant yells back,
'Cos I'm telling ya, sober up first.'
'Sober Up first eh,' says Dipso Dan,
'So much for the minister's hunch.'
He lies down on the bed, 'Sober Up first, eh,
Thank gawd I didn't back Lunch!'

A MEMORY OF BREAKER MORANT

A.B. 'BANJO' PATERSON

Amateur racing, for some reason or other, has always had some sort of encouragement from the Rosehill proprietary, and that club is the only metropolitan institution that caters for the 'lily-whites'. Their annual race at Rosehill is a sort of 'Custer's last stand'.

They used to also run an amateur steeplechase, and one of these was to some extent memorable, for among the riders was Harry Morant, whose tempestuous career was ended by a firing squad in the South African war.

Plucky to the point of recklessness, he suffered from a theatrical complex which made him pretend to be badly hurt when there was, really, not much up with him.

Morant was breaking in horses and mustering wild cattle somewhere up in the west, and he had been accustomed to ride after hounds in England.

Arriving in Sydney at the time of the amateur steeplechase, he set out to look for a mount.

Mr Pottie, of the veterinary family, had a mare that could both gallop and jump, but she was such an unmanageable brute that none of the local amateurs (and I was one of them) cared to take the mount.

Morant jumped at the chance, but as soon as they started the mare cleared out with him and fell into a drain, rolling her rider out as flat as a flounder.

He was carried in, supposed to be unconscious, and I was taken up to hear his last wishes.

The doctors could get nothing out of him, but after listening to his wanderings for a while I said, very loudly and clearly, 'What'll you have Morant?' and he said, equally clearly,

'Brandy and soda.'

CORN MEDICINE

HARRY 'THE BREAKER' MORANT

'A well-bred horse! but he won't get fat,
Though I've done the best I can;
He keeps as poor as a blessed rat!'
Said the sorrowful stable-man.
'I've bled and I've blistered him, and to-day
I bought him a monster ball;
But, blow the horse! Let me do what I may,
He won't get fat at all.
'I've given him medicines galore,
And linseed oil and bran,
And yet the brute looks awfully poor,'
Said the woebegone stable-man.
One glance the intelligent stranger threw
At the ribs of the hollow weed,
Then asked, with an innocent air, 'Did you
Remember to give him a feed?'

YOU CAN'T LOSE

JIM HAYNES

Back in the days before doping tests came in, a trainer was spotted by a steward slipping a pre-prepared 'speed-ball' to his horse before a race.

'What did you give that horse?' demanded the steward.

The trainer, who had several more of the pills in his pocket, replied, 'Oh, they're just homemade boiled lollies,' and he popped one into his mouth and went on, 'My missus makes 'em and the horse loves them. I'm having one myself,' he said, 'here, do you wanna try one?'

'Okay,' said the steward as he took the pill, looked at it and put it in his mouth, 'but I've got my eye on you.'

Minutes later, as the trainer legged him aboard, the stable jockey asked, 'Are we all set, boss, everything as planned?'

'Yes,' the trainer replied, 'money's on and he'll win. If anything passes you, don't worry, it'll just be the Chief Steward or me!'

HOW THE FAVOURITE BEAT US

A.B. 'BANJO' PATERSON

This is a parody of a famous Adam Lindsay Gordon poem called 'How We Beat the Favourite' and it's even written in exactly the same rhyme and metre as that celebrated poem. It's the classic yarn of a bloke who decides to pull up his horse because he can't get a decent price about her, but gives the jockey the wrong signal by mistake. A 'brown', incidentally, is a penny, or any copper coin. The advice 'win when you're able' is still the best advice any owner or trainer can follow!

***

'Aye,' said the boozer, 'I tell you it's true, sir,
I once was a punter with plenty of pelf,
But gone is my glory, I'll tell you the story
How I stiffened my horse and got stiffened myself.

''Twas a mare called the Cracker, I came down to back her,
But found she was favourite all of a rush,
The folk just did pour on to lay six to four on,
And several bookies were killed in the crush.

'It seems old Tomato was stiff, though a starter;
They reckoned him fit for the Caulfield to keep.
The Bloke and the Donah were scratched by their owner,
He only was offered three-fourths of the sweep.

'We knew Salamander was slow as a gander,
The mare could have beat him the length of the straight,
And old Manumission was out of condition,
And most of the others were running off weight.

'No doubt someone "blew it", for everyone knew it,
The bets were all gone, and I muttered in spite,
"If I can't get a copper, by Jingo, I'll stop her,
Let the public fall in, it will serve the brutes right."

'I said to the jockey, "Now, listen, my cocky,
You watch as you're cantering down by the stand,
I'll wait where that toff is and give you the office,
You're only to win if I lift up my hand."

'I then tried to back her—What price is the Cracker?
"Our books are all full, sir," each bookie did swear;
My mind, then, I made up, my fortune I played up
I bet every shilling against my own mare.

'I strolled to the gateway, the mare in the straight way
Was shifting and dancing, and pawing the ground,
The boy saw me enter and wheeled for his canter,
When a darned great mosquito came buzzing around.

'They breed 'em et Hexham, it's risky to vex 'em,
They suck a man dry at a sitting, no doubt,
But just as the mare passed, he fluttered my hair past,
I lifted my hand, and I flattened him out.

'I was stunned when they started, the mare simply darted
Away to the front when the flag was let fall,
For none there could match her, and none tried to catch her—
She finished a furlong in front of them all.

'You bet that I went for the boy, whom I sent for
The moment he weighed and came out of the stand—
"Who paid you to win it? Come, own up this minute."
"Lord love yer," said he, "why, you lifted your hand."

''Twas true, by St Peter, that cursed "muskeeter"
Had broke me so broke that I hadn't a brown,
And you'll find the best course is when dealing with horses
To win when you're able, and *keep your hands down*.'

MY RACING PROBLEMS

C.J. DENNIS

Now that the racing season gathers to its exciting climax, a unique racing problem that has interested me for a number of years again presents itself for solution.

You are quite wrong if you imagine that my problem has anything to do with my own puny efforts to 'spot stone morals' with a view to pecuniary gain. It is far more impersonal than that. Punting to me presents no problem at all! It is a perfectly simple process.

When I wish to have a little flutter I merely bid a last farewell to a ten shilling note and give it to a bookmaker. (At the precise moment of its passing one gently intones over the ten shillings the name of some favoured horse.) For this sum the bookmaker sells me a little piece of pasteboard bearing his name and certain indecipherable characters that look like Coptic Roots, or something.

This piece of pasteboard I cling to religiously—even fanatically until the race is over. Then I tear it into little pieces, throw these to all or any of the four winds that happen to be blowing at the time, and the transaction is completed.

I have heard it rumored that, should the animal I fancy win the race (which is absurd) the bookmaker will then buy back my piece of pasteboard at a price more or less in advance of what it cost me. Some day I should like to have an opportunity of testing this contention.

But, even without this happy consummation, the mere purchase of the pasteboard provides me with a mild thrill. For, if the horse I have chosen manages to beat at least one other horse in the race, a distinct glow of satisfaction flatters my prescience and unexpectedly shrewd judgement.

I should like to know how to capitalise this; for I feel that I have a unique flair for selecting certain horses that are frequently well able to run faster than certain other horses, or at least one other horse.

But my real problem is far more baffling than anything presented by the simple mechanical rights of punting. It is this: —

Why is it that a large proportion of regular racecourse frequenters have extremely fat necks?

I know immediately what you would answer: that thin necks are also much in evidence; but I hope to be able to explain that also at a later date.

I wish it understood that I exclude from this enquiry all owners and trainers.

The men I refer to are very evidently gamblers who 'follow the game' with a queer devotion worthy of an even nobler aim; and their fat necks are abnormally fat. Look about you next time you are on a racecourse.

I had taken my problem to various learned men without getting much satisfaction; and then I remembered Percy Podgrass. Percy is a friend of mine and a scientist of sorts—of very many sorts, in fact; he attends guild lectures.

I have propounded my perplexing problem to Percy (alliteratively, like that) and he has promised to chew it over and bring back to me a working hypothesis. At least, I think it is a hypothesis and certainly not a hypothenuse; though Percy himself laughingly referred to it, with his quaint, diffident humor, as his hippopotamus.

I shall be glad, later, to afford readers the benefit of the Podgrassian research.

THE OIL FROM OLD BILL SHANE

C.J. DENNIS

I got the oil: too right. A cove called Shane.
    Yes; ole Bill Shane. You've 'eard of 'im, of course.
Big racin' 'ead. There's no need to explain
    The things he don't know about a 'orse.
Good ole Bill Shane. They say he's made a pile
    At puntin'. Shrewd! I wish I 'ad 'is brain.
An' does 'e know the game? Well, I should smile.
    They can't put nothin' over ole Bill Shane.

Yes; Shane, Bill Shane . . . Aw, listen, lad. Wake up!
    Why everybody's 'eard of ole Bill Shane.
They say he made ten thousan' on the Cup
    Last year, an' now he's got the oil again.
Wot? Owner? Trainer? Nah! Who 'eeds their guff?
    Bill's a big racin' man—a punter. See?
Top dog. I alwiz sez wot's good enough
    For ole Bill Shane is good enough for me.

Yes; he gave me the oil. I got it straight—
    Well, nearly straight. Of course, I've never spoke
To Bill 'imself direck. I got a mate
    Wot knows a bloke wot knows another bloke
Wot's frien's with Shane, an' so—you un'erstand.
    Wot? me give you the tip? Aw, take a walk!
Yeh think I'd do a thing so under'and?
    Bill Shane would kill me if I was to talk.

Well, listen . . . Now, for gosh sake, keep it dark.
    An' don't let no one know it came from Shane.
Keep it strick secret. I would be a nark
    To let you chuck yer money down the drain . . .
Wazzat you said? He's scratched? 'Ere! Lemme look!
    Scratched! Ain't that noos to knock a man clean out?
I alwiz said this puntin' game was crook . . . .
    Who? Shane? Aw, I dunno. Some racin' tout.

A-MAIZING ESCAPE

A.B. 'BANJO' PATERSON

Here is another of Banjo Paterson's yarns about country race meetings, written in 1914. This time it's a memory of a meeting on the South Coast of New South Wales.

***

The most vivid memory that abides with me of south-coast racing is of a meeting held many years ago in the Shoalhaven District.

The attendance consisted mostly of the local agriculturalists, horny-handed sons of the soil quite formidable in appearance and character. The foreign element was provided by a group of welshers, side-show artists, prize-fighters and acrobats who followed the southern meetings as hawks follow a plague of mice.

The centre of the course consisted of a field of maize fully ten feet high and when one bookmaker decided to 'take a sherry with the dook and guy-a-whack' (a slang expression meaning to abscond without paying), he melted into the maize and took cover like a wounded black duck.

The hefty agriculturalists went in after him like South African natives after a lion in the jungle. For a time nothing could be seen but the waving of the maize and nothing could be heard but the shouts of the 'beaters' when they thought they caught sound or scent of their prey.

After a time all and sundry took a hand in the hunt; so the 'wanted man' simply slipped off his coat and joined in the search for himself, shouting and waving his arms just as vigorously as anybody else.

When the searchers got tired of the business and started to straggle out of the maize he straggled out too, on the far side, and kept putting one foot in front of the other till he struck the coach road to Sydney.

FLYING KATE

ANONYMOUS

If you think Henry's Lawson's yarn about the horse trained to poke out his tongue in Part 8 of this collection is well beyond credibility, here is the most outrageous racing yarn of all time. It's about a mare so good that she raced while she was in foal and then . . . oh look, read it for yourself and find out! It's by that well-known Aussie poet A Nonymous.

***

It makes us old hands sick and tired to hear
Them talk of their champions of today,
Eurythmics and Davids (yes, I'll have a beer)
Are only fair hacks in their way.

Now this happened out West before records were took,
And 'tis not to be found in the guide,
But it's honest—Gor' struth, and can't be mistook,
For it happened that I had the ride.

'Twas the Hummer's Creek Cup, and our mare, Flying Kate,
Was allotted eleven stone two;
The race was two miles, you'll agree with me mate,
It was asking her something to do.

She was heavy in foal, but the owner and me
Decided to give her a spin,
We were right on the rocks, 'twas the end of a spree,
So we needed a bit of a win.

I saddled her up and went down with the rest,
Her movements were clumsy and slow,
The starter to get us in line did his best,
Then swishing his flag he said, 'Go!'

The field jumped away but the mare seemed asleep,
And I thought to myself, 'We've been sold,'
Then I heard something queer, and I felt I could weep,
For strike me if Kate hadn't foaled.

The field by this time had gone half-a-mile,
But I knew what the old mare could do,
So I gave her a cut with the whip—you can smile,
But the game little beast simply flew.

'Twas then she showed them her wonderful speed,
For we mowed down the field one by one,
With a furlong to go we were out in the lead,
And prepared for a last final run.

Then something came at us right on the outside,
And we only just scratched past the pole,
When I had a good look I thought I'd have died,
For I'm blowed if it wasn't the foal.

THE STUTTERING STABLEHAND

JIM HAYNES

One of my favourite politically incorrect racetrack stories concerns an old stablehand, the iconic desperate old battler, who was a victim of *Alalia syllabaris*, that is, he stuttered.

This character appears in front of a bookmaker who is frantically writing out tickets and taking money hand-over-fist just before a big race.

'Waddya want, mate?' asks the bookie.

'I b-b-b-b-b-backed . . .' stammers the stablehand.

'Come on, mate,' says the bookie, 'you backed what?'

'I b-b-b-b-b-backed . . . a f-f-f-f-f-f-five t-t-t-t-t-t . . . ' the flustered stablehand manages to get out, his face growing red in the process.

''Struth, mate,' says the impatient and insensitive bookie. 'You backed what!?'

'I b-b-b-b-b-backed . . . a f-f-f-f-f-f-five t-t-t-t-t-to . . . ' comes the slow stuttering reply.

'Look, mate,' says the bookmaker, 'I haven't got time to hear your story now. You backed a five-to-one winner and lost your ticket or something . . . here's $50, I hope that's near enough, now get out of the way will you?'

The old stablehand is walking back to the horse stalls when he meets the trainer he works for. The trainer sees the $50 in his hand and asks, 'Bloody hell, where did you get $50?'

'W-w-w-w-w-well,' replies the stutterer, 'I ww-w-w-went t-t-t-to t-t-t-tell that b-b-b-bookie, old M-M-M-Mr S-S-S-Samuels I b-b-b-b backed . . . your f-f-f-five t-t-t-t-ton h-h-horse float over his M-M-M-Mercedes . . . and he gave me f-f-f-fifty b-b-b-bucks!'

THE OLD TIMER'S STEEPLECHASE

A.B. 'BANJO' PATERSON

Here is another classic tale from Banjo about the days when races of 3, 4 and even 5 miles were common, especially in steeplechasing. This meant that several laps of the track had to be made, and thus the opportunity to 'take a lap off' arose if there was some bush along the course and you were clever enough. Of course, there was always a chance there was someone cleverer than you!

***

The sheep were shorn and the wool went down
At the time of our local racing:
And I'd earned a spell—I was burned and brown—
So I rolled my swag for a trip to town
And a look at the steeplechasing.

'Twas rough and ready—an uncleared course
As rough as the pioneers found it;
With barbed-wire fences, topped with gorse,
And a water-jump that would drown a horse,
And the steeple three times round it.

There was never a fence the tracks to guard,
Some straggling posts defined 'em:
And the day was hot, and the drinking hard,
Till none of the stewards could see a yard
Before nor yet behind 'em!

But the bell was rung and the nags were out,
Excepting an old outsider
Whose trainer started an awful rout,
For his boy had gone on a drinking bout
And left him without a rider.

'Is there not one man in the crowd,' he cried,
'In the whole of the crowd so clever,
Is there not one man that will take a ride
On the old white horse from the northern side
That was bred on the Mooki River?'

'Twas an old white horse that they called The Cow,
And a cow would look well beside him;
But I was pluckier then than now
(And I wanted excitement anyhow),
So at last I agreed to ride him.

And the trainer said, 'Well, he's dreadful slow,
And he hasn't a chance whatever;
But I'm stony broke, so it's time to show
A trick or two that the trainers know
Who train by the Mooki River.

'The first time round at the further side,
With the trees and the scrub about you,
Just pull behind them and run out wide
And then dodge into the scrub and hide,
And let them go round without you.

'At the third time round, for the final spin
With the pace, and the dust to blind 'em,
They'll never notice if you chip in
For the last half-mile—you'll be sure to win,
And they'll think you raced behind 'em.

'At the water-jump you may have to swim—
He hasn't a hope to clear it—
Unless he skims like the swallows skim
At full speed over, but not for him!
He'll never go next or near it.

'But don't you worry—just plunge across,
For he swims like a well-trained setter.
Then hide away in the scrub and gorse
The rest will be far ahead of course—
The further ahead the better.

'You must rush the jumps in the last half-round
For fear that he might refuse 'em;
He'll try to baulk with you, I'll be bound,
Take whip and spurs on the mean old hound,
And don't be afraid to use 'em.

'At the final round, when the field are slow
And you are quite fresh to meet 'em,
Sit down, and hustle him all you know
With the whip and spurs, and he'll have to go—
Remember, you've *GOT* to beat 'em!'

The flag went down and we seemed to fly,
And we made the timbers shiver
Of the first big fence, as the stand flashed by,
And I caught the ring of the trainer's cry:
'Go on! For the Mooki River!'

I jammed him in with a well-packed crush,
And recklessly—out for slaughter—
Like a living wave over fence and brush
We swept and swung with a flying rush,
Till we came to the dreaded water.

Ha, ha! I laugh at it now to think
Of the way I contrived to work it.
Shut in among them, before you'd wink,
He found himself on the water's brink,
With never a chance to shirk it!

The thought of the horror he felt beguiles
The heart of this grizzled rover!
He gave a snort you could hear for miles,
And a spring would have cleared the Channel Isles
And carried me safely over!

Then we neared the scrub, and I pulled him back
In the shade where the gum-leaves quiver:
And I waited there in the shadows black
While the rest of the horses, round the track,
Went on like a rushing river!

At the second round, as the field swept by,
I saw that the pace was telling;
But on they thundered, and by-and-by
As they passed the stand I could hear the cry
Of the folk in the distance, yelling!

Then the last time round! And the hoofbeats rang!
And I said, 'Well, it's now or never!'
And out on the heels of the throng I sprang,
And the spurs bit deep and the whipcord sang
As I rode! For the Mooki River!

We raced for home in a cloud of dust
And the curses rose in chorus.
'Twas flog, and hustle, and jump you must!
And The Cow ran well—but to my disgust
There was one got home before us.

'Twas a big black horse, that I had not seen
In the part of the race I'd ridden;
And his coat was cool and his rider clean,
And I thought that perhaps I had not been
The only one that had hidden.

And the trainer came with a visage blue
With rage, when the race concluded:
Said he, 'I thought you'd have pulled us through,
But the man on the black horse planted too,
And nearer to home than you did!'

Alas to think that those times so gay
Have vanished and passed for ever!
You don't believe in the yarn you say?
Why, man! 'Twas a matter of every day
When we raced on the Mooki River!

I HAVE A DREAM!

JIM HAYNES

While we are roaming the realms of pure fantasy, here is a racing yarn that I heard years ago but cannot corroborate.

The scene was suburban Melbourne a few years back.

A bloke bumped into a neighbour on the tram going home.

'Hello, Bill,' said the friend, 'where have you been?'

'I've been to the races,' Bill replied.

'You don't usually go to the mid-week meetings, do you?' said the neighbour.

'No,' said Bill, 'I only went today because I had a very vivid dream early this morning. I saw sunshine through fluffy clouds and a voice kept repeating "number seven . . . number seven . . ." So I looked in the paper and there was a horse carrying saddlecloth seven, coming out of barrier seven, in the seventh race at Sandown, at 7 to 1. So I went to the track and put $777 dollars on it.'

'What happened?' asked the neighbour.

'It ran seventh,' replied Bill.

FLASH JACK'S LAST RACE

A.B. 'BANJO' PATERSON

Here is yet another yarn from the pen of Banjo Paterson, in prose this time. This incident took place not far from where Banjo spent his childhood. He went to school at Binalong, not far from Jugiong, New South Wales.

***

It was at the hamlet of Jugiong that an event occurred, which is perhaps unique in turf history.

It was a publican's meeting, which means that the promoter was less concerned with gate money than with the sale of strong liquor.

The unfenced course was laid out alongside the Murrumbidgee River and one of the Osborne family, graziers in the district, had entered a mare which was fed and looked after on the other side of the river.

Off they went, and the mare made straight for home, jumping into the river and nearly drowning the jockey who was rescued by a young aboriginal boy.

Meanwhile Mr Osborne, under a pardonable mistake, was cheering on another runner in the belief that it was his mare.

Then there came a splashing sound at the back of the waggonette and Mr Osborne, looking around, was astonished to see his jockey.

'Well, I'll be damned,' he said. 'What are you doing here? Where's the mare?'

'She's home by now,' said the boy, a bush youngster known locally as 'Flash Jack from Gundagai'.

'And I'm going home too,' he added, 'I've had enough of it. In the last race my moke fell in front of the field and there was me lying on the track with nothing but horses' heels going over my head for half an hour and this time I was nearly drowned. I'd sunk four times when that black boy came in after me.

'I'd like a job, Mr Osborne, picking up fleeces in the shed if you ain't full up; but Flash Jack has rode his last race.'

THE FASTER RACEHORSE

BETTY LANE HOLLAND

Why is it so often thought
An owner's knowledge can be sought,
By all and sundry at the track,
Who are offended if knocked back?
A stranger blocks an owner's way,
'I see your horse is in today,
Should I have a bet or not?'
The owner's pride is on the spot.

'My horse is fit and win it may,
But play it safe and bet each way.'
The stranger goes to find a mate,
Such inside knowledge to relate,
The mate in turn will then pass on,
This information come upon.
And each repeat will escalate,
Until, 'He'll win by half the straight.'

Later they'll come back to him,
'What went wrong? It didn't win.'
They speak as if he was to blame,
As if to question his good name.
The owner says (to save his pride),
'Perhaps the jockey rode too wide.'
Or, 'Perhaps he had too great a weight,'
Or, 'Got blocked-in into the straight.'

But one owner had enough,
Decided it was all too rough
It was not some urger's place to know
Why his horse had been too slow.
Why should he have to tell them why?
Give a reason—he wouldn't try,
When queried why his was the 'last-er',
He snapped back, ''cos the rest were faster!'

WRONG DIAGNOSIS

JIM HAYNES

The Western Districts of Victoria are a great area for racing. This story was told to me by a good old yarn spinner at Port Fairy, near Warrnambool. He swore it was true but couldn't give me any names or details.

It seems that an old cocky trainer once turned up at a jumps meeting with a tough old steeplechaser, but with no jockey to ride it.

As the lad he had engaged for the ride didn't show up, the old trainer approached one of the professional city jockeys and asked if he would take the ride.

The jockey looked the old bloke up and down with a bored expression on his face and said, 'All right, Pop, I'll take him around for you I suppose, the moke I was booked for has been scratched and it will warm me up for the important races later in the day.'

As the old bloke legged the jockey aboard, he whispered urgently, 'Now listen carefully, this horse will win easily if you remember one thing.'

'I'll do a good job on him, Pop,' the jockey said impatiently. 'Don't worry, I do know how to ride you know.'

The old trainer persisted, 'This is important, listen. As you approach each jump you must say, "One, two, three . . . jump." If you do that he'll win.'

The jockey was already moving the horse away from the old trainer as this advice was given. 'Sure, Pop, it'll be all right, don't you worry,' he called back over his shoulder.

Of course the smug city jockey took no notice of the old trainer's advice. Away went the field and the tough old chaser was up with the leaders as they approached the first fence. When the horse made no preparation at all to jump, the jockey desperately attempted to lift him. The horse belatedly rose to the jump, struck heavily and almost dislodged the startled 'professional'.

This incident caused them to fall right back through the field, the horse being lucky to stay on his feet and the jockey using all his skill to stay in the saddle. The jockey's mind was now racing to remember the old man's advice and, at the next jump, he succeeded in calling out, 'One, two, three . . . jump!' and the horse easily accounted for the fence.

The jockey repeated the process at each jump and the horse jumped brilliantly, making up many lengths, but just failing to catch the winner at the post.

On his return to the enclosure, the jockey was confronted by the old trainer who said, 'You didn't listen to me, did you? You didn't say, "One, two, three . . . jump" at the first fence.'

'Yes, I did, Pop,' lied the jockey, 'but perhaps I didn't say it loudly enough the first time. He didn't hear me, he must be deaf.'

'He's not deaf, you bloody fool,' replied the old trainer laconically. 'He's blind.'

FLEW IT LIKE A BIRD

JIM HAYNES

It was the district's annual meeting, the cup and steeplechase.
And one prospective entry seemed a little out of place.
He wore a monocle and pantaloons and rode in dressage style.
'You sure you want to enter?' asked the steward, 'it's four mile?'

'Look here, my man,' the new chum said, 'I may look out of place,
And I'm new here in this district, but my horse can win this race.'
'But you have no race experience,' said the old man, with a frown,
'And are you sure this horse of yours can jump and not fall down?'

'We'll fly them like a bird,' said the new chum, 'he can leap,
Logs and hedges, post and rail, he'll jump 'em in his sleep!
Around the Sydney countryside we had some lovely fun,
I rode him with the Sydney hunt, he can jump and run.'

The old man listened to the words, and slowly scratched his chin,
'But this is on a racetrack, mate, this race you're entering.'
'I know, I know,' the new chum said, 'we'll fly 'em like a bird!'
He repeated the assertion as if the old man hadn't heard.

The steward walked around the beast, he wasn't often fooled,
'How long has he been jumping? How long has he been schooled?'
'I've ridden him cross country, over creeks and logs and such,
So I doubt your racetrack fences will worry him too much!'

'He'll take 'em in his stride,' he said. He savoured every word,
And spoke again the well-worn phrase; 'we'll fly 'em like a bird!'
'I hope you're right,' the old man said, 'and I admire your pluck,
But a four-mile chase, for your first race? Oh well, I wish you luck.'

'I'll be fine,' the new chum said, and climbed aboard his horse,
And trotted him genteelly to the start out on the course.
The flag went down and off they went, racing tight and fast,
Unused to such a hectic pace, the new chum followed—last.

The first jump in the home straight was right before the stand
But the new chum couldn't see too well, it wasn't as he'd planned.
The rumps of thirty racing horses quite obscured his vision,
Then they all rose, the jump appeared, and his horse made a
  decision.

The result was such a spectacle, it brought applause and cheers
The racing crowd who saw it talked of it for years.
'I will say this,' the old man said, 'He was true to his word,
For when his horse stood still—that new chum flew it like a bird!'

ASK THE HORSE

A.B. 'BANJO' PATERSON

Bill Kelso was an old-time trainer, a very direct-spoken man and if you didn't like what he said you could leave it.

I was doing some amateur writing and falling about over steeplechase fences and, like a lot of other young fellows, I began to fancy myself as a judge of racing. So, one day I asked old Kelso, 'Mr Kelso, what will win this race?'

'Well,' he said, 'I'll tell you something. Do you know what I was before I went in for training?'

I said, 'No.'

He said, 'I was working for a pound a week and I might be working for a pound a week still, only for young fools like you that will go betting. You leave it alone or get somebody to sew your pockets up before you come to the races.'

Well, it wasn't very polite but it was good advice.

The committee had him in once to explain the running of a race, before the days of stipendiary stewards. It took them a lot of trouble to get the committee together and they sat down, prepared for a good long explanation.

'Mr Kelso,' said the chairman, 'can you tell us why your horse ran so badly today?'

'No, I'm afraid I can't,' he said, 'you'll have to ask the horse. He's the only one that knows.'

THE URGING OF UNCLE

C.J. DENNIS

No; I ain't got a talent for races.
  I ain't no frequenter of courses;
But I've lately been watchin' the paces
  Of some of these promisin' 'orses
Huh! promise? if 'orses 'ave uses,
  'Tain't bringin' no joy to the faces
Of uncles wot 'arks to abuses
  From nieces wot follers the races.

It's this 'ow. A friend of my niece's
  Is friends with a friend wot rejoices
In knowin' a cove wot increases
  'Is wealth thro' 'is wise racin' choices.
So we gits the good oil. But reverses
  Leaves me with three thruppeny pieces,
While riches pours into the purses
  Of friends of friends' friends of me nieces.

Now, I ain't a great reader of faces
  Nor wise to the wiles of the courses;
But when I gits out to the races
  I meets a nice feller wot forces
Acquaintance, an' w'ispers advices
  Concernin' dead certainties w'ich is
All startin' at much better prices
  Than wot my niece tips. So I switches.

Now, I ain't so much 'urt that our riches
Is down to three thruppeny pieces
Because from sure winners I switches;
It's them narsty remarks of my niece's.
'Ot anger within 'er it surges,
She sez, at an uncle wot places
'Is faith in a feller wot urges . . .
No; I ain't got much talent for races.

NO CHANCE

JIM HAYNES

It was a country race meeting with small fields and only a few bookies fielding on the six races.

Just before the last race, a handicap with five starters, a well-dressed 'squatter' type cockie approaches one of the bookies who has come up from the big smoke to the meeting.

'I want a hundred on Blue Peter,' he says, 'what are the odds?'

'You can have ten to one,' says the bookie and the bloke is quite happy with that and hands over the money.

Five minutes later the cockie is back, having visited the other five or six bookmakers fielding that day.

'Do you still have Blue Peter at tens?' he asks.

'Look mate,' says the bookie, 'you can have twelves if you like, but I have to tell you, I don't think he has a chance.'

'That's okay,' says the cockie, 'I only want the bet, not the advice.' And he pulls out another hundred and gets his ticket.

Just as the race is about to start he is back again, 'What price Blue Peter now?' he asks.

'Mate, you can have twenty to one but I have to tell you, I own Blue Peter and we brought him up for the run. The horse is running off weight and being trained for much longer races—he hasn't much hope at all in this race. I've already got two hundred quid of your money, I don't want to rob you blind!'

'That's okay,' says the cockie, unperturbed, 'I'll have another hundred at twenties.'

The bookie shrugs and writes the ticket.

The five-horse field is despatched by the starter and in a very slowly run race, Blue Peter wins by 2 lengths.

The bookie is stunned, he pays out and says to the cockie, 'How the hell did you work that out? We only brought the horse up here to run him into some condition! I told you I owned him, and you still knew he could win. What did you know that we didn't?'

'Well,' said the cockie, stuffing the money into his pockets, 'I knew that I owned the other four runners.'

OUR NEW HORSE

A.B. 'BANJO' PATERSON

The boys had come back from the races
    All silent and down on their luck;
They'd backed 'em, straight out and for places,
    But never a winner they struck.
They lost their good money on Slogan,
    And fell, most uncommonly flat,
When Partner, the pride of the Bogan,
    Was beaten by Aristocrat.

And one said, 'I move that instanter
    We sell out our horses and quit,
The brutes ought to win in a canter,
    Such trials they do when they're fit.
The last one they ran was a snorter—
    A gallop to gladden one's heart—
Two-twelve for a mile and a quarter,
    And finished as straight as a dart.

'And then when I think that they're ready
    To win me a nice little swag,
They are licked like the veriest neddy—
    They're licked from the fall of the flag.
The mare held her own to the stable,
    She died out to nothing at that,
And Partner he never seemed able
    To pace it with Aristocrat.

'And times have been bad, and the seasons
  Don't promise to be of the best;
In short, boys, there's plenty of reasons
  For giving the racing a rest.
The mare can be kept on the station—
  Her breeding is good as can be—
But Partner, his next destination
  Is rather a trouble to me.

'We can't sell him here, for they know him
  As well as the clerk of the course;
He's raced and won races till, blow him,
  He's done as a handicap horse.
A jady, uncertain performer,
  They weight him right out of the hunt,
And clap it on warmer and warmer
  Whenever he gets near the front.

'It's no use to paint him or dot him
  Or put any "fake" on his brand,
For bushmen are smart, and they'd spot him
  In any sale-yard in the land.
The folk about here could all tell him,
  Could swear to each separate hair;
Let us send him to Sydney and sell him,
  There's plenty of Jugginses there.

'We'll call him a maiden, and treat 'em
  To trials will open their eyes,
We'll run their best horses and beat 'em,
  And then won't they think him a prize.
I pity the fellow that buys him,
  He'll find in a very short space,
No matter how highly he tries him,
  The beggar won't *race* in a race.'

***

Next week, under 'Seller and Buyer',
  Appeared in the *Daily Gazette*:
'A racehorse for sale, and a flyer;
  Has never been started as yet;
A trial will show what his pace is;
  The buyer can get him in light,
And win all the handicap races.
  Apply here before Wednesday night.'

He sold for a hundred and thirty,
  Because of a gallop he had
One morning with Bluefish and Bertie,
  And donkey-licked both of 'em bad.
And when the old horse had departed,
  The life on the station grew tame;
The race-track was dull and deserted,
  The boys had gone back on the game.

***

The winter rolled by, and the station
  Was green with the garland of spring
A spirit of glad exultation
  Awoke in each animate thing.
And all the old love, the old longing,
  Broke out in the breasts of the boys,
The visions of racing came thronging
  With all its delirious joys.

The rushing of floods in their courses,
  The rattle of rain on the roofs
Recalled the fierce rush of the horses,
  The thunder of galloping hoofs.
And soon one broke out: 'I can suffer

No longer the life of a slug,
The man that don't race is a duffer,
Let's have one more run for the mug.

'Why, everything races, no matter
Whatever its method may be:
The waterfowl hold a regatta;
The 'possums run heats up a tree;
The emus are constantly sprinting
A handicap out on the plain;
It seems like all nature was hinting,
'Tis time to be at it again.

'The cockatoo parrots are talking
Of races to far away lands;
The native companions are walking
A go-as-you-please on the sands;
The little foals gallop for pastime;
The wallabies race down the gap;
Let's try it once more for the last time,
Bring out the old jacket and cap.

'And now for a horse; we might try one
Of those that are bred on the place,
But I think it better to buy one,
A horse that has proved he can race.
Let us send down to Sydney to Skinner,
A thorough good judge who can ride,
And ask him to buy us a spinner
To clean out the whole countryside.'

They wrote him a letter as follows:
'We want you to buy us a horse;
He must have the speed to catch swallows,
And stamina with it of course.
The price ain't a thing that'll grieve us,

It's getting a bad 'un annoys
The undersigned blokes, and believe us,
We're yours to a cinder, "the boys"'.

He answered: 'I've bought you a hummer,
A horse that has never been raced;
I saw him run over the Drummer,
He held him outclassed and outpaced.
His breeding's not known, but they state he
Is born of a thoroughbred strain,
I paid them a hundred and eighty,
And started the horse in the train.'

They met him—alas, that these verses
Aren't up to the subject's demands—
Can't set forth their eloquent curses,
For Partner was back on their hands.
They went in to meet him in gladness,
They opened his box with delight—
A silent procession of sadness
They crept to the station at night.

And life has grown dull on the station,
The boys are all silent and slow;
Their work is a daily vexation,
And sport is unknown to them now.
Whenever they think how they stranded,
They squeal just like guinea-pigs squeal;
They bit their own hook, and were landed
With fifty pounds loss on the deal.

THE GUDGEONS GO TO RANDWICK

LENNIE LOWER

(Adapted from Here's Luck*)*

I had a feeling of impending trouble. As the browsing lamb sees the shadow of the hawk on the grass, so I saw trouble.

Gradually the clock forced itself on me. It ticked at me. Its little hand went around. Every tick was a second nearer the grave; my life was ebbing away, ebbing away—second by second. I was in a very bad state.

There was a loud knock on the door, and my son, Stanley, appeared. At the sight of him my fit of abstraction vanished and my mind resumed business at the same old stand.

'Well?' I queried.

'Daisy just phoned and said she's going to the races with Maureen and she wants us to come and meet her out there. You'll have to hurry. I'm almost ready. Don't bother about a shave. Come on, hurry up.'

'Races? What races?'

'Randwick Races. Get a collar on and a coat. I'll have to get you a hat somewhere. Look lively or we'll be late.'

He scurried out of the room, and the bedroom door, the front door and the gate slammed almost simultaneously behind him.

I rose to my feet. I didn't want to go to the races. I just wanted to sit down and think. Besides, I had only about eight pounds and I wasn't going to be financially butchered to make a holiday for the gimme-girls. I was a respectable married man whose wife had merely left to live with her sister. I sat down again. A loud crashing of doors and gates resounded through the house and Stanley suddenly appeared in the room like a stage demon.

'Not dressed yet!' he squeaked breathlessly.

'I'm not . . .'

'Here's a hat of Temple's I've borrowed for you from next door,' he gasped, and threw it to me.

'I'm not . . .'

'Come on. Get on your coat. I've phoned for a taxi; it will be here any moment.'

'I'm not going!' I shouted.

'Don't be silly, Dad. This collar looks clean enough. I found it in the hall. Got your studs?'

'Listen to me, Stanley. I am not going. Don't try these tornado tactics on me; I'm not going.'

'Aw, be yourself, Dad! You're not working. There's no money coming in. Daisy knows an absolute cert for today. Opportunity only knocks once. Come on!'

The doorbell rang.

'That's the taxi-man!' he exclaimed. 'Here, put your coat on.'

I clambered into my coat as he rushed out of the room. He was back in something under a second with my tie and studs.

'You can put these on in the car,' he gasped, slamming a hat on my head. He grasped me by the arm, swung me out of the room, out of the front door, out the gate and into the taxi.

'Randwick!' he cried. 'Drive like hell!' and the car leapt forward.

'Keep close to that car in front,' I added, 'and if it stops, shoot to kill.'

I struggled out of the hat, which was much too small and jammed down on my ears.

'What are you talking about?' said Stanley. 'What car in front?'

'There's always a car in front,' I replied testily. 'A black closed-in car, and it winds in and out streets until it pulls up at a deserted house and they all get out and carry the unconscious girl into the cellar and we surround the house and capture the Master Mind who turns out to be the butler.'

He stared at me. 'You're mad!' he said.

'Have it your own way,' I replied, and proceeded to adjust my collar.

I made no complaint to Stanley for literally dragging me out of the house and throwing me into a taxi. I had been practically abducted—shanghaied; but the thing was done. It was no use objecting. It was all of a piece with my presentiments and I sensed the presence of the finger of fate.

I am a fatalist and believe that what will be, will be; what is, is; and what was, was; and so on through the verbs. I am not alone in my belief; the modern trend of thought is more and more in that direction and I sometimes suspect that even the Railway Commissioners operate their passenger services on the same principle.

Stanley must have been thinking on similar lines. He had been gazing at the taximeter, a thing I never do in a taxi as it takes half the pleasure out of the ride. He seemed to be fascinated by the cold-blooded inexorableness of the thing.

'You know, Father,' he said, 'all life is a gamble.'

'A highly original remark, my boy,' I replied, 'I suppose then that a Randwick race-meeting is the quintessence of life and a royal routine flush would be the peak of existence?'

'It would be the end of your existence if you were playing at the camp with the boys. Wouldn't it be funny if we won a thousand pounds today?'

'Funny! The braw laddies of the Highland Society would laugh their sporrans off. May I inquire the basis of these hopes for fun? How are we to participate in this huge joke?'

'Don't try to be sarcastic, Father. It lessens my respect for you.'

'Your respect for your poor old father is already a minus quantity. It only appears on pay-days. You haven't answered my question.'

He leaned over and clutched my ear.

'Daisy had a stone moral,' he whispered.

'A stone moral.'

'Ssh!'

'What's a stone moral?'

'Don't talk so loud. It's a certainty. It can't be beaten. There's only one horse in it.'

'Oh, well, in that case,' I said, leaning back in my corner, 'it certainly must win.'

'Of course it'll win; you can put your undies on it.'

'Seems rather strange, though,' I ruminated, 'having only one horse in the race. Any fool ought to see that it must win.'

'Arrgh!'

I relapsed into my corner again.

The taximeter, foaming at the mouth, demolished another shilling and gnashed its teeth in anticipation of the next. The tick menace is not confined to our country districts.

'Who is going to pay this lightning calculator?' I asked, pointing to it.

'That's all right. I'll see that,' replied Stanley with a contemptuous flirt of his hand that must have greatly disheartened the meter. 'It's only twelve shillings,' he added.

'Where did you get it?' I exclaimed.

'Temple. Good feller your neighbour. Stung him for a couple.'

'Great!' I cried. 'Serves him damn well right!' I had begun to dislike Temple and to hear of his lending money to Stanley was sweet music to mine ears. Anything lent to Stanley can be lined up with the Pyramids, the Sphinx, the national debt and such-like time-defying monuments.

'Leger reserve, sir?'

The driver spoke through the back of his neck after the manner of his kind. The car pulled up and we decanted ourselves onto the pavement. Stanley paid the driver and we walked towards the entrance.

'Synagogue rules,' he said. 'Take yourself in and pay for yourself.'

We clattered through the turnstiles. A horde of racebook sellers detonated in our faces.

'Book! Book! Book! Bookertherazes! Book, sir?'

I bought two and handed one to Stanley.

'That squares us,' I said. 'You paid for the taxi and I've paid for the programmes.'

'If there's a harder man than you,' he said, taking the book, 'I'll bet he stands on a pedestal in Hyde Park, wrought in solid bronze.'

'Where have we to meet Daisy?' I said coldly.

'Over by the first stand—there she is!'

I looked as he pointed, and saw Daisy and Maureen with two men, one of whom seemed to be drunk.

'Who are those men?' I asked, waving my hand at the same time to Daisy.

'Dunno,' he answered in a puzzled voice.

As we drew nearer to them a strange feeling of apprehension stole over me. Their faces left me perturbed. I felt that the only way these men could attain popularity in a civilised community would be for them to become radio announcers, unseen and gravely announcing a glut of onions in the market. Later, when I heard their voices, I was forced to deny them even this faint hope. We doffed our hats and greeted the ladies.

'So glad you came,' said Maureen in an enthusiastic voice. 'I don't think you've met our friends. Mister Simpson; Mister Gudgeon. Mister Stanley Gudgeon—Mister Slatter—Gudgeons. Mix!'

As we shook hands I made a mental note of Stanley's perfidy in divulging my name. Smith is good enough for me.

'Gonna back all the winners?' asked Mr Slatter pleasantly. Or as pleasantly as he could. He was not the type of man I usually associate with. He was tall and very broad about the shoulders, attired in a silvery-grey suit and a hard hat. His features reminded me of the cliffs at South Head, and his nose, which had evidently been broken at some time, had a disposition to lounge about his face. I pictured him shaving with a hammer and a cold chisel.

'I hope so, Mr Slatter,' I replied.

'Call me Woggo,' he said, spitting over my shoulder. 'All the boys call me that. Where's Dogsbody?' he added, gazing around.

I concluded that 'Dogsbody' was the inebriated Mr Simpson's trade name and turned to see him a little distance away, leaning on Stanley and breathing very confidentially into his face.

'Come on, Dosb'dy,' bawled Woggo. 'We're going inter the ring.'

I took Daisy's arm and moved off towards the betting-ring.

'Your friend has evidently been looking on the wine when it was red,' I remarked to her.

'He'd look on it if it was purple and had frogs in it.' She squeezed my arm. 'Glad you came, honey,' she said.

'Have you known Mr Slatter long?' I asked.

'Woggo? He's all right. We get the dinkum oil off him. He knows all the jockeys and trainers and everything. He was born in a horse-trough and carried round in a nosebag when he was a child. You don't want to worry about him.'

'What does he know for this race?'

She stopped and put her mouth close to my ear. 'King Rabbit,' she whispered. 'He's an outsider and he'll be any old price. Put a couple of pounds on for me.'

She kissed me on the ear. She was a just a gimme-girl, but twenty years of life fell from me, and I kicked them out of the way as I walked on.

The frantic clamour of the bookmakers roared around us as we entered the ring. Men and women surged about the stands hurling money away with both hands. Punters pleaded to be allowed to lay odds on the favourite and elbowed each other out of the way in their earnest desire to be robbed.

Tip-slingers, urgers and whisperers slunk like jackals through the crowd, and grave and massive policemen placed their furtive bets. I shrunk from the ordeal, but how can man die better than by facing fearful odds? The rest of the gang came up and, with a parting glance at Daisy, I plunged into the riot.

Pausing at a stand, I addressed the open mouth of a bawling bookmaker.

'What price King Rabbit?'

'Oo? King Rabbit? Never 'eard of it. King Rabbit? Ar, yer, four to one, King Rabbit.'

I turned away.

'Well, eight to one,' he bawled. 'Tens!'

I continued on my way.

'Fifteens!' he yelled. 'Twenties! Well, go to blazes!'

I emerged at long last with my head throbbing under Temple's hat and the dust of conflict clinging to my boots. Daisy was waiting for me, with Maureen. I handed her a ticket.

'Sixty-eight pounds!' she shrieked. 'He must have been thirty-three to one!'

'You went to a good school,' I said.

'Gimme half if it wins,' pleaded Maureen.

Daisy impaled her with a glance.

'This is my ticket,' she said coldly. 'Stanley will get yours.'

'But he's only putting ten shillings on for me,' wailed Maureen.

'Faulty work,' said Daisy succinctly. 'Come and we'll watch the race, honey,' she added, taking my arm.

Never, never shall I forget that race. When I am old and peevish, sans teeth, sans hair, and shod with elastic-sided boots, I shall be content merely with the memory of that race. When St Peter asks me my greatest display of charity and fortitude on earth, my answer will be that I refrained from choking Daisy when King Rabbit won the Grantham Stakes.

When the barrier went up, the jockey seemed quite oblivious to the fact that I had four pounds on his mount. He appeared to go to sleep on the horse's neck. They wallowed round the bend behind everything else that had legs. The jockey seemed to be about as useful as a wart on the hip and I groaned aloud.

To this day, I believe the horse heard me. He laid his ears back, opened his mouth and accelerated. He threw his legs about in wild abandon. His hoofs touched the turf merely here and there. He flung himself along like a thing gone mad. His tail stood out. Like a chestnut bullet he sped past the field, past the favourite, past the winning-post, and twice around the course before he could be pulled up. Doped, of course.

The great, beautiful, brave beast, may he live for a hundred years and die in a lucerne paddock surrounded by his progeny.

Hoarse with shouting, my hands sore from beating the railing, I assisted the almost unconscious Daisy out of the crowd. The stricken punters were very, very quiet and the happy laughter of the bookmakers plunged the iron into their souls.

Thirty-three to one! Even now my hand trembles as I write.

One hundred and thirty-six pounds I collected, and sixty-eight for Daisy. If horses have halos when they die, King Rabbit should look like a zebra. We were joined by the rest of the party. I wanted to go home. I was padded with notes. Daisy was crying on my shoulder; Maureen was in the charge of the matron in the ladies' waiting-room; Stanley and the drunken Simpson were dancing like bears in the midst of an interested crowd.

Woggo Slatter stood aloof and not a pore of his skin opened or shut. Not a smile disturbed his granite face. A cigarette hung from the corner of his mouth, and when I sighted him he was buying a packet of chewing gum. Chewing gum! Fancy him being able to chew.

I parked Daisy in the grandstand and went to him.

'Thanks for the tip, old man,' I said, grasping him by the hand. 'Thanks very much.'

''Sall right,' he drawled. 'We has our lucky days. I might want ter put the fangs inter you for twenty or so one er these days. What are you goin' to do now?'

'I'm going home.'

He shifted his cigarette to the other side of his mouth.

'Don't go yet,' he said. 'Got another one. Be a short price, but it's good.'

He tipped his hat over one eye and walked away.

Stanley touched my arm.

'Hello!' I said. 'Corroboree finished?'

'The police stopped it,' he whispered.

'What are you whispering for? Are they after you?'

'No,' he said in an almost inaudible voice, 'it's my throat. I couldn't talk at all a while ago. I don't care if I'm never able to yell again. Wasn't it wonderful?'

'Oh, fair performance, I suppose. What are you going to do now?'

'I'm going home if I can get away from Maureen,' he whispered.

I studied the nail on my little finger for a moment. 'Don't go yet,' I said. 'Got another one. Short price, but good,' and tilting my hat over my forehead I strolled away and left him gaping.

Returning to the stand, I found Maureen and Daisy sitting with their heads close together. Their talk ceased suddenly as I came up to them. I know women. I buttoned my coat and sat down warily.

'Oh, gee!' sighed Maureen. 'Wasn't it just too lovely! Whatever are you going to buy me with all that money?'

'If you'll excuse me, Maureen,' said Daisy in a chilly voice, 'Jack is *my* friend. Go and find Stanley.'

'I like Stan,' murmured Maureen, 'but I don't value his friendship half as much as Jack's. Besides, he's only a boy, really, isn't he?'

I felt that I was being haggled over. Stanley had evidently been weighed in the balance and found to be under the limit.

'What about Woggo?' I suggested.

'Woggo!' they echoed. 'Ha! Ha!'

That let Woggo out. He was either a member of the syndicate or an abandoned mine.

'Do you know what this next winner is going to be?' I asked, to change the subject.

'Dunno,' answered Daisy. 'Woggo will tell you when the time comes. Here he is now.'

Woggo strolled into view and halted before us. Fixing his gaze on the horizon, he slowly stroked his left ear with three fingers, spat aimlessly in the general direction of the betting-ring and moved on. Maureen and Daisy hurriedly turned the pages of their racebooks.

'Number three, Useless Annie!' they gasped in unison.

'What about her?' I queried, looking around.

'That's it,' gabbled Maureen. 'That's the pea. Where's Stanley?' She jumped to her feet and scurried away.

'What do I do now?' I asked, turning to Daisy.

'All you've got to do now is to empty the roll out on Useless Annie—and make it snappy. Off you go! I'll wait here.'

'The whole lot!' I gasped.

'Absolutely,' she said, giving me a push. 'Put a pony on for me.'

I hurried away and burrowed into the betting-ring. A striving elbow bored into my ear as I squirmed through the crowd. It was Stanley. I might have known that with practically the whole population of Sydney collected in one place, Stanley would single me out for injury.

I stamped heavily on his foot.

'Sorry, Stan,' I said, patting him on the shoulder, 'it's the crowd you know. What's a pony?'

'Thassall right, Dad,' he replied, 'that wasn't my foot. A pony is a little horse.'

He was swept away on a wave of punters before I could land him one. Useless Annie, as Woggo foretold, was a short price. One Hennessy, on the outer edge of the ring, who may possibly have been one of the lost tribe, offered to lay me fifty pounds to forty and I passed up the money. He made a quivering stab with his pencil at the betting-ticket and passed the result down to me.

'What's this?' I asked, staring at the Morse code on the ticket.

'Useless,' he snapped, glaring at me. 'A pony, fifty pounds to forty. That's vat you vant, ain't it?'

'Useless Annie?' I inquired meekly.

'Ah, Gor!' he moaned. 'Can't you read?'

'All right, all right,' I muttered, and wandered away to the bar.

A flying barman, handling glasses like a nervous octopus, extracted the order from between my teeth before I could utter it, and sped away.

'Snappy, eh?' commented Stanley. He was at my elbow. Ubiquitous.

'Stanley,' I said, producing the ticket, 'what do you make of this?'

'Useless Annie,' he said, glancing at it. 'Who put you onto that zoo fodder?'

'Slatter.'

'The urger with the ironstone complexion?'

I nodded uneasily.

'One born every day,' he muttered, shaking his head at his glass. 'One a minute.'

'What's wrong with it?' I demanded.

He leaned towards me. 'Useless Annie's in the bag,' he whispered. 'I've backed Bonser Baby. Get on while you've got time.'

'But . . .' I faltered, waving my ticket.

'Well, of course, if you don't want to—don't,' he said, shrugging his shoulders.

'Do you think I ought to?'

He glanced at me pityingly. 'Anyone picked your pocket yet?'

'No.'

'Hmm, funny,' he said. Then fiercely he added, 'Go and get your money on. Leave your drink; I'll look after that.'

I gulped my drink and hurried away with my mind in a whirl.

The bookmakers were howling that they were prepared to lay five to one against Bonser Baby and I took a hundred and fifty to thirty pounds in three bets. I stood to win one hundred and fifty, or flay my thirty pounds' worth out of Stanley. Something seemed to tell me that I would win. I felt confident. I decided to avoid Daisy for the nonce, and took up a position near the track to watch the race.

It wasn't a race. Some dissatisfied gentleman close to me remarked that it was 'a mere sanguinary, lightning-struck, blasted, confounded and unmentionable procession.' Useless Annie might have been sired by a rocking-horse, and as regards its dam, it was damned by all present. The jockey made a ferocious display with his whip and then realistically fell off and left his horse to browse the track.

Bonser Baby was in front, with another horse gaining on it rapidly and for a moment it looked as if the jockey of that horse would have to fall off too. Fortunately Bonser Baby, with the fear of the bone-yard in him, speeded up his lollipop and staggered past the post amid a chorus of congratulatory groans. The race had not the thrill of the previous one, and although I was pleased to collect my winnings, I was not excited. My presentiments were returning.

I sought Daisy and handed her the ticket for Useless Annie. 'I put fifty on for you,' I said with a wry smile, 'the remainder I put on for myself.'

I sat down heavily beside her.

'Oh, what a pity!' cried Daisy. 'You poor thing! Are you absolutely broke?'

'Penniless,' I muttered.

'And you put fifty on for me! That was sporty of you, Jack. Here, you'd better take this fiver.'

I waved it aside.

'Don't be foolish,' she said, pressing it into my hand. I took it and thanked her.

'Hard luck,' I groaned.

'Absolutely.'

The stand was half full, but she put her arm round my neck, and drawing my head close to her mouth kissed me on the chin. 'There's possibilities in you, honey,' she whispered.

''Ullo! Wot's this?' grated a harsh voice.

I looked up and quickly declutched. Slatter was glaring at me and chewing his lip. He looked, to put it mildly, discontented. I felt an empty feeling in my stomach as I rose to my feet. It looked like an even chance of my becoming a co-respondent or a corpse.

'It's all right,' cried Daisy, rising.

Keeping my eyes on Slatter, I edged, crabwise, away from him.

'Well, so long,' I called, waving my arm.

''Ere!' growled Woggo.

I hurried on.

'Come 'ere. I want yer!' he bawled savagely.

I broke into a trot.

''Ell!' he bellowed, and started after me.

It was then that the benefits of living a more or less clean life came to my aid. There, on that day, without thought of honour or reward, I put up a performance that would have given any Olympic Games aspirant a lesson. I flashed past Stanley, who was strolling towards the gates with Maureen clinging to his arm like some parasitic growth.

'Father!' he yelled.

'Pace me, boy,' I gasped.

'Hey!' called a policeman, dashing towards me.

I slowed down as Stanley came beside me.

'Whatever you've pinched,' he panted, 'hand it over to me. They're bound to search you.'

'What's all this?' boomed the constable.

'It—it's his wife,' gasped Stanley. 'She's dying. We must get a taxi.'

I caught a glimpse of Woggo temporarily off the scent in the crowd.

'Dying?' queried the constable.

'Yes,' I gulped.

'While the Spring Meeting's on!' he gasped incredulously.

I nodded vigorously. Woggo had sighted us.

'My gore!' said the policeman. 'You can't beat women.'

'Come on, Stanley!' I cried, and bounded towards the gate.

''Ere!' shouted Woggo.

'Stop!' bawled another policeman.

'Taxi, sir,' queried an angel in uniform, as we dashed out the gate.

I hurled Stanley in and threw myself on top of him.

'Woollahra!' I yelled. 'Drive like hell!'

Stanley sat down and straightened his tie as the car bounded away. 'Referring to the car in front,' he said, 'do we shoot to kill, in the event of its stopping?'

'If you're trying to be funny, Stanley,' I said, scrambling to my knees, 'you have selected an inopportune time and run a grave risk of disfigurement for life.'

'Well, what's it all about?'

'Woggo was going to assault me,' I hissed, seating myself.

'Was he? And yet when I first saw him I didn't like him. Funny how you can be mistaken about a feller.' He shook his head and sighed. 'And I helped you to get away,' he muttered.

FATHER RILEY'S HORSE

A.B. 'BANJO' PATERSON

'Twas the horse thief, Andy Regan, that was hunted like a dog
By the troopers of the Upper Murray side,
They had searched in every gully—they had looked in every log,
But never sight or track of him they spied,
Till the priest at Kiley's Crossing heard a knocking very late
And a whisper, 'Father Riley—come across!'
So his Reverence, in pyjamas, trotted softly to the gate
And admitted Andy Regan—and a horse!

'Now, it's listen, Father Riley, to the words I've got to say,
For it's close upon my death I am tonight;
With the troopers hard behind me I've been hiding all the day
In the gullies, keeping close and out of sight.
But they're watching all the ranges till there's not a bird could fly,
And I'm fairly worn to pieces with the strife;
So I'm taking no more trouble, but I'm going home to die,
'Tis the only way I see to save my life!

'Yes, I'm making home to mother's, and I'll die a Tuesday next
And be buried on the Thursday—and, of course,
I'm prepared to meet my penance, but with one thing I'm perplexed
And it's—Father, it's this jewel of a horse!
He was never bought nor paid for, and there's not a man can swear
To his owner or his breeder, but I know,
That his sire was by Pedantic from the Old Pretender mare
And his dam was close related to The Roe.

'And there's nothing in the district that can race him for a step;
He could canter while they're going at their top:
He's the king of all the leppers that was ever seen to lep,
A five-foot fence—he'd clear it in a hop!
So I'll leave him with you, Father, till the dead shall rise again;
'Tis yourself that knows a good 'un; and, of course,
You can say he's got by Moonlight out of Paddy Murphy's plain
If you're ever asked the breeding of the horse!

'But it's getting on to daylight and it's time to say goodbye,
For the stars above the east are growing pale.
And I'm making home to mother; and it's hard for me to die!
But it's harder still, is keeping out of gaol!
You can ride the old horse over to my grave across the dip
Where the wattle bloom is waving overhead.
Sure he'll jump them fences easy; you must never raise the whip
Or he'll rush 'em! now, goodbye!' and he had fled.

So they buried Andy Regan, and they buried him to rights,
In the graveyard at the back of Kiley's Hill;
There were five-and-twenty mourners who had five-and-twenty fights
Till the very boldest fighters had their fill.
There were fifty horses racing from the graveyard to the pub,
And their riders flogged each other all the while.
And the lashin's of the liquor! And the lavin's of the grub!
Oh! poor Andy went to rest in proper style.

Then the races came to Kiley's—with a steeplechase and all,
For the folk were mostly Irish round about,
And it takes an Irish rider to be fearless of a fall;
They were training morning in and morning out.
But they never worked their horses till the sun was on the course
For a superstitious story kept 'em back,
That the ghost of Andy Regan, on a slashing chestnut horse,
Had been training by the starlight on the track.

And they read the nominations for the races with surprise
And amusement at the Father's little joke,
For a novice had been entered for the steeplechasing prize,
And they found it was Father Riley's moke!
He was neat enough to gallop, he was strong enough to stay!
But his owner's views of training were immense,
For the Reverend Father Riley used to ride him every day,
And he never saw a hurdle nor a fence.

And the priest would join the laughter, 'Oh,' said he, 'I put him in,
For there's five-and-twenty sovereigns to be won.
And the poor would find it useful, if the chestnut chanced to win,
And he'll maybe win when all is said and done!'
He had called him Faugh-a-ballagh (which is French for 'Clear
the course'),
And his colours were a vivid shade of green:
All the Dooleys and O'Donnells were on Father Riley's horse,
While the Orangemen were backing Mandarin!

It was Hogan, the dog poisoner—old man and very wise,
Who was camping in the racecourse with his swag,
And who ventured the opinion, to the township's great surprise,
That the race would go to Father Riley's nag.
'You can talk about your riders—and the horse has not been schooled,
And the fences is terrific, and the rest!
When the field is fairly going, then ye'll see ye've all been fooled,
And the chestnut horse will battle with the best.

'For there's some has got condition, and they think the race is sure,
And the chestnut horse will fall beneath the weight,
But the hopes of all the helpless, and the prayers of all the poor,
Will be running by his side to keep him straight.
And what's the need of schoolin' or of workin' on the track,
When the saints are there to guide him round the course!
I've prayed him over every fence—I've prayed him out and back!
And I'll bet my cash on Father Riley's horse!'

Oh, the steeple was a caution! They went tearin' round and round,
And the fences rang and rattled where they struck.
There was some that cleared the water, there was more fell in and
drowned,
Some blamed the men and others blamed the luck!
But the whips were flying freely when the field came into view,
For the finish down the long green stretch of course,
And in front of all the flyers—jumping like a kangaroo,
Came the rank outsider—Father Riley's horse!

Oh, the shouting and the cheering as he rattled past the post!
For he left the others standing in the straight;
And the rider—well they reckoned it was Andy Regan's ghost,
And it beat 'em how a ghost would draw the weight!
But he weighed in, nine stone seven, then he laughed and
disappeared,
Like a banshee (which is Spanish for an elf),
And old Hogan muttered sagely, 'If it wasn't for the beard
They'd be thinking it was Andy Regan's self!'

And the poor of Kiley's Crossing gave their thanks at Christmastide
To the chestnut and his jockey dressed in green.
There was never such a rider, not since Andy Regan died,
And they wondered who on earth it could have been.
But they settled it among 'em, for the story got about,
'Mongst the bushmen and the people on the course,
That the Devil had been ordered to let Andy Regan out
For the steeplechase on Father Riley's horse!

Note: I find this poem very amusing in an Irish accent. It is the only poem I know of Paterson's, apart from 'A Bush Christening', where he uses zany 'Irish humour' with jokes such as 'a banshee (which is Spanish for an elf)' and 'He had called him Faugh-a-ballagh (which is French for "Clear the course")'. Faugh-a-ballagh is an ancient Irish battle cry which means, in Gaelic, 'Get out of the way' or 'clear the way'. It is the motto of the Royal Irish Regiment.

HARRY CALLS A WINNER

WAYNE PEAKE

From Wayne's collection of humorous racing stories, The Gambler's Ghost, *Ascot Press, 2012*

***

Harry Trump had been a race-caller for more than thirty years. He had started out in the days when broadcasters were banned from racecourses, and had had to rely on their own inventiveness to call races from the outer. He had called the 1937 Melbourne Cup from half way up a tree on the far side of the Maribyrnong River, and in the excitement of the finish had fallen out and almost hanged himself on the microphone lead.

He had called from the top of removalists' vans, mounted on fire-engine ladders, lowered from a French aviator's dirigible airship, and on one memorable occasion on a trampoline, when he'd had to time his bounce so that he was in the air as the horses passed the post. He had called camel races in North Africa with the Second AIF. During a fact finding tour of world racing venues in 1957, he had outraged the British by falling down the grandstand steps blind drunk at Royal Ascot (his dislodged top hat landing in the lap of the Queen Mother), and bemused the Americans at the Kentucky Derby, on spotting the dirt track, by commenting that he'd never seen a racecourse in worse condition, even in Woop-Woop. He advised any who cared to listen (and many others who would rather have not) that they should transfer the Derby to another course until the grass had had a chance to grow back.

Harry's manner of speech was colourful and dotted with turf metaphors, and he invariably addressed his interlocutors as 'sport', or 'brother', which saved him the bother of remembering names. His clothes were equally idiosyncratic, whether observed at the bar of the local RSL or the races; two-tone shoes with pointy toes, voluminous bottle green trousers, vest and hound's-tooth sports jacket with red-rose buttonhole, felt hat turned down at the front. From beneath the hat wafted the elusive scent of an exotic hair oil. He had a glossy art-deco haircut like Bill Ponsford the 1920s cricketer that reflected the light like a wet road at night.

On race days Harry was preceded through the entrance to the commentary box by a battered old Gladstone bag. The bag contained the four tools of the trade to which Harry attributed his great success. These were a set of ancient but excellent binoculars, a little battery operated fan, a facecloth steeped in Eau De Cologne, and a bottle of black label scotch.

As the years passed this last item increasingly diverted Harry's attention from the first three. It would perhaps have been going too far too describe Harry as a booze hound—he would have scoffed at the idea himself—but a lot of listeners came to feel that Harry's first call of the day usually had much greater clarity than the last.

One Thursday morning in the late 1960s Harry was not particularly surprised to be summoned to radio 2RAW station manager Joe Jones's office. Though he was seriously hung-over, he had some recollection of an unfortunate incident the previous day at Randwick, something to do with the last race, maybe . . .

Joe Jones quickly provided the forgotten details. 'You called the wrong horse the winner, Harry!' he said, pointing at the photo-strip of the finish in the racing paper.

'Oh, yeah—I remember now. Sorry, sport. You know it was that bloody silly old "Crasher" Gates's fault. If a trainer's goin' to start two horses in a race, why doesn't he make sure that their colours are different? Where's the sense in using the stable colours on both and puttin' a white cap on one jockey, and a yellow cap on the other? Eh? Askin' for trouble, I reckon. But look—sorry—I'll be more careful here-on-in.'

'It's not that easy, Harry. Do you know who owns that horse you called the winner?'

'Nope—enlighten me.'

'Never noticed a bloke being chauffeur-driven to the front door here in a silver Rolls Royce?'

'Little shifty lookin' bloke with beady eyes in a homburg hat?'

'That is he. Sir Reginald Barry is his name—ring a bell? He happens to be the owner of this station. Yes, he's the man who's been covering your gambling losses these last twenty years. He also happens to be the owner of that nag you called the winner of the last race. However, as the morning paper reveals, it did not win, but rather ran twenty-eighth in a field of twenty-nine.'

'Big field, that,' Harry pointed out.

'Big mistake, I'm afraid, Harry.' Jones sighed as he opened a drawer in his desk and withdrew a sealed envelope. He handed it to Harry. 'Sorry to do this to you, old boy.'

'What's this—tickets to the opera or somethin'?' asked Harry, looking with distaste at the envelope.

'No, it's your final cheque, Harry. You're fired.'

'Fired!'

'Effective immediately. Please clear your desk and be off the premises within the hour.'

'Hang on, don't I get a second chance? This is the first blue I've made since that triple dead heat in the '56 Hotham Handicap.'

'Sir Reginald doesn't give second chances, especially when the mistake is one that affects his pocket. He laid out big on that horse yesterday Harry, and as he couldn't be at the track, he listened in on the radio. Do you get the picture?'

'You mean he was listening to me—and I called his horse the winner when it wasn't? S'truth, no wonder he's a bit dirty on the world.'

'He's more than dirty, Harry—he's as cranky as a jockey forced to waste at Christmas. And Mr Barry is a very mean man. He's so careful I heard he found a band-aid once and cut himself because he couldn't wait to use it straight away. And, what's more, he's decided that you were shickered when you called that race.

He's a typical big businessman; vindictive, doesn't like to be let down by underlings. Really, you're lucky he's decided to break only your contract and not your legs as well.'

'Still, it isn't my fault that 'is horse is a hay bandit,' Harry replied.

Joe Jones's craggy features softened slightly. 'You understand this isn't my doing, Harry. I hate to turn a legend like you out on the streets with the finishing post almost in sight. But it's out of my hands—you see?'

'Yeah, yeah,' responded Harry absent-mindedly, suddenly wishing that he had opened a savings account thirty years ago rather than last week. For Harry knew what this sacking meant. Race-callers, unlike brickies' labourers or short-order cooks, are not advertised for each morning in the *Herald*. Opportunities are finite and limited. And if word got out that he'd been full on the job . . . which it had by lunchtime . . .

***

It was a day some six months later when Harry Trump, a couple of days' growth on his chin, approached the entrance of his bank. In his hand was a cheque in his favour drawn against the account of his sister Beryl. He had received several similar cheques in recent months, the amount each time smaller than last. He was now firmly advised that this was the last of its kind that he could expect to receive. The family, he was told, was no longer prepared to pay for his stabling.

It had been a tough six months, Harry reflected. As he had anticipated, offers of work were not forthcoming. Doors slammed in his face with cyclonic ferocity. In the first weeks Harry had gathered up what little assets he could claim as his own and converted them to cash money. His aspiration was to eke out a modest existence punting. But Harry found that he had little talent for identifying winners—a fairly essential component of the skill-set of a successful professional punter.

It dawned on Harry for the first time that he had always been a lousy judge—good race-caller, but a lousy judge. What winners he had backed were almost always the result of inside information he'd received at the track. He was suddenly aware, albeit without any sense of guilt, of the financial deprivations that anyone who had followed his tips for any length of time must have suffered. How many marriages had he sent down the gurgler, he wondered.

There was just one other customer in the bank when Harry entered, an elderly gentleman in a hat, who was already being attended to by one of the tellers. Harry waited his turn at the top of the otherwise empty queue.

'Next, please,' called the other teller, who was now free. He smiled at Harry.

Harry began to move forward, but he happened to look down and notice that one of his shoelaces had worked free.

'Bugger!' he said to himself. 'Hang on, mate,' he called to the teller. 'I've loosened a plate here! I'll 'ave to be reshod! Be with you in a moment.'

Harry noticed an artificial palm tree in the corner of the bank. It was housed in a planter box which he judged was just the right height, if rested on, to enable him to re-tie his shoelace. He shuffled over to the box with this in mind.

Now, as a race-caller, there was one area where the public always agreed that Harry had it all over his rivals. He had an uncanny ability to call the 'swoopers'—the horses finishing fast from the rear in the last half furlong in big fields—much earlier than anyone else.

Although Harry just took this talent for granted he was in fact blessed with exceptionally good peripheral vision. At that moment, courtesy of this great gift, he was aware of a sudden, violent movement almost directly behind him. And even as this movement registered in his brain, it was joined by an instinctive suspicion that whatever was its source, it bode no good for Harry Trump.

It was well known among returned servicemen that while with the Second AIF in North Africa Harry had also developed great expertise in finding cover, even in the seemingly featureless desert, to avoid contact with the enemy, and he didn't hesitate to put that skill to good use now. He had already begun to bend down to tie his lace, but now he modified that movement into a neat forward tumble that carried him over the planter box and out of sight behind the palm tree.

Harry quickly righted himself and looked forward into the bank from between two palm fronds. He was certain that the tree would conceal his presence from anyone standing in the public section of the floor.

He saw three men wearing masks rush into the bank. The foremost was waving a sawn-off shot gun at the bank officials and the lone customer.

'Property is theft!' he cried in a gravelly voice. 'You pair!' he called to the tellers. 'Turn around and put your hands up! Now!'

'Right, lads,' he said to his two accomplices, 'get over the counter and get the cash—and don't muck around. They've probably hit the alarm already.'

As his partners leapt the counter, the man with the gun and gravelly voice turned to the elderly customer. 'OK, old man, you can reach, as well,' he ordered. Then he grabbed the lapel of the old man's suit and rubbed it between his thumb and index finger. 'Say, great bag of fruit this! Top of the range cloth, that. Bet this didn't come off the rack at Solly Cohen's cheap-and-cheerful menswear, eh? You're some sort of capitalist, I'll warrant. Hand over your roll so I can redistribute some of your surplus of production!'

'This is an outrage!' spluttered the Suit.

'*Nyet*, Rockefeller,' responded the robber, firing a shot into the air, then bringing the butt of his rifle down on the customer's head. As that person crumpled to the floor, he reached inside the victim's coat and removed a plump wallet which he replaced in his own pocket.

'Jeez, I'm well out of this,' said Harry to himself, concealed behind his tree. 'Worse than bloody Tobruk.'

Then Harry heard the sound of a distant siren, rapidly drawing nearer. The gang-leader heard it too, and he cocked his head, as though to discern which direction the sound came from.

'Fall back, boys, it's the cops,' he yelled to his henchmen.

Obediently his deputies leapt out and sprinted for the door. Gravel Voice backed behind them providing cover. As he reached the door he called to the bank clerks, 'Come after me and I'll blow a God-damn hole in you!' Then he turned and ran off.

Moments later three policemen entered the bank. Once it was clear that the robbers had fled two of them set off in pursuit. The third, a young man of self-confident bearing, had been at the scene several minutes before Harry decided it was safe to emerge from his hiding spot. With a rustle of palm fronds he stepped out into the open. The policeman, who had begun interviewing the tellers, turned at the sound.

'Hello, where have you come from?' he asked Harry.

'Oh, I'd forgotten. This gentleman was in the line before the robbers struck,' said one of the tellers. His eyes narrowed. 'Perhaps he is an accomplice!'

'Accomplice nothin',' Harry said, 'I just came here to cash me tight sister's *Kleine* cheque.' He noted a safe, its door swinging open, its interior empty. 'And I suppose that plan's a late scratchin', and all, judging by the hungry look of that cashbox.'

'Never mind about that,' said the policeman. 'I was just about to ask these fellows for a description of the criminals.'

But the bank men could offer little help, as they had been made to face the wall during most of the raid. Both also frankly admitted that they had been too scared to notice much anyway.

The police officer looked Harry up and down, then asked none too hopefully, 'I don't suppose that you, sir, would be able to describe—'

Harry cleared his throat like he used to when the runners were moving into the starting barrier.

'Maybe I can at that, captain,' he said. 'Now: there were three of these blokes. The first—the one who thought he was Ned Kelly holdin' up the bank at Euroa—was wearing a sort of khaki blouse with a belt around it, and a houndstooth floppy cap like the pommy workers wear.'

'Hey, that's right!' confirmed one of the tellers. 'I remember now.'

'The second bloke,' continued Harry, 'was wearing white and

blue striped seersucker trousers, and a tan jacket with white arm-bands.'

'That's the fellow!' agreed the teller again. 'Bloody crook dresser, he was!'

'And the last one,' went on Harry again, closing his eyes, 'green gabardine trousers with white contrast stitching, blue body shirt with dark blue yoke and inlays under the armpits. White footie beanie with red stripes and pom-pom.'

'Pop, you ought to be a race-caller,' said the police officer, busily scribbling notes onto a pad. 'You've got a great memory for colours.'

'As a matter of fact, Chief Inspector, I'm Harry Trump, the legendary broadcaster who—'

'Some other time,' cut in the policeman. 'What about the height, weight—distinguishing features—of these offenders?'

'Pah! Statistics! Such things mean nothing to me. I'm a colours man.'

'You should try to be more versatile, like Bill Collins. He sings and dances on the telly, as well as calls races and wrestling at the Olympics!' said the policeman, who Harry now suspected of being a Melburnian.

At that point the other policemen returned to report they had lost the robbers. The first told them to call an ambulance for the injured customer, who was still lying unconscious on the floor.

The policeman barked out a few more orders to his colleagues. For some reason he then took Harry Trump into his confidence. 'Of course, we'll never get them now. Got away scot-free. Who knows where they're heading?'

'As a matter of fact, major, I might be able to help you there as well,' said Harry.

'Oh! And how is that?'

'Look, one of those characters had a race-book sticking out of his sky-rocket.'

'So what?'

'It was for a provincial trot meeting run later this afternoon—a non-TAB meeting. Now, most blokes only carry a form guide if they're planning to have a bet, see, and as this meeting's non TAB—and as you and I both know, field marshal, there's no such thing as SP betting—then I reckon maybe—'

'Are you trying to tell me that if we go to this race meeting we're going to find these fellows there betting on the trots?'

'It might be a rough chance, brother,' said Harry to the constable, 'but these long shots get up some times—that I can vouch for better than any man alive.'

'If these fellows operate on the trots it would explain why they've taken to robbing banks,' put in one of the tellers. 'Now I think of it, too, the leader sounded a bit like a revolutionary; he shouted something about the redistribution of wealth on his way out. That might account for the poor taste in clothes.'

'Cripes, a trots man and a commie!' Harry exclaimed. 'Talk about drawing an outside barrier twice!'

'All right, I'll call the sarge and see what he thinks,' said the constable. 'Meanwhile, old timer, I'll take some personal details from you, if you don't mind.'

***

That night Harry received a call from the jubilant police constable to tell him that what had quickly become known as the 'red-hots gang' had been picked up during the afternoon at the trot meeting. After observing the activities of the threesome for some time, undercover police moved in and made an arrest. The credit was due entirely to Harry, said the policeman generously.

'We've recovered the entire proceeds of the bank robbery, as well as the wallet of the gentleman who was assaulted during the raid,' went on the constable. 'We've also got a fair bit of cash above and beyond that.'

The policeman had taken a shine to Harry. Again he became matey and confidential. 'Believe it or not, those crims had backed the first three winners straight at long odds before we caught up with them. Half the bookies had jumped in their Valiants and headed for the hills. Our undercover boys didn't arrest the gang straight away—decided to see if their luck held. Fair dinkum, they got the next two up as well, both at ten-to-one. Our boys collected from the tote, went to the bar for a round of drinks, and then moved in. The bookies stood to a man and cheered when they saw those blokes being led off the course in handcuffs. By the way, the wallet has been returned to the victim of the assault, and he has been informed of the major part you played in its recovery.'

'How is the old coot, anyway,' asked Harry, though not in fact much interested.

'Oh, he's not doing so badly,' said the police constable. 'In fact, the hospital's released him. He's a big shot, you know. He'd like to meet you. Could you arrange to call in down here at the station tomorrow morning? I reckon he has some kind of a reward in mind.'

'Beauty! What time do you open?' asked Harry quickly.

'Harry, we're not like the pub—we don't have licensed hours. But he asked if you could make it at about 10 o'clock.'

'I'll be there, you can take the odds to that,' promised Harry.

Next morning Harry was shown into the sergeant's office. Seated before the desk was a man whose small head was swathed in a large bandage. Harry guessed correctly that it was the man from the bank, whom he had not really looked at closely before. Now as he studied the gentleman, it occurred to him there was something vaguely familiar about the fellow—his small stature, bristling moustache, and beady eye.

Harry started slightly as he recognised the man as his erstwhile employer, Sir Reginald Barry. Barry himself had a sharp intake of breath, which indicated to Harry that recognition had been mutual.

'Anything wrong, sir?' asked the police sergeant, noting the wealthy man's reaction.

'Er—no sergeant. It's just that this man is a former employee of mine who lost his position as a consequence of—well, I needn't go into that.'

Sir Reginald turned to Harry.

'Mr Trump, I have been informed by the police that my billfold, which contained some very important personal effects, as well as a large sum of cash, was restored to me primarily because of a remarkable piece of observation on your part, as well as a very sharp piece of deductive reasoning.'

'No worries,' responded Harry magnanimously.

'It had been my intention, sergeant, to make a substantial cash award to this person, in order to express my gratitude. I think, however, that in these extraordinary circumstances, I can do better than that. It is clear, Trump, that you have lost none of the skills of your calling, of, er, *calling*. It would be a great pity to continue to see them go to waste. I think it would be best for everyone if you came back to work for us.'

'Mind you, Harry, there's been a changing of the guard in your absence,' said Sir Reginald later, when they were alone for a moment. 'I'm afraid you won't be the top dog anymore. Broderick Kent, who has come up from our sister station in Victoria, is now the number one race-caller.'

Harry was at the point of telling Sir Reginald that in his opinion Broderick Kent could not call a hungry hog to a feed, but he wisely decided that a policy of diplomacy and humility was better value, so he kept this assessment to himself. Which was as well, for Kent was Sir Reginald's nephew.

Instead Harry responded, 'Think nothing of it, your honour; I know I'm no longer the stable favourite, but I need regular racing. Being in the spelling paddock when the races are on is no good to me.'

'You will, of course, have to be done with this debilitating dependency on alcohol—'

'Haven't touched a drop these six months, so help me!' lied Harry easily, glad that his flask of Corio 'Five Star' Whisky was safely out of sight in his coat pocket.

'Very well, then. Report for duty to Joseph Jones in the morning. He will be expecting you.'

'Goodo, sport—er, boss, that is.'

'Yes.'

And while it is not true that a bottle of black label whisky never again ascended from the old Gladstone bag on race days, Joe Jones gave Harry an assistant whose primary task, apart from placing Harry's bets, was to ensure it stayed more or less out of play until after the last race. At the time of his retirement some years later, Harry had accumulated a 'cunning kick' sufficient to keep him in comfort the rest of his days.

Part 5
THE CUP IS MORE THAN A HORSE RACE

INTRODUCTION—A BRIEF HISTORY OF THE CUP

That Cup Day and Anzac Day are the most iconic cultural events in our national calendar is self-evident. For better or for worse, these two days are the ones that Australians have taken to their hearts and singled out as special celebrations of our lifestyle, heritage and national character.

The Cup is surrounded every year by a media frenzy, which includes masses of trivia, history, statistics, tall tales and drama from the past, and a myriad of myths and legends.

Since the Cup was first run in 1861 the Australian public have clamoured to believe the most ridiculous and romantic tales of coincidence, supernatural premonition and divine intervention. Each year brings new examples of heroism and perseverance as horses and jockeys and trainers battle, overcoming seemingly insurmountable odds, to achieve victory.

The Cup was, in a sense, born out of rivalry between two racing clubs: the Victoria Turf Club and the Victoria Jockey Club. It was the brainchild of Captain Standish, Chief Commissioner of Police in Melbourne and VTC Chairman at the time.

Until 1854 Melbourne races were run annually in the autumn. Then the Victoria Turf Club decided to hold a spring meeting as well. The Cup was first run in November 1861 at Flemington, which had originally been called Melbourne Racecourse and was first used as a racecourse as far back as March 1840.

The new race attracted top inter-colonial horses, including the winner, Archer, from New South Wales. This began a great Cup tradition of interstate rivalry, or inter-colonial rivalry as it was back then.

One of the main reasons for the Cup being established was to assert Melbourne's superiority over Sydney both as a city and as a sporting capital. For many years, from the time of the gold rushes, Melbourne was the most populous and richest city in Australia. Victorians were keen to establish Melbourne as the sporting capital, as well as the financial capital, of all the colonies.

So the Victoria Turf Club announced the running of a great new race. It was to be an egalitarian affair with the best horses carrying extra weight to make the race more equal. The trophy was a gold watch and the prizemoney, of £710, was the most ever put up for a race in the colonies. The wonderful aura of myth, legend and history that surrounds the Cup developed right from the start.

The legend of Archer's two wins, and the myths surrounding those events, the fictitious story of Peter St Albans riding the first female horse to win the Cup—these have become the stuff that dreams are made of. Later came Carbine's famous win under a massive weight, after a brave second the year before with a damaged hoof, and the only undefeated Cup winner Grand Flaneur.

Other Cup folklore has William Evans weighing in unconscious after wasting more than 10 pounds (4.5 kg) in a week to ride the 1907 winner Apologue at 7 st 9 lb (48.5 kg). Evidently the totally exhausted jockey collapsed after the horse passed the post and was placed unconscious on the scales.

Let us hope that Dame Nellie Melba and famous English contralto Dame Clara Butt, whose combined presence on the lawn was the social highlight of Cup Day 1907, were not unduly distressed by witnessing the poor jockey's plight!

The Cup was already well established as the high point of Melbourne's social calendar when poor Evans passed out past the post. Indeed, once the race had recovered from the debacle of 1863 and the two rival race clubs of Melbourne combined to form the Victoria Racing Club (VRC) in 1864, the race quickly developed into far more than a mere rich handicap where horses from all colonies could compete.

The dream of the creators of the race, Captain Standish and the committeemen of the Victoria Turf Club, was to show the Victorian colony's supremacy over New South Wales in all matters, especially sporting matters, by running the richest race on the continent. This was looking like becoming reality as crowd numbers for the event went to 25,000-plus in the first decade of the race's history and had reached a regular 100,000 by the end of the second decade.

Although Melbourne gave way to Sydney as the financial capital of Australia and the most populous city in the 150 years after the Cup was created, it remains the true sporting capital of the nation, largely due to the iconic status of the Melbourne Cup.

Racing has always been a focus for literature, art and romance since the earliest times of the sport in Britain. There is something in the nature and history of the sport which brings to the surface the more imaginative and romantic aspects of our humanity. The nobility and beauty of the horse, the drama of the competition, mere men controlling large and powerful animals—all these things inspire awe and wonder.

The whole fickle and glorious nature of the human drama is intensified and crystallised in the sport of thoroughbred racing. What is it that draws us to the sport? The vicarious thrill of the risks involved? The possibility of making and losing fortunes? The snob appeal of the involvement of the nobility? The possibility that the sport may make a prince from a pauper, and vice versa?

Whatever it is, it is typified and made easy for Australians via the Melbourne Cup. Each year all Aussies can get a massive dose of 'whatever it is' in early November and then return to the humdrum of normality. Those of us afflicted by the 'racing bug' habitually raise our eyebrows at this seasonal invasion of the uneducated into 'our world' and instead enjoy the event as the culmination of the racing season which, for us, lasts twelve months in every year.

The general Australian population of some 23 million can, with the help of the media, enjoy the annual human and equine drama and suspense as the Cup approaches. They are told the usual stories of potential 'rags to riches' battlers, the horses that might compete become characters, and Cup history and mythology is retold to a point that a collective sigh of relief goes up when the gates spring open on that first Tuesday afternoon in November.

After the race comes a week of reflection on the winners and losers. Recent examples of Cup 'drama' being used to create more Cup folklore and provide millions of words in 'human interest' journalism are the amazing stories of Tommy Woodcock and Reckless in 1977, and the spine-tingling win of Damien Oliver and Media Puzzle in 2001, a week after the racetrack death of Damien's brother, Jason. Plus of course, Makybe Diva's three wins and Bart's twelve.

Perhaps the true magic of the Cup is that everyone throughout the country has a way of being involved in racing once a year, in some way or another. Every Aussie gets something from the Cup, has a feeling or opinion about it, and has a way of looking at it.

After all the media attention and the build-up, when the human and equine drama and romance has been played out to the minute, the nation waits for what is the most universally anticipated instant in horseracing each year.

Everyone is carried away by the magic of the Cup, none more than racing people and writers from overseas. Nat Gould was a Cup fanatic during his time in Australia and wrote glowingly about the magic of the Cup and the superior nature of Australian racing when compared to British racing. The most famous and popular writer in the world, Samuel Clemens, or 'Mark Twain', was 'blown away' by the Melbourne Cup.

It is lucky for us that Clemens fell upon hard times and lost his fortune, and his wife's inheritance, by investing everything in his own publishing business and a mechanical typesetting machine that was cutting edge technology at the time but was prone to breakdowns. Before it could be perfected, the system was made obsolete by the linotype machine and the publishing house failed. Clemens was forced to go on the lecture circuit and write travel books, thus he came to Australia and wrote about the Melbourne

Cup! He thought that Cup Day was the supreme day of celebration anywhere in the world.

As the horses are loaded into the starting stalls for the Cup, the entire nation stops. All of us—racing fanatics, totally uneducated once-a-year-mug-punters, the party generation swaying drunk in their stilettos and cheap suits, and prudish aunties with two-dollar sweep tickets—wait for the barrier gates to open.

The nation breathes as one.

Then, with a roar from the course that echoes from every television and radio in the land, and a universal gasp from the rest of us, the gates spring open, our hearts stop and . . . *They're off!*

CUP COUPLETS

C.J. DENNIS

Out of great wisdom, long stored up,
I would write me a rhyme of the Melbourne Cup.
With words of wisdom then let us begin;
For many shall wager, but few shall win.
And first a warning: Go slow this trip,
For there's many a slip 'twixt the Cup and the *tip*.
And the sport of Kings, tho' it capture the town,
Is never for one with but *half-a-crown*.
And this oft is the rule when the lucky man sups:
He is in on the Cup and he's on in his cups.
So this is the motto to hold and to hug:
There is but one Cup; but there's many a *mug*.
So, out or in, if you still can grin,
Here's a glorious day to you, lose or win!

THE LEGEND OF ARCHER

JIM HAYNES

The story of Archer's two victories in the first two Cups is the stuff of legend. This all began with the unlikely tall tale of Archer's long walk to Melbourne to win the Cup, two years in a row. This 'walk' never happened the first time around, let alone twice.

To suggest that Australia's most successful trainer, Etienne de Mestre, would have sent his valuable horse on such an arduous marathon walk is laughable. Yet, many believe it, despite accounts from the time that Archer, like all other normal human beings and horses, made his way to Melbourne by sea.

Newspaper accounts of the day show that Archer left Sydney on 18 September 1861 on the steamer *City of Sydney*, together with two stablemates, Exeter and Inheritor, and arrived at Port Melbourne three days later.

Also on board were Etienne de Mestre, and jockey Johnny 'Cutts', who was, in fact, John 'Cutts' Dillon, one of the most respected jockeys in New South Wales. Despite stories to the contrary, Cutts was not from the Nowra district and never lived there, although his brother-in-law Walter Bradbury worked for de Mestre, and lived at Terara, on de Mestre's property.

This pretty much puts a hole in the theory, or 'legend', that Johnny Cutts was born and raised in the area around Nowra, supposedly one of many Aboriginal stockmen who replaced the stockmen of European descent when they left to join the gold rushes.

There is even a more ridiculous 'legend' that Archer's strapper, Dave Power, not only walked him to Melbourne, but rode him under Cutts' name in the Cup . . . and was of Aboriginal descent.

Perhaps Power walked Archer to the nearest port of embarkation from his home on the south coast of New South Wales, or perhaps he walked him from the Port Melbourne docks to the hotel stables at South Yarra, where he was trained for the first Cup; but he certainly never walked him to Melbourne from his home near Nowra, nor did he ride him in the Cup.

Archer went by steamboat from Sydney to Melbourne three times to compete in Victorian races, in 1861, 1862 and 1863.

De Mestre's horses usually boarded the steamer at Adam's Wharf near his property at Terara, on the Shoalhaven River. However, floods in 1860 altered the course of the river channels and made navigation dangerous. So, from 1860 to 1863, horses needed to be walked to the wharf at Greenwell Point 13 kilometres to the east. Perhaps this was the origin of the 'walking to Melbourne' legend.

The longest distance Archer ever walked was the 250 kilometres from the end of the railway line at Campelltown to his owners' paddock near Braidwood when he retired from racing in 1864.

Etienne de Mestre, cunning as he was, may have enjoyed spreading the ridiculous rumour about the walk as part of his plan to empty the pockets of Melbourne's bookmakers. It is more obvious, however, that he achieved his goal by keeping the horse away from prying eyes and training him in what was then known as St Kilda Park, opposite the Botanical Hotel, where he was stabled in South Yarra.

If looked at devoid of its myths and fairytales, the first Melbourne Cup was a rough-and-tumble affair. One horse bolted off the course during the race, three of the seventeen runners fell and two died. Two jockeys were seriously injured and suffered broken bones.

Archer defeated the favourite, and local champion, Mormon, by 6 lengths in the slowest time in Cup history, 3 minutes 52 seconds, in front of the smallest crowd ever, 4000 people.

Archer had previously defeated Mormon over 2½ miles in the Australia Plate at Randwick. So the form was there to see and de Mestre's betting coup was a real triumph over local pride. An injury to Archer, real or feigned, leading up to the race may have helped the price get out to an appetising 8 to 1 before de Mestre pounced and reduced the odds to 6 to 1.

Archer had won his last seven starts in Sydney, but those wins were spread out over a year and 'inter-colonial' form was not always well known. It was the Cup that would eventually bring Australian champions together from around the continent and give us a real 'Australian racing scene'.

De Mestre single-handedly backed his victorious horse in from 8 to 1 to 6 to 1, with the result that the bookmakers of Melbourne were left reeling and more grist was added to the mill of interstate rivalry, or inter-colonial rivalry, as it then was. A further irony, which modern racegoers may not realise, is that there was no prize at all for running second.

The following day Archer won again, taking out the Melbourne Town Plate, also run over 2 miles.

Neither the handicapper nor the bookmakers of Melbourne missed Archer the following year. Of course, he added another chapter to Cup history by winning yet again, this time defeating Mormon by 8 lengths in spite of carrying 10 st 2 lb (64.5 kg).

The second year the odds were not as juicy. Archer won by 8 lengths, a feat not equalled until Rain Lover won by the same margin in 1968. His trainer took home £810 and another watch. Mormon again ran second and this time collected £20.

The story of how Archer missed running in a third Melbourne Cup is also part of the Cup legend.

In the true spirit of colonial rivalry, Archer was given the massive weight of 11 st 4 lb (72 kg) by the handicapper in 1863. De Mestre had paid the first acceptance fee of 5 sovereigns and was incensed when weights were announced. However, he eventually relented and Archer and another runner from his stable, Haidee, left by steamboat for Melbourne on 16 June.

De Mestre's agents reminded him on 1 July that he needed to send final payment and acceptance that day, so a telegram was sent to the Melbourne office of George Kirk & Co., asking them to accept on his behalf. De Mestre sent the telegram himself, as the due date was a normal working day in New South Wales, and records show it was received at Melbourne Telegraph Office at 1 p.m.

However, Wednesday 1 July was a public holiday in Melbourne, and the telegram was not delivered to George Kirk until 7.30 p.m.

Acceptances closed at 8 p.m. and, when George Kirk handed the telegram to the stewards at the Turf Club the next morning, those honourable sporting men, having found a loophole to stop Archer once and for all, decided it was too late and the entry was not accepted.

This decision caused a furore at the time; even Victorian owners lobbied the club to accept the entry, but to no avail. Mind you, it was highly unlikely that Archer, carrying 11 st 4 lb (72 kg), could have won anyway, and the Victorian owners doubtless realised this. If he had run it would have been the biggest weight carried in the history of the Melbourne Cup.

All the interstate entrants pulled out in protest and only seven local horses ran in what is considered the worst and weakest Cup in history. It was won, in front of 7000 people, by Banker, carrying 5 st 4 lb (34 kg).

It is both fitting and ironic that the public holiday that enabled this unsportsmanlike decision to be made was Separation Day, the day that Victoria celebrated its official separation from New South Wales in 1851.

The original success of the new race, followed by the debacle of 1863, eventually led to the end of the rivalry between the two race clubs, which merged to become the Victoria Racing Club in 1864. The VRC has run the Cup at Flemington every spring without fail since that time, as its feature race for the year.

Archer was taken by train to Ballarat in August 1863 and ran poorly in a sweepstakes race. He was suffering from fever and an injured fetlock and returned to Sydney to recover and be trained for the Metropolitan Handicap of 1864. He broke down once more on the eve of the race, however, and never raced again.

Although Archer is shown in the record books as being owned by de Mestre, he was actually leased by de Mestre and was always owned by an old school friend of de Mestre's, J.T. Roberts, in partnership with his brother-in-law and two nephews. He raced in his trainer's famous colours, which were, rather ominously for the bookies of Melbourne in 1861, all black.

Archer was retired to stand at his owners' property, Exeter Farm, near Braidwood, where he was foaled, for a fee of 10 guineas, but his progeny failed to win a stakes race, bearing out, perhaps, de Mestre's opinion that Archer was not among the best horses he had ever trained.

Archer died, aged sixteen, in 1872. An ornament made from his tail hair, coiled into a horseshoe shape and set in silver and mounted on red satin, can be seen at the Australian Racing Museum in Melbourne.

Etienne de Mestre had developed land his father was granted at Terara, near Nowra, into a successful training and breeding establishment. Archer's stable is still there. In fact, it's a bed and breakfast establishment today and, if you are prepared to believe Cup and local folklore, you can spend a weekend sleeping where Archer was supposedly stabled for most of his racing life.

Maybe you believe he walked to Melbourne, too.

WESTWARD HO!

HARRY 'THE BREAKER' MORANT

Extract

***

The night's a trifle chilly, and the stars are very bright,
A heavy dew is falling, but the tent-fly is rigged right;
You may rest your bones till morning, then, if you chance to wake,
Give me a call about the time that daylight starts to break.
We may not camp tomorrow, for we've many a mile to go,
'Ere we turn our horses' heads round to make tracks for down below.
There's many a water-course to cross, and many a black-soil plain,
And many a mile of mulga ridge 'ere we get back again.
That time five moons shall wax and wane we'll finish up the work,
Have the bullocks o'er the border and truck 'em down from Bourke,
And when they're sold at Homebush, and the agents settle up,
Sing hey! A spell in Sydney town . . . and Melbourne for the 'Cup'.

THE CUP IS MORE THAN A HORSE RACE

LES CARLYON

'Mort from Chicago'—that's how he introduced himself to me in an hotel dining room four years ago in Lexington, Kentucky. If the name sounds Runyonesque, Mort wasn't. He was that peculiarly American creature, the urban horse investor. From the big city, he sent his money to Kentucky where thoroughbreds ate it, but in a tax-effective way.

Mort owned pieces of several swish yearlings to be sold in the pavilion across from Blue Grass Airport, where the Arab buyers had already parked in their jets much as we park Commodores. After we had been talking half an hour, Mort suddenly said: 'Yeah, I bred a Melbourne Cup winner once.' It was less than a boast—more like you or I confessing to having once kicked a goal for Mount Pleasant seconds.

Years earlier, Mort and his partners had sold a yearling to Sheikh Hamdan Bin Rashid Al Maktoum of Dubai, dreaming the colt would make them famous in the Derby at Epsom, England, or the Arc de Triomphe at Longchamp, France. The colt ran second in a big German race and third in the Rome Derby before being bundled off to Australia. As At Talaq, he won the 1986 Melbourne Cup. Mort felt things could have turned out better.

I told him that while the Cup wasn't as famous as the races he coveted, it was a lung-buster, perhaps the most honest staying race in the world, and never won by a soft horse. Cup day, I told him, was one of the world's great booze-ups, a public holiday no less. Then I hit him with the clincher: kids from Moonee Ponds went along dressed as the Pope. Mort didn't say much. I'm sure he thought it was Mt Pleasant seconds.

It's hard to explain the Cup to an outsider. Most of the turf's fabled events were got up by racing insiders for themselves. The Epsom and Kentucky Derbies are about the supremacy of genes and the buying power of the ruling classes. The public is allowed to join in for the crowd scenes. The best colt of the year usually wins and is hustled off to the breeding shed. Sheikh What's-His-Name doesn't get too excited about the stake money because he's worth a couple of billion anyway. Besides, he spent $20 million on yearlings that year, so he's still behind, but who's counting?

Our Cup is quirky. Got up for people, it is: a cross between a horse race and a folk festival. And it mocks good order because it's a handicap. This gets rid of the preordained factor: just about any runner can win. It's the best sporting idea anyone ever had in this town—if only because racing is international and AFL footy isn't.

And the Cup is folksy. Ray Trinder, the Tasmanian owner who won in 1972, was seen outside the course holding the Cup in a cardboard box and trying to hail a cab. It doesn't go like this at Epsom or Longchamp. In Melbourne, the script is by Shakespeare. The Cup is a saga about horses and the human condition, about lowbrows and highbrows, toffs and villains, irony and rough humour. And the improbable.

In 1987, Harry Lawton had bought Kensei out of a New Zealand paddock for $15,000. Now the chestnut had won the Cup. 'Looked like a yak when I bought him,' said Harry. 'Had a coat about 3 inches long.' Harry used to be a fitter and turner, and played footy for Preston at $4 a game. Rosedale, a bay stallion owned in America by Nelson Bunker Hunt, once thought to be the richest man in the world, ran third to Kensei. 'Tell Bunker I'm sorry I knocked him off,' said Harry. It only goes like this in Australia.

As the Cup field paraded last year, the crowd, as it always does, fell silent. When Fraar, owned by the above-mentioned Sheikh Hamdan, reached the top corner of the yard, a falsetto voice cried out: 'I love you, Fraar.'

Next time around, Michael Jackson cried out even louder. 'I want to marry you, Fraar.'

Only on such a day can a wag from Werribee, or wherever, make thousands laugh. When, around 15 minutes later, Ireland's Vintage Crop came back the winner, a joker in white Arabic robes rose, arms outstretched, to welcome him. Here, having a day out, was Lawrence of Nunawading, or possibly Sheikh Akbar Bin Merv of Wagga. In 1992, maybe the same gent came as Batman. Next Tuesday he could be Roseanne. Only in Australia.

Cup crowds always seem bigger than AFL Grand Final crowds because racegoers need to move around more. Last year I was looking for an old friend, the Irish journalist Robin Park. I couldn't find him. But when Vintage Crop swooped on the leaders, I heard Robin's voice. Somewhere in that throng of 80,000, he was yelling as only a patriot with a bookie's ticket can. I didn't find his body until an hour later. Robin flushed and short in his action, mainly because of all the money he was carrying.

One reason the Cup has endured so well is that it keeps reinventing itself. In the early 1980s, it began to look worn. Too often it was won by mere handicappers, game horses but not the stuff of legend. People said the Cox Plate at Moonee Valley had more class. Without fanfare, the VRC began to handicap the Cup as a 'quality handicap', which favoured good horses. Up popped winners as classy as Empire Rose, Kingston Rule and Let's Elope. Then, last year, the VRC attracted two European runners and took the race to the world.

So it was that in the wind and rain we heard Irish accents at the winner's stall. Back came Vintage Crop, a long chestnut with a sheepskin noseband and a plaited mane. Hauntingly Irish, it was: the light soft and grey, the grass bruised and squelching, the rain incessant.

Back, too, came Mick Kinane, Vintage Crop's jockey, mud spattered across his shoulders, face and crotch. He had struck the chestnut just five times with the whip. He had gone out along its neck, kept his head low, and helped the gelding to the line. Behind him, local jockeys were sitting up, flailing away, and generally demonstrating why Australian jockeys are no longer as popular as they once were in Europe. Vintage Crop changed the nature of the Cup. Kinane's example may yet change the way Australian jockeys ride.

As usual, the return to scale made the running of the bulls at Pamplona, Spain, seem dull. Eventually Rod Johnson, the then VRC chief executive, took Dermot Weld, Vintage Crop's trainer, and some of the print journalists to a bar. Here, we met a chameleon. One moment Weld would talk as clinically as a surgeon, explaining how he had planned the whole thing, which he had. Next, he was a romantic, reciting bush poetry. Can you imagine the winning trainer on Derby day at Epsom holding forth on Michael Magee, who owned a shanty on the outer Barcoo?

They drink at the Cup. Leaving the course in the dark after phoning in your story, you feel like the lone wowser at a Roman orgy. Cans rattle, glass crunches underfoot, tote tickets flutter, car boots gape. The air reeks of stale beer and you have to step around the bodies. Feeling absurdly chaste, one makes it to the street and hails a cab. Except the driver doesn't stop at once; he slows down and peers. 'Why didn't you stop right away?' I ask as we head for town. 'Got to be careful who you pick up here,' he says.

The carousing starts early. Arriving at the Cup one year, the first human I saw on the course was a youth, dead drunk and wearing only shorts, stretched out along the limbs of a shrub near the birdcage entrance, like a South American sloth but with tattoos. Far away a pipe band played 'Scotland the Brave'. There were similar wildlife displays all over the course. The runners were going out for race one.

Long ago before the police brought precision to breathalyser queues, a knight of the realm was leaving the Cup in his Rolls with a crony. Both had enjoyed a top day of betting, drinking and lying. They were waved into the queue to be tested by the new-fangled breathalyser. Both at once tumbled into the back seat.

A policeman strode up. 'Get this car moving . . .' he started. 'What's going on? Who's driving?'

'It's the damned chauffeur,' said Sir M. 'Just got out and ran away when we were signalled to stop. Must have been drinking.'

'Well, one of you move the car,' the policeman demanded. 'You're holding up the line.'

'We can't possibly do that, officer,' said Sir M. 'We're pissed.'

Broadly speaking, four classes of people go to the Cup. A few men come in morning suits and toppers. They are the last surviving members of a class to which they never belonged—the English aristocracy. They look more self-conscious than the working-class kids who come dressed as Madonna. There are the thousands of women who dress so elegantly. You think of the Rome's Via Veneto, then notice the lady is standing next to a drunk in a gorilla suit. And there is the suburban middle class. They stake out patches on the Flemington lawns. Things are so territorial here one thinks of the rookery scene in nature documentaries. Plots are marked out by a tartan rug on one's corner, a Great Western bottle on another. Oh, and there are the racing diehards. They mostly hate Cup day.

The Cup is a reference point. Grand Flaneur, ridden by the crack Tommy Hales, won in 1880, days before they hanged another useful horseman, Edward Kelly, after a $30 trial. By 1895, Grand Flaneur was champion sire and no one knew where Ned's body had been thrown. The wounded from Gallipoli limped around Flemington to see Patrobas win in 1915, the year Australia bought its nationhood with blood. Russia, a chestnut stallion, won in 1946, as the Allies realised they had licked Hitler only to inherit Stalin. Equally poetic, Think Big won in 1975, days before Gough Whitlam was sacked as PM by Sir John Kerr. A few years later at the Cup presentation, Kerr, slurring and looking like something gone to seed, tried to upstage a horse on Cup day.

In the country towns of my youth, the Cup was the reference point. A squint-eyed farmer would say: 'We haven't had a crop as good as this since . . . buggered if I can remember . . . when The Trump won the Cup.'

One of the townsfolk was a defrocked jockey who once rode a double at Flemington. In Cup week people bought him beers and took him seriously. For the rest of the year we treated him for what he truly was: a derelict.

But, in the end, and rightly, we remember only the horses. Who can forget Light Fingers nosing out Ziema in 1965? Light Fingers, the mare, small and finely chiselled. Ziema, the gelding, big and homely. Roy Higgins throwing everything at the little girl, asking her to crash through the wall. Johnny Miller cuddling Ziema, who was inclined to give up if passed. Two bobbing white bridles, two hearts close to bursting.

And what about Empire Rose in the muggy heat of 1988? She was huge like the Himalayas and had a lot of bad disposition. With joints like water melons, she should have broken down, yet she won our hardest race, neck down low, ears laid back threateningly. Laurie Laxon, her trainer, said she won because she had a 'good aggressive attitude'. What Laurie meant was that she hated other horses.

In 1960, the Centenary Cup, 101,000 of us turned up because Tulloch, the best horse most of us will ever see, was going around. That's just what he seemed to do: go around. Neville Sellwood took him via Footscray Tech and he flashed home seventh. Hi Jinx, the winner at 50 to 1, came back in silence. I was young and idolised Tulloch. I couldn't understand what had happened. I have matured a bit since; I think I now understand what happened.

In 1989, a new prince of trainers arrived: Lee Freedman. People will tell you afterwards they knew their horse would win; Lee told anyone who wanted to listen the Saturday before, after Tawrrific had run in the Mackinnon. Freedman stood watching the bay being cooled down. Each time the horse passed, he would say: 'I love him, I love him. He's a toughie, my favourite horse. He can win the Cup.' On Cup day, Freedman, his collar smudged with lipstick, said quietly: 'I told you so'. He was, and is, a man with faith in himself.

In 1976, the year Van Der Hum won in a cloudburst, I stood with my mate Mick from Queensland and watched the field parade. We had a wonderful view because no one else was dumb enough to stand in the rain. After the pneumonia passed, we felt we had matured a lot. In 1985, the two of us again watched the parade and agreed on one thing: What A Nuisance couldn't win because his coat was too dull. He won, and we matured some more. We felt better when we learned Johnny Meagher had trained the horse from a paddock.

Bart Cummings had trained nine Cup winners. His finest performance was perhaps Kingston Rule in 1990. With the look of eagles in his eye and copper lights in his coat, Kingston Rule seemed too pretty, too brittle, to be a contender. Bart made him one.

Kingston Town almost won the Cup in 1982. Tommy Smith, his trainer, and David Hains, his owner, thought he had, then the wrong number went up. The pair came down the steps with the uncomprehending looks of people herded out of a hotel fire at 3 a.m.

Johnny Letts, who won on Piping Lane in 1972, hadn't ridden at Flemington before and asked other riders where he should make his run. 'Go at Chiquita Lodge,' they told him. Letts assumed Chiquita Lodge to be a '30-storey motel' rather than a single-storey stable block at the 1000-metre post. He never saw it. He decided to go when he saw Roy Higgins send Gunsynd forward. Higgins had gone Chiquita Lodge. It only goes like this in Australia.

While I never convinced Mort from Chicago, Mick Kinane a few months ago told an English journalist of his ride down the Damascus road: 'It gets as much hype as the Derby and the Arc put together, and though I never dreamt as a child of winning the race—like I did the Derby—I'd recommend it to anyone.'

So would I.

30 October 1994

GALLOPING HORSES

C.J. DENNIS

C.J. Dennis was able to convey the effects of Cup Week on all and sundry. In 1932 he even wrote about the effect of the Spring Carnival obsession on himself and other poets.

***

Oh, this is the week when no rhymster may rhyme
On the joy of the bush or the ills of the time,
Nor pour out his soul in delectable rhythm
Of women and wine and the lure they have with 'em,
Nor pen philosophic (if foolish) discourses,
Because of the fury of galloping horses.

Galloping, galloping thro' the refrain—
The lure and the lilt of it beat on the brain.
Strive as you may for Arcadian Themes,
The silks and the saddles will weave thro' your dreams.
Surging, and urging the visions aside
For a lyrical lay of equestrian pride,
For the roar of the race and the call of the courses,
And galloping, galloping, galloping horses.

A cigarette card featuring The Barb.

Archer pictured in a newspaper sketch of the day, carrying Etienne de Mestre's famous all-black colours. (AJC)

A cigarette card featuring Briseis. (ARM)

Off to the Melbourne Cup, c.1880. (VRC)

Carbine wins the Melbourne Cup in 1890. (AJC)

A newspaper artist's impression of the 1891 Cup atmosphere at Flemington. (VRC)

The Cup-day crowd watch Bravo win the 1889 Melbourne Cup. (VRC)

Brighton Pony Racecourse in 1900. (WAYNE PEAKE/STATE LIBRARY OF NSW)

He Flew It Like a Bird, Stuart Allen c.1910. (DAY FINE ART)

C.J. Dennis.

14.1 Handicap at Rosebery, 11 December 1918, won by Dol Merv. (WAYNE PEAK/STATE LIBRARY OF NSW)

Crowd at Kensington racetrack c.1920. (WAYNE PEAK/STATE LIBRARY OF NSW)

Ascot racecourse in 1926. (AJC)

Trivalve c.1927. (AJC)

Light Fingers (outside) defeats stable mate Ziema by a nose in the 1965 Melbourne Cup. (NEWSPIX)

Reckless and Tommy Woodcock share a stable bedroom before the 1977 Melbourne Cup. (BRUCE POSTLE/FAIRFAX PHOTOS)

This is the week for the apotheosis
Of Horse in his glory, from tail to proboscis.
That curious quadruped, proud and aloof,
That holds all the land under thrall of his hoof.
All creeds and conditions, all factions and forces,
All, all must give way to the galloping horses.

Galloping, galloping—sinner and saint
March to the metre, releasing restraint.
If it isn't the Cup it's the Oaks or the Steeple
That wraps in its magic the minds of the people.
Whether they seek it for profit or pleasure,
They all, willy-nilly, must dance to the measure.
The mood of the moment in all men endorses
The glamorous game and the galloping horses—
Galloping horses—jockeys and courses—
They gallop, we gallop with galloping horses.

THE TALE OF PETER ST ALBANS

JIM HAYNES

Cup folklore includes the tale of the twelve-year-old 'Aboriginal' boy named Peter riding Briseis, the first female horse to win, in 1876.

The story goes that Peter was born on the St Albans Stud property near Geelong to an Aboriginal mother; perhaps he was the son of St Albans' owner, Jim Wilson Snr, or his son, also Jim. Another version has the boy being left as a baby on the doorstep of the home of one of St Albans' grooms, Michael Bowden, to be raised by him and his wife.

As he had no 'real' surname, so the story goes, he was given the name of the property and became Peter St Albans, youngest jockey and first Aboriginal rider to win the Cup!

Unfortunately, this wonderful story, like Archer's walk to Melbourne with his Aboriginal 'strapper/jockey', has more holes in it than a Swiss cheese.

Two elements of the story are true. He was known as Peter and he was very young, in fact he was only twelve and, oddly enough, this fact explains the whole wonderful concoction.

Aged only twelve, the boy had ridden Briseis, as a two-year-old, to three victories at Randwick earlier in the year, including an incredible win in the Doncaster Handicap where he rode her at 5 st 7 lb (35 kg). However, the VRC rules did not allow jockeys to ride in the Cup until they were aged thirteen, and Peter was a few days shy of his thirteenth birthday on Cup Day 1876.

The regular jockey for St Albans' horses was the legendary Tom Hales, who could not make the Cup weight at 6 st 4 lb (39.5 kg).

As Briseis won most of her big races as a two- and three-year-old, she was given very light weights to carry, which meant that a good lightweight jockey was required.

Few grown men could ride at those weights, but Peter was an excellent rider who knew the horse as a stableboy at St Albans and had ridden her to victory in three races in Sydney. So, cunning old Jim Wilson came up with the 'cock-and-bull' story of Peter's origins to allow him to ride Briseis in the Cup. He argued to the VRC that both the boy's birth date and parents were unknown, but he was probably older than thirteen.

'Peter St Albans' was actually born in Geelong on 15 November 1864, and there is a birth certificate to prove it. He was the son of Michael Bowden and his wife and, though christened Michael, he was known as Peter from an early age. There is a painting at the State Library of Victoria by Frederick Woodhouse showing Peter as a youth, looking very white and European, standing alongside Briseis with Tom Hales in the saddle.

Michael 'Peter St Albans' Bowden was a successful jockey for several years around Geelong and also rode successfully interstate until a bad fall at age nineteen saw him switch to training. He died in 1900 at the age of 35. The Geelong Thoroughbred Club awards the Peter St Albans Trophy each year to the jockey who rides the most winners at the Geelong track.

CUP MEMORIES

NAT GOULD

To chronicle all I have seen on the turf in Australia would fill two or three volumes, so I shall merely give reminiscences and incidents likely to interest the reader.

Bravo won the Melbourne Cup in 1889 and when I arrived in Melbourne that year one of the first men I met was the late Mr Chapman, a racing journalist who wrote as 'Augur' for *The Australasian*. He was a good fellow and he told me he had backed Bravo at the forlorn odds of a thousand to one.

It appears some rash bookmaker, more in a spirit of bravado than anything else, had offered to lay a thousand pounds to a sovereign against Bravo and Mr Chapman had stood in with a friend and taken a quarter of the bet and won £250 for his five shillings.

I was more interested in the fate of a horse called Chicago. He was a good horse and a Caulfield Cup winner; but, somehow, I managed to back him in the wrong race.

Bravo had been reported as so lame that his starting was regarded as out of the question. A few days before the race Bravo came into the market again and was well backed. The bookmakers who had been taking liberties with him felt uneasy, and a lot of the money they had laid against him at long odds was hedged at a loss.

The Melbourne Stakes on the Saturday had produced a terrific race between Abercorn, Melos and Carbine, who passed the post in that order. Abercorn on that day was at his best and I never saw him run a better race. At this particular time he was even better than Carbine, but it must not be forgotten that the son of Musket had one of his fore-hoofs tightly bound up due to a cracked heel, and was not at his best.

After his forward running in the Stakes on the Saturday, Melos was naturally a great favourite for the Cup, as he had a lot less weight to carry, yet Bravo's Cup win was not such a surprise as many people imagined, for the horse was well backed at twelve to one on the day of the race. He beat Carbine and Melos, who finished in that order.

Bravo's win put a good stake in the pocket of his owner, Mr W.T. Jones of Ballarat, a good racing man.

The next year's Cup was won by Carbine.

Carbine was the best racehorse I ever saw during my residence in Australia.

He won the Champion Stakes, three mile, as a three-year-old, beating Abercorn, who was then a four-year-old, at wfa [weight-for-age]. He won several races that season, including the Sydney Cup, in which he carried nine stone, or within four pounds of Abercorn, who finished third. This race goes far to prove he was a better horse than Abercorn, as he was receiving only four pounds, and giving away a year.

As a four-year-old he ran second to Bravo in the Melbourne Cup, with ten stone on his back, giving the winner 1 stone 7 pounds. He again won the Sydney Cup, carrying 9 stone 9 pounds and performed the great feat of winning five of the principal races at the AJC Autumn Meeting in four days, including Sydney Cup and four wfa races.

It was a treat to see the way in which Carbine tackled his opponents. The horse fairly revelled in his work, and his rush at the finish was marvellous. I have never seen a horse of his size cover so much ground in his stride.

If Carbine was a wonder up to four years old, what shall we say for his five-year-old career, which fairly eclipsed all that he had previously done. He ran eleven times, and was beaten once, when he ought to have won. He won his memorable Melbourne Cup this season.

When the saddling bell rang before the Cup race there was intense excitement, and Carbine held his position as favourite firm as a rock, and Highborn was at thirty-three to one. Ramage rode Carbine, and Egan, a tiny lad, Highborn. 'Old Jack' was fairly mobbed as he was being saddled, but as usual he took no notice of the crowd. When he came onto the track there was a terrific burst of cheering. Carbine stood still and looked round, and then declined to go to the post.

His trainer, Mr Hickenbotham, gave him a push behind, and Carbine moved a few paces. This was a slow process. At last Ramage threw the reins over the horse's head, and Mr Hickenbotham fairly dragged him up the course. I never saw a more sluggish horse until he commenced to race, and then there was a different tale to tell. Mr Forrester was very confident Highborn would beat him.

I shall never forget that race.

Carbine held a good position throughout, but did not get well to the front until they were in the straight. At the home turn Highborn looked to have a chance second to none, and the hopes of his backers were high. No sooner, however, did Carbine see an opening than he shot through, and after that it was a case of hare and hounds. On came 'Old Jack', with his 10 stone 5 pounds, and at the distance he had the race won.

Cheer after cheer rent the air, and people went almost frantic with excitement. It was a wild scene. For months Carbine had been backed by the public, and at last the suspense was over. It was a glorious victory, and everyone knew it, but none better than Mr Forrester, whose crack Highborn finished a couple of lengths behind him. Not only did Carbine carry 10 stone 5 pounds, but he ran the two miles in 3 minutes 28.5 seconds, the fastest time on record for that distance in the colonies.

I had special opportunities of learning a good deal more about that race before it came off than most people. Mr William Forrester, of Warwick Farm, had in his stable a horse called Highborn that he had specially kept for this event. Mr Forrester was then, and, I am proud to say, still is, a great friend of mine; and I also knew Mr Hickenbotham, the trainer of Carbine, very well.

I went to Warwick Farm from Sydney, about an hour's ride in the train, to have a peep at the horses. Warwick Farm is a snug place, and the house and stables join on to Mr Oatley's private racecourse. Mr Forrester is brimful of hospitality, and a born gentleman if ever there was one. When we came to Highborn's box, Mr Forrester said, 'What do you think of him?'

I was looking at a lanky, flat-sided common gelding, as black as coal, with a wall eye that made him look wicked. Honestly, I could not say I thought much of him. It was wonderful how he improved upon acquaintance. 'He's no beauty,' I replied, or words to that effect.

Mr Forrester smiled, and gave me to understand if I did not have a few pounds on 'the black fellow' in the Melbourne Cup I should regret it. Knowing 'the Squire's' propensity for practical joking, I thought he was trying it on, but I soon found he was serious. He had specially kept Highborn for this particular race, and when the weights came out with Carbine 10 stone 5 pounds and Highborn 6 stone 8 pounds, there was much joy in the Warwick Farm camp.

The preparation of both horses went on satisfactorily, but Carbine's trainer had a lot of trouble with the horse's feet, and had a very anxious time of it. Mr Forrester and some of his friends were quietly putting money on Highborn at very long odds months before the race. Highborn's trial was good enough to win with nearer nine stone up than 6 stone 8 pounds, so no wonder they were sanguine. When I reached Melbourne that year for the Cup meeting, I saw Carbine do his winding-up preparations on the track at Flemington. One morning he easily beat his stable-mate, Megaphone, for whom Mr Wallace had given two thousand guineas or more after he ran Carbine such a great race at Randwick.

Meeting Mr Hickenbotham after the gallop, I remarked what a good go it was.

'Yes,' he replied, 'and weight or no weight, bar accidents, he'll win the Cup.'

I had an idea he could go near it, but doubted if he could give 3 stone 11 pounds to a horse like Highborn. About a week before the Melbourne Cup was run, I met Mr Forrester, and he asked me to go up to Oakleigh Park, as they were going to give Highborn a run there. I went, to my sorrow, for Highborn was just beaten by Mr James Redfearn's Malvolio. I remarked to Mr Forrester, after the race, that a beating like that was not good enough to win a Melbourne Cup.

'Don't make any mistake,' was his reply. 'Malvolio's Redfearn's crack three-year-old, and he'll win the next Melbourne Cup with him.'

Sure enough his words came true, for I saw Malvolio win it the following year.

To show how good the performance of Carbine was, I have only to allude to Highborn's performances afterwards. Highborn won the Australian Cup, the Sydney Cup, and the Anniversary Handicap, and ran fourth in the Melbourne Cup the following year with nine stone up. He was sold to go to India, and when the property of the Maharajah of Cooch Behar he won two Viceroy's Cups in succession.

In 1891, Malvolio beat Sir William and Strathmore to win the Cup. His sire was the 1884 Cup winner, Malua, and his dam was Madcap. Malvolio was bred, owned and trained by Mr James Redfearn and ridden to victory by his son.

There was some trouble about paying over the stakes in the 1891 Cup. Mr Etienne de Mestre put in a claim for them on the grounds that he owned Madcap, the dam of Malvolio, and had merely lent her to Mr Redfearn. This Mr Redfearn denied and I think Mr de Mestre was ill-advised to make the claim he did. Malvolio's owner got the stakes, and rightly so.

On the return journey from Melbourne in 1891 we had a fire alarm on the train. Lord Jersey, the Governor, was in a special car behind ours and the attendant roused us and said to me, 'There's a fire, sir! You'd better get out!'

'No, you don't,' I replied. 'It's not time to turn out yet.'

The attendant has a knack of rousing you up early in order to make the beds in the car. I fancied his fire alarm was a happy inspiration on his part to get me out.

When I saw the train had stopped and people were hurrying out of the car I felt it was time to make a move. Then a sudden thought occurred to me: I felt I could earn undying fame as a staunch supporter of our great Empire, so I sang out, 'Save the Governor!'

An old Scotsman was in the berth over mine, and he growled out, 'Save the Governor be damned! Where's me boots?'

Evidently the gentleman from the north did not coincide with my views and just wanted to make tracks.

Happily no great harm was done, only one side of the car was burned, through some of the rods being overheated.

An amusing account of the incident appeared in the Melbourne paper *Bohemian*. Here is the extract, which I happened to come across:

> The true story of the fire on board the Sydney express, about a week ago, has not yet been told. No one has yet ventured to describe the scene in the interior of the car after the alarm was sounded.
>
> The alarm of 'Fire', when uttered in a shrill voice in the small hours of the morning, never fails to have the desired effect on the soundest sleeper, especially if the cry be uttered by a female. On this occasion it had the desired effect on every soul in the carriage.
>
> A lady who slept in a berth by the door heard it first and, running out into the passage that traverses the carriage in her robe de nuit, was confronted by the stalwart figure of Dibbs, the new Premier, who was vainly trying to find his way into the trousers of Nat Gould, the author of The Double Event.
>
> Nat Gould is fat and short and Dibbs is a big fellow, and slim with an altitude of six feet three inches. When the alarm was given, Gould promptly seized hold of Dibbs's clothes and made straight for the open air. By the time Dibbs got his eyes open there was only one pair of trousers available and they were Gould's.
>
> When he met the hysterical female in the curl papers, the New South Wales Premier had only got one leg into Gould's unmentionables, but he struggled manfully to cover the other leg with a newspaper.
>
> Gould's plight was even worse. He had got his legs into the sleeves of Dibbs's shooting-jacket and, when he was discovered out on the line a few minutes later by the guard, he was carrying over his arm a set of ladies' overalls, which he had borne off triumphantly in his flight.

Such is the account given of this memorable episode involving myself and the Governor of New South Wales.

What an awful Cup it was in 1892.

I have been at race-meetings in all sorts of weather in the old country and elsewhere, but I never recollect a more uncomfortable day than when Glenloth won the Cup. Torrents of rain came down and deluged everybody and turned the course into a quagmire on the far side.

All the fashionable world turned out as usual. Nothing short of an earthquake would prevent Melbourne people from going to the Cup, and even then, when the course was clear, they would sit on the ruins of the stands and watch the race!

The lawn became very slippery and it was amusing to see the numerous spills as some well-dressed swell measured his length in the mud and then got up to shake himself like a Newfoundland dog.

The rain poured down like a second deluge when the horses came out. The mud flew up in a shower in the preliminary canter and in the actual race it can easily be imagined what it was like. I was in the press box on the top of the grandstand and at the back of this, some distance away, is 'the hill', which was crowded with a wet, miserable mass of people.

Umbrellas were put up by some people on the top of the stand, but loud shouts from the people on the hill ordered them to be shut. Many declined to close their umbrellas and a shower of mud in lumps came rattling down on them from the irate crowd on the hill. This had the desired effect. On the flat there was a perfect forest of umbrellas and it was a strange sight as seen from our box. As for seeing the race, it was well nigh impossible and, when the horses flashed past the post there was a cry of 'What's won?'

When Glenloth's number went up it put the finishing touches on backers' misery. The horse was a rank outsider and fifty to one could have been had about him in places.

Glenloth was a good stamp of a horse, but the wet day was all in his favour. He might have won under any circumstances, but the heavy going assisted a horse of his build.

An incident that happened to me over this race shows how unwise it is to put a man off backing a horse when he fancies it.

Before I left my hotel in the morning, one of the waiters asked me to put a pound on Glenloth for him. I laughed at him, and told him to keep his money in his pocket. He did, with the result that he was about fifty pounds worse off after Glenloth won, as he would have procured that amount to his pound.

I shall never forget the mournful look with which he regarded me after the event. I had serious thoughts about changing my table, in case a concoction of arsenic fell into my soup by mistake. Thinking to make things better, I advised him to back Trieste in the Oaks. He did, and she lost, though she ought to have won, which only made matters worse.

Moral: always keep your information to yourself, and then you will be the only sufferer.

The year following Glenloth's wet Cup I again found myself in Melbourne for the two big meetings at Caulfield and Flemington.

The 1893 Cup was won by another outsider, Tarcoola. Once again I had a bad time, as I backed Carnage for the double, the Derby and the Cup. Carnage won the Derby all right, but just failed in the Cup as he ran second after making nearly all the running.

It is curious how men sometimes miss a good win. One morning I was coming off the track with Mr Frank Wilkinson, a well-known pressman and handicapper, when he turned around and said, 'Stop a minute, Nat; here's Tarcoola going for a spin.'

'Hang Tarcoola,' I said, 'I'm in a hurry for breakfast.'

Frank had, however, got his watch on them, and I waited until the gallop was over.

'By Jove! That's a great go!' said Frank, looking at his watch. 'It's worth taking a few pounds about Tarcoola at one hundred to two or three.'

I said, 'We'll think about it. You can get a bit of money in the Club, and I'll go you halves.'

Unfortunately, Frank did not get the money and, a day or two after, Tarcoola did such a bad gallop I forgot all about him until I saw him beating my pet fancy, Carnage, in the Cup. I believe

Frank wired the result of the good gallop to a friend in Sydney who won a thousand pounds on Tarcoola. Such is luck.

Tarcoola won cleverly from Carnage and Jeweller, with Loyalty well up close, and again the public were floored, as Tarcoola started at a very long price.

The last Cup I saw, before sailing for London, was in 1894. Again an outsider landed the race when Patron won, and it was a most extraordinary victory, as I will endeavour to show.

Patron was a very good three-year-old and, naturally, he was backed early in the season for the Cup. On paper his chances looked as good as anything in the race. Some of the first double-event wagers booked were for Paris in the Caulfield Cup and Patron in the Melbourne Cup.

Before the date for the Cup arrived Patron went wrong, and his name gradually receded from the betting list until, shortly before the race, long odds could be had about his chances.

Dawes, the jockey who rode Patron, had not much faith in his mount either and Mr Purchas, the owner, also laid off as much of his money as he could. I believe as late as the evening before the race it was not decided whether Patron would run or be scratched. This was certainly not encouraging to anyone who had backed the horse.

It was, however, decided to start the horse and let him take his chance, and, much to the surprise of everyone, he won the Cup after a good race with Devon and Nada.

Bravo and Patron were both sired by the only unbeaten Cup winner in history, Grand Flaneur, who won in 1880 and started nine times for nine wins.

CARBINE'S MELBOURNE CUP, 1890

ANONYMOUS

The race is run, the Cup is won, the great event is o'er.
The grandest horse that strode a course has led them home once
more.
I watched with pride your sweeping stride before you ranged in line,
For far and near a ringing cheer was echoed for Carbine.

The start was made, no time delayed before they got away,
Those horses great, some thirty-eight, all eager for the fray.
No better start could human heart to sportsmen ever show
As Watson did, each jockey bid get ready for to go.

With lightning speed, each gallant steed along the green track tore;
Each jockey knew what he must do to finish in the fore.
But Ramage knew his mount was true, though he had ten-five up,
For Musket's son great deeds had done before that Melbourne Cup.

No whip, nor spur, he needs to stir a horse to greater speed;
He knew as well as man can tell when he could take the lead.
So on he glides with even strides, though he is led by nine;
But Ramage knows before they close he'll try them with Carbine.

The bend is passed; the straight at last: he takes him to the fore.
The surging crowd with voices loud the stud's name loudly roar.
The jockey too, he full well knew the race was nearly o'er,
As on his mane he slacked the rein: no need to urge him more.

Brave horse and man who led the van on that November day!
Your records will be history still when ye have passed away.
For such a race, for weight and pace, has never been put up
As that deed done by Musket's son in the 1890 Cup.

DREAMING TO WIN

JIM HAYNES

Dreams and premonitions have long been a part of Cup folklore. There are many accounts, mostly unsubstantiated, of people dreaming the winner. Shearers riding miles but arriving too late to place a bet having dreamed the winner in an isolated shearing shed; housewives telling husbands the name of the winner before the race due to women's intuition, a premonition or cryptic dream, only to be ignored or laughed at by the husband until proven right on race day.

The most famous Melbourne Cup dream story is the one concerning Walter Craig, owner of the 1870 winner, Nimblefoot.

Craig was the owner and the licensee of Ballarat's Royal Hotel. He had purchased the hotel in 1857, at the height of the gold boom. It was originally known as Bath's Hotel but, after Alfred Duke of Edinburgh stayed there in 1867, it became known as the Royal.

In the same year legendary horseman and poet, Adam Lindsay Gordon, took over management of the hotel's substantial stables and livery business. Walter Craig and his horses are mentioned several times in Gordon's verse.

In August 1870 Craig dreamed that he saw his horse, Nimblefoot, winning the Melbourne Cup. The horse carried Craig's violet silks but the jockey was wearing a black armband in the dream.

Craig recounted the dream to several people and died within days of the premonition. An account of this strange event did appear in *The Age* just prior to the running of the Cup, which lends some credibility at least to this piece of Cup folklore.

Needless to say, the horse subsequently won the Cup with the jockey wearing a black crepe armband to mark the passing of the owner.

Walter Craig's death is the central feature of another piece of Melbourne Cup mythology. It seems that Craig and a group of friends, including well-known bookmaker Joseph Slack, were drinking at Craig's hotel in February 1870 when Craig asked the bookmaker what odds he would give on an AJC Metropolitan Handicap–Melbourne Cup double featuring Croydon and Nimblefoot.

The bookmaker, in a spirit of conviviality, offered to bet £1000 against a round of drinks for the group and Craig duly obliged. Although the double proved successful, Craig died before the result was finalised and, according to the unwritten rules of gentlemanly sportsmanship, death cancels out debts of honour.

Legend has it, however, that Joseph Slack chose to honour the bet made with his friend and paid Craig's widow the £1000. A second account of the story has the bookmaker paying £500 to the widow in order to appear honourable while still acknowledging the accepted rules of sportsmanship surrounding such verbal, or 'handshake', bets.

Stories of 'dreaming the winner' had become such an accepted feature of the annual Cup publicity barrage by 1886 that a young Banjo Paterson was able to use the idea as the basis of a comic poem, 'A Dream of the Melbourne Cup'. Published in *The Bulletin* just prior to the Cup of that year, the poem has several interesting elements.

For one thing it demonstrates Paterson's parochial support for his home colony of New South Wales and reminds us just how fierce the rivalry was between that state and Victoria.

Paterson, who was a member of the first New South Wales polo team to play against Victoria, sees the race in his dream as a match between the New South Wales champion, Trident, and the great Victorian stayer, Commotion.

When the actual race was run, some weeks after the poem appeared in *The Bulletin*, it was a pyrrhic victory for Paterson's 'dream horse' Trident, who finished fourth, but well ahead of Commotion, who came in 21st in a field of 28 runners.

The result that year would have pleased young Banjo Paterson, however, as the race was won by the New South Wales bred, trained and owned horse, Arsenal.

Even more pleasing to New South Welshmen would have been the fact that Arsenal's previous owner was a Victorian, Mr W. Pearson, who also owned Commotion.

Pearson was a wealthy sportsman who owned a large team of horses in Melbourne and had dreadful luck in attempting to win the Cup. Commotion had finished third behind Martini-Henry in 1883 and second behind Malua in 1884.

Pearson then purchased Arsenal, who was bred at Tocal Stud near Maitland, for 625 guineas. The horse won the VATC Criterion Stakes and performed well in lead-up races to the Cup of 1885, in which the three-year-old was given the featherweight handicap of 6 st 9 lb (42 kg). In spite of all his promise, however, Arsenal ran a shocker in the big race, finishing 31st in a field of 35.

Disgusted with both his poor luck and the horse, Pearson sold Arsenal to Mr W. Gannon, a Sydney racing man, for a mere 375 guineas. Trained by Harry Rayner and ridden by inexperienced jockey W. English, Arsenal won the Cup in 1886, soundly defeating Commotion, carrying the Pearson colours.

The poem, only the third of Paterson's verses to be published in *The Bulletin*, also pokes fun at the typical punter's fear of picking a winner but not being paid. The poet also has some fun with the various old wives' tales concerning which foods give us restless nights and vivid dreams.

Above all, the poem demonstrates the 22-year-old writer's enthusiasm for racing.

A DREAM OF THE MELBOURNE CUP

A.B. 'BANJO' PATERSON

Bring me a quart of colonial beer
And some doughy damper to make good cheer,
I must make a heavy dinner;
Heavily dine and heavily sup,
Of indigestible things fill up,
Next month they run the Melbourne Cup,
And I have to dream the winner.

Stoke it in, boys! the half-cooked ham,
The rich ragout and the charming cham.
I've got to mix my liquor;
Give me a gander's gaunt hind leg,
Hard and tough as a wooden peg,
And I'll keep it down with a hard-boiled egg,
'Twill make me dream the quicker.

Now I am full of fearful feed,
Now I may dream a race indeed,
In my restless, troubled slumber;
While the night-mares race through my heated brain
And their devil-riders spur amain,
The tip for the Cup will reward my pain,
And I'll spot the winning number.

Thousands and thousands and thousands more,
Like sands on the white Pacific shore,
The crowding people cluster;
For evermore it's the story old,
While races are bought and backers are sold,
Drawn by the greed of the gain of gold,
In their thousands still they muster.

***

And the bookies' cries grow fierce and hot,
'I'll lay the Cup! The double, if not!'
'Five monkeys, Little John, sir!'
'Here's fives bar one, I lay, I lay!'
And so they shout through the livelong day,
And stick to the game that is sure to pay,
While fools put money on, sir!

And now in my dream I seem to go
And bet with a 'book' that I seem to know—
A Hebrew money-lender;
A million to five is the price I get—
Not bad! but before I book the bet
The horse's name I clean forget,
Its number and even gender.

Now for the start, and here they come,
And the hoof-strokes roar like a mighty drum
Beat by a hand unsteady;
They come like a rushing, roaring flood,
Hurrah for the speed of the Chester blood;
For Acme is making the pace so good
There are some of 'em done already.

But round the back she begins to tire,
And a mighty shout goes up, 'Crossfire!'
The magpie jacket's leading;
And Crossfire challenges, fierce and bold,
And the lead she'll have and the lead she'll hold,
But at length gives way to the black and gold,
Which away to the front is speeding.

Carry them on and keep it up—
A flying race is the Melbourne Cup,
You must race and stay to win it;
And old Commotion, Victoria's pride,
Now takes the lead with his raking stride,
And a mighty roar goes far and wide—
'There's only Commotion in it!'

But one draws out from the beaten ruck
And up on the rails by a piece of luck
He comes in a style that's clever;
'It's Trident! Trident! Hurrah for Hales!'
'Go at 'em now while their courage fails';
'Trident! Trident! for New South Wales!'
'The blue and white for ever!'

Under the whip! with the ears flat back,
Under the whip! though the sinews crack,
No sign of the base white feather;
Stick to it now for your breeding's sake,
Stick to it now though your hearts should break,
While the yells and roars make the grand-stand shake,
They come down the straight together.

Trident slowly forges ahead,
The fierce whips cut and the spurs are red,
The pace is undiminished;
Now for the Panics that never fail!
But many a backer's face grows pale
As old Commotion swings his tail
And swerves—and the Cup is finished.

***

And now in my dream it all comes back:
I bet my coin on the Sydney crack,
A million I've won, no question!
Give me my money, you greedy hog
Give me my money, bookmaking dog
But he disappeared in a kind of fog . . .
And I woke with 'the indigestion'.

CUP DAY IS SUPREME

MARK TWAIN

The things which interest us when we travel are, first, the people; next, the novelties; and finally, the history of the places and countries visited. Novelties are rare in cities which represent the most advanced civilisation of the modern day. When one is familiar with such cities in the other parts of the world he is in effect familiar with the cities of Australasia. There may be shades of difference, but these can easily be too fine for detection by the incompetent eye of the passing stranger.

Even in the famous so-called 'larrikin', for instance, the traveller will not be able to discover a new species, but only an old one met elsewhere, and variously called loafer, rough, tough, bummer, or blatherskite, according to his geographical distribution. The larrikin differs by a shade from those others, in that he is more sociable towards the stranger, more kindly disposed, more hospitable, more hearty, more friendly.

As I have suggested, novelties are rare in the great capitals of modern times. Even the wool exchange in Melbourne could not be told from the familiar stock exchange of other countries. Wool brokers are just like stockbrokers; they all bounce from their seats and put up their hands and yell in unison . . . though no stranger can tell what they yell. Then the president calmly says, 'Sold to Smith and Co, threepence farthing . . . next!' when probably nothing of the kind happened; for how should he know?

Melbourne spreads around over an immense area of ground. And what was the origin of this majestic city and its efflorescence of palatial town houses and country seats? Its first brick was laid and its first house built by a passing convict.

Australian history is almost always picturesque; indeed, it is so curious and strange, that it is itself the chiefest novelty the country has to offer, and so it pushes the other novelties into second and third place. It does not read like history, but like the most beautiful lies, and all of a fresh new sort, no mouldy old stale ones.

Australian history is full of surprises, and adventures, and incongruities, and contradictions, and incredibilities; but they are all true, they all happened.

Melbourne is the largest city of Australasia, and fills the post with honour and credit. It is a stately city architecturally as well as in magnitude. It has an elaborate cable-car system; it has museums, and colleges, and schools, and public gardens, and electricity, and gas, and libraries, and theatres, and mining centres, and wool centres, and centres of the arts and sciences, and boards of trade, and ships, and railroads, and a harbour.

Melbourne has social clubs, and journalistic clubs, and racing clubs, and a squatter club sumptuously housed and appointed, and as many churches and banks as can make a living. In a word, it is equipped with everything that goes to make the modern great city.

Yet, Melbourne has one specialty that must not be jumbled in with those other things. It is the mitred Metropolitan centre of the Horse Racing Cult. Its raceground is the Mecca of Australasia.

On the great annual day of sacrifice—the fifth of November, Guy Fawkes's Day, business is suspended over a stretch of land and sea as wide as from New York to San Francisco, and deeper than from the northern lakes to the Gulf of Mexico; and every man and woman, of high degree or low, who can afford the expense, put away all their other duties and come to the racetrack.

They begin to swarm in by ship and rail a fortnight before the day, and they swarm thicker and thicker day after day, until all the vehicles of transportation are taxed to their uttermost to meet the demands of the occasion, and all hotels and lodgings are bulging outward because of the pressure from within.

They come a hundred thousand strong, as all the best authorities say, and they pack the spacious grounds and grandstands and make a spectacle such as is never to be seen in Australasia or elsewhere.

It is the 'Melbourne Cup' that brings this multitude together.

Their clothes have been ordered long ago, at unlimited cost, and without bounds as to beauty and magnificence, and have been kept in concealment until now, for unto this day are they consecrate. (I am speaking of the ladies' clothes; but one might know that.)

And so the grandstands make a brilliant and wonderful spectacle, a delirium of colour, a vision of beauty. The champagne flows, everybody is vivacious, excited and happy.

Everybody bets, and gloves and fortunes change hands right along, all the time. Day after day the races go on, and the fun and the excitement are kept at white heat; and when each day is done, the people dance all night so as to be fresh for the racing in the morning.

At the end of the great week the swarms secure lodgings and transportation for next year, then flock away to their remote homes and count their gains and losses, and order next year's Cup-clothes, and then lie down and sleep for two weeks, and get up sorry to reflect that a whole year must be put in somehow or other before they can be wholly happy again.

The Melbourne Cup is the Australasian National Day. It would be difficult to overstate its importance. It overshadows all other holidays and specialised days of whatever sort in the colonies.

Overshadows them? I might almost say it blots them out. Each special day gets attention, but not everybody's attention. Each holiday evokes interest, but not everybody's interest. Each of them rouses enthusiasm, but not everybody's enthusiasm. In each case a part of the attention, interest, and enthusiasm is a matter of habit and custom, and another part of it is official and perfunctory.

Cup Day, and Cup Day only, commands an attention, an interest, and an enthusiasm, which are universal and spontaneous, not perfunctory.

In America we have no annual supreme day, no day whose approach makes the whole nation glad.

We have the fourth of July, and Christmas, and Thanksgiving. None of them can claim primacy; none of them can arouse an enthusiasm which comes near to being universal. Eight grown Americans out of ten dread the coming of the fourth of July, with its pandemonium and its perils, and they rejoice when it is gone . . . if they are still alive.

The approach of Christmas brings harassment and dread to many excellent people. They have to buy a cart-load of presents, and they never know what to buy to hit the various tastes. People put in three weeks of hard and anxious work, and when Christmas morning comes they are so dissatisfied with the result, and so disappointed, that they want to sit down and cry. Then they give thanks that Christmas comes but once a year.

The observance of Thanksgiving Day, as a function, has become general of late. The thankfulness is not so general. This is natural. Two-thirds of the nation have always had hard luck and a hard time during the year, and this has a calming effect upon their enthusiasm for giving thanks.

We have a supreme day, a sweeping and tremendous and tumultuous day, a day which commands an absolute universality of interest and excitement; but it is not annual. It comes but once in four years when the President is elected; therefore it cannot count as a rival of the Melbourne Cup.

In Great Britain and Ireland they have two great days, Christmas and the Queen's birthday. But they are equally popular; there is no supremacy.

I think it must be conceded that the position of the Australasian Day is unique, solitary, unparalleled, and likely to hold that high place a long time.

Cup Day is supreme, it has no rival. I can call to mind no specialised annual day, in any country, which can be named by that large name . . . Supreme!

I can call to mind no specialised annual day, in any country, whose approach fires the whole land with a conflagration of conversation and preparation and anticipation and jubilation. No day save this one; but this one does it.

THE NARK

C.J. DENNIS

Wait till after Chewsday, wife.
'Taint far ahead to look,
A change is comin' in your life,
Or else I'm much mistook,
I'll buy you rugs an' furs an' things
An' di'monds by the ton.
We're 'ome at last when Chewsday's past
An' Melbun Cup is run.

Wait till after Chewsday, Bill.
You're silly if you frets;
I'll pay that quid; you know I will;
An' settle all me debts.
The tip's cert; the 'orse can spurt
An' last the distance too.
I'm 'ome all right by Chewsday night
When all me dreams come true.

I knows, I knows; too well I knows
I've said it all before;
But blokes 'as got to learn I s'pose;
I'll never switch no more.
Me mind's made up. This Melbun Cup
You'll 'ave no chance to scoff.
I mean to stick to my first pick
An' never git put off.

So wait till after Chewsdy, mate.
Till after Chewsday, wife.
A man can't be the fool of fate
For all 'is nach'ril life.
An' yet, an' yet, I can't forget
Past years, an' nags I backs.
In pichers grim I visions 'im,
That coot wot dogs me tracks—

Never the same bloke year by year,
'E waits there on the course
To pour 'is poison in my ear—
That 'ound wot knows a 'orse.
'E knows a man wot knows a man
Wot knows the stable well.
'E knows, 'e knows—Lord! Wot 'e knows
'Ud take a book to tell.

An' must I meet 'im once again—
My Jonah, still disguised?
An' must I 'ark to that dead nark
An' stand there, 'ipnertised?
Keep 'im away! Keep me, I pray,
From speakin', still bewitched,
The bitterest word a man 'er 'eard:
'I 'ad it, but I switched.'

CUP CASUALTIES

C.J. DENNIS

'A man can never tell.' This, I find, is a favourite phrase in the mouths of Australian sportsmen who 'follow the game' more or less as a regular habit. It indicates a mildly philosophic mental attitude that is commendable, and a state of fitting humility before the gods. A man—a mere man—never can tell.

I commend the sentence now to the notice of those countless thousands of amateur sportsmen who, shortly after the publication of these words, will be suffering all the slings and arrows of a faith betrayed, and bearing fardels of confidence misplaced.

I refer to those myriads who backed a loser in the race for the Melbourne Cup.

But who would fardels bear when the slogan of the true sport is available to all as a solace and a shield against the barbs of vain regret? 'A man can never tell.'

Yet those doleful losers, even at the moment, possibly, when these lines swim into their ken, are already imagining vain things and painting in absurdly glowing colours ridiculous pictures of vanished might-have-beens.

But, believe me, a man never can tell. And to such jaded Jonahs as these—also the joyless Jeremiahs and lamenting Lears—I here offer these few soothing bromides to lay, as unction, to their aching souls. (I am not sure that this is the orthodox manner of applying bromides, but it really doesn't matter much.)

Yes, my fellows in adversity. The phrase betrays me; for I fear greatly that I, too, will very soon be counted amongst you. I have risked my paltry all upon the chances of a horse named James

Aitch because he seemed to offer the richest rewards. But even at this stage strange misgivings begin to assail me. But let us to our cases.

Take that of my friend, Selwyn X. Shad, who won £300 in Manfred's year. The efficient chief accountant of a prosperous city firm, Selwyn had long nursed in secret the desire to possess a business of his own. That £300 helped him to realise his ambition, and he rejoiced. At the end of two years, Selwyn (a far better servant than master, as events proved) failed in business, and now, after humbling himself greatly, fills a minor position at reduced salary with his old firm. Whereas, if he had not backed the winner—But, of course, you apprehend.

Behold my bosom pal, Peter A. Fittlebrush, painfully propelling homeward his fevered feet after losing his last lone sixpence at a bygone Cup meeting.

Upon his painful pilgrimage he enters a secluded suburban street. A gaily garbed little girl dandles a doll by the edge of the road. Suddenly a baker's careering cart dashes dangerously around a corner, swerves and side-slips straight upon the beautiful babe. Urged by an inflexible will, Peter propels fevered feet aforesaid with sudden speed, snatches, in the nick of time, the babe from beneath those horrible hooves.

From where a palatial pile stands in its own gorgeous grounds near by, sounds first a woman's shriek, then a strong man's hoarse cry of horror. The mother and father rush into the street to receive from Peter's trembling hands their cherished child—unscathed. Peter, whose only good suit, foul with the gutter's grime, is ruined beyond repair, is urged to come within. Here a touching scene ensues. The beauteous babe throws adoring arms about Peter's neck and cries that her preserver must never leave her.

Who today does not know the magic name of Peter A. Fittlebrush, the marmalade magnate, who once saved from dreadful death the youngest daughter, and subsequently wedded the eldest daughter, of the millionaire manufacturer whose right-hand man and partner he is today? Yet, had he backed but one winner . . . Need I elaborate?

But, as I write, the Melbourne Cup is yet to be run and won; and still I toy with the lingering hope that perhaps this James Aitch may—Ah well; a man really never can tell.

Note: James Aitch finished last of the eighteen runners in the 1933 Melbourne Cup won by Hall Mark.

A POST CUP TALE

C.J. DENNIS

When Trivalve won in 1927, Dennis wrote 'A Post Cup Tale', a sequel to 'The Nark'. In 'A Post Cup Tale' everything the protagonist in 'The Nark' feared would happen, does happen! The wonderful thing about Dennis's poem about Trivalve's Cup win is that it has outlived any other poems written about Cup winners in various years because it contains a greater human story and captures an elemental truth about all punters, anytime, anywhere. It is one of the most recited and anthologised of all Dennis's poems.

***

I 'ad the money in me 'and!
Fair dinkum! Right there, by the stand.
I tole me wife at breakfus' time,
Straight out: 'Trivalve,' I sez, ''is prime.
Trivalve,' I sez. An', all the week,
I swear there's no one 'eard me speak
Another 'orse's name. Why, look,
I 'ad the oil straight from a Book
On Sund'y at me cousin's place
When we was talkin' of the race.
'Trivalve,' 'e sez. ''Is chance is grand.'
I 'ad the money in me 'and!

Fair in me 'and I 'ad the dough!
An' then a man 'as got to go—
Wot? Tough? Look, if I 'adn't met
Jim Smith (I ain't forgave 'im yet)
'E takes an' grabs me by the coat.
'Trivalve?' 'e sez. 'That hairy goat!'
(I 'ad the money in me 'and
Just makin' for the bookie's stand)
'Trivalve?' 'e sez. 'Ar, turn it up!
'Ow could 'e win a flamin' Cup?'
Of course, I thort 'e muster knoo.
'Im livin' near a trainer, too.

Right 'ere, like that, fair in me fist
I 'ad the notes! An' then I missed—
Missed like a mug fair on the knock
Becos 'is maggin' done me block.
'That hairy goat?' 'e sez. 'E's crook!'
Fair knocked me back, 'e did. An' look,
I 'ad the money in me 'and!
Fair in me paw! An', un'erstand,
Sixes at least I coulder got—
Thirty to five, an' made a pot.
Today I mighter been reel rich—
Rollin' in dough! Instid o' which,
'Ere's me—Aw! Don't it beat the band?
I 'AD THE MONEY IN ME 'AND!
Put me clean off, that's wot 'e did . . .
Say, could yeh lend us 'arf a quid?

AS UNLUCKY AS SHADOW KING

JIM HAYNES

'As unlucky as Shadow King' was a common saying in Australia in the 1930s and 1940s. True, it was mostly a racetrack saying but, as Shadow King was six times a player in that most Australian of all events, the Melbourne Cup, it was a saying that all Australians understood.

Shadow King was a son of Comedy King, the first imported horse to win the Melbourne Cup. Comedy King had arrived in Australia as a foal. Mr Sol Green purchased his dam, Tragedy Queen, in Britain in 1906. She was in foal to the famous English Derby winner, Persimmon, and the resulting foal was Comedy King, who dominated Australian racing in 1910 and defeated another great horse, Trafalgar, in the Melbourne Cup of that year. Indeed, he defeated Trafalgar on eight occasions.

Comedy King also proved to be an outstanding sire. Two of his sons won the Cup—Artilleryman (1919) and King Ingoda (1922)—and he was grandsire on the dam side to Comic Court, who won in 1950. Artilleryman was reputed to be the best looking horse ever seen on an Australian racetrack and many feel he could have been the greatest racehorse of his era. He won the Cup as a three-year-old but was tragically dead from illness before the season ended.

Shadow King's dam, Beryllia, was by the Irish stallion Land of Song from the English mare, Berylium, so he was truly of migrant stock, yet the racing public loved him as the archetypal Aussie battler.

It has been much discussed that our premier race is a handicap rather than a true test of quality. A brief study of the race's history will show it is exactly that element that has made the Cup the great Australian event that it is.

We want to see if our champions can overcome the odds and win with the weight, and we love our champions whether they win or lose the Cup. Wakeful, Kingston Town, Gunsynd and Phar Lap in 1931 were cheered from the course, gallant in defeat.

We want to know if the three-year-olds can run above their experience with the smaller weights. We also want to see if that dour battling old stayer we have watched over the years can run a brave race against the odds.

Americans, it is said, love winners, and the British love quality and breeding. Australians appreciate these things too but, perhaps because of certain elements in our history and heritage, we are different: we believe everyone should be given a 'fair go' and our greatest sporting event is a handicap race.

If the Melbourne Cup is a celebration of the Australian's love of 'giving everyone a go', then Shadow King truly represents the 'everyone' we are talking about.

Shadow King was a 'trier'; he always 'had a go'. Trained by popular 'battling' trainer Elwood Fisher, the dark bay gelding ran in his first Melbourne Cup as a four-year-old in 1929. Nightmarch won the Cup that year, from Paquito and the three-year-old Phar Lap, who was even-money favourite.

Most experts think that Phar Lap lost the 1929 Cup by pulling all through the early stages so badly that his jockey that day, the fifty-year-old Bobby Lewis, had little choice but to let him have his head and stride away at the 6-furlong post. This enabled Nightmarch to run him down in the straight. Shadow King followed them in a respectable sixth.

The following year Phar Lap, ridden by Jim Pike, won the Cup easily, carrying a record weight for a four-year-old and at the prohibitive odds of 11 to 8 on. It was the only time in history that the bookies sent a horse out at odds-on in the Cup.

The appropriately named Second Wind was 3 lengths away in second place and Shadow King was there, earning £1000 for his owner, Mr Schillaber, by finishing three-quarters of a length away in third place.

The following year Phar Lap was asked to carry the record weight of 10 st 10 lb (68 kg), which proved to be too much even for that great horse. White Nose, with the featherweight of 6 st 12 lb (43.5 kg), finished 2 lengths ahead of a gallant Shadow King, who carried 8 st 7 lb (54 kg). Phar Lap finished eighth. Prizemoney had been reduced due to the Depression and Shadow King took home just a little more than he had for finishing third the year before, £1250.

There was no Phar Lap in 1932. Instead of the 'Red Terror' there was the showy golden chestnut with the silver mane and tail, Peter Pan. With the standard three-year-old's weight of 7 st 6 lb (47 kg), Peter Pan started favourite and defeated Yarramba, a five-year-old who carried the even lighter weight of 7 st 3 lb (46 kg), in a close finish. Two lengths behind them came Shadow King, now officially 'aged' and carrying 8 st 12 lb (56 kg). Third prizemoney was £750.

Now we come to the highlight of Shadow King's Cup career, the Cup he really should have won.

In 1933 Shadow King was eight years old. Only one eight-year-old had ever won the Cup up to that time, the mighty little grey Toryboy, in 1865. (The New Zealander, Catalogue, would become the only other eight-year-old to win the Cup, in 1938.)

The two best horses in Australia at the time were Peter Pan and Hall Mark. Peter Pan had come back from his Cup win in 1932 to win the AJC St Leger, Cumberland Plate and AJC Plate but he was out for the spring with a severe bout of muscular rheumatism.

Hall Mark had won the premier two-year-old races in Victoria in 1932 and also the Fairfield Handicap, Sires Produce and Champagne Stakes in Sydney. As a three-year-old he won the AJC and VRC Derbies and he would race on to win a Doncaster in 1935.

Hall Mark was surely a champion but he was under an injury cloud with a leg infection on Cup Day 1933. Finally, at 1.30 p.m. Hall Mark was passed fit to run by the VRC vet and he took his place at the start carrying 7 st 8 lb (48 kg). Shadow King carried 8 st 9 lb (55 kg).

It was one of the closest finishes in Cup history. Hall Mark raced on the pace in sixth position throughout and made a run to take the lead at the furlong post. Shadow King raced back in the field, struck dreadful trouble on the turn and was almost flattened. His jockey, Scobie Breasley, managed to get him balanced again and he made a long run in the straight from well back and just failed to catch Hall Mark, who won by a head. Topical and Gaine Carrington dead-heated for third, a further head behind Shadow King, who again earned £1250 for running second.

Two weeks later Shadow King won the Williamstown Cup, at his fifth attempt, at the good odds of 12 to 1. Despite the fact that few had backed him, he was cheered into the winners' enclosure.

Peter Pan returned to win his second Cup in 1934 but, for the first time in six years, Shadow King was not fit enough to take his place in the Cup field.

When the Cup came around in 1935 Peter Pan was favoured early but he disappointed in the Melbourne Stakes on the Saturday before the Cup. Marabou, who had been placed in the Caulfield Cup and the Melbourne Stakes, started favourite on the day.

That is to say, Marabou started the 'money' favourite. There was no doubt who was 'favourite' with the crowd, despite being quoted at 100 to 1 in the betting ring.

In a wonderful gesture the VRC allowed Shadow King, ten years old and carrying saddlecloth number 7, to lead the field onto the track for the Melbourne Cup of 1935, and how the crowd of 110,739 cheered!

Marabou won carrying 7 st 11 lb (50 kg). Shadow King, ridden again by the great Scobie Breasley, flew home to run fourth and create a Melbourne Cup record that will never be beaten: six starts for two seconds, two thirds, a fourth and a sixth.

In those six Melbourne Cups, Shadow King competed against three of the greatest horses to ever draw breath in Australia in Hall Mark, Peter Pan and Phar Lap. He was never the 'money' favourite. He started at 10 to 1 in 1929, ran third at 50 to 1 in 1930, second at 25 to 1 in 1931, third at 25 to 1 in 1932, second at 33 to 1 in 1933, and fourth at 100 to 1 in 1935! But there was no horse the punters would rather have seen win, whether they lost their money or not.

Apart from his 1933 Williamstown Cup win, Shadow King was a good enough stayer to also win the Hotham Handicap in 1929, the Coongy Handicap and the Moonee Valley Gold Cup in 1930, and the Herbert Power Handicap in 1931.

After all that, he didn't get to retire to a lucerne paddock somewhere. As a gelding with good temperament he was still a useful horse and he was retrained after he quit racing and became a police horse.

One advantage of being a trooper's horse was that Shadow King was called upon to do ceremonial police duty at the Melbourne Cup each year and he attended every Cup until he passed away in 1945. He was buried beneath a little headstone at the Bundoora Police Depot.

Back in the 1930s and 1940s 'as unlucky as Shadow King' was a common saying. It is forgotten today, along with most of the horses that have won the Melbourne Cup.

Every November the media remind us about some of the great names in Cup history. There are trivia contests on radio and the same famous names are usually referred to.

Among the names remembered by average Aussies, when they are reminded, are Phar Lap, Peter Pan and maybe Carbine, along with a few of the winners of recent years. The rest of the winners are long forgotten.

Oh . . . and there's another name everyone seems to remember too, whenever the Cup comes around, which seems odd, because he never won the Cup . . . his name is Shadow King.

THE BARBER'S STORY

C.J. DENNIS

In the year of Phar Lap's victory, 1930, C.J. Dennis produced one of his funniest Spring Carnival poems, written from the point of view of a barber who, the day after the Cup, attempts to make conversation with a surly customer who has, rather obviously, backed the second favourite, Tregilla. Many punters backed Tregilla, with 7 st 9 lb (48.5 kg), to beat Phar Lap, who carried the huge weight of 9 st 12 lb, 15 pounds over weight-for-age. Tregilla was a talented Sydney four-year-old who had won the Australian Derby and finished second to Phar Lap in the Cox Plate and the Melbourne Stakes.

Phar Lap won by 3 lengths slowing down. Tregilla started at 5 to 1 and ran seventh. Dennis's verse appeared in the Melbourne Herald the following day.

***

'Mornin',' I sez to 'im. Gloomy, 'e seemed to be.
Glum an' unsociable, comes in the shop
'Mornin',' I sez to 'im, 'e don't say anythin'.
'You're next,' I sez; and 'e sits with a flop.

'Great Cup?' I sez to 'im. Shakin' the wrappin's out.
He don't say nothin'; but jist give a grunt.
'Great win?' I sez to 'im, Smilin' encouragin'.
'Wonderful way that 'e come to the front.'

He don't reply to me. Sits sorta glarin' like.
'Phar Lap,' I sez to 'im. 'Wonder 'orse, what?
Have a win yestidy?' Still 'e don't answer me.
'Phar Lap,' I sez, 'He made hacks of the lot.'

'Champeen,' I sez to 'im. 'Wonderful popular . . .
This 'ere Tregilla, 'e never showed up . . .
Phar Lap,' I sez to 'im, 'Must be a wonder 'orse.
But that Tregilla run bad in the Cup.'

'What?' 'e come back at me, lookin' peculiar,
Red in the face, so I thought 'e would choke.
'Cab-horse!' 'e sez to me, nasty an' venomous,
Real disagreeable sort of a bloke.

'Tregilla!?' 'e sez to me, glarin' real murderous.
'Tregilla!!?' 'e barks at me. 'That 'airy goat!'
Surly, 'e seemed to me, man couldn't talk to 'im . . .
'Hair-cut?' I sez to 'im. 'No!' 'e sez . . . 'Throat!'

THE EVE OF THE CUP

A.B. 'BANJO' PATERSON

I had intended to say something about men and manners outback, but, this being the eve of the Melbourne Cup, I thought I ought to say something about horseracing.

I don't know which is the hardest, the human race or the horserace. You can tell pretty well what a horse will do but when a man starts backing horses you never know what he'll do.

Now, here's an instance. A lady friend of mine, a fine sensible woman, went into a big drapery store just before the last Metropolitan. She bought a lot of goods and they sent a small boy out with her to carry her parcels to the car.

On the way out to the car the boy said, 'Now, listen, lady. If you want a good bet, put all you've got on Strength for the Metropolitan. It's a snip. Now I'm telling you. Don't listen to anybody else. Back Strength.'

If it had been anything except horseracing she'd have given him a lift under the ear and told him to mind his own business, but people think there's some kind of magic about horseracing. She put a pound on Strength and won fifty pounds and then she said to me, 'Now, how did that boy know Strength was going to win?'

I said, 'He didn't know. He was just guessing.'

'Oh,' she said, 'that's nonsense. He must have known. Look how sure he was.'

So then I thought I'd try her on another tack and I said, 'What was the boy like?' She described him and I said, 'Oh, I know about that boy. He's a bit of a phenomenon. They keep him here to tell them what the fashions will be next season.'

'Ah,' she said, 'don't be silly. How could he know what the women's fashion would be? An ignorant little boy like that!'

'Well,' I said, 'how could he know what would win the Metropolitan?'

It was no use. She's going down to that same shop this week to buy the same goods and get the same boy to carry them, and she thinks she'll get the winner of the Melbourne Cup at fifty to one. I've no doubt that ninety per cent of you that are listening to me would do the same thing if you knew what shop it was.

This betting complex is an interesting study in human psychology. People think there's some magic about it. Well, it's like the poetry. It's an inheritance from the old tribal days, when every tribe had its magician. A magician in those days would tell a man that he was going to die in a fortnight and if the man's health continued to be good, the magician would knock him on the head some dark night. Then, when the body was found in the morning, the tribe would say, 'Isn't that magician a wonder! How did he know the man was doing to die?'

Even intelligent people like the Romans would not go into battle until the soothsayers had killed some chickens and studied their entrails to see whether the Romans were going to win the battle. It's not much over a couple of hundred years since the English were burning people for witchcraft, and millions of people believe in fortune tellers, and divining rods for finding water, and quack doctors that can cure anything. You know, even now any quack doctor can go into a country town and take away two or three hundred pounds in cash, while the local professional men can't get in a bob. It's the same complex we have on the turf, the magician complex.

Talking of doctors, a doctor friend of mine started betting pretty heavily and I said, 'What are you betting on, doctor? What makes you think you can beat the books?'

'Oh,' he said, 'I've got hold of a wonderful chap. He knows when they are going to back their horses. They tell him . . .' (I thought to myself, 'I'm sure they would') 'and, although I never listen to trainers, who are mostly a lot of mugs, this cove knows.'

So then he went to go away, and I said, 'Where are you going to, doctor?'

'Oh,' he said, 'I'm going down town to pay for a suit of clothes for this fellow. He hasn't got any clothes fit to go to the races in.'

Well, there you are. Can you beat it? The magician complex again.

Coming now to this year's Melbourne Cup, I've been very friendly with Mr Moss, owner of the second favourite, Veilmond, for many years, and I asked him whether he thought Phar Lap could give his horse twenty-five pounds.

Do you know what he said? He said, 'I don't know.' If he'd been a small boy in a shop he'd have known offhand.

About this business of knowing winners, I was at Randwick one day with a lady friend of mine—I seem to have a lot of lady friends, don't I—and she stopped a trainer and she said, 'Oh, Mr So-and-so, tell me what will win this race.'

Now the trainer hadn't been going too well, and he said, 'Look, lady, if I knew the winners of races, do you think I'd train horses for a living? Do you think I'd get up at four o'clock in the morning and get my feet wet, and run to the telephone all day explaining to owners why their horses didn't win? I would not. I'd come down here and win all the money I wanted and I'd go fishing all day, and I'd play cards all night. I wouldn't go to bed till four o'clock in the morning. On with the dance: that'd be my motto.'

So when he went away this lady said, 'There's a nice ungrateful hound for you. My husband used to have horses with that man, and now he won't tell me anything.'

So I said, 'I think he told you a lot.'

Betting is like drinking and card playing; it's all right in moderation but I have seen too many decent fellows got to ruin and some of them got to gaol because they get this betting complex. But the Latin poet Horace says, '*Dulce est desipere in loco* . . . It is pleasant to make a fool of yourself occasionally,' so I think I'll probably make a fool of myself by betting a bit with Mr Moss on Veilmond mainly for old acquaintance sake.

I think Phar Lap may beat himself by fighting for his head in the early part of the race. But keep that to yourself. Don't tell anybody I told you.

Note: Veilmond did finish ahead of Phar Lap in the 1931 Cup, to which Paterson refers here but, unfortunately for 'The Banjo', he was fifth and Phar Lap eighth behind White Nose. Veilmond was at least a model of consistency in the Cup, having also finished fifth behind Phar Lap in 1930. And, incidentally, although Paterson was an astute judge of horses, it was common knowledge that Phar Lap was prone to over-race and be difficult to ride at times; he probably lost the 1929 Cup by fighting for his head early, and finished third.

LISTEN, ELAINE!

C.J. DENNIS

One of C.J. Dennis's favourite devices was the 'one-sided conversation' in which the reader is presented with only one voice in a conversation and the humour comes, in part, from guessing the obvious 'other side' of the dialogue.

In 'Listen, Elaine' the husband is slowly stripped of his Cup Day punting money by a wife keen on using the Cup as the excuse to obtain an entire new wardrobe. The only voice we hear is that of the husband, making unsuccessful attempts to keep his wife in her old dress. Of course, the punter's need for betting money is of no concern to a fashion-conscious wife. Some things don't change.

***

Listen, Elaine. Tho' I'm not mad on racing,
I like a little flutter now and then;
But I maintain you would not be disgracing
The family, or look like some old hen
If you just wore . . . Now, just a minute, please . . .
That pinkish frock . . . No, wait! Let me explain.
That pinkish frock with spots . . . You wouldn't *freeze*!
You've got your furs. Aw, listen, please, Elaine!

Now, look. We've twenty pounds. Don't let us quarrel.
  Surely we can be sane and quite grown-up.
If you take most of that, what of the 'moral'
  That Percy Podgrass gave us for the Cup?
Of course he's sure to win. What are vain dresses
  Compared . . . My dear! I did not call *you* vain!
Nor selfish either. Gosh! What married messes
  Start over clothes, and . . . Listen, please, Elaine.

We're partners, aren't we? Well, then, listen, darling.
  We might discuss this calmly, don't you think?
Now! Please be sensible . . . I am not *snarling*!
  Rubbish! Of course, you do look nice in pink.
I always thought that spotted pink looked dandy,
  And comfy, too. Supposing it should rain.
Nice sight you'd look in . . . What's it called . . . organdie . . .
  I was not *wishing* . . . Listen, please! Elaine!

Women just dress to spite some other tabby.
  Who said you were a cat? One moment, pet.
Of course, I wouldn't have my wife look *shabby*.
  Take what you need. We'll make a smaller bet . . .
Eight . . . ten . . . twelve quid! Whew! Not much left for betting.
  Still, just a flutter and expenses . . . *What*?
Listen, Elaine. What could I be *forgetting*?
  Hat? Stockings? Shoes to match? . . . Here . . . Take the lot!

BART CUMMINGS: THE KING OF THE CUP

BRUCE MONTGOMERIE

There are three factors which made Bart the 'Cups King', with an unprecedented twelve Melbourne Cup wins over a period of 44 years.

Firstly, there is his understanding of training for stamina. Secondly, his amazing knack of timing horses' campaigns. Lastly, his dedication to the welfare of his horses.

If you count Bart's involvement as the track rider and strapper of 1950 winner Comic Court, trained by his father James, he has been involved in thirteen Cup wins over a 60-year period. Now, that's a feat that will surely never be repeated.

The future 'Cups King' had an inauspicious start to his Melbourne Cup career when his first runner, Asian Court, at 40 to 1, finished twelfth in 1958.

Bart's first Melbourne Cup success came with a quinella seven years later, at his fourth attempt, in 1965, when one of his favourite horses, Light Fingers, won and another of his runners, Ziema, finished second.

Bart spotted Light Fingers as a yearling at Pirongia Stud in New Zealand. He did not think the foal was much to look at but as she took off across the paddock it was a different story. As soon as he saw her move Bart said he noticed the mighty stride of a natural galloper.

'She had tremendous will to win and would strain every limb in her body to do so,' Bart recalled.

Light Fingers almost missed the Cup in 1965. In the Caulfield Stakes she clipped the heels of Winfreux and almost fell, causing her to rick a muscle in her shoulder. It looked like the end of her spring campaign and she was forced to miss the Caulfield Cup, but the magic of Bart Cummings had her ready to run on the first Tuesday in November.

Bart had three runners in the 1965 Melbourne Cup: the big, tough stayer Ziema, another hardened character The Dip (winner of the AJC Metropolitan Handicap), and Light Fingers. It looked like Ziema would take the Cup until Light Fingers emerged from the pack to challenge. The tiny chestnut mare and the big black gelding went to the line locked together and Light Fingers won by a lip.

Light Fingers was raced on lease by Melbourne grain merchant, Wally Broderick, who owned her older full brother, The Dip. The two were well named, being by the French stallion Le Filou, which translates as 'pickpocket'. 'Dip' is an old Aussie slang term for just that, a pickpocket. Light Fingers' name was clever and an obvious choice as a full sister to The Dip.

Light Fingers was originally named Close Embrace by her owners, the Dawson family. This name came from her female lineage; her dam, granddam and great-granddam raced as Cuddlesome, Fondle and Caress. Wally Broderick preferred the name to come from the sire's side to match her full brother, and re-registered her before she raced in his famous colours of white with royal blue spots and cap.

Bart then went on to chalk up three Melbourne Cups in a row, with Galilee and Light Fingers adding another quinella in the 1966 race and Red Handed winning in 1967.

Bart's second quinella in the race saw the owners of the unlucky Ziema, the Baileys, win with Galilee; while it was Wally Broderick's turn to finish second, again with little Light Fingers.

Galilee was an astute buy twelve months before Bart's first Cup win with Light Fingers. His success on the track is an example of Bart's eagle eye and training ability.

Galilee threw his offside front leg out at a 45-degree angle, which produced an awkward, almost laughable, gait; but Bart noticed that Galilee was not knock-kneed but pigeon-toed, and that he actually put his hooves down perfectly. Good training and shoeing could overcome the condition. The Baileys trusted Bart and consequently won the Melbourne Cup in 1966 after going within a whisker the year before with Ziema.

In the spring of 1966 Galilee had an arthritic condition, and as the rumour spread he drifted from 6 to 1 to 14 to 1 for the Caulfield Cup. However, there was no indication of soreness when Galilee unleashed his withering finish to beat Gala Crest by a length and a half to give Bart his first Caulfield Cup victory.

Bart attacked the 1966 Melbourne Cup with two starters: Galilee and Light Fingers. Bart brought Light Fingers to Melbourne rather short of condition, with only four lead-up runs in which she had been second twice and third once.

Once again history was made when Bart became the first trainer to quinella the Melbourne Cup twice. With little more than a furlong to run Light Fingers stormed to the front. For a moment it seemed she would triumph until Bart's better-conditioned runner, Galilee, breezed past her for an easy 2-length win.

Galilee was a champion. He became the first racehorse since Even Stevens in 1962 to win the Caulfield–Melbourne Cup double and was recognised as the best horse in Australia since Tulloch.

'Not only is Cummings the man of the moment but also at least the racing man of the decade,' one newspaper claimed. 'His Cups win climaxed a run of successes, as no other Australian horse trainer has known.'

Cummings's success in major races surpassed even that of Sydney's Tommy Smith, who had broken almost every training record.

Racing historians were astounded at Bart's feat of claiming the Caulfield, Melbourne and Sydney Cups with Galilee. In more than a century no trainer had prepared one horse to win that hat-trick.

Bart's most astonishing, and highly profitable, 1966–67 season, with a small but strong team of horses, set a Commonwealth training record—winning $358,918 in stakes money.

Bart finished the season with seven cups to his credit. He had quinellaed the Melbourne and Adelaide Cups, and won the

Caulfield, Sandown, Sydney, Brisbane and Queens Cups. It was one of the most sensational training performances in Australian racing history, a record that may never be equalled.

No man had trained three Cup winners on the trot. But soon after Galilee won the 1966 Melbourne Cup Bart forecast he had another 'good thing'. He announced that Red Handed would win the 1967 Melbourne Cup.

Again Bart's expert knowledge of horses stood him in good stead when he had settled for an 'ugly duckling' chestnut colt by Le Filou, lot 202 at the 1963 New Zealand yearling sales.

Bart had tried to prepare Red Handed for Galilee's 1966 Melbourne Cup but then, as a four-year-old, he fell in the Geelong Cup in October, breaking a bone in the near hock, which ruled him out of the Cup. It was only with careful nursing and skilled veterinary care that the chestnut stayer was brought back to racing ten months later.

Red Handed was a frail-looking, plain customer.

Few people noticed that Red Handed almost fell in the straight the first time around in the 1967 Melbourne Cup while travelling wide and looking for a position. He was well back in the field for most of the race but hit the front 400 metres from home. With 100 metres to go he seemed beaten when Red Crest passed him and forged clear. However, Red Handed fought back, drew closer with each stride and went on to win by a neck.

Bart had become the first trainer in the 107-year history of the Melbourne Cup to train three successive winners of the race. The normally unflappable, deadpan trainer admitted Galilee had given him a big thrill when he won in 1966, but said the pleasure was far greater when Red Handed completed the hat-trick. It was also the first time Bart's stable colours—the now-famous green and gold diagonal stripes with a white cap—had been carried to Melbourne Cup victory.

Bart's third Melbourne Cup had come along just when some people were saying his luck had run out and he owed his success in 1965 and 1966 to two horses 'anyone could have trained'.

Red Handed's win was a typical example of Bart's earnest pursuit of perfection—patience and care, attention to detail, homework and hard work have always been essential to the Bart Cummings style of training.

Bart claimed he did not believe in luck, but he admitted he gave Red Handed a helping hand by using Light Fingers' bridle on him in the 1967 Melbourne Cup.

By Melbourne Cup time the following spring Bart had trained plenty of winners, but his four runners in the Flemington marathon were all beaten out of the placings. It was the first time in four years he had failed to get a winner or a placed horse.

'I don't suppose a man can go on expecting to train the Melbourne Cup winner year after year,' he philosophised laconically.

Bart opened a permanent stable in Melbourne during 1968 with enough space for 60 boxes. Since 1965 he had been making two raids a year on Melbourne's rich purses, and the new set-up was his first step in his plan to become the first trainer to operate self-contained stables in three capital cities: Adelaide, Melbourne and Sydney.

By the late 1960s Bart was getting among the big prizemoney just as he planned. He was soon to feature in one of the most stunning incidents in the history of the turf in Australia.

Leading up to the 1969 Melbourne Cup Bart had four acceptors in the big race: Big Philou, Swift General, General Command and The Sharper. The first of a series of sensations occurred when Big Philou was beaten into second place by Nausori in the Caulfield Cup.

Cummings entered a protest against Nausori, which was upheld. For only the second time in the history of the Caulfield Cup, the result was altered by the stewards to place Big Philou first.

Big Philou was to be withdrawn suddenly, just 45 minutes before the start of the 1969 Melbourne Cup. Bart noticed the horse scouring profusely in his stall and advised the stewards that the horse was distressed. It was one of the most sensational dramas in Cup history.

Big Philou had been nobbled, and the repercussions dragged on for more than a year. After receiving the result of the urine samples and droppings taken from Big Philou, it was discovered that the gelding had been administered a drug called Danthron.

Bart did not know how Big Philou had been 'got at'. VRC stewards swabbed fourteen of Bart's horses between November 1969 and August 1970 but all swabs returned negative findings.

In 1974 Bart was involved in a battle with Tommy Smith to become the first Australian to train horses to win more than 1 million dollars in stakes money before the season ended on 31 July.

On 17 June Bart pipped Tommy to reach the million-dollar mark. Bart picked up $200 in the first race at Caulfield when Lady Antoinette finished fourth, and even though Hello Honey was unlucky to finish second in the Birthday Handicap at Warwick Farm, the $1200 prizemoney she won did the trick. His runners went on to earn $12,250 in four starts—Eagle Farm, Warwick Farm, Caulfield and Victoria Park—that day, giving him a total of $1,011,252 for the season.

Bart had few better years than 1974. His stable took $272,360 over four days at the Melbourne Cup Carnival at Flemington, winning a staggering $432,430 from the time the Carnival opened with the Caulfield Guineas on October 12. His nine winners and a dead heat in the four days of the Melbourne Cup meeting were a training record for Victoria.

In 1974 Bart spearheaded his effort to win his first Melbourne Cup since 1967 with the great mare Leilani and the aptly named Think Big.

Leilani was easily his highest stakes-winner, with $143,550 from wins in the Toorak Handicap, Caulfield Cup, Mackinnon Stakes and Queens Cup. Astonishingly, Bart was to quinella the 1974 Melbourne Cup with horses he had cleverly acquired in 1972.

The trainer with a special eye for stayers had taken a chance at the New Zealand sales on a good-looking yearling and made the successful $10,000 bid. This on-the-spot decision was to prove as astute as his choice of Light Fingers, Galilee and Red Handed in previous years.

On Bart's arrival back in Australia, a Malaysian banker and property developer, Dato Tan Chin Nam, from Kuala Lumpur, asked him to buy a horse, preferably a stayer, and Bart suggested Think Big. At the same time as he bought Think Big he liked the look of a filly by Oncidium from the good race mare Lei. Bart snapped her up on lease and registered her as Leilani.

Leilani became the eleventh mare in history to win the Caulfield Cup, giving Bart his third victory in the race. Her Caulfield Cup win had been so convincing that she became a short-priced favourite to win the 1974 Melbourne Cup.

On the other hand, Think Big's 1974 Melbourne Cup campaign was unimpressive. He finished last in the AJC Metropolitan at Randwick on 7 October, failed in the Coongy Handicap at Caulfield on 16 October on a heavy track and was eighth in the Moonee Valley Cup on 26 October.

It rained heavily on the morning of the Melbourne Cup, but the track was still officially 'good' and Leilani was made 7 to 2 favourite.

Leilani loomed into contention in the straight and appeared to have the Melbourne Cup in her keeping until Think Big wound up and charged home to win by three-quarters of a length. Think Big had given the trainer his fourth Melbourne Cup, and with Leilani's second placing he had managed to quinella the race for the third time.

In May 1975 Bart shifted to new AJC stables at Randwick Racecourse and named the yard 'Leilani Lodge'. In June that year he chalked up his thirteenth Derby victory when Bottled Sunshine won the Queensland Derby.

During the 1974–75 season horses trained by Bart earned $1,399,182 in five states, creating another Australian record. The Cummings magic carried on into the 1975–76 season, and Bart approached the 1975 Melbourne Cup with three chances: Holiday Waggon, Leica Lover and Think Big.

Bart was confident of winning his fifth Melbourne Cup with either Leica Lover or Think Big. Think Big had again been unimpressive in lead-up races, beating only one horse home in the Mackinnon Stakes.

With 100 metres to go in the Cup Think Big grabbed the lead and the only challenge came from his stablemate, Holiday Waggon, who tried hard before finishing three-quarters of a length away second. Think Big knew only one thing—how to stay. It was another Melbourne Cup quinella and Bart's fifth Melbourne Cup, making him the first man to achieve five Cup wins in the twentieth century.

Think Big never won another race in nineteen starts. Bart was preparing the six-year-old for a tilt at the 1976 Melbourne Cup when the gelding broke down and was retired.

Bart had 30 horses entered for the 1976 Melbourne Cup, but his only runner come post time was Gold And Black. All eyes were on Bart's runner but a freak deluge—5 inches (12 cm) of rain accompanied by lightning and thunder just 30 minutes before the start of the Cup—had punters rushing to back the New Zealand mud-lark, Van Der Hum, into 9 to 2 favouritism.

Van Der Hum surged through the slush to score by 2 lengths from Gold And Black.

In 1977 Bart's chances of winning the Melbourne Cup were boosted when Gold And Black zoomed home for a half-length second in the Mackinnon Stakes.

The galloper was in line to become the first racehorse in the twentieth century to win a Melbourne Cup after being runner-up the previous year. Punters were not convinced and allowed Gold And Black to drift to 11 to 2 in the betting.

Gold And Black and Reckless, trained by Phar Lap's legendary strapper Tommy Woodcock, were destined to fight out the 1977 Melbourne Cup, with Gold And Black finishing just the stronger.

In claiming the race Bart had become the first trainer in history to prepare six Melbourne Cup winners.

He had now won six Melbourne Cups and also had five seconds, two fourths, a fifth and two sixths from the 32 runners he had started in fifteen Melbourne Cups since 1958. No wonder he was being called the Cups King.

Bart's four starters in 1978—Panamint, Vive Velours, Belmura Lad and Stormy Rex—did nothing to add to the legend, with Panamint at tenth the closest of the four at the finish.

In 1979 it was an older horse with leg problems, the 1977 Melbourne Cup placegetter, Hyperno, that was to add the next chapter to the legend.

The Cups King was at first reluctant to take on the horse, reasoning that it was hard enough to win races with sound horses, let alone with unsound ones. But Bart's methods suited Hyperno, who responded to the trainer's patient care even though his legs swelled badly after running in the Toorak Handicap of 1978.

On the Tuesday before the 1979 Melbourne Cup, Bart trialled the problem horse in blinkers and the gallop pleased him enough to believe he had another Cup winner. Hyperno went on to give the maestro his seventh Melbourne Cup. Hyperno's win also put paid to any suggestions that Bart had lost his touch.

Bart quinellaed the 1980 Caulfield Cup with Ming Dynasty and Hyperno but failed to get a placegetter in the Melbourne Cup, with Ming Dynasty finishing 17th.

Bart was awarded an Order of Australia for his services to horseracing in 1982, an honour for both him and his industry. It seemed that springtime in Melbourne belonged to Bart Cummings. His record of seven Melbourne Cups seemed destined to remain intact for years to come.

Between 1979 and 1986, however, Bart's Cups fortunes slumped and his only placing was Mr Jazz—third in 1983.

Bart finished the 1985–86 season eleventh on the Sydney trainers' list, the lowest he had been since opening his Sydney stable, and the 'knockers' were out again. 'They' said he was not putting enough effort into his horses and he was washed up as a trainer.

Unbelievably, in 1989, Bart found himself faced with a debt of more than $22 million when an ambitious syndication scheme he had hoped to get off the ground that year failed during an economic recession and he was left to pay for more than 80 yearlings.

Despite all his problems Bart won the 1989–90 Sydney trainers' premiership—his first in that city—and finished the season with six Group 1 wins, second to Colin Hayes with thirteen. However, Bart did not have a runner in the 1989 Melbourne Cup.

When 1990 rolled around, Bart had not prepared a winner of the Melbourne Cup for a decade, since Hyperno in 1979.

Bart put that decade of Melbourne Cup failures behind him in decisive fashion when he trained the 7 to 1 favourite, Kingston Rule, to win in 1990, and made it two in a row when Let's Elope won in 1991, with Shiva's Revenge finishing second to give him his fifth quinella in the race.

Let's Elope was the first mare to take the Caulfield–Melbourne Cups double since Rivette in 1939. Let's Elope was a duffer on rain-affected ground and, luckily for Bart, the spring of 1991 and the autumn of 1992 were seasons of fine, dry weather. The mare began a seven-race winning streak with the Turnbull Stakes in October, taking both Cups, and the Mackinnon, and returned in the new year to take the Orr Stakes, St George Stakes and Australian Cup, in course record time.

Bart had achieved what no other trainer had done. He had now won eight Melbourne Cups. Was there any stopping him from continuing to dominate the legendary staying event? He was certainly making it his race. Surely at his age he could not win another one!

Then, in 1996, along came a mighty stayer named Saintly. Darren Beadman wore the now-famous Dato Tan Chin Nam colours—black and white check with yellow sleeves—that day in November. It seems the born-again jockey sang a few hymns to the aptly named Saintly as they left the rest of the Melbourne Cup field in their wake. That was Cup number ten.

A new method of discovering ulcers in horses helped Western Australian galloper Rogan Josh to win the Melbourne Cup in 1999, giving J.B. Cummings his eleventh Melbourne Cup winner in the process.

Bart was the first to use a video gastro-endoscope machine, which offered a way of checking for ulcers in a horse's stomach. He used the process to sort out the health problems suffered by Rogan Josh and guided the gelding to a famous Cup victory.

In racing, fortunes are bound to fluctuate over time and even champion trainers have lean spells. Bart's top race wins dried up during the 2000–01 season in what was the start of one of his worst losing patches.

The Cups King went twelve months without a Group 1 winner and did not even have a runner in the 2000 Melbourne Cup. He had six Melbourne Cup hopes—Crown Mahal, Matriculate, Philidor, Indian Ridge, Darne Cath and Ringleader—start in the Saab Quality in an effort to qualify one or two of them in the 2000 Melbourne Cup through a win or second placing, but they all failed to run a place. The closest he came to having a runner in the Cup that year was with Philidor, who had qualified 36th, and Matriculate, who had been 27th in order of entry in the race.

Going into his 2002 Melbourne Cup campaign, Bart had only one Group 1 victory for the season.

The fickle punters were quick to write Cummings off, suggesting that he had passed his best and age was catching up with him. He failed to have a placegetter in the Melbourne Cup between 2001 and 2007. Despite Bart's apparent rise to glory again with Rogan Josh in 1999 it wasn't proving to be another golden era.

It was during the 2002 Melbourne Spring Carnival that Bart claimed all the overseas gallopers coming to Australia were making it difficult for local trainers to get a start in the Melbourne Cup. These comments were misconstrued as sour grapes in some quarters. What Bart really feared was that Australasian breeders and owners were not bothering to breed good stayers and keep them in training.

Bart was thankful for more support from his old friend, Dato Tan, when the 2008 Melbourne Cup approached. The two were now 'old men', and many saw both as dinosaurs of the turf. But Dato Tan owned the middle-distance galloper Viewed and Bart saw the chance to make him a Cup horse.

How could you bet on Viewed? He came into the race with a reputation as a wet tracker and the form in his four starts leading up to the Melbourne Cup read eighth of 15 at Flemington, seventh of 13, tenth of 17 in the Caulfield Cup, and last of 11 in the LKS Mackinnon Stakes.

Viewed went out at 40 to 1 and was supported by only the most loyal followers of J.B. Cummings. He hit the front at the 350-metre mark in the Melbourne Cup and was 2 lengths clear with 200 metres to run. When he began to tire with 100 metres to go, his 21-year-old jockey, Blake Shinn, thought he had gone too early.

Shinn said he could hear the Luca Cumani–trained Bauer closing in. Many thought the grey import had snatched victory but Bauer died slightly on his run as he closed rapidly and just failed to run out the final few metres to the finishing post.

The crowd roared as the English invader drew closer and the gap narrowed. For Bart it was an odd déjà vu, almost a carbon copy of the 1965 Melbourne Cup when his first Cup winner, Light Fingers, won by the narrowest of margins from stablemate Ziema. This time, however, the rival was an overseas horse, not a stablemate.

This made victory all that much sweeter for the two old friends, Dato Tan Chin Nam and Bart Cummings, both in their 80s.

After Viewed and Bauer crossed the line together and the agonising wait was over, the photo finish gave Viewed the race by a whisker.

The Cup eluded Bart in 2009, although he dominated the Spring Carnivals across Australia with an amazing run of wins in Group 1 races; including the Cox Plate and the AJC Derby, to take his tally of Group 1 wins to 257, more than double that of second-placed contemporary trainer Lee Freedman.

Bart had nothing else to achieve. He was inducted into the Sport Australia Hall of Fame in 1991, was an inaugural inductee into the Australian Racing Hall of Fame and has since been elevated to the status of Legend—and the only other Legend is Phar Lap.

The only active racing trainer to be given life membership by the Victorian Racing Club, Bart revolutionised Australian racing with his complete dominance of Australia's most famous race.

He passed away on 30 August, 2015, aged 87.

Bart's Melbourne Cup Record:

81 runners, 12 winners, 9 other placegetters
15 per cent strike-rate win
11 per cent strike-rate place
26 per cent strike-rate win/place
5 quinellas

THE MELBOURNE CUP

LESBIA HARFORD

It is hard to imagine Lesbia Harford knowing much about horses, she was hardly the type to study a form guide or be seen in a marquee during the Spring Carnival. But she was a Melbourne girl and everyone loves the Cup!

Born in Melbourne in 1891 she suffered from a congenital heart defect and tuberculosis. She graduated in law in 1916 from Melbourne University in the same class as Robert Menzies. A radical socialist and champion of working women, she wrote wonderful poetry which she never bothered to publish. She died of tuberculosis in 1927, aged 36.

***

I like the riders
Clad in rose and blue;
Their colours glitter
And their horses too.
Swift go the riders
On incarnate speed.
My thought can scarcely
Follow where they lead.
Delicate, strong, long
Lines of colour flow,
And all the people
Tremble as they go.

QUEENS OF THE CUP

JIM HAYNES

Many would argue that Makybe Diva, three times Melbourne Cup winner, is the greatest staying mare of the modern era. Others would say that she was one of the greatest stayers ever—regardless of age, era or gender.

Makybe Diva was bred and born in Britain and so was always six months out of sync to her Australian rivals. This made it near impossible to train her for classic two- and three-year-old races, as she was six months younger than all Australian horses of the same official age.

After she was born, Makybe Diva was offered for sale at the famous Tatts Newmarket sales but, luckily for Tony Santic, she was passed in and so was shipped out to Australia with her mother, Tugela, who had been bought in foal to Desert King by Santic, an Aussie who migrated from Croatia as a child and made his money in the tuna fishing industry in South Australia before moving full-time into the thoroughbred industry.

Santic had Tugela taken to Dick Fowlston's Britton House Stud in Somerset before being sent on to Australia, and Makybe Diva was born there on 21 March 1999.

The filly's name was derived from the first two letters of the names of five women who worked in Santic's office and she raced in his now famous colours, a combination of the Croatian and Australian flags. Apart from two starts in Japan, she did all her racing in Australia.

With two lines back to Northern Dancer on her sire side and Northern Dancer and Nasrullah twice on her dam side,

Makybe Diva was line-bred to stay all day and had plenty of Carbine blood.

She was broken in and conditioned in two spells at Scone with legendary horseman Greg Bennett. Like all the thousands of horses he has educated, Bennett taught her 'to be a horse' before she became a racehorse. 'I think there's more to life than running around a racetrack,' Bennett often said.

Makybe Diva stood out as special when it became obvious she could carry Bennett's 85 kilograms up 'Heartbreak Hill', the rough rise at the back of his Scone property, and not even be blowing. Plenty of horses don't even get halfway, according to Bennett.

Bennett, a tough man who admitted he cried when the great mare won the Cox Plate, remembered she was 'very smooth to ride'.

'You could almost sit on her back,' he said, 'canter along, roll a smoke and drink a cup of tea at the same time.'

As she never started in the classic races at two and three, it is hard to line up a comparison between the tough bay mare and other great staying fillies and mares. She started once at three and finished fourth. She then went on a winning spree and won six in a row, starting with a maiden at Wangaratta and concluding with wins in the Werribee Cup and Queen Elizabeth Stakes of 2002. Although classed as a four-year-old mare, Makybe Diva was actually a three-year-old filly when she won those major races. The win in the Queen Elizabeth Stakes qualified her for the Melbourne Cup the following year and meant that her trainer, David Hall, could plan a light autumn and toughen the horse up slowly for her first attempt at the Melbourne Cup.

After two unplaced runs in the autumn she was rested for her spring campaign of 2003. She returned to run a series of fourth placings, culminating in the Caulfield Cup, and then took out her first Melbourne Cup by a length and a half carrying 51 kilograms.

This pattern was repeated in the autumn of 2004. Trained by Lee Freedman, after David Hall left to train in Hong Kong, she ran unplaced in the Chester Manifold Stakes and Australian Cup, third in the Carlyon Cup, and then went to Sydney where she finished third in the Ranvet and the BMW before winning the Sydney Cup.

In the spring the familiar pattern emerged again, with the mare running four times before winning the Melbourne Cup for two unplaced runs and two seconds, notably a close second, from barrier 18, to Elvstroem in the Caulfield Cup.

She returned for the most successful autumn campaign of her career in 2005. After an unplaced run in the C.F. Orr Stakes, she was a close second to Elvstroem in the St George Stakes, before winning the Australian Cup in record time. She then won the BMW in Sydney in a remarkable fashion, coming from the tail of the field to make up 10 lengths and run down Gai Waterhouse's old warhorse Grand Armee. The Diva was sent to Japan and ran seventh in two international races over 2000 metres and 3200 metres, carrying 56 kilograms and 59 kilograms.

After her disappointing overseas campaign it appeared she was being weighted out of handicaps and had perhaps reached the twilight of her great career, but the best was yet to come.

In her final campaign, the spring of 2005, the great mare won the Memsie Stakes first-up; then ran second, beaten a nose by a great middle-distance horse in Lad Of The Manor, in the Feehan Stakes.

She then won the Turnbull Stakes and showed her class by winning the WS Cox Plate, coming six wide around the field on the turn to win running away from Lotteria and two-time winner Fields Of Omagh.

From that moment on, all talk was about the great mare winning her third Melbourne Cup. If she did, she would become the only horse in history to win three Cups; and only four others had ever won it twice! She would also have to smash her own weight-carrying record of 55.5 kilograms for a winning mare by lumping top-weight of 58 kilograms, and she would have to do it from barrier 14.

The nation was in a state of expectation and every aspect of the great mare's life was examined in detail. Her relationship with jockey Glen Boss, who first rode her in the 2003 Caulfield Cup and was to be her jockey for eighteen of her subsequent 24 starts, was told from all angles by the media. The fairytale of the migrant fisherman made good and the great mare bred to northern hemisphere time became the main media story of the spring in Australia in 2005. The whole nation was 'Makybe Diva mad' as the Cup approached and it seemed the entire population had backed the great mare.

Of course, we all know that she did it, with relative ease, ridden perfectly by Glen Boss, and was then immediately retired to Tony Santic's stud, appropriately named after her, where a life-size statue of the great horse stands at the gate. There are also statues of her at Flemington and in Tony Santic's hometown of Port Lincoln.

In a great piece of tactical riding, Glen Boss had The Diva on the rails as they came down the straight the first time and he 'put her to sleep' and then brought her into the race five-deep at the turn. The euphoria that gripped the nation as Makybe Diva hit the lead and then dug deep under her record weight to race into immortality by over a length would be hard for anyone not versed in the history of the Cup to understand.

Australia had found a new idol and a new legend was born; one broadcaster called it 'the greatest Melbourne Cup win of all time' as she passed the post.

Her first foal, a colt by Epsom Derby winner Galileo, sold for $1.5 million at the Inglis Easter Yearling Sales in 2009 and her second, a filly by Kentucky Derby winner Fusaichi Pegasus, fetched $1.2 million the following year.

Makybe Diva's career differed from that of some other great race mares in that she was always conditioned in shorter races for her victories in longer races. This makes her win and place rates look poor in comparison to some other great mares, like Wakeful and Sunline. The Diva started 36 times for fifteen wins, four seconds, three thirds, six fourths, and eight other unplaced runs. So, while Sunline and Wakeful have win rates of 69 per cent and 61 per cent respectively, Makybe Diva's win rate was 41.5 per cent and her place rate 69 per cent, compared to 94 per cent and 93 per cent for Sunline and Wakeful.

Of course, when you make history by winning three Melbourne Cups, such statistics become meaningless and, as has been stated several times in this collection, comparing champions of different eras is mere folly, but we all do it anyway!

The nature of racing and weight allocation has changed dramatically in the 200-year history of Australian racing. The nature of the Melbourne Cup, too, has changed throughout its history.

Three fillies and eleven mares have won the Melbourne Cup and several others probably deserved to win it.

Of the three three-year-old fillies that won the Cup, one was great, one was pretty good, and the third was good enough.

Sister Olive had won only once before taking out the big race, in the Maribyrnong Trial as a two-year-old. She had run well for a fourth in the Caulfield Cup and carried a light weight, as you would expect for a horse with few credentials. She was good enough to defeat John Wren's good stayer The Rover, three Sydney Cup winners in Eurythmic, David and Kennequhair, a WS Cox Plate winner, Violoncello, and a Caulfield Cup winner in Purser, so she took some good scalps on that day in November 1921.

Auraria, the Cup winner of 1895, was a good filly that won the South Australian Derby and ran third in the VRC Derby behind Carbine's best son, Wallace. She then won the Cup at 33 to 1 and won the Oaks two days later. She was a daughter of the great stayer Trenton and therefore a granddaughter of Carbine's sire, Musket. She also carried the blood of the great imported stallion Fisherman on both sides. Her full brother, Aurum, was a champion on the track and at stud in England, but could not emulate his sister, although he ran third in the Cup carrying a record weight for a three-year-old in 1897.

The greatest three-year-old filly to win the Cup was Briseis, the first of her sex to win the race, in 1876, and she was probably the best three-year-old filly ever to start in the race.

At two Briseis, a daughter of imported stallion Tim Whiffler, went to Sydney and won the Doncaster Handicap, a flying handicap, and the All-Aged Stakes, at weight-for-age, in a week. She then set a record that has never been broken by winning the VRC Derby, Melbourne Cup and Oaks, all within six days. In the Derby she took 1.75 seconds off the race record and ran the second-fastest time ever recorded for the distance, in the world.

Sadly Briseis died in a freak accident in the breeding barn. Hobbled for her first mating, to King Of The Ring, she reared up, slipped over and fractured her skull, and it was left to her full sister, Idalia, to carry the bloodline successfully into the future.

The first tough staying mare to win the Cup was the 1904 winner Acrasia. She was aged seven and had run fourth in the Cup two years before. Her sire was Gozo, who also sired full brothers Gaulus and The Grafter to win the Cup in 1897 and 1898.

Acrasia was owned by colourful Sydney bookmaker Humphrey Oxenham, who bred her from his Sydney Cup-winning mare Cerise And Blue. He famously lost her to Lord Cardigan's owner, John Mayo, in a card game on the eve of the Caulfield Cup and bought her back for £2000. Lord Cardigan, carrying 6 st 8 lb (41.5 kg), had defeated the mighty Wakeful, carrying 10 st (63.5 kg), in the Melbourne Cup the previous year.

The tables were turned by the fair sex in 1904 with Lord Cardigan, carrying 9 st 6 lb (60 kg), chasing home Acrasia, carrying 7 st 6 lb (47 kg). The tough mare equalled Carbine's race record, but sadly, Lord Cardigan ruptured himself in his effort to catch her with his big weight and died several days later.

After Acrasia's win there was a gap of seventeen years before another female horse, the filly Sister Olive, won the great race in 1921. Then there was an even longer gap of eighteen years before Rivette came along to make history in 1939.

Rivette had an interesting pedigree: she had the great sire Isonomy on both sides through her two granddams, and her dam, Riv, was a granddaughter of Carbine's Epsom Derby-winning son Spearmint. Isonomy started fourteen times for ten wins, two seconds and a third, and his wins included two Ascot Gold Cups, in 1879 and 1880. He then became a highly influential sire.

Rivette was bred, owned and trained by an amazing man, Harry Bamber. Oddly enough, the only other Cup winner to be bred, owned and trained by one man was the first female winner, the black filly Briseis, who was owned, trained and bred by Jim Wilson, of the famous St Albans Stud near Geelong.

Harry Bamber was the archetypal 'battling trainer'. He was a blacksmith by trade and served in the Light Horse in World War I. As a dairy farmer on a soldier-settler block he studied veterinary science, and he and his brother and a friend bought Rivette's dam for 200 guineas at auction. She was originally named Riverside and raced as a '14.2 hand pony', winning many races on the unregistered tracks.

Bamber thought the little mare was good enough to race against thoroughbreds. She had the required pedigree, although she was not in the stud book, so he raced her at Sandown and she duly won. At registered meetings she raced as Riv, since the name Riverside was not available.

The Depression forced the Bamber brothers off their farm, and Harry milked cows to pay the agistment for his mare and her foals, the second of which was Rivette.

Bamber then acquired stables at Mordialloc, and his training techniques were considered quirky. He walked his horses and didn't over-train them, but kept them in work far longer than other trainers. In fact, he trained much more like a 'pony' trainer than a thoroughbred trainer.

Rivette did not start at two as she was injured while training on the road. She had her first win at Packenham late in her three-year-old season and was being prepared for the Caulfield–Melbourne Cups double of 1938 when she cut herself badly while rolling on the beach and had to be spelled.

The following year she was in training from February right through to the Melbourne Cup. She started ten times in welters and handicaps and never missed a place. When the pressure was on she responded and, on that odd preparation, easily won both the Caulfield and Melbourne Cups, making history by being the first mare, and only the third horse, to do so. Had she not completely missed the start in the Moonee Valley Gold Cup, in which she finished third within a length of the winner Gilltown, she would undoubtedly have made more history by being the first horse to win all three Cups.

At the Melbourne Cup presentation ceremony she kicked the holy grail out of Harry Bamber's hands, but he didn't mind one bit. 'She set me up for life,' the battling trainer said.

Rivette had a career severely interrupted by injury, but she was a good hard racehorse who made history in winning the Cups double in the early, dark days of World War II. Her offspring were not registered, as she was not eligible for the stud book.

Racing was severely interrupted in the eastern states during the war, and completely banned in South Australia, which certainly affected the career of Rainbird, the next mare to win the Cup, just after the war ended in 1945.

Rainbird was owned by South Australian racing identity C.H. Reid, whose brother had bred the mare. Rainbird's dam, Sequoia, was a daughter of the great Australian champion Heroic, and she was by the imported stallion The Buzzard, who also sired the 1940 Cup winner, Old Rowley. The Buzzard was a son of Epsom Derby winner Spion Kop, who was himself a son of an Epsom Derby winner Spearmint, who was by Carbine. It is an amusing reflection on Australian prudery that The Buzzard raced, quite successfully, in Britain as The Bastard. His name was changed when he came to Australia.

When racing was closed down in South Australia in 1942, Rainbird's trainer, Sam Evans, moved to Victoria where he trained the filly to win the Wakeful Stakes of 1944 and run an unlucky second in The Oaks.

Rainbird went home to win the 1945 South Australian St Leger, the first since 1941, and her training schedule was again interrupted by lack of shipping at the end of the war. Most trading vessels had been taken over by the navy and took ages to return to normal duties, which meant Rainbird did not arrive back in Melbourne until late September. Although 'under done' she ran a good second in the Caulfield Cup.

She then ran unplaced on a heavy track in the Moonee Valley Gold Cup, and Evans thought that the only thing that could prevent her winning the Melbourne Cup was rain. Like the later great champion Rain Lover, Rainbird was, ironically, a duffer in the wet! The weather stayed fine for the big race, however, and she won the Cup easily by 2½ lengths.

Rainbird went on to win the Port Adelaide Cup and ran second in the Sydney Cup, before heading to the breeding barn where she was a great success. Her daughter Raindear won the South Australian Oaks, and her descendants include the great sire Centaine, the good staying mare Allez Wonder, and many others.

The well-named mare Evening Peal won the Cup a decade after Rainbird, in 1956. She was by the great sire Delville Wood out of Mission Chimes, and had the Spearmint/Carbine/Musket bloodline on both sides of her pedigree.

She was a bonny mare who won eleven races from 51 starts. Her wins included the Wakeful Stakes and the VRC, Queensland and AJC Oaks (then known as the Adrian Knox Stakes). She often raced against mighty horses like Redcraze and Rising Fast and carried a record-winning weight for a female of 8 st (50.5 kg) to beat Redcraze, carrying 10 st 3 lb (65 kg), by a neck in record time in the Melbourne Cup of 1956.

The New Zealand mare Hi-Jinx had one of the least distinguished records of any Melbourne Cup winner. She started three times only in Australia, running unplaced in the Caulfield Cup and a good second in the Moonee Valley Cup before winning the historic 100th Melbourne Cup at 50 to 1.

There was great hype around the 100th Cup and record prizemoney. Hi-Jinx's win was an anticlimax for the crowd, who had hoped to see the mighty Tulloch carry 10 st 1 lb (64 kg) to victory. Tulloch, who had returned to racing after two years spent overcoming a crippling illness, ran seventh; it was the only time he was unplaced in 51 starts.

Hi-Jinx, a plain mare described as the ugliest horse in the race by one unkind journalist, returned to one of the mildest receptions in Cup history. She had the breeding to win, however, being bred at the famous Trelawney Stud in New Zealand from a Foxbridge mare, Lady's Bridge. Trelawney Stud had produced three previous Melbourne Cup winners—Hiraji, Foxzami and MacDougal—all from mares by the great sire Foxbridge. Hi-Jinx cost 500 guineas as a yearling, and took out the largest prize ever offered for a race in Australia when she won $40,000 for her Cup victory.

The brave little chestnut mare Light Fingers was spotted as a yearling in New Zealand by Bart Cummings and raced on lease in the white with royal blue spots and cap of Wally Broderick, a Melbourne grain merchant who owned her older full brother, The Dip, also trained by Bart.

The two were well named, being by the French stallion Le Filou, which translates as 'pickpocket', out of a New Zealand mare Cuddlesome. In fact, Light Fingers was originally named Close Embrace by her breeders, the Dawson family, but Broderick wanted a name from the sire's side to match her full brother, so he changed her name before she raced.

Changing a horse's registered name is supposed to be unlucky, but Broderick and Bart struck it lucky with Light Fingers. She was an out-and-out champion, considered 'the best since Wakeful' by older racing men. She started four times at two for three wins and a second, beaten a head. In her three-year-old season she started twelve times for seven wins, two seconds and two thirds; the wins included the VRC Wakeful, Manifold and Oaks Stakes, the Sandown Guineas, and the AJC Princess Handicap and the Oaks.

Light Fingers suffered a serious virus attack, which delayed her return to racing in the spring of 1965. She also was plagued by back problems and missed the Caulfield Cup after she won but pulled a shoulder muscle in the Craiglee Stakes. She went into the Melbourne Cup on the limited preparation of just five starts.

In one of the greatest Cup finishes of all time the tiny chestnut mare defeated her huge black stablemate, Ziema, by a lip to give Bart his first Cup win and his first Cup quinella.

Her bad back worsened after her four-year-old season, which meant Bart needed all his skill and care to keep her racing. She went into the 1966 Cup carrying a massive weight, on an even lighter preparation than 1965, just four starts; Bart's better-conditioned champion, Galilee, defeated her by 2 lengths even though she ran a great race, hitting the front halfway down the straight and hanging on for a gallant second to give Bart his second Cup quinella in a row.

The racing public loved the little mare and sent her out at 10 to 9 for her final victory in the Sandown Cup, carrying 9 st (57 kg) on a bog track. Light Fingers' record overall was 33 starts for fifteen wins, eight seconds and five thirds.

It was to be another 23 years before a female would win another Melbourne Cup, but mares won two out of four Cups between 1988 and 1991—who could forget those two mighty chestnuts, Empire Rose and Let's Elope?

Although bred on different lines, Empire Rose and Let's Elope were similar in many ways. Both were bred and owned in New Zealand, both were huge chestnut mares (Empire Rose only just fitted in the barrier stalls and Let's Elope was not much smaller), and both were mighty tough stayers.

Empire Rose was by the great Sir Tristram out of a Sovereign Edition mare and won good races on both sides of the Tasman, including the New Zealand Cup and Trentham Stakes in New Zealand, and Australia's Mackinnon Stakes and Melbourne Cup of 1988.

Her record in the Melbourne Cup is getting towards the 'Shadow King' level. She started four times in the great race for a fifth in 1986, a second in 1987, a win in 1988, and a final unplaced run as a seven-year-old, behind Tawriffic, in 1989.

Although Empire Rose's overall record of nine wins and eight placings from 48 starts is not equal to that of some other great staying mares, Laurie Laxon's efforts to condition the huge mare to win major races and race on well into her seven-year-old season is remarkable. He was helped in his training by wife Sheila, who rode Empire Rose in her trackwork and would later become the first female trainer to win a Melbourne Cup, appropriately with a mare.

Having watched the huge chestnut mare go around in four Melbourne Cups, the racing public could have been forgiven for thinking she had returned, in different racing colours, two years after her final run in 1989, when Let's Elope took out the Cup.

Let's Elope was by the American stallion Nassipour out of a New Zealand-bred mare by the good English sire Battle-Waggon. In spite of the multinational nature of her pedigree, a look at her breeding confirms that she had three crosses to Nearco, two via Nasrullah and one via Dante, and also had Bois Roussel on her sire side, which means she had an abundance of Carbine blood.

Let's Elope did not start at two, but showed some promise at three while racing in New Zealand. She won her first start and then struggled to win again until taking out a Group 3 event and being sold. Her new owners transferred her to Bart Cummings in Australia, and the 'Cups King' conditioned her for a spring campaign in Melbourne, in 1991, as a four-year-old.

Although she was a duffer in the wet, she showed good staying ability in her first three starts for Bart. Then the weather cleared and the mighty mare went on a winning rampage.

Let's Elope won four races in a row in the spring: the Turnbull Stakes, the Mackinnon and the Melbourne–Caulfield Cups double—the first mare since Rivette to do so.

She then returned in the autumn to win three in a row: the C.F. Orr Stakes, St George Stakes and Australian Cup.

Injury and controversy plagued Let's Elope for the rest of her career. A damaged fetlock kept her out of racing until she returned to defeat the champion Better Loosen Up in a match race at five. She was then relegated from close second to fifth for causing interference to that same horse in the 1992 W.S. Cox Plate, won by Super Impose.

She bled in the Japan Cup and again while racing in the USA, where on two occasions she was first past the post but was again relegated for interference, including from first to third in a Group 1 race.

The second bleeding attack and a fractured cannon bone forced her into retirement in 1993. She produced the good stayer Ustinov from a mating to Seeking The Gold but, despite her matings with the best US sires, her other progeny did not do well on the track.

In 1998 another two great New Zealand mares fought out a memorable Melbourne Cup finish when Jezabeel, winner of the Auckland Cup and a daughter of that great producer of stayers, Sir Tristram's son Zabeel, defeated another daughter of Zabeel, Champagne, in an unforgettable finish.

Jezabeel was typical of the dour Zabeel offspring who took time to mature and race into condition; she won seven of her 26 starts and was placed another five times. Jezabeel had Northern Dancer blood via her sire's dam, Lady Giselle, and Nasrullah on her dam side, so she fits the 'Cup-winning' pattern of Carbine blood on both sides.

Having helped husband Laurie to win the Cup with Empire Rose in 1988, Sheila Laxon returned in triumph as a trainer in her own right to take the Cups double with Ethereal in 2001.

Owned and bred by the Vela brothers at Pencarrow Stud, Ethereal was sired by US Breeders' Cup winner, Rhythm, the champion US two-year-old of 1989 and a son of the hugely influential sire Mr Prospector. Completing Ethereal's multinational pedigree was her dam, Romanee Conti, a Hong Kong Cup winner and daughter of Sir Tristram, who carried both Wilkes and Le Filou blood on her dam side.

With a pedigree made to order for a stayer with a turn of foot, Ethereal proved to be just that. She took out four classic races at Group 1 level in winning the Caulfield–Melbourne Cups double, the Queensland Oaks and the Tancred Stakes (now the BMW).

At stud Ethereal produced the handy filly Uberalles, from a mating to Giant's Causeway. Uberalles won at Group 2 level and was third in the New Zealand Derby. Ethereal's other progeny have sold for huge prices, with a colt by Stravinsky fetching $1.3 million at the Karaka sales, but have not excelled as yet on the track.

Two years after Ethereal's Cups double, the history of 'mares and the Melbourne Cup' was to be changed forever when Makybe Diva won the first of her three.

But what of mares who never won the Melbourne Cup? How do Wakeful, Carlita, Desert Gold, Tranquil Star, Flight, Chiquita, Leilani, Surround, Emancipation and Sunline compare to those who did?

Surround, Emancipation and Sunline were great champions, but they were not true stayers, although Surround looked like having the potential to be a great stayer at three. She won the VRC Oaks and Queensland Oaks, but failed in the Brisbane Cup at 3200 metres. After an amazing three-year-old season, in which she started sixteen times for twelve wins, she was retired at four, the age at which Makybe Diva won her first race.

Emancipation, for all her brilliance and toughness up to a mile, failed to run beyond 2000 metres. Her tally of Group 1 wins—seven—equals The Diva's, but she was certainly no stayer.

Sunline won almost twice as many times as The Diva at Group 1 level, but she was powerful only over the shorter distances—the longest distance at which she ever competed was 2040 metres—and she was never a candidate for a 2-mile Cup.

Carlita won the VRC Derby and Oaks as well as the Rosehill Guineas and the Craven Plate, and the Kings Plate at weight-for-age by a massive 25 lengths. She ran third in the Cup of 1915 carrying 8 st 5 lb (53 kg), and sixth in 1916, with 9 st 5 lb (59.5 kg), behind Sasanof who was carrying only 6 st 12 lb (43.5 kg).

Desert Gold also raced in World War I and won nineteen races in a row. She won 36 times from 59 starts and carried top-weight of 9 st 6 lb (60 kg) to finish eighth in the Cup of 1918. It was one of only six unplaced runs in her 59-start career.

Tranquil Star was tough as old boots, starting 111 times and winning two Cox Plates, three Mackinnons, and the St George Stakes, Caulfield Stakes, Lloyd Stakes and so on. She carried a record-winning weight for a mare to take out the Caulfield Cup with 8 st 12 lb (56 kg) in 1942, and then carried a whopping 9 st 3 lb (58.5 kg) to run twelfth on a bog track behind Colonus, carrying 7 st 2 lb (45 kg), in the Melbourne Cup that year. She even raced on successfully after recovering from breaking her jaw, winning a Memsie Stakes, a William Reid Stakes and her third Mackinnon!

Flight never started in a Melbourne Cup, but could stay. She won the Cox Plate, Mackinnon Stakes, AJC Oaks, Colin Stephen Stakes and Champagne Stakes, and ran third in a Sydney Cup. At middle distance she was often up against Bernborough, but still ended her career with a respectable record of 24 wins and 28 other placings from 65 starts. Although she was a granddaughter of Heroic, she was famously bought for just 60 guineas and won more than a thousand times her purchase price in wartime when prizemoney was very low. Her daughter, appropriately named Flight's Daughter, produced Derby winners Skyline and Sky High, who established a bloodline of world significance when standing at stud in the USA.

The bonny black mare Chiquita won eleven times at three, including the Manifold Stakes, Thousand Guineas, Wakeful Stakes and the VRC Oaks. She found one better in the Jim Cummings-trained Comic Court, however, who defeated her often, including in the Mackinnon Stakes and Melbourne Cup of 1950, where she ran second both times; she also ran second in the Caulfield Cup behind Grey Boots. She had the satisfaction of one win over Comic Court in the Craiglee Stakes over a mile, and their daughter, Comicquita, ran second to Even Stevens in the 1962 Melbourne Cup.

Leilani was a great staying mare, winning six times at Group 1 level in a relatively short career. Her fourteen wins, six seconds and six thirds from 28 starts is a great record for a stayer, and her wins included the AJC Oaks, Caulfield Cup, Toorak Handicap, and the Mackinnon, St George, C.F. Orr and Turnbull Stakes. Bart Cummings's decision not to start her in the Cup with 59 kilograms means we will never know if she could have been up there with the great mares who won it.

For my money it comes down to Wakeful and Makybe Diva as the two greatest staying mares in our racing history.

Both mares started racing late and missed the classic fillies races for different reasons. Wakeful was amazingly versatile and won the sprint double of the Oakleigh Plate and Newmarket early in her career, at four. Makybe Diva, on the other hand, having never won first-up and never won a race under a mile in distance, came out at seven and won the Memsie Stakes first-up over 1400 metres.

Wakeful won over 4800 metres, a feat not possible in Makybe Diva's day. She also won ten races that would be Group 1 today, compared to Makybe Diva's seven. On the other hand, she started twice in the Melbourne Cup and never won; Makybe Diva won three. The Diva raced a century after Wakeful and much had changed in that time; she never carried the weights Wakeful had to, and her record overall does not match that of Wakeful.

So, it all depends on how you look at it and which facts and figures you want to use. The greatest staying mare to ever compete in the Melbourne Cup? Maybe it was Wakeful, or maybe it was Makybe Diva.

The greatest mare to win the Cup? Well, history says that it's Makybe Diva . . . and maybe it always will be.

AN ANTICIPATORY PICTURE

C.J. DENNIS

This poem, written in Cup Week 1931, gives us all the excitement of the race and concludes with a blank space in which we can live out our own Cup dream.

***

The scene upon the frock-flecked lawn
Is, as you please, a picture fair,
Or just a hunk of human brawn,
With blobs of faces here and there.
Stilled are the clamours of the Ring;
The famous race is on at last;
All eyes are on the lengthening string
Of brilliant jackets moving fast.

Torn, trampled tickets mark the birth
Of broken hopes all now would mend,
As quickening hoof-beats spurn the earth,
And the field thunders to the bend.
All men are equal for the nonce,
Bound by an urgency intense,
And eager questionings win response
From strangers tiptoe with suspense.

'What's that in front?' All faces yearn
Toward the track in serried rows.
The field comes round the homeward turn,
As, wave on wave, the murmuring grows,
Waxes and swells from out that host
Till pandemonium begins,
And flecks of colour pass the post
To mighty cries of '(__________*) wins'.
[N.B.—Write your own ticket.]*

Part 6
A PUNT ON THE PONIES

INTRODUCTION—THE FORGOTTEN RACING GAME

Pony racing is a forgotten part of our racing history. Many people today assume that thoroughbred racing is the only form of horseracing we've ever had, but 'unregistered' or 'pony racing' was huge in Sydney and Melbourne, and other cities and towns, from the 1890s to the 1930s, and many horses were trained in suburban backyards for these races, although many 'pony trainers' had huge stables.

Prior to World War II there were six racetracks between the CBD and Botany Bay in Sydney. Apart from Randwick there was Kensington, where the University of New South Wales is now; Rosebery, which became a housing estate in the 1960s; Ascot, which made way for the airport, Victoria Park, which is now another housing estate near Moore Park; and Moorfields out towards Kogarah. These were exclusively designed as 'non-thoroughbred' or 'pony' tracks.

Other racetracks, which provided events for unregistered horses, were to be found at Glebe, Menangle, Parramatta, Hornsby and other suburbs. These tracks operated from the late nineteenth century as pony tracks.

I am deeply indebted to Wayne Peake for the inclusion here of 'A Brief History of Pony Racing'. Wayne's comprehensive history of this almost forgotten form of racing, *Sydney's Pony Racecourses—An Alternative Racing History*, is the definitive work on the subject and we owe a debt of gratitude to Wayne for preserving the social history of this other, hugely popular, form of racing.

Men such as Sydney Lord Mayor Joynton Smith, owner of Victoria Park racecourse, and John Wren, Melbourne's political powerbroker and pony track owner, were larger than life characters who shaped our social history in the early twentieth century.

Pony racing was deeply embedded as part of the fabric of life in our cities for 75 years, in an era when the only access to legal betting was *at* the racetrack.

While the gentry at Randwick watched five races, contested by small fields of 'blue-bloods', and enjoyed long lunches (the luncheon break at AJC meetings was often more than an hour and there was an hour between races), the hoi polloi packed Ascot, Kensington, Rosebery and other pony tracks to watch fifteen races with large fields, and bet and booze to their heart's content. Pony racing, although perhaps loosely governed and slightly shady, was dangerous, exciting, accessible, affordable and *fun*!

Characters such as 'Baron' Bob Skelton are the stuff of legend. The Baron, and others such as bookmakers Andy Kerr the 'Coogee Bunyip', 'Lordy' Angles and Rufe Naylor, as well as jockeys Andy Knox and Alf Stanton, are now almost forgotten as the phenomenon of pony racing fades into the mists of time, unheralded except by historians like Wayne Peake.

The legendary T.J. Smith, a bush kid from Wagga Wagga, began his career as a trainer in Sydney living in a stable on the Kensington pony track. His one horse, Bragger, occupied the stable next door! Legendary jockey Billy Cook was one of many famous thoroughbred riders who rode countless winners 'at the ponies'.

Jim Bendrodt was another great character in the heyday of both pony racing and, later, thoroughbred racing. He was a flamboyant entrepreneur in the 1920s and 1930s, an owner of dance halls and racehorses who later trained thoroughbreds himself with great success. Bendrodt was also a great writer of true adventure stories, and was my favourite author when I was a boy.

Several of his stories appear in other sections of this collection, along with David Hickie's biography of the man himself. In this section, you will find Bendrodt's story, 'Passella', which describes the events which first introduced him to the world of racing, via the pony track at Kensington.

This section also contains Banjo Paterson's hilarious send-up of the greatest turf writer of all time, Nat Gould.

Gould more or less invented the 'racing novel'; later to become a specific genre of fiction of which Dick Francis was the king. Born in Manchester in 1857, Gould came to Australia in 1884 and worked as a reporter in Brisbane and Sydney before spending eighteen months at Bathurst as editor of *The Bathurst Times*. While there he wrote his first novel, *With the Tide,* which was published in England under the title of *The Double Event* and was an immediate success. It was dramatised in Australia and had a long run as a play in 1893.

In 1895, after eleven years in Australia, Gould returned to England and began steadily writing an average of more than four books a year. All up, he wrote more than 130 novels and his sales ran into many millions of copies.

Gould was a great raconteur who didn't take himself or his work too seriously. His modesty and sense of humour shine through in the accounts of his visits to Melbourne for the Spring Carnival, such as 'Cup Memories', featured in another section of this collection.

While his novels had no great originality of plot and tended to be melodramatic in the extreme, they were rattling good yarns and stand as proof that racing is a wonderful subject for authors.

Under the pen name 'Knott Gold' Banjo Paterson, who was a friend of Gould's, wrote a very funny piece parodying the Nat Gould style. Set in the pony racing world of inner Sydney, it is titled 'Done for the Double', a humorous reference to the title of Gould's most famous novel, *The Double Event*, and it still makes me laugh out loud to read it today.

The pony tracks were closed, to be used by the military in World War II, and simply never re-opened for unregistered racing. The McKell state government took the opportunity to legislate for their permanent demise and then created the Sydney Turf Club.

A PUNT UPON THE PONIES

JIM HAYNES

There's no movement in the suburbs, the silence is profound,
For the kids are at the Sat'day arvo flicks.
The missus has her mother and her sisters coming round,
So you won't get tea till after half past six.

So with suit and tie and hat on you hurry from the door
To the tram stop, where you meet up with your cronies,
And you feel alive and happy, like a single man once more,
'Cos you're off to have a punt upon the ponies.

For they're racing down at Moorefields, Kensington, Ascot,
Or at Rosebery, or at Victoria Park.
So you take a hard-earned quid or two and maybe lose the lot
And face the music when you get home after dark.

But, then again, you might get lucky, get the good oil from a mate,
Make a pile and shout and boast and win some more,
And arrive back home in what's called 'an inebriated state',
With some chocolates for the 'minister for war'.

Yes, a punt upon the ponies is a working man's reward,
Helps you tolerate your work . . . your kids and wife.
It's the thing that keeps you going, keeps you looking forward.
Through the six-and-a-half-day misery of life.

A BRIEF HISTORY OF PONY RACING

WAYNE PEAKE

Pony racing was a form of horseracing conducted at regular meetings in Australia from the 1880s to the 1940s. This article concentrates on Sydney pony racing, which was undoubtedly its bastion in the twentieth century, but it was also significant in Melbourne (in particular), Brisbane, Perth and rural New South Wales.

I use this term 'pony racing' with some reluctance, as it seems to give people the wrong idea of what it was. They get visions of little kids riding Shetland ponies in hay bale hurdle races at agricultural shows or pony clubs. In fact in its most popular years around the First World War and the 1920s, at a pony race meeting conducted by the Associated Race Clubs (ARC) in Sydney, on a card of seventeen races as many as twelve would have been open to Thoroughbred horses of any height. But the alternative term for pony racing, 'unregistered proprietary horse racing', is too much of a mouthful. So pony racing it must be.

What was, for racing purposes, a pony? The usual definition was a beast that measured less than 14.2 hands (a hand is about 10 centimetres) at the wither. Those between 14.3 and 15 hands were called galloways—a usage that gradually disappeared in the 1920s. Anything over 15 hands was an 'all heights'. In the early years the racing press often referred to restricted heights competitors as 'littl'uns'. By the 1920s the colloquial name was a 'macker', a term derived from the rhyming slang 'macaroni'.

'Littl'uns' was a fair enough description of the participants in pony races when a regular circuit became fully established in the 1890s. There was a myriad of classes based on height, and races for midgets of 12 hands or less were not unusual. Such events were often given twee names like the 'Tom Thumb' or 'Lilliputian' handicap. The competitors were a fairly motley lot, with the influence of pony breeds such as the Timor and the Welsh evident, but already Thoroughbred blood was becoming preponderant. As pony racing evolved, Thoroughbred dominance increased to the point that a modern racegoer would be hard-pressed to pick the difference between a meeting at Randwick in the 1920s and one say at the Victoria Park racecourse. All of the major blood horse sires were well represented at the ponies.

How did this phenomenon of pony racing come about? It is ironic that it was an indirect result of the rise of the Australian Jockey Club (AJC) to the role of principal club and regulatory body of racing in New South Wales. The irony lies in the fact that the AJC came to loathe pony racing like the squatter members of its Committee detested the rabbit plague.

Pony racing was a form of private 'for profit' racing—racing's equivalent of the 1908 Rugby League breakaway. In the early 1880s the only race meetings in Sydney were non-proprietary and all took place at Randwick. On most Saturdays there was no racing and there was an obvious opportunity for someone to supply the undoubted demand for more.

In 1884, the Canterbury Race Club, adopting the model established some years earlier by the Cox family in Melbourne, gained registration to race on vacant Saturdays under AJC rules. Meanwhile the Agricultural Society had built a small racecourse at Moore Park on which trotting meetings took place. A few years later these were supplemented and ultimately replaced by races for gallopers that were graded on the basis of height. These first pony meetings at Moore Park were not registered with the AJC.

Canterbury began racing one Saturday a month and its success soon encouraged imitators at the new Rosehill (1885), Warwick Farm (1888) and Moorefield (1888) racecourses in suburban Sydney. Each ran meetings under AJC rules, which demanded certain standards for racecourse size, prizemoney, etc. Restricted heights races were not allowed.

At that time there was no government licensing of racecourses so there was nothing to stop sports entrepreneurs from building racecourses when and where they pleased. So long as they did not seek AJC registration they could set their own standards. These more transient promoters tended to gravitate towards the cheaper pony racing, establishing what the AJC regarded as 'black market' racing.

New racecourses for pony racing sprung up at Woodlands near Liverpool (1889), Lillie Bridge (1890), Botany (1891), the first Rosebery Park (1895), Brighton (1895), and Belmore (1900). The Kensington racecourse also opened for pony racing in 1893, across the road from Randwick. It was a much more ambitious venture than the others and boasted a first-class racecourse and grounds.

Surprisingly, in the 1880s and 1890s the AJC allowed its registered clubs to also conduct pony meetings, mostly on Wednesdays. It is a little known fact that pony racing once took place regularly on the Rosehill, Canterbury, Warwick Farm and Moorefield racecourses. Remarkably, the pony meetings at these tracks often drew larger crowds than those held there under AJC rules, probably because there were usually more races and larger fields, and thus provided better value for money. The AJC closed this loophole in 1898.

In the unregulated racing environment of early twentieth-century Sydney, racing was conducted on 235 days a year at up to a dozen racecourses. Wowser elements of society were appalled by this explosion and gradually gained the state government's ear. At the end of 1906, a year in which the splendid new Ascot pony racecourse opened, the government passed new gaming and betting legislation which restricted metropolitan racing dates, outlawed racecourses under 6 furlongs and prohibited the construction of new racecourses within 40 miles of the Sydney GPO.

This meant the end of gallops meetings at the Epping and old Rosebery racecourses, although their owners were allowed to transfer their licences to the new Victoria Park (1908) and second Rosebery (1907) racecourses respectively. All the other pony racecourses except Kensington had already closed. Victoria Park was rated the second best course in Sydney behind Randwick.

There were three eras of pony racing in Sydney. The first, from 1888 to 1906, was the unlicensed and unregistered period. It took place at either the small, relatively primitive tracks like Liverpool and old Rosebery, at the suburban AJC racecourses, or at the independent Kensington course, which imagined itself pony racing's equivalent of the AJC. The second era began with the introduction of government licensing and regulation of pony racing in 1906. The four surviving clubs formed the ARC to rationalise its administration.

In addition to the meetings at Ascot, Rosebery, Victoria Park and Kensington on Wednesdays and 28 Saturdays a year, pony racing took place at provincial racecourses registered with the ARC such as Menangle, Richmond and Tuggerah. These meetings were on Tuesdays and Thursdays. This was the 'golden age' of pony racing. The third era began in 1933, when the ARC clubs, seeking protection from the damaging effects of the Great Depression, obtained AJC registration. The AJC amended its by-laws to again allow restricted heights races on registered racecourses.

Pony racing was by then in decline and its courses, denied maintenance, began to deteriorate. The dangerous course of the war in early 1942 caused restrictions on racing. Pony racing bore the brunt of these. And each of its racecourses was occupied by the military. In 1943 Premier McKell created the Sydney Turf Club and invited it to take its pick of the proprietary racecourses. The pony companies were allowed a few years to wind up.

The last race meeting at Rosebery took place on 10 July 1940, at Kensington on Christmas Eve 1941, at Victoria Park on 14 February 1942 and at Ascot on 22 August 1942. Ascot was retained for training until 1948, and then resumed for the east–west runway of Sydney Airport. Construction of the University of New South Wales began on Kensington in the late 1940s. Victoria Park remained open for training until 31 August 1952, and then was redeveloped to become the Leyland Automotive plant that opened in 1960. Barrier trials and training continued at Rosebery until mid-1962. It became a housing development that included the new Eastlakes shopping centre.

It is the period of the independent ARC, 1907–1932, that most people associate with pony racing. The racecourses were much larger and better appointed than the early pony courses; Victoria Park was, for example, over 2000 metres in circumference (many registered racing people and journalists were of the opinion that the AJC should have sought to acquire it for registered racing).

Pony racing in Sydney was extraordinarily popular in this period. Indicators such as journalist's attendance estimates, photographs published in the press, numbers of tram cars deployed, and betting turnover attest that many racegoers preferred the pony brand to the AJC meetings run on the suburban racecourses (although Randwick meetings remained unchallenged).

Betting turnover on an Ascot meeting might be double that at Canterbury on the same day. In part this ascendancy was due to the ease with which the pony racecourses could be reached compared with the registered suburban courses. However, there was also a genuine fondness for pony racing, as it was a stimulating racing experience. This is, I think, captured nicely in a verse penned by a *Sportsman* journalist:

On racedays from the city far,
I'd travel with some dear old cronies,
All eager as true sportsmen are,
To win a fortune on the ponies.
My cobbers talked of naught but horse—
Of horse at Redfern, horse at Mascot,
Nor ceased they till we reached the course,
To revel in the joys of Ascot.

Taking these light-hearted lines as a starting point, attending a meeting at Ascot in 1920 may have been something like this: the tram left Botany Road at Lord's Road just past Mascot and passed over a level crossing with the Botany goods line to a terminus loop adjacent to the Paddock entrance gates. If you were a male, as the great majority of pony racegoers were, it cost 14 shillings to enter the Paddock or 5 shillings to the Leger (as the average wage at that time was around 3 pounds a week, the cost of a day at the races was substantial). These charges matched those at Randwick. A racebook cost 1 shilling.

Ascot racecourse stood on 101 acres. It was an attractive venue on a fine day. An advertisement described it as 'popular, pure and pretty; fringed with lofty pines, the verdure is refreshing to the eye. In the distance are the limpid waters of Botany Bay'. The course proper was 1 mile and 90 yards in circumference and 90 feet wide. The track had chutes for 1 mile and 4-furlong races. Races at other distances—over 6, 6½, 9 and 12 furlongs—started from the course proper. Each start could accommodate twenty horses.

Ascot's amenities in 1920 were second only to Victoria Park and far superior to those provided at the Melbourne pony courses. They included: a two-storey timber members' stand, a brick, twin-gabled paddock stand that accommodated 600 and a similar timber structure for 1500 in the Leger. Drinking was not the essential racecourse activity it became after World War II, but for the thirsty there were bars located under the public stands in both enclosures. There was also a separate open-air bar in the Paddock. There were stand-alone tearooms in either enclosure serving light meals, as well as a snack bar and tobacconist's kiosk. The Paddock lavatories boasted water closets but Leger inmates had to make do with pans.

There was no trouble in getting a bet on. There were 100 bookmakers in the Paddock and about 150 in the Leger. At Ascot the main Paddock betting ring was on the lawn between the course proper and the public stand. The Ascot club had opened stand-alone totalisators in each enclosure, which incidentally paid different dividends, in 1917. The betting options available were win, place, concession and doubles.

Ascot, 6 miles from the GPO, was the most distant of the Sydney pony racecourses. After the last, one of the 150 tram cars set aside for the inbound return journey would return racegoers to Central Station in about 25 minutes.

***

The writers David Hickie and Jack Pollard were in the habit of describing Sydney's pony racecourses as the haunts of the 'Needy and the Greedy' and the 'Quick and the Dead'. Similarly, some Edwardian journalists who worked on newspapers of the Establishment such as *The Sydney Morning Herald* and *The Sydney Mail*, and the AJC men, secretary Tom Clibborn and chairman Adrian Knox, spoke of the pony courses as if they were *Kasbahs* packed with low-lifes, which respectable people entered at their peril.

While Hickie and Pollard's calumnies may have been true of the Great Depression years when pony racing was in its terminal decline (and even then only in part), and the earlier comments refer to the 'roaring days' before the Associated Race Clubs brought good governance, nevertheless they have given the reputation of the sport a somewhat unwarranted black eye.

However, it is certainly true that the pony racecourses were interesting and fascinating places where things tended to happen. This second article on Sydney pony racing selects just a few of the events and aspects of its culture that warrant inclusion in the broader memory of horseracing.

A dangerous profession

In the early days of pony racing the deaths of jockeys were regularly reported in the newspapers, though they hardly made the headlines. A small paragraph announcing funeral arrangements or a whip-around on behalf of dependants at the end of the racing column was the usual practice. Not that there was a lot of public sympathy wasted on the deceased; jockeys in general were held in low esteem, and *pony* jockeys were regarded as little better than street hoodlums in fancy dress.

There were a number of factors that contributed to the carnage. The unregistered pony racecourses of the late-Victorian and early Edwardian period like the first Rosebery Park and Lillie Bridge were inherently dangerous places to ride. Although an imaginative journalist once described Rosebery as 'Flemington in reverse', it was little more than 4 furlongs in circumference and featured sharp bends. Lillie Bridge was even smaller, and its turn out of the home straight so severe that riders strapped padding to their left legs to protect themselves from contact with the running rail as they cut the corner.

Collisions with rails, made of unforgiving hardwood, were a major cause of death and injury. Other contributors to a death rate that today would be considered monstrous were a lack of protective clothing (skull caps were not made compulsory until 1914 and skull fractures were the most common cause of death), the absence of stewards' observation towers around the track to discourage foul riding, a laissez faire approach to the licensing of jockeys, the uneven and largely unimproved surface of some courses, and primitive first aid facilities.

The number of names on the role of those known to have lost their lives between 1890 and 1906 is not inconsiderable. The first Rosebery, which had a reputation as a place of death that rivalled that of the Maroubra speedway a generation later, contributed the most: J. Elliot and G. Fewings at the inaugural meeting in 1895, G. Clayton (1896), T. Rooke (1897), P. Maughlin (1899), J. Allen and W. Cohn (1901), and T.W. Adams (1905). Deaths also occurred at other pony courses. John Driscoll Jr, whose father won the 1867 Melbourne Cup on Tim Whiffler, was killed at the Driving Park in 1890, W. Cartwright at Forest Lodge in 1902, T. Gardiner (1897) and E. Julius (1906) at Kensington.

Eventually the frequency of fatalities at the proprietary courses (Canterbury's record was as bad as the ponies) troubled even the phlegmatic members of the New South Wales parliament. One demanded more stringent government regulation of racecourses, citing the example of Lillie Bridge, which he said was not big enough to allow a game of cricket or the proverbial swinging of a cat.

No immediate action was taken, but the *1906 Gaming and Betting Act*, which caused the creation of the Associated Race Clubs with its painstaking stewardship of racing, as well as the construction of the larger and better maintained second-generation pony racecourses, proved a godsend. Over the next 25 years jockey mortality at the pony tracks was markedly lower than in AJC racing.

The pony racecourses were sometimes dangerous places *off* the track as well. There were the occasional robberies and assaults, although the ARC racecourse detective, Mr Jackson, was a vigilant and respected man well equipped for throwing louts off the course. Such occurrences were unusual but not unprecedented perils of the type that racegoers at all tracks were more or less prepared for. However, a stand collapsing beneath your feet was rather a different matter.

This was what happened at the second Rosebery racecourse on 5 May 1928. The Rosebery cup meeting was in progress. It was a rather unpleasant day, on which an important meeting was also in progress at Rosehill. Despite this a very large attendance was at Rosebery and up to the running of the Trial Stakes well-backed horses had been faring well. Consequently few people had left the course.

A large squadron of young men had momentarily gathered in the Leger betting ring on the lawn in front of the stand to watch the race. The less peripatetic females and elderly racegoers had secured sheltered positions in the stand—a rather rickety wooden structure that had been transported from the old Rosebery racecourse and was more than 30 years old. Witnesses later testified it was already near, if not beyond, its safe capacity.

Just prior to the advertised race time a squall of unusually heavy rain swept into the faces of the men on the lawn. They quickly retreated onto the walkways and lower ramparts of the stand, forcing the incumbents to concentrate in the centre. Following immediately on a loud crack, the lower-centre decks of the stand collapsed several feet into the tearoom below and a large hole appeared.

As a result people were thrown from their feet and some seriously injured. Many of the men last in from the rain quickly evacuated the sinking stand, even if this meant stomping on the injured. A number were not content upon reaching the apparent safe haven of the lawn, but jumped the fence onto the course proper to avoid any crush. Perhaps they thought there had been an earthquake.

The stand's collapse was front-page news the following Monday. The papers criticised the stampeders for displaying less than Anzac standards of bravery, and for the lack of concern they showed injured females and elderly. The disaster did ultimately bring benefits for racegoers though. Rather than simply construct a new stand, the Rosebery club virtually rebuilt the entire racecourse and lengthened and widened the course proper, to such good effect that both Bill Cook and Edgar Britt named it among the best tracks in Sydney.

The 'Mackers'

We now know much less about the equine competitors in pony racing than its human participants. This is not surprising, as it had no absolute standouts to provide a pantheon of legendary champions as Carbine, Phar Lap, Bernborough and Tulloch have for registered racing. The truth was that for the most part they were either pygmies that never graduated from restricted class racing (if 'restricted heights' races can be thought of in this way) or 'all heights' that had either failed to measure up in registered racing, were past their prime, or had been judged so unpromising they were consigned immediately to pony trainers.

Nevertheless *in their own time* the best ponies had large followings. The most admired were those ponies that had the ability to overcome massive weights and concede several stones to low weighted rivals, and to win races outside their own heights category. Most celebrated of all were those who were able to beat their bigger registered cousins on their own turf.

Thus when the 14.1 hand Sydney pony Jack Marsh was able to beat a 'particularly smart' field in the Truganinni Handicap at the registered Williamstown racecourse, Melbourne, in 1920 at 50 to

1, it was reported as a lead story in *The Argus* next day and a major talking point around the haunts of 'sportsmen', such as hotels and clubs. Jack Marsh won more than 40 races. Other ponies that proved very competitive on registered racecourses included:

- Cinderellen, a galloway that won the 1896 Kensington Cup carrying 10 st 13 lb. It ran unplaced in a Toorak Handicap, but second in a £200 race on Caulfield Cup day and also a Hobart Cup. Later Cinderellen won the 10-furlong Maribyrnong Cup at that registered Melbourne racecourse.
- Djin Djin, which won the 1898 Epsom Handicap.
- Fitzroy, which Adrian Knox admitted to admiring, ran second in a Hobart Cup and fifth in an Australian Cup.
- Other ponies and galloways that achieved fame within their milieu included Precious Dust, Adam Bede, Bruce, Currawong, Lady Liddell, Marabeau, Moorefield Lass, Pearl Powder, Scarpa Flow, Prince Bruce, Scooter, Silver Grist, Silver Rose and Woy Woy.

Pony humour

If the Depression brought problems for pony racing that ultimately proved fatal for it, it also generated a great deal of grim humour. These stories are largely to blame for the 'needy and greedy' label referred to earlier and were hardly representative of the total culture of the sport. That being said, they are certainly worth recounting.

Bert Lillye told a delightful story about an unlicensed bookmaker who set up business on the 'outer' above Kensington racecourse. Defaulting bookmakers were not unknown at that venue so punters viewed with favour the disabled man, his leg in a plaster cast, who obviously could not out-run a pursuit. Consequently business was very good; in fact disconcertingly good for the bookie, as favourite after favourite won. He knew if the next was successful he would be unable to pay. Sure enough it charged away to the cheers of the outer crowd, who then turned to line up for payment. To their chagrin they saw their man rapidly receding into the distance. Before them lay the discarded cast. It had been a 'falsie'.

Lillye told another story of a desperate trainer who hid in a bush near the 5-furlong start at the back of the Kensington racecourse. Just as the barrier was raised the trainer leapt from his hide and gave his horse a resounding smack on the backside with a stockwhip. Not surprisingly the horse sped off down the track and duly won the race.

Clive Inglis, the auctioneer, also had some neat stories. The jockeys Alby Callinan and Ernie Henry were close mates and suspected by the public of being in cahoots in planning races. One day a horse to be ridden by Henry blew ominously in the market. The stewards smelt a rat and substituted Callinan—to the disgust of one punter, who informed them: 'You mugs, you take off Ned Kelly and put on his brother Dan.'

Callinan's mount ran an 'unlucky' second. As the jockey returned to scale, the same humourist was in position on the rail with his head bowed and hat over his heart. Callinan could not resist asking what it meant. 'I always show my respect for the dead,' he responded (I have heard this 'respect' story told against a number of jockeys but Callinan was the earliest of them and I suspect this is the origin of the yarn).

Inglis also told of an incident that occurred soon after the stewards' observations towers were first used. The pony jockey Alf Stanton had evidently forgotten about them, for soon after, as he passed one riding a horse that was pulling double, he shouted to a colleague, 'How far will this win by when we let it go next time?' His reward was a lengthy suspension.

I hope this gives an impressionist view of the phenomenon that was pony racing in Sydney. If you would like to read a deeper analysis of it, I would refer you to my book *Sydney's Pony Racecourses: An Alternative Racing History*.

A RULE OF THE A.J.C.

A.B. 'BANJO' PATERSON

Come all ye bold trainers attend to my song,
It's a rule of the A.J.C.
You mustn't train ponies, for that's very wrong
By the rules of the A.J.C.
You have to wear winkers when crossing the street,
For fear that a pony you'd happen to meet
If you hear one about, you must beat a retreat,
That's a rule of the A.J.C.

And all ye bold owners will find without fail
By the rules of the A.J.C.
The jockey boys' fees you must pay at the scale,
It's a rule of the A.J.C.
When your horse wins a fiver, you'll laugh, I'll be bound,
But you won't laugh so much by the time that you've found
That the fee to the boy is exactly ten pound!
That's a rule of the A.J.C.

And all ye bold 'Books' who are keeping a shop,
In the rules of the A.J.C.,
There's a new regulation that says you must stop!
That's a rule of the A.J.C.
You must give up your shop with its pipes and cigars
To an unlicensed man who is thanking his stars,
While you go and bet in the threepenny bars,
That's a rule of the A.J.C.

And all ye small jockeys who ride in a race,
In the rules of the A.J.C.
If owners' instructions are 'Don't get a place',
By the rules of the A.J.C.,
You must ride the horse out, though, of course, if you do
You will get no more mounts, it's starvation to you.
But, bless you, you'll always find plenty to chew
In the rules of the A.J.C.

PASSELLA, BY PASSING BY—SWEET ELLA

JIM BENDRODT

You wouldn't have known when the police came in, but I did.

To you the giant dance hall would have seemed about as usual. But your big-time dance-hall operator always knows. Sometimes I've wondered if there isn't some affinity between a showman and a wild forest creature. Neither of them needs much warning when unusual things occur.

I took a golden cigarette case from the pocket of a coat my tailor said was faultless. I opened it and chose a cigarette, and my men came past and didn't stop, but whispered as they passed me from the corners of their mouths, 'It's the cops, boss,' and I answered softly, 'Sure, I know.'

I lit my cigarette, and looked out over the dance floor where undulating thousands moved to the music of a waltz. I shifted my gaze casually to the shadows near the doorways and watched the big men take position. I knew the phones were covered and the exits and the stairs. I knew that in the avenue outside the patrol cars and the wagons would be waiting. The stage was set.

I lit another cigarette and turned away. A deep voice said, 'So it's selling sly grog now, Jim, is it. Well, you can come along with me.'

Then another voice bit into the silence like a file, 'Forget it, copper. It wasn't 'im that sold it. It was me.'

Well, there it was. Liquor is worse than dynamite in public dance halls. You had to have it at a function such as this one was, but you didn't sell it. You had good sense enough for that. You let your patrons bring it in, and then you watched them. You limited the quantity they could take.

You didn't have the profit motive, so you didn't care. But someone had sold liquor here tonight for profit, that was certain. Someone who couldn't smell 'Police' beneath a tailed coat and white bow tie. And here at my side was a tiny chap with high-bridged nose and myopic eyes who said in his acrid voice, ''E didn't sell it, copper, I did.'

I hadn't spoken. This was a situation when I thought a still tongue might pay dividends. The big inspector didn't know that he was wrong. It wouldn't have been the slightest use my telling him that I hated grog in a place like this just as much as he did.

He looked at me for a long time. He knew the tricks of evidence, the difficulties in a court of law. I knew he had to take the little man in all the circumstances. There wasn't any other thing for him to do.

I smiled and said gently, 'Well, Inspector, I couldn't tell the answer. It's up to you.'

He glared at me, then beckoned with a finger, and two large, good-humoured fellows ranged up on either side of the little man, and he walked away between them with his head at about the level of their knees. I noticed that his legs were bowed, and that he had little narrow feet.

In the morning an unsympathetic magistrate told him, 'Ninety pounds or thirty days,' but in the meantime my big boys had found the real culprit, so my cashier peeled the notes off, and brought the little fellow back to me.

I told him to sit down, and smiled at him while he picked with stubby fingers at a pack of cigarettes.

'What's the name, lad?' I inquired.

'Tom,' he said. He didn't say Tom White or Tom Some-other-thing, he just said, 'Tom.'

'Well, Tom,' I went on, 'what did you do it for? You didn't sell the wine, and you don't know me. But you thought I had sold it, didn't you?'

'Sure.' He grinned. 'Why wouldn't you?'

'Well, Tom,' I said, 'the answer to that one would probably be very involved from your point of view. We'll skip it. Now tell me, why did you say you sold it?'

He looked at me with his hard little face set stubbornly, and then he grinned. 'Well, I'll tell you, boss. Your caterer put me on the casual waiter staff last night. I knew the set-up when the cops came in, and I figured you'd be generous if I took the rap for you.'

I nodded. 'An opportunist, eh, Tom? And apparently an honest one. That's very interesting.'

So that was it. He had come from a hard school, this one. You only had to look at him to know that. 'But, Tom,' I continued, 'you're no waiter. Now tell me just what are you?'

'Waiter be damned!' he said indignantly. 'I was broke, so I took the job to get a feed. I'm a jockey.'

'Jockey? But, Tom, if you're a jockey, why don't you work at it?'

He shuffled his feet uneasily, and peered at me with his round myopic eyes, and then he grinned.

'The stewards 'ad me in,' he said, 'and afterwards I figured I might as well buy a one-way ticket out of town.'

He grinned again, but looked at me in astonishment when I asked, 'But why one way only, Tom?'

He studied me suspiciously, and then he asked, 'Say, boss, do you know anything about horses or jockeys?'

'Nothing, Tom. I've never seen a racecourse.' His face cleared as if a great light had burst upon him.

'Well,' he said, 'I've 'eard of folks like you, but you're the first I've ever met. Whadda you do on Saturdays? Perhaps you'll understand when I tell you I rode forty-two favourites in succession and got beat on every one. Does that mean anything to you?'

'Not a thing, Tom.'

He peered at me again. 'Well, I'll be damned!' he said. 'I don't believe it does, boss,' and he shook his head in a puzzled way.

'Well, Tom,' I said, 'let's forget it. For reasons best known to yourself, you have become a waiter and you don't like it. Now what would you like to do if you had a choice?'

He answered instantly, 'Train a 'orse.'

I looked at him. His object had been purely mercenary, but the fact remained that but for him my name would have figured prominently in the morning papers in connection with sly grog.

'How would you go about that, Tom?'

He looked at me disgustedly for a time before he answered. 'Buy a 'orse I know of,' he said at last. 'A pony mare by Passing By out of Sweet Ella. 'Er name's Passella. A 'undred quid will buy 'er. Then I'd rent a stable and . . .' He paused. 'Aw, hell,' he finished indignantly, 'anyone but you would know the rest of it! It don't seem possible that *you* don't.'

I laughed. Then I said, 'OK, Tom. Perhaps I *should* know. There's a stable behind this building. Take it. Here is a hundred pounds. Go and buy your mare. By Passing By out of Sweet Ella, I think you said. If there's anything else you want to train her, just let me know.'

Well, that was the start of it. A queer entrance to the Sport of Kings.

It wasn't long before Tom had her ready. She was a pretty mare with a sweet true head, just 14.1 hands.

'Now, boss,' Tom said in the inevitable highly confidential manner of all trainers of a horse, 'this mare's in at Kensington tomorrow with 8 stone 1, and she's a moral. What I want you to do is just go out quiet like and put about four 'undred on 'er, and she'll come 'ome smoking her pipe.'

The old, old story in the same time-honoured vernacular. How many men have fallen for a yarn like that! The confidence, the bland assurance, the fantastic triumph of hope over experience these little fellows always have.

'But, Tom,' I said, 'four hundred is a lot of money. What makes you so sure she'll win?'

'Sure?' Tom exclaimed with considerable asperity. 'Sure? Of course I'm sure.' Then with the crackpot logic of his kind, ''Aven't I told you she's a moral? Run three in thirty-seven she did this morning, touching the outside fence, with 'er 'eavy irons on. There's a thing called Pretty Sweet in it, which of course Passella will leave for dead, but they'll make a price for us. Well, 'ow about it, boss? 'Aven't lost your nerve, I 'ope?'

I remember that I felt a little bit ashamed. After all, this lad should know. Hadn't he been beaten on forty-two favourites in a row? Wasn't he steeped to his very ears in the chances of the racecourse? He had gone to what seemed to me a prodigious amount of trouble to get this mare ready.

He was so confident. He spoke with such finality about so many intriguing aspects of the art of training horses. It appeared almost ludicrous to imagine this horseman wouldn't know. Moreover, he was an amateur psychologist. He'd said, ''Aven't lost your nerve, boss, I 'ope?' A remark like that to a man like me! Just dynamite!

Well, I went to Kensington, and Tom hovered at my elbow.

'Now what do I do?' I asked.

Tom said, 'There's Jack Shaw, he'll bet you. 'E's a 'eavy better, 'e'll take the lot.'

'The lot, Tom?'

'Yes, ask 'im for the odds to four 'undred quid.'

So I did as I was told, and Mr Shaw bet me eight hundred pounds to four hundred, and I put the indecipherable ticket in my pocket.

'Now what, Tom?'

He looked at me, as a mother will a backward child.

'Get into the stand,' he answered, 'and watch 'er win it.' And he trotted off.

So I sat down in the stand and they brought the ponies out, and the jockeys mounted in their flaunting colours. And there was a chap called Bill Cook in *my* colours, which I'd never seen before.

I didn't know it then because I didn't know horses, but she was a bonny little mare, this Passella. I could see the way she fought to reach the bay mare, Pretty Sweet, all the long way up that straight. I didn't know a horse, but I knew a fighter when I saw one. I heard the crowd roar, and I saw the sign hoisted on the signal box. It read, 'Dead Heat'.

I went to look for Tom, and when I found him I asked in some puzzlement, 'What now, Tom?'

'We'll run it off,' he said.

'Run what off, Tom?'

He glared at me. 'Yeah, run it off in an hour's time. 'Ere, you go and 'ave a drink.'

He muttered something under his breath I couldn't catch, and hurried off as if he wanted to get away from me, which was unusual.

Well, they came up that straight a second time, locked together, in a bitter struggle, those two game midget horses with their nostrils flaring, and their ears resting in their straining necks, with the jockeys flailing at them with their whips and the people shouting.

They were very close together, so very close that in the last few desperate yards they seemed to lean over at an angle as if sheer weariness forced them to seek support. But Pretty Sweet won. No doubt of that. By the bare three inches. Her number showed in the signal box, and Tom came running and whispered urgently, 'Protest.'

'Protest, Tom?' I echoed. 'About what? To whom?'

'Aw, hell!' he snarled, and scuttled off, and as the ponies came trotting in I heard the crowd roar, 'Protest!' I looked at the signal tower where a green flag fluttered, and under it the word 'Protest' showed in black and white.

I waited, and in a little time I saw another flag go up, and another legend underneath, 'Protest upheld'.

I saw Tom coming at a run, with a grin upon his face, and when he reached me I asked him, 'What now, Tom?'

His excited chatter stopped as if I'd hit him with a board.

He took his hat off, and ran his stubby fingers through the remnants of his hair, and then in a voice devoid of hope, he said disgustedly, 'Aw, hell! You run and collect your eight 'undred quid and then go 'ome.'

The story's true. You can read the records if you want to.

BOTTLE QUEEN

TRADITIONAL/JIM HAYNES

Here is a yarn that I heard often as a kid. It concerns pony racing. The classic tale is about a pony which was trained by a couple of 'bottle-oh's' and used on the bottle cart when not racing, and I've put it into verse. My version is based in Botany or Mascot, Sydney, but I have seen versions of this yarn from as far afield as New Zealand. Obviously the joke is that the horse was also trained to stop to collect bottles!

***

We bred her in the suburbs and we trained her after dark,
Sometimes down the Botany Road and sometimes in the park,
And the way we used to feed her, it often led to rows,
We pinched the chaff from stables and the green stuff from
the Chows.

Now her sire was imported but we never knew from where
And her mother Black Moria, was a bottle dealer's mare.
We bought a set of colours; they were second hand and green,
And we had to call her something, so we called her Bottle Queen.

In the evenings when we galloped her I usually took the mount,
We didn't have a stopwatch, so me mate he used to count.
She showed us four in forty-nine, one-forty for the mile,
But she coulda done much better, she was pulling all the while.

Now that's something like a gallop, on the sand with ten stone up,
It'd win the English Derby! Or the Wagga Wagga Cup!
And when we thought we had her just as fit as she could be,
Me mate, he bit his sheila for the nomination fee.

We bunged her in a maiden and they dobbed her seven stone,
Talk about a 'jacky', she was in it on her own!
So we worked her on the bottles when the cart was good and light,
It was bottles every morning and training every night.

We walked her down to Kenso on the morning of the race,
The books had never heard of her, we backed her win and place,
Then we rubbed her down and saddled her and led her to the track,
And told that hoop his fee was good . . . if he brought a
winner back!

Well, they jumped away together but The Queen was soon in front,
As for all the others, they were never in the hunt!
She was romping past the leger; she was fighting for her head,
When some bastard waved a bottle . . . and our certainty
stopped dead!

Now when folks who know hear, 'Bottle-Oh', they say, 'There's poor
old Jim,
He mighta made a fortune, but the bottle did him in.'
Yes we shoulda made a motza, my bloody oath we should,
Except I guess you might say that The Queen was trained too good!

So, don't talk to me of racing, you can see I've had enough.
It's a game for men with money and for blokes who know
their stuff.
And if someone tries to tell you that the racing game is clean . . .
Just remember what I told you, my tale of Bottle Queen.

'BARON' BOB SKELTON

WAYNE PEAKE

Robert Skelton was larger than life. He so dominated pony racing in Sydney in the 1920s that he is perhaps best described as unregistered racing's equivalent of T.J. Smith, the famous post-war Randwick trainer whose career began two decades later, at Kensington, in 1942.

Known as 'the Baron' or 'Baron Bob', Skelton was the embodiment of the phrase 'colourful racing identity' before it became merely a euphemism used by the press to identify a mobster, although for decades Skelton was indeed a plentiful source of copy for racing journalists.

He was a participant in at least three racecourse brawls and a minor riot at the Richmond races, and was a weekly visitor to the stewards' room, from whence, like a Saturday cinema-matinee hero, he routinely escaped seemingly hopeless entrapments.

His two-storey home and stable, known as 'the Castle', which dominated the skyline on Barker Street, overlooking the back straight of Kensington racecourse, was, like Smith's 'Tulloch Lodge' in later year, as much campaign headquarters as training establishment.

Skelton was so dominant in the years between 1918 and 1925 that his career needs to be seen, again like Smith's, as atypical. It is important this is appreciated, for he is the source of much of what is known or supposed about pony trainers.

There are many possibly apocryphal stories about the exploits of Skelton. One suggests he once misled the ring by having a leading jockey change his name by deed poll; another relates how he sold a block of ice to finance a day at the course, and won an enormous amount. Although some of these stories have probably grown in the telling, there is no doubt Skelton enjoyed devising gothic schemes aimed at obtaining a better price for a horse that had been prepared to win.

His brinkmanship tested the ARC's rules of racing and he constantly flirted with suspension. Among his more straightforward devices was the bogus sale of horses that had been racing in poor form to a close associate, such as Barney Goldstein. The horses often won at their next starts in new colours after being heavily commissioned. Later the horse would return to Skelton's ownership.

Another often-told parable is said to illustrate how he escaped censure over a first-to-last performance by his horse by pointing out that test cricketer Herbert Collins, at that time an ARC steward, had recently scored a duck directly after a century—which he said amounted to the same thing as his horse's inconsistent form.

Skelton was twice suspended for twelve months in 1919, but on both occasions appealed successfully to the usually unresponsive ARC appeals board. He was always on a war footing to engage with bookmakers and sometimes their skirmishes became more than intellectual. In 1933 he was escorted from the course after assaulting a bookmaker who had chaffed him over an unsettled debt.

In the 1920s Skelton's ascendancy among pony trainers was even more pronounced than premiership statistics suggest, as many immediately below him were in fact AJC trainers who, by the anomalous rules of the time, were allowed to race their smaller thoroughbreds in restricted heights races on ARC racecourses.

Unfortunately for ARC trainers this border hopping did not apply bilaterally. AJC trainers who profited from the opportunity included Joe Burton, Joe Cook and Chris O'Rourke, a steel-grey headed veteran Randwick trainer who made numerous successful raids on the ARC racecourses with horses like Little Lady, the champion 14.1 hand pony of the mid-1920s, while continuing to prepare feature-race winners on AJC tracks. John Donohoe, an AJC trainer and member of the family associated with Victoria

Park, had the 14.0 hand flyer Valora. Donohoe was also the master of the champion rider Billy Cook who was, coincidentally, the first AJC apprentice to gain a permit to ride in ARC restricted heights races.

Skelton was a plumber before he became first a pony punter, then an owner and finally, a trainer, by at least 1916. He even dabbled in bookmaking for a short time. Initially he trained only a small number of his horses, preferring to send most to outside trainers such as Charlie Rudd. To a degree he owed his success to a deal he made with Les Bower, the racing manager of the leading registered owner John Brown (who raced under the name 'J. Baron'), for Skelton to lease the undersized produce of Brown's studs, particularly the progeny of champion sire Wallace, to race on the pony tracks. For this association Skelton was originally nicknamed 'Baron Junior'.

Skelton owned and trained in order to gamble. One of the earliest of the assaults on the betting ring for which he became noted occurred on 28 July 1920 at Kensington, when he prepared four winners, The Student (12 to 1), Smart Scribe (7 to 1), Precious Dust (10 to 1) and Prince Elect (4 to 5).

Skelton was a loner and he resisted attempts by the Pony Owners and Trainers Association (POTA) to make him place the corporate interests of his brother trainers before his own, yet by 1923 he had somehow become an unlikely president of the POTA.

He resigned the position after a bitter dispute with other delegates in which they accused him of using POTA membership fees to pay gambling debts. The ARC was inevitably drawn into this argument. The POTA requested that the ARC reject nominations received from outside the POTA membership, a proposal clearly intended to isolate Skelton. The ARC received legal advice that they could not refuse an entry unless the nominee had been found guilty of malpractice or a breach of the ARC rules of racing.

When they advised the POTA of this, the trainers called a strike. The first boycotted meeting happened to include the rich Rosebery Cup. Despite a picket line at the ARC office, Skelton and a handful of other non-POTA trainers were able to make sufficient entries for the meeting to go ahead, although it drew a much smaller attendance than usual.

Skelton won every race except for the Cup. The POTA strike continued at a second meeting at Ascot four days later, but thereafter the resolve of its members faltered and the strike petered out. Several of Skelton's fellow trainers and the editor of the *Sportsman*, Sam Mackenzie, believed that for a time after the POTA strike Skelton entries received generous handicaps and other favourable treatment from the ARC.

While enmity towards Skelton, rather than economic or industrial conditions, was the direct cause of the strike, it was nevertheless an expression of class-consciousness and the trainers' dissatisfaction with the way in which they believed financial surplus generated by unregistered racing was divided.

Despite his frequently reported betting successes, Skelton became insolvent in 1933. This did not end his career, however, and he continued to be one of the best-known faces on Sydney racecourses until the late 1950s.

While he was a student of form, he also sometimes gambled most irrationally, in the manner of what are known as 'mug' punters: 'Bob was so keen to have a bet, when he felt lucky, that, on one occasion, when Rufe Naylor refused to bet him an even thousand on the favourite . . . he offered to bet the bookmaker the same amount to the same odds that the favourite wouldn't win,' recalled Joe Andersen.

He also liked to bet on the fluctuating odds during the running of a race, as he, other gamblers and bookmakers gathered in the area reserved for licensed persons in the grandstand.

Baron Bob died almost penniless but had sustained himself in some comfort off the bounty of the racecourse for almost 40 years; a long career denied to most who follow that vocation.

A DISQUALIFIED JOCKEY'S STORY

A.B. 'BANJO' PATERSON

You see, the thing was this way—there was me,
That rode Panopply, the Splendor mare,
And Ikey Chambers on the Iron Dook,
And Smith, the half-caste rider on Regret,
And that long bloke from Wagga—him that rode
Veronikew, the Snowy River horse.
Well, none of them had chances—not a chance
Among the lot, unless the rest fell dead
Or wasn't trying—for a blind man's dog
Could see Enchantress was a certain cop,
And all the books was layin' six to four.

They brought her out to show our lot the road,
Or so they said: but, then Gord's truth! you know,
You can't believe 'em, though they took an oath
On forty Bibles that they'd tell the truth.
But anyhow, an amateur was up
On this Enchantress; and so Ike and me,
We thought that we might frighten him a bit
By asking if he minded riding rough—
'Oh, not at all,' says he, 'oh, not at all!
I learned at Robbo Park, and if it comes
To bumping I'm your Moses! Strike me blue!'

Says he, 'I'll bump you over either rail,
The inside rail or outside—which you choose
Is good enough for me'—which settled Ike.
For he was shaky since he near got killed
From being sent a buster on the rail,
When some chap bumped his horse and fetched him down
At Stony Bridge; so Ikey thought it best
To leave this bloke alone, and I agreed.

So all the books was layin' six to four
Against the favourite, and the amateur
Was walking this Enchantress up and down,
And me and Smithy backed him; for we thought
We might as well get something for ourselves,
Because we knew our horses couldn't win.
But Ikey wouldn't back him for a bob;
Because he said he reckoned he was stiff,
And all the books was layin' six to four.

Well, anyhow, before the start the news
Got around that this here amateur was stiff,
And our good stuff was blued, and all the books
Was in it, and the prices lengthened out,
And every book was bustin' of his throat,
And layin' five to one the favourite.
So there was we that couldn't win ourselves,
And this here amateur that wouldn't try,
And all the books was layin' five to one.

So Smithy says to me, 'You take a hold
Of that there moke of yours, and round the turn
Come up behind Enchantress with the whip
And let her have it; that long bloke and me
Will wait ahead, and when she comes to us
We'll pass her on and belt her down the straight,
And Ikey'll flog her home—because his boss

Is judge and steward and the Lord knows what,
And so he won't be touched; and, as for us,
We'll swear we only hit her by mistake!'
And all the books was layin' five to one.

Well, off we went, and comin' to the turn
I saw the amateur was holding back
And poking into every hole he could
To get her blocked; and so I pulled behind
And drew the whip and dropped it on the mare.
I let her have it twice, and then she shot
Ahead of me, and Smithy opened out
And let her up beside him on the rails,
And kept her there a-beltin' her like smoke
Until she struggled past him, pullin' hard,
And came to Ike; but Ikey drew his whip
And hit her on the nose, and sent her back
And won the race himself—for, after all,
It seems he had a fiver on The Dook
And never told us—so our stuff was lost.
And then they had us up for ridin' foul,
And warned us off the tracks for twelve months each
To get our livin' any way we could;
But Ikey wasn't touched, because his boss
Was judge and steward and the Lord knows what.

But Mister—if you'll lend us half-a-crown,
I know three certain winners at the Park—
Three certain cops as no one knows but me;
And—thank you, Mister, come an' have a beer
(I always like a beer about this time) . . .
Well, so long, Mister, till we meet again.

DONE FOR THE DOUBLE

A.B. 'BANJO' PATERSON—WRITING AS 'KNOTT GOLD' (AUTHOR OF *FLOGGED FOR A FURLONG, WON BY A WINKER* , ETC.)

Part 1—Wanted, a Pony

Algernon de Montgomery Smythers was a merchant, wealthy and beyond the dreams of avarice. Other merchants might dress more lavishly, and wear larger watch chains, but the bank balance is the true test of mercantile superiority, and in trial of bank balances Algernon de Montgomery represented Tyson at seven stone. He was unbeatable.

He lived in comfort, not to say luxury. He had champagne for breakfast every morning and his wife always slept with a pair of diamond earrings worth a small fortune in her ears. It is things like these that show true gentility. All others are shoddy.

Though they had been married many years, the A de M Smythers had but one child—a son and heir. He was brought up in the lap of luxury. No Christmas Day was allowed to pass by his doting parents without a gift to young Algy of some trifle worth about £150, less the discount for cash. He had six playrooms, all filled with the most expensive toys and ingenious mechanical devices. He had a phonograph that could hail a ship out at the South Head, and a mechanical parrot that sang 'The Wearing of the Green'. And still he was not happy.

Sometimes, in spite of the vigilance of his four nurses and six under-nurses, he would escape into the street, and run about with the little boys that he met there. One day he gave one of them a sovereign for a locust. Certainly the locust was a 'double-drummer', and could deafen the German Band when shaken up judiciously; still, it was dear at the price of a sovereign.

It is ever thus.

What we have we do not value, and what other people have we are not strong enough to take from them.

Such is life.

Christmas was approaching, and the question of what should be given to Algy as a present agitated the bosom of his parents. He had nearly everything a child would want, but one morning a bright inspiration struck Algy's father. Algy should have a pony.

With Mr Smythers to think was to act. He was not a man who believed in allowing grass to grow under his feet. His motto was, 'Up and be doing—somebody'. So he put an advertisement in the paper that same day.

> Wanted, a boy's pony. Must be guaranteed sound, strong, handsome, intelligent. Used to trains, trams, motors, fire engines, and motor buses. Any failure in above respect will disqualify. Certificate of birth required as well as references from last place, when calling. Price no object.

Part 2—Blinky Bill's Sacrifice

Down in the poverty-stricken portions of the city lived Blinky Bill the horse dealer. His yard was surrounded by loose boxes made of any old timber, galvanised iron, sheets of roofing felt, and bark that he could gather together. He kept all sorts of horses, except good sorts. There were harness horses that wouldn't pull, and saddle horses that wouldn't go—or, if they went used to fall down; nearly every animal about the place had something the matter with it.

He kept racing ponies, and when the bailiff dropped in, for the rent, as he did every two or three weeks, Bill and the bailiff would go out together, and 'have a punt' on some of Bill's ponies, or on somebody else's ponies—the latter for choice. But the periodical punts and occasional sales of horses would not keep the wolf from the door. Ponies keep on eating whether they are winning or not and Blinky Bill had got down to the very last pitch of desperation when he saw the advertisement mentioned at the end of the last chapter.

It was like a ray of hope to him. At once there flashed upon him what he must do. He must make a great sacrifice; he must sell Sausage II. What, the reader might ask, was Sausage II? Alas, that such a great notability should be anywhere unknown!

Sausage II was the greatest thirteen-two pony of the day. Time and again he had gone out to race when, to use William's own words, it was a blue duck for Bill's chance of keeping afloat unless the pony won; and every time did the gallant race pony pull his owner through. Bill owed more to Sausage II than he owed to any of his creditors.

Brought up as a pet, the little animal was absolutely trustworthy. He would carry a lady or a child, or pull a sulky; in fact, it was quite a common thing for Blinky Bill to drive him in a sulky to a country meeting and look about him for a likely 'mark'; if he could find a fleet youth with a reputedly fast pony, Bill would offer to 'pull the little cuddy out of the sulky and run yer for a fiver.' Sometimes he got beaten but, as he never paid, that didn't matter. He did not believe in fighting, except under desperate circumstances, but he would always sooner fight than pay.

But all these devices had left him on his uppers in the end. He had no feed for his ponies, and no money to buy feed; the corn merchant had written his account off as bad, and had no desire to make it worse. Under the circumstances, what was he to do? Sausage II must be sold.

With heavy heart Bill led the pony down to be inspected. He saw Algernon de Montgomery Smythers and measured him with his eye. He saw it would be no use to talk about racing to him, so he went on the other tack.

He told him that the pony belonged to a Methodist clergyman, who used to drive him in a 'shay.' There are no shays in this country; but Bill had read the word somewhere, and thought it sounded respectable. 'Yus, sir,' he said, ''e goes lovely in a shay,' and he was just starting off at twenty words a second, when he was stopped.

Mr A de M Smythers was brusque with his inferiors, and in this he made a mistake. Instead of listening to all that Blinky Bill said, and disbelieving it at his leisure, he stopped his talk. 'If you want to sell this pony, dry up,' he said. 'I don't believe a word you say, and it only worries me to hear you lying.'

Fatal mistake! You should never stop a horse dealer's talk. And call him anything you like, but never say you doubt his word.

Both these things, Mr Smythers did; and though he bought the pony at a high price, yet the insult sank deep into the heart of Blinky Bill.

As the capitalist departed leading the pony, Blinky Bill muttered to himself, 'Ha! Ha! Little does he know that he is leading Sausage II, the greatest thirteen-two pony of the century. Let him beware how he gets alongside anything. That's all! Blinky Bill may yet be revenged!'

We shall see.

Part 3—Exit Algy

Christmas Day came. Algy's father gave orders to have the pony saddled, and led round to the front door. Algy's mother, a lady of forty summers, spent the morning superintending the dinner. Dinner was the principal event in the day with her. Alas, poor lady! Everything she ate agreed with her, and she got fatter and fatter and fatter.

The cold world never fully appreciates struggles of those who are fat—the efforts at starvation, the detested exercise, the long, miserable walks. Well has one of our greatest poets written, 'Take up the fat man's burden'. But we digress.

When Algy saw the pony he shouted with delight, and in half a minute was riding him up and down the front drive. Then he asked for leave to go out in the street, and that was where the trouble began.

Up and down the street the pony cantered, as quietly as possible, till suddenly round a corner came two butcher boys racing their horses. With a clatter of clumsy hoofs they thundered past. In half a second there was a rattle, and a sort of comet-like rush through the air. Sausage II was off after them with his precious burden.

The family dog tried to keep up with him, and succeeded in keeping ahead for about three strides. Then, like the wolves that pursued Mazeppa, he was left yelping far behind.

Through Surry Hills and Redfern swept the flying pony, his rider lying out on his neck in Tod Sloan fashion, while the ground seemed to race beneath him. The events of the way were just one hopeless blur till the pony ran straight as an arrow into the yard of his owner, Blinky Bill.

Part 4—Running the Rule

As soon as Blinky Bill recognised his visitor, he was delighted. 'You here,' he said, 'Ha, ha, revenge is mine! I'll get a tidy reward for taking you back, my young shaver.' Then from the unresisting child he took a gold watch and three sovereigns, which he had in his pocket. These he said he would put in a safe place for him, till he was going home again. He expected to get at least a tenner ready money for bringing the child back, and hoped that he might be allowed to keep the watch into the bargain. With a light heart he went down town with Algy's watch and sovereigns in his pocket. He did not return till daylight, when he awoke his wife with bad news.

'Can't give the boy up,' he said. 'I moskenoed his block and tackle, and blued it in the school,' meaning that he had pawned the boy's watch and chain, and had lost the proceeds at pitch and toss. 'Nothing for it but to move,' he said, 'and take the kid with us.'

So move they did.

The reader can imagine with what frantic anxiety the father and mother of little Algy sought for their lost one. They put the matter into the hands of the detective police, and waited for the Sherlock Holmeses of the force to get in their fine work. They heard nothing.

Years rolled on, and the mysterious disappearance of little Algy was never solved. The horse dealer's revenge was complete. The boy's mother consulted a clairvoyant, who said, 'What went by the ponies, will come by the ponies,' and with that they had to remain satisfied.

Part 5—The Tricks of the Turf

It was race day at Pulling'em Park, and the ponies were doing their usual performances. Among the throng the heaviest punter is a fat lady with diamond earrings. Does the reader recognise her? It is little Algy's mother. Her husband is dead, leaving her the whole of his colossal fortune, and, having developed a taste for gambling, she is now engaged in 'doing in on the ponies'. She is one of the biggest betters in the game.

When women take to betting they are worse than men.

But it is not for betting alone that she attends the meetings. She remembers the clairvoyant's 'What went by the ponies will come by the ponies.' And always she searches in the ranks of the talent for her lost Algy.

Here comes another of our dramatis personae—Blinky Bill, prosperous once more. He got a string of ponies and punters together. The first are not much use to a man without the second; but, in spite of all temptations, Bill has always declined to number among his punters the mother of the child he stole. But the poor lady regularly punts on his ponies, and just as regularly is 'sent up'—in other words, loses her money.

Today she has backed Blinky's pair, Nostrils and Tin Can, for the double. Nostrils has won his race, and Tin Can, if on the job, can win the second half of the double. Is he on the job? The prices are lengthening against him, and the poor lady recognises that once more she is 'in the cart'.

Just then she meets Tin Can's jockey, Dodger Smith, face to face. A piercing scream rends the atmosphere, as if a thousand school children drew a thousand slate pencils down a thousand slates simultaneously. 'Me cheild! Me cheild! Me long-lost Algy!'

It did not take long to convince Algy that he would be better off as son to a wealthy lady than as a jockey subject to the fiendish caprices of Blinky Bill.

'All right, Mother,' he said. 'Put all you can raise on Tin Can. I'm going to send Blinky up. It's time I had a cut on me own, anyway.'

The horses went to the post. Tons of money were at the last moment hurled onto Tin Can. The books, knowing he was 'dead', responded gamely, and wrote his name till their wrists gave out. Blinky Bill had a half-share in all the bookies' winnings, so he chuckled grimly as he went to the rails to watch the race.

They're off. And what is this that flashes to the front, while the howls of the bookies rise like the yelping of fiends in torment? It is Dodger Smith on Tin Can, and from the grandstand there is a shrill feminine yell of triumph as the gallant pony sails past the post.

The bookies thought that Blinky Bill had sold them, and they discarded him forever. He is now a bottle-oh!

Algy and his mother were united, and backed horses together happily ever after; and sometimes out in the back yard of their palatial mansion they hand the empty bottles, free of charge, to a poor old broken-down bottle-oh. It is Blinky Bill. Thus has his revenge recoiled upon himself.

BETTING AND BEER

J.G. MEDLEY

Put three or four quid on the horses,
And a couple of pounds on the trots;
Ten bob for the dogs in their courses,
And something or other for spots—
And if there is anything over
That hasn't been got by the cats,
What ho! for a future in clover
By way of a ticket in Tatts.
Oh! Betting and Beer are the basis
Of the only respectable life.
Much better to go to the races
Than moulder at home with the wife.
I'd much sooner go to the races
Than take all the kids to the sea.
My family knows what their place is,
And that is at home—without me.

Part 7
RACING CHARACTERS

INTRODUCTION—KINGS AND DEADBEATS

Racing breeds 'characters', and characters make great stories.

Racing has been called 'the sport of kings . . . and deadbeats' and the term 'colourful racing identity' is used as a euphemism in Australia for a major criminal who, though he is known to be a crook, hasn't been caught yet.

In living memory, 'Hollywood' George Edser, Perce Galea, Abe Saffron and many others fit into this category and colonial racing had many more.

Almost everyone I know in racing is a character with a story worth telling, often many stories. Every trainer, from the flamboyant, ever-positive Gai Waterhouse, to the dour and implacable John O'Shea, are 'characters' in one way or another.

Jockeys are certainly characters—every one. It's an odd profession for a start, and a dangerous one, which attracts men with a certain personality due to their smallness. Cheeky, chirpy types like George Moore and Chris Munce are loved by the media, Tommy Berry is a noted practical joker, Jack Thompson was known to never smile, and Darren Beadman was renowned as a devout Christian, rather an anomaly for a jockey.

These days there are almost as many female riders as there are men and they have brought a certain glamour and freshness to racing, after battling for decades to gain respect and be accepted—there are some great stories there!

But it's often the owners who are the real characters of racing. Owners range from the great men and women on the world stage, such as the Queen, the Aga Khan and Sheik Mohammed, to larger-than-life characters like the Inghams brothers, Tony Santic and John Singleton, and true Aussie battlers such as Joe Janiak, owner-trainer of Takeover Target, and schoolteacher Wendy Green who bought Rogan Josh for $13,000 and won the Melbourne Cup.

We mustn't forget the punters, characters like Louis the Possum and the Legal Eagles, a small punting squad masterminded by Don Scott that terrorised bookies in the 1970s and included Clyde Packer, lawyer Clive Evatt and racing aficionado Bob Charley. Then there are the bookies; in the Sydney ring the personalities range from the high-rolling Waterhouses to stony-faced Eric Conlon, who always risks a point or two more than the rest. And who could forget that larger-than-life character, the late Kerry Packer, who once bet a million dollars on a race at Rosehill?

Then there are the coat-tuggers, touts and whisperers who haunted racetracks in 'the good old days'. And we shouldn't forget the stablehands, trackwork riders and clockers, and the race-callers and tipsters who become media personalities, like Ken Howard, Bert Bryant, Kenny Callander and a hundred more.

Enough to fill many books with great stories; here are just a handful.

THE MAN WHO PREFERRED HORSES TO CHILDREN

JIM HAYNES

Etienne de Mestre was one of ten children of a fascinating character in our history, Prosper de Mestre.

The son of a French officer fleeing the Revolution, Prosper de Mestre was born at sea on a British ship after his father's death. He was raised and educated in America after his mother remarried and he lived and traded in China, India and Mauritius before arriving in Sydney, where his right to trade as a 'foreigner' was challenged and he subsequently became the first person ever to be naturalised as an 'Australian', or at least a British subject in Australia!

Prosper married Mary Anne Black, daughter of the ex-convict Mary Hyde and stepdaughter of the successful ex-convict merchant Simeon Lord, with whom Prosper was in partnership. After Simeon Lord died, Mary Hyde-Lord famously sued the city of Sydney for resuming land and a water supply granted to her husband which prevented her mill at Botany from continuing to operate. She took her case to London and it was upheld by the Privy Council.

Etienne was the third son from the marriage. He was born in 1832 in George Street, in the house where his mother was born, on land that backed onto the Tank Stream.

Etienne developed a love of racing while spending school holidays working with thoroughbred horses at Exeter Farm at Jembaicumbene, which was owned by the family of his school friend Thomas Roberts. The two boys remained lifelong friends and the Roberts family actually owned Melbourne Cup winners

Archer and Tim Whiffler, though the horses were leased by de Mestre and raced in his famous stable colours of all black.

Etienne developed into an excellent horseman and won his first race as a jockey in 1847, at the age of fifteen, on one of the Roberts' horses, Sweetheart. He later leased, trained and rode Nancy, a daughter of Sweetheart, to win several races in the Shoalhaven district.

When Etienne was seventeen or eighteen, he fathered a child with an Aboriginal girl, Sarah Lamb. Little is known about Sarah but their daughter, Helen, born about 1850, lived into her 80s and died in 1934 at Wallaga Lake Aboriginal settlement. Helen had four sons with her first husband, a tracker named Jacky Bond, and three children with her second husband, Chinese market gardener James Ahoy. Her son Andy Bond, Etienne's grandson, served in the 33rd Battalion in World War I and her grandson Ted 'Guboo' Thomas, Etienne's great-grandson, was a famous Aboriginal leader and statesman, an elder of the Yuin people, and the last initiated tribal elder on the South Coast of New South Wales. One of Helen de Mestre's great-grandchildren is renowned Aboriginal artist Lloyd Hornsby.

Etienne's oldest brother, also named Prosper, had taken over the family merchant business when their father died in 1843 and, in 1851, Etienne went into partnership with his elder brother Andre and they leased a section of the land their father had been granted at Terara, on the Shoalhaven River, from their mother.

They built stables and a racetrack where unofficial meetings were held and set up a stud and training business. When their mother died in 1861 they inherited the property and expanded their operations into the finest training and breeding operation in the colony.

Etienne became the most successful jockey of his day and then bred and trained many winners of feature races including four AJC Derbies, three VRC Derbies, two Sydney Cups (including the first ever run), eight AJC Queen's Plates and an Epsom Handicap. He trained Archer to win the first two Melbourne Cups and, with his three other Cup winners, he set a record of five wins in the great race, which lasted for 99 years, until Bart Cummings broke it in 1977.

In 1857 de Mestre won the Liverpool Members Plate on George Taylor Rowe's horse Plant and then trained Rowe's horse Veno to win the first inter-colonial Champion Challenge at Flemington in 1859. Veno defeated the Melbourne mare Alice Hawthorn. The match race, staged in front of 20,000 spectators, was a precursor to the Melbourne Cup, which began two years later.

Etienne built his reputation as a trainer from 1857 to 1860 with horses like the Tom Roberts-bred colts Mariner and Sailor, and soon owners throughout the Shoalhaven and Sydney districts sent him their best horses to train. Although he bred many horses himself, he also trained others such as Archer, Tim Whiffler, Sailor and Mariner for the Roberts family, Plant and Veno for the Rowe family, and Yattendon and Chester for noted Sydney sportsman James White.

Archer and two other de Mestre horses were sent to contest the first Melbourne Cup and Archer famously won the first and second Cups and was then infamously prevented from starting in the third by the machinations of the Victoria Turf Club who used a technicality to refuse the entry. All the interstate entrants pulled out in protest and only seven local horses ran in what is considered the weakest Cup in history. This was a wake-up call to the VTC and the club merged with old rivals the Victoria Jockey Club (VJC) to form the Victoria Racing Club (VRC) in 1863 and get the Cup back to its original standing.

Although de Mestre had claimed he would never enter the Cup again, he returned for the 1867 Cup and set a record by winning for a third time with another horse he leased from the Roberts family, Tim Whiffler.

In 1872 de Mestre's rival 'Honest' John Tait beat his record by winning his fourth Cup. Etienne tried hard to catch Tait with Cup wins and was certain he had the horse to do it in 1876. That horse was Robin Hood, the best horse he ever trained, according to Etienne, but Robin Hood and ten other horses were lost at sea when the steamer *City Of Melbourne* encountered a ferocious storm on the voyage to Melbourne and it was not until 1877 that de Mestre was able to match the record, by winning the Cup with James White's horse Chester.

In 1878 he won again with his own horse Calamia and set a record of five wins, which would last for 99 years.

De Mestre encountered many financial and health problems in the early 1880s. He had invested heavily in Queensland property and then severe drought in Queensland, and also on the Shoalhaven, broke him financially and his health began to fail. At the age of 51, in 1883, his property at Terara was auctioned off to pay his debts, and the all-black livery of the Terara stable disappeared from the colonial racing world.

Friends organised a successful benefit race meeting for him and the proceeds enabled him to live quietly yet comfortably with his large family on the family dairy farm, Garryowen, at Moss Vale.

In 1873 Etienne, aged 41, had married Clara Eliza Rowe, known as Eliza. She was the 21-year-old daughter of his friend George Taylor Rowe and sister of George W.S. Rowe, secretary of the Rosehill Racing Club. Eliza bore ten children, of whom nine survived infancy. The younger children were born and grew up on the dairy farm at Moss Vale and, according to descendant Jeanne de Mestre, all of Etienne's children 'had to make their own way in life while he concentrated on his horses'.

The eldest child, Etienne George, became a trainer in England and the third son, Hurtle Edwin, went to the Boer War and later managed a stud farm in South Africa. The youngest child, Leroy Leveson Laurent Joseph de Mestre, was a sickly pampered child who became a gifted artist and musician and played viola with the Sydney Orchestra. He changed his name to Roy De Maistre and became one of Australia's greatest painters and a legendary figure in the world of post-impressionist art. Knighted in 1962, Roy was a close friend of Patrick White and the painter Roland Wakelin and, in spite of joining the army three times in World War I and being discharged due to physical weakness from congenital tuberculosis, he lived to be 73 and died in London in 1968. His famous *Stations of the Cross* series hangs in Westminster Cathedral.

Etienne de Mestre died at Moss Vale on 22 October 1916 at the age of 84, and was buried in the Church of England cemetery at Bong Bong. He was inducted into the Australian Racing Hall of Fame in September 1992.

TOM HALES

NAT GOULD

Tom Hales, one of the ten children of a blacksmith, was born in Portland, Western Victoria, and grew up in Penola, South Australia. Forbidden to be a jockey by his father, he ran away from home at twelve and found work on Edward Stockdale's station, Lake Hawden, and met Adam Lindsay Gordon, who was working as a horse-breaker. Later, when Gordon was a police trooper, he arrested Hales for throwing stones at cattle in the Penola stockyard, but released the offender when he realised who he was.

Hales rode his first winner at thirteen and went on to win three Sydney Cups, six AJC Derbies, seven AJC St Legers, seven Victoria Derbies and ten St Legers, six Australasian Champion Cups and the Melbourne Cup on Grand Flaneur. Between 1872 and 1894 he rode 1678 times for 496 wins, 332 seconds and 195 thirds. In an age of corrupt racing he was renowned as an honest and incorruptible jockey. He died aged 54 in 1901.

***

When I first went to Australia Tom Hales was at the height of his fame as a jockey, but of late years he has almost given up riding and is rarely seen in the saddle. His record stands alone, and he has ridden more winners than any other jockey in the colonies. He has won nearly every race of importance on the Australian turf, and his classic wins are too numerous to mention.

As a rider of two-year-olds Hales may be placed on a par with that master of the art, Tom Cannon. Hales has a wonderful sympathy with the horse he rides, and he and his mount appear to understand each other thoroughly. In such races as the Derby, Hales's judgement stands him in good stead, and his knowledge of pace was never better displayed than when he beat Carbine on Ensign in the Derby of 1888.

It was in this type of race for the late James White that Hales scored his biggest wins, and he rode scores of winners for the Newmarket stable.

Tom Hales, in my humble opinion, is one of the best men I ever saw ride a racehorse. He has marvellous hands, a clear, cool head, and is a wonderful judge of pace, a great finisher, and has a good seat. Above all, he is as honest as the day, and there has never been a whisper of suspicion against him during his long career in the saddle.

I have known Hales a long time, and his modest and unassuming manner and thorough straightforwardness have always favourably impressed me. Many happy hours have I spent with him, both on the turf and off, more especially in his beautiful home, Acmeville, at Moonee Ponds, near Melbourne.

Acmeville is a charming residence, luxurious without being ostentatious. Tom Hales at home is the hospitable host and Mrs Hales, a daughter of South Australia's most successful breeder of horses, is a model wife.

Unfortunately Tom Hales is a great sufferer from asthma and is anything but strong. His love of riding, however, is as keen as ever. The last time I was at Acmeville he returned with me to Melbourne in order to go on that night to Caulfield to ride one of his own horses at work next morning.

'I never consider any trouble or inconvenience it may cause me, when there is work to be done,' he said, when I asked him why he left his comfortable home to go out to Caulfield. 'I have always made it a practice through life to be on the spot when I'm wanted. I have done this for the owners I have ridden for, now I am doing it for myself.'

Tom Hales is a wealthy man, and has acquired his money in an honest manner, and has worked very hard for it, I'm afraid to the detriment of his health.

He has a fine stud farm at Halesville, near Albury, in lovely country near the banks of the Murray, and there he is devoting much of his time to the breeding of bloodstock.

'HONEST JOHN'

JIM HAYNES

John Tait was born in 1813 at Melrose near Edinburgh. The son of Robert Tait, a jeweller and engraver, he trained as a jeweller before deciding on a new life in Tasmania and emigrating in 1837, at the age of 24, with his young wife Janet and their daughter.

They arrived in Hobart aboard the *Hindo* in November 1837 and ran several businesses successfully. The adventurous and enterprising Tait found Hobart rather slow, however, and moved to New South Wales in 1843, where he became the licensee of the Albion Inn at Hartley. He began training horses and racing them in the district and, like many publicans, held race meetings at his pub at Hartley, and later at the Black Bull Inn at Bathurst, which he took over in 1847. His skill in the art of boxing and his sense of fair play helped him to run pubs successfully and deal with troublesome drinkers.

The enterprising Scotsman was approaching 40 when he moved to Sydney in 1851 to train horses and become licensee of the Commercial Hotel on Castlereagh Street.

In 1847 he won his first St Leger at Homebush with a horse named Whalebone and was soon training and managing racehorses for some very important Bathurst district owners and horse breeders, men such as pastoralist George Lee and Thomas Icely, a landowner famous as a breeder and importer of cattle, sheep and horses who exported cavalry remounts to India and developed the merino sheep breed.

Tait's racing business grew quickly and he hired Noah Beale as a trainer and James Ashworth as his stable jockey. From 1851 to 1854 he won races with prizemoney totalling about £2500 at Bathurst, Parramatta, Homebush and Penrith, including two more St Legers with Cossack and Surplice and three Queen's Plates with Cossack (twice) and Sportsman.

Big money was available in horseracing by this time, but it was not a game for the faint-hearted. In a match race at Homebush in 1854, Tait's horse Sportsman defeated Cooramin, owned by pioneer grazier John Eales; the two men bet each other £1000 on the result.

In 1855 Tait sold his horses and visited England, accompanied by Ashworth, to choose breeding stock. By this time he had made some rich and powerful friends and had formed a partnership with Alfred Cheeke, crown prosecutor and later Supreme Court judge of New South Wales. They imported three British horses, Warwick, New Warrior and Magus, who sired Clove, winner of the first AJC Derby in 1865.

On his return to Sydney in 1857, Tait set up a stud farm at Mount Druitt, in partnership with Cheeke, and chose his new racing colours of yellow jacket and black cap. Perhaps his old colours, black jacket and red cap, were too close to those of his rival Etienne de Mestre whose horses, including the famous Archer, raced in all black.

Unlike many other racing men, who saw themselves as 'sportsmen', Tait always said he 'went into racing as a business'. The success of his business depended on winning races and he used scientific methods of feeding and training. He supervised the training and preparation of all the horses in his stables and his horses were always fit, healthy and raced in top condition.

He owned two triple-derby winners: Fireworks, who won twelve of his sixteen starts including the 1867 AJC Derby and the VRC Derby in 1867 and 1868 (when the race date was changed to 1 January), and Florence who won the AJC Derby, VRC Derby and Queensland Turf Club Derby in 1870–71. The great filly Florence also won the VRC Oaks.

As well as The Barb, Tait trained three other Melbourne Cup winners: Glencoe (1869) who also won the AJC Derby, The Pearl (1871) and The Quack (1872). He trained Goldsbrough to win the

Epsom–Metropolitan double in 1875, and his last win in a big race came when Amendment won the 1877 Metropolitan.

Between 1865 and 1880 Tait won something like £30,000 in prizemoney alone. That in itself was a fortune at the time and when you remember that added 'sweepstakes' and side bets were commonplace back then, you can imagine just how profitable his 'business' was!

John Tait was given his nickname, 'Honest John', because he only ever protested once, in the Sydney Cup of 1866. Even then he protested out of a sense of justice, not to gain the race, which was won by Yattendon. Tait's horse Falcon was blatantly 'taken out' when Pitsford crossed and 'hocked' him; Thompson, the offending jockey, was disqualified.

When The Barb weighed in 2 pounds light in the Queen's Plate of 1868, he offered £100 reward to anyone who could prove foul play. The race was given to Etienne de Mestre's Tim Whiffler, which had finished second.

Tait and de Mestre dominated racing in New South Wales for two decades, being the first trainers to bring commercial principles and good management practices to the sport of racing. Between 1861 and 1878 the two great Sydney trainers won half of the Melbourne Cups contested, with de Mestre taking the Cup five times and Tait four times.

The Barb's Melbourne Cup victory, as a three-year-old, in 1866 was the first of Tait's four Cup victories. It was a controversial Cup. There were two horses named Falcon engaged. One of them, also trained by Tait, finished third behind The Barb but the judge would not declare a third place, as the colours carried by the 'Sydney Falcon', yellow jacket and red cap, did not match any of the entries given to the judges on the official race card.

Tait had substituted a red cap on his second runner to differentiate the colours from those carried by The Barb, but evidently he didn't notify the judge officially. The following day at 4 p.m. the stewards declared 'Sydney Falcon' had been placed third, but many bookmakers refused to pay out on the horse, arguing that only the judge had the power to 'place' horses officially.

Tait retired from training in 1880 due to poor health. His wife Janet died that year and this enabled Tait to marry Christian Ann Swannell, a widow who had already borne him six children. This they did on 18 August 1880 while visiting London.

The couple were known for their hospitality and lived in a fine house called Toddington, on the Boulevard, at Petersham. John had been a justice of the peace from 1879, he also served on the committee of the Animals Protection Society, and represented New South Wales as commissioner at the 1887 Adelaide and 1888 Melbourne exhibitions.

'Honest John' Tait collapsed and died of heart disease in May 1888 and was buried in Waverley cemetery without religious rites. Survived by his second wife, four of their children, and two sons and a daughter from his first marriage, he left an estate valued at £24,000.

THE BANJO

JIM HAYNES

We all know 'The Banjo' as the man who wrote two famous poems and a song! But there are so many other elements to Andrew Barton Paterson's life apart from him being the author of 'Clancy', 'Snowy River' and 'Waltzing Matilda'. He was a remarkable man!

I guess most people think Paterson was born and raised in the bush, but he lived there on the family property for just the first decade of his life and left home in 1874, at the age of ten, to live with his literary-minded grandmother in Sydney and attend Sydney Grammar School.

After leaving school he trained to become a solicitor, and started writing poetry about current affairs, sporting events and tragic bush tales and sending them to *The Bulletin*. His first published poems were about the Sudan War, the Melbourne Cup and a lost child dying in the bush.

He was a very 'sporty' type and a very good rider. He always said the broken arm he suffered as a child was his secret; his shortened arm gave him a light touch on the reins. His 'nurse' was an Aboriginal girl who was too scared to tell the family she'd dropped the baby and the arm had to be treated in several painful operations years later.

Paterson was known as 'Barty' to family and friends, but he used the name of a station racehorse as his nom-de-plume, 'The Banjo'.

Even after 'The Man From Snowy River' caused a stir in *The Bulletin*, nobody knew who 'The Banjo' was until his first book was released. Later he was so famous that the pen name 'The Banjo' was shortened to 'Banjo' and added to his name.

He played in the first New South Wales Polo Team ever assembled and they defeated Victoria 2–0. He won the Polo Challenge Cup, a race for polo ponies, at Rosehill racetrack in 1892, on his horse called The Shifter. His poem 'How The Favourite Beat Us' was printed in the racebook for the Rosehill meeting of 9 November 1894.

Banjo was a member of the Sydney Hunt Club and rode winners at Randwick and Rosehill as an amateur jockey, including the Hunt Club Steeplechase Cup at Rosehill on Black Tracker in May 1896. His racing colours were lilac and yellow quarters with a quartered cap in the same colours. These colours are carried today by horses raced by the Banjo Paterson syndicate, whose horses are mostly named after Paterson's characters and poems.

Paterson wrote a long treatise on racing which was never published during his lifetime. More than a hundred pages long, it contains a complete explanation of everything to do with racing, from understanding the stud book, to buying a yearling, training, bookmaking, a history of early racing, punting and even comparing English champions to Australian-bred horses. He also wrote a novel about racing called *The Shearer's Colt*.

The Paterson estate contains many paintings and lithographs and also the trophies that he won, along with photos of his much-loved horses and portraits and photos of Paterson himself in his racing colours.

A solicitor by trade, he helped Henry Lawson and Breaker Morant with legal matters at times. For six years he was engaged to the daughter of the head of the law firm he worked for, but the marriage never happened and it was many years before he married someone else. He became bored as a solicitor and later worked as a journalist, editor and broadcaster.

He travelled to distant parts of Australia and the Pacific and wrote articles on pearl fishing, hunting, new colonies, and many other things. In 1899 he travelled with a troopship carrying men and horses to the Boer War and wrote extensively about the war. As a war correspondent Paterson developed sympathy for the Boers and became opposed to the war.

He returned home and in 1900 travelled via the Northern Territory to China to report on the Boxer Rebellion, which was over when he arrived. In China he met fellow Australian George 'Chinese' Morrison, the hero of the Boxer Rebellion and the man Banjo regarded as the most impressive man he ever met (a big call as he met Cecil Rhodes, Winston Churchill, Conan Doyle, Kipling and others!).

Paterson then visited France and Britain and, as ever, took every opportunity to visit racecourses and talk to racing men. His approach to different cultures may seem old-fashioned today and very 'British' to modern readers, but he was, in fact, open-minded for his time and always looked for the positive in other lifestyles. Here is his summation of the French approach to horseracing, after spending a day observing the natives at a race meeting in Marseilles:

> A day's racing in France is something to remember. In Australia racing is a business, and everyone who goes out goes with bent brows and an anxious mind, to try and unravel what is to him a serious problem. But with the Frenchman, a day's racing is a light-hearted holiday. He closes his shop at one o'clock, and goes out with his wife, in a trap drawn by a little pony with jingling bells and harness, and rattles away through the clear crisp air, with the dry aromatic smell of the autumn leaves all round, down the long avenue of sycamores out to the course. The tram-cars, loaded with the happy laughing crowds, go thundering along the streets. Motor cars rush past at a pace that would not be tolerated for an instant in any Australian or English community; on the seat of each motorcar, alongside the driver, sits a large black French poodle, sagely contemplating the moving scene around him.
>
> Everyone is laughing, and everyone looks on the racing in a light-hearted way, quite foreign to our idea. They have left dull care behind them for the day, and they will back a horse because they like the look of his tail or the colours of his jockey, and then say it is treachery if they lose their money!
>
> A dashing young Frenchman, with waxed moustache, tall hat and fur-lined coat, was sitting in the stand near us with a party

of three superbly dressed ladies. As the horses started he fixed his glasses on the race and sprang to his feet, his face working with emotion. He had backed a big chestnut horse, which was running well up with the leaders. Every time the chestnut drew to the lead the Frenchman's face lit up, his chest expanded, and he turned with the air of a conqueror to the females behind him, saying, 'Il gagne! Il gagne!'

Round the turn they came. He clutched the rail in front of him, and clenched his teeth, and fairly shook with the strain that was put on him. As the horses flashed past the post, with his chestnut beaten by a neck, he dropped back on the seat with the air of a man whose hopes in life are crushed. He was too heartbroken to speak for a long time. It turned out afterwards that he had five francs (four and tuppence) on the chestnut in the place totalisator, so he had saved his money, but it was the defeat of his judgement that annoyed him.

That is the right way to go racing, to squirm and yell when your horse gets ahead, and prance about the paddock after a win of one and sixpence. The French do not know much about racing, but they get a lot of fun out of it.

Banjo was editor of *The Sydney Evening News* and the *Town and Country Journal* from 1904 to 1908. Then, after a trip to the United Kingdom, he decided to move with his family to a 40,000-acre property near Yass.

In 1914 Paterson enlisted, at the age of 51, to fight in World War I and was disappointed when he was made an ambulance driver on the Western Front. He asked to do something more useful and was given command of the 2nd Remount Division, in charge of bringing horses from Australia via India to the war. He became a major, saw service in the Middle East and became quite ill, but continued serving until the end of the war, with his wife Alice who joined the Red Cross and served close to her husband.

After the war Paterson travelled to Britain and China and then returned home, lived in Sydney, and kept writing and broadcasting until his death in 1941.

He was never a part of the bohemian group of Sydney writers who owed their fame to *The Bulletin*, but he met Conan Doyle and was friendly with Rudyard Kipling and developed a friendship with artist Norman Lindsay—they went for weekend rides 'through the bushland' . . . at Cremorne, which is now an inner suburb of Sydney!

A STEEPLECHASE RIDER

A.B. 'BANJO' PATERSON

He was a small, wiry, hard-featured fellow, the son of a stockman on a big cattle-station, and began life as a horse-breaker; he was naturally a horseman, able and willing to ride anything that could carry him. He left the station to go with cattle on the road, and having picked up a horse that showed pace, amused himself by jumping over fences. Then he went to Wagga, entered the horse in a steeplechase, rode him himself, won handsomely, sold the horse at a good price to a Sydney buyer, and went down to ride it in his Sydney races.

In Sydney he did very well; he got a name as a fearless and clever rider, and was offered several mounts on fine animals. So he pitched his camp in Sydney, and became a fully enrolled member of the worst profession in the world. I had known him in the old days on the road, and when I met him on the course one day I inquired how he liked the new life.

'Well, it's a livin',' he said, 'but it's no great shakes. They don't give steeplechase riders a chance in Sydney. There's very few races, and the big sweepstakes keep horses out of the game.'

'Do you get a fair share of the riding?' I asked.

'Oh, yes, I get as much as anybody. But there's a lot of 'em got a notion I won't take hold of a horse when I'm told (that is, pull him to prevent him winning). Some of these days I'll take hold of a horse when they don't expect it.'

I smiled as I thought there was probably a sorry day in store for some backer when the jockey 'took hold' unexpectedly.

'Do you have to pull horses, then, to get employment?'

'Oh, well, it's this way,' he said, rather apologetically, 'if an owner is badly treated by the handicapper, and is just giving his horse a run to get weight off, then it's right enough to catch hold a bit. But when a horse is favourite and the public are backing him it isn't right to take hold of him then. I would not do it.'

This was his whole code of morals, not to pull a favourite; and he felt himself very superior to the scoundrel who would pull favourites or outsiders indiscriminately.

'What do you get for riding?' I asked him.

'Well,' he said, looking about uneasily, 'we're supposed to get a fiver for a losing mount and ten pounds if we win, but a lot of the steeplechase owners are what I call "battlers", men who have no money and get along by owing everybody. They promise us all sorts of money if we win, but they don't pay if we lose. I only got two pounds for that last steeplechase.'

'Two pounds!' I made a rapid calculation. He had ridden over eighteen fences for two pounds, had chanced his life eighteen times at less than half a crown a time.

'Good Heavens!' I said. 'That's a poor game. Wouldn't you be better back on the station?'

'Oh, I don't know, sometimes we get laid a bit to nothing, and do well out of a race. And then, you know, a steeplechase rider is somebody, not like an ordinary fellow that is just working.'

I realised that I was an 'ordinary fellow who was just working', and felt small accordingly.

'I'm just off to weigh now,' he said. 'I'm riding Contractor, and he'll run well, but he always seems to fall at those logs. Still, I ought to have luck today. I met a hearse as I was coming out. I'll get him over the fences, somehow.'

'Do you think it lucky, then, to meet a hearse?'

'Oh, yes,' he said, 'if you *meet* it. You mustn't overtake it, that's unlucky. So is a cross-eyed man unlucky. Cross-eyed men ought to be kept off racecourses.'

He reappeared clad in his racing rig, and we set off to see the horse saddled. We found the owner in a great state of excitement. It seemed he had no money, absolutely none whatever, but had borrowed enough to pay the sweepstakes, and stood to make something if the horse won and lose nothing if he lost, as he had nothing to lose.

My friend insisted on being paid two pounds before he would mount, and the owner nearly had a fit in his efforts to persuade him to ride on credit. At last a backer of the horse agreed to pay two pounds ten shillings, win or lose, and the rider was to get twenty-five pounds out of the prize if he won.

So up he got; and as he and the others walked the big muscular horses round the ring, nodding gaily to friends in the crowd, I thought of the gladiators going out to fight in the arena with the cry of 'Hail, Caesar, those about to die salute thee!'

The story of the race is soon told. My friend went to the front at the start and led nearly all the way, and 'Contractor!' was on everyone's lips as the big horse sailed along in front of his field. He came at the log fence full of running, and it looked certain that he would get over. But at the last stride he seemed to falter, then plunged right into the fence, striking it with his chest, and, turning right over, landed on his unfortunate rider.

A crowd clustered round and hid horse and rider from view, and I ran down to the casualty room to meet him when the ambulance came in. The limp form was carefully taken out and laid on a stretcher while a doctor examined the crushed ribs, the broken arm, and all the havoc that the horse's huge weight had wrought.

There was no hope from the first. My poor friend, who had so often faced Death for two pounds, lay very still awhile. Then he began to talk, wandering in his mind, 'Where are the cattle?' his mind evidently going back to the old days on the road. Then, quickly, 'Look out there, give me room!' and again, 'Five-and-twenty pounds, Mary, and a sure thing if he don't fall at the logs.'

Mary was sobbing beside the bed, cursing the fence and the money that had brought him to grief. At last, in a tone of satisfaction, he said, quite clear and loud: 'I know how it was . . . *there couldn't have been any dead man in that hearse!*'

And so, having solved the mystery to his own satisfaction, he drifted away into unconsciousness, and woke somewhere on the other side of the big fence that we can neither see through nor over, but all have to face sooner or later.

LOUIS THE POSSUM

JIM HAYNES

One of the strangest true stories of the Australian Turf concerns the uncanny punting ability of a Chinese market gardener, Jimmy Ah Poon. It is believed that he came to Australia for the last major gold rush in Victoria, the Berringa Gold Rush, which started in 1897. The odd thing about this story is that, to the best of anyone's knowledge, Jimmy only ever backed one horse, and only when he won.

You see, Jimmy Ah Poon's appearance on Sydney's racetracks coincided with the career of the mighty champion Poseidon in the early years of the twentieth century.

As a three-year-old Poseidon won eight times and ran second three times. His wins included two Derbies, two Caulfield Cups, the Melbourne Cup, and the AJC and VRC St Legers, and it seems that Jimmy backed him on every one of the eight occasions that he won as a three-year-old, but never when he ran second. He invested all of his winnings every time and never backed other horses.

Jimmy's first bet on Poseidon was at his first start at three, a handicap over the Randwick mile, which the horse duly won at 3 to 1—Jimmy's stake was £50. He then invested all his winnings when Poseidon won another race in the lead-up to the AJC Derby and did the same when the horse won the Derby at 7 to 1.

When Poseidon started in the Metropolitan, racing against older horses for the first time, Jimmy was not seen at the racetrack. Poseidon ran second. His trainer Ike Earnshaw then took him to Melbourne to win the Eclipse Stakes, Caulfield Cup, VRC Derby and Melbourne Cup in the Spring, and the St. Helier Stakes, VRC

St. Leger and the Loch Stakes in the Autumn. Jimmy invested every cent of his winning every time. When the horse ran second in the VRC Champion Stakes over a mile, however, Jimmy was not at the track!

Back in Sydney Poseidon won the AJC St. Leger at the prohibitive odds of 25 to 1 on! Jimmy wagered over £33,500 to make his total winnings on the horse over £35,000. Jimmy was never seen again. Legend has it that he returned to China and lived like a Mandarin for the rest of his days on the fortune he acquired due to his uncanny prescience—or was it luck?

With Jimmy nowhere to be found, Posiedon ran second in his last start as a three-year-old, his total prizemoney earnings for that year was £12,000.

Jimmy, from the Sydney suburb of Bankstown, was known as 'Louis the Possum' by bookmakers because he could not pronounce the name of the horse which won him an untold fortune. Every time Poseidon was due to win, Jimmy would turn up at the track and ask the bookmakers, 'What price Possumum?' Why they called him Louis is anyone's guess, but probably Jimmy never officially introduced himself and the bookies just chose a name for him.

Punters used to follow Jimmy around and treat him as kindly as possible to see if he was going to bet or not. I believe this is the origin of that odd saying still heard on Aussie racetracks when a punter cannot pick a winner for love or money—'My luck's lousy today, I must have killed a Chinaman.'

Note: There was a minor gold rush at Tarnagulla, west of Bendigo in 1906, just after the Melbourne Cup. More than 3000 ounces of gold nuggets were mined from a strip of ground 25 metres long. It was named 'The Poseidon Rush', after the Cup winner. Seventy years later the nickel boom of the same name caused the minor 1906 discovery to fade into history.

FRANK MCGRATH

BRUCE MONTGOMERIE

Setting out in his career in racing as an amateur jockey, the young Frank McGrath rode his first winner at nine years of age for his father. On his nineteenth birthday he survived the worst race fall in Australia's history when his horse and fifteen others crashed to the turf in the 1885 Caulfield Cup. One rider died and many were badly injured, including Frank.

After recovering from his injuries the following year, he returned to race riding. By 1890 McGrath had given up the saddle for the stopwatch and field glasses and had begun a career spanning 65 years in which he produced many champion racehorses and won almost every major race in Australia.

Frank McGrath, master racehorse trainer of his era, won three Melbourne Cups with two of his outstanding thoroughbreds—Prince Foote in 1909 and Peter Pan in 1932 and 1934.

McGrath also prepared Melbourne Cup placegetters—Abundance, third in 1902, Antonius, second in 1906, and Beau Vite, third in 1941.

After being well conditioned by McGrath, Abundance developed into Australia's top three-year-old of the 1901–02 season, winning six of his twelve starts—the Tattersall's Club Hampden Stakes at Randwick, the Chelmsford Stakes, the AJC Derby, the VRC Victoria Derby, the VRC St Leger Stakes and the AJC St Leger Stakes.

Abundance broke the Australian record when he won the 1902 VRC Victorian Derby in 2 minutes 36.2 seconds.

The colt's second in the VATC Caulfield Stakes on October 10 helped make him 4 to 1 equal favourite for the 1902 Melbourne Cup. The horse was to give McGrath his first placing in the great race. Walter Jennings, McGrath's apprentice, rode the colt at 7 st 6 lb (47 kg). McGrath later told the Press that 'Walter did not have the strength to finish the race strongly after the battering he suffered in the race.'

Abundance had been knocked from pillar to post throughout. McGrath always felt the colt would have won if he had had a stronger rider aboard to cope with the interference. Entering the straight Lieutenant Bill led with Abundance in fifth place just behind The Victory, who went on to win by a neck from Vanity Fair with Abundance a half-length away third. The other 4 to 1 equal favourite, The Persian, beat four home.

As Abundance was nearing the end of his racing career, another top-liner stepped in the stables. As a two-year-old Antonius won four of his starts and was even more prominent as a three-year-old, winning eleven of his fourteen starts during the 1906–07 season including the 1906 VRC Sires Produce Stakes.

McGrath thought he had broken his Melbourne Cup drought when Antonius went into the Cup at 9 to 4. Antonius made a mighty effort to tumble Poseidon, who as a three-year-old was fresh from winning the AJC Derby, the Victoria Derby and the VATC Caulfield Cup. Antonius was beaten into second place by 1½ lengths.

Antonius had some great duels with Poseidon, with one of his best efforts a fast-finishing second by a length-and-a-quarter in the 1906 VRC Victoria Derby. He also ran third to Poseidon in the 1906 AJC Derby.

In 1909 McGrath at last achieved his ambition with a racehorse that pundits claimed was too small to win a Derby or Melbourne Cup. He was Prince Foote, the 15.1 hands high three-year-old who ran all over his opposition in the 1909 AJC and VRC Derby double. Prince Foote's effort was all the more remarkable when it was found that he had raced with a damaged heel in the Victoria Derby, winning it by 6 lengths, and had suffered two checks during the AJC Derby. His exceptional season continued with wins in the AJC and VRC St Legers, AJC Sires Produce Stakes, AJC Doncaster, AJC Cumberland Stakes and AJC Plate. Prince Foote's victories in his lead-up to the Melbourne Cup included the first of his two Tattersall's Chelmsford Stakes.

Jockey Billy McLachlan thought during the running of the 1909 Melbourne Cup that he was destined to lose the race. After the Cup McLachlan described his mount as a fine racehorse but a 'lazy bugger'.

McLachlan lost all hope when Prince Foote was at the rear of the field and not responding to the whip. It seemed an impossible task.

McLachlan said: 'I couldn't get him to shift for a long time and I began to get anxious. I got away pretty well but I couldn't see much chance by the time we reached the turn near the saddling paddock. I was lying somewhere near last. There was plenty of bumping. I got knocked back but I didn't give up hope. I started to make up ground along the back-stretch near the river. I looked out for a position and after trying hard I could not gain a yard. Prince Foote would not answer to the spur and I knew it was only his laziness.

'He brightened up a bit and I improved my position. I was on the outside and it was just as well because if I had been inside I would have been bumped and never got out. I saw a chance and I didn't waste time. It was the ride of my life. Just after the turn into the straight Alawa and Trafalgar were six lengths clear. I was still on the outside and about three furlongs from the finishing post. I got out the whip and you would have thought it was another horse.

'As soon as I touched him he started to sprint. He went past Alawa and Trafalgar like a flash. I don't remember anything else except that stretch of course between me and the finishing post. He's a beauty to go when he likes and is one of the gamest horses I have ridden in my life.'

Although Prince Foote was not a big horse he had a huge heart. Winning by 3 lengths, he was the fifth three-year-old to win the Melbourne Cup, recording 3 minutes 27.2 seconds and running a second faster than Carbine's 1890 Cup time. At last Frank McGrath had his first Melbourne Cup . . . and there were more to come.

One racehorse who should have won a Melbourne Cup for McGrath was his 'warrior', Amounis—the toughest and best galloper he ever trained. Amounis completed an incredible seven full seasons winning up to a mile-and-a-half with great staying power.

Amounis won 33 of his 79 starts. His busiest season was when he won ten races as a seven-year-old. These victories included the VRC Cantala Stakes, the VRC Linlithgow Stakes, the VRC C.B. Fisher Plate, the VATC Futurity Stakes and the AJC All-Aged Stakes. As an eight-year-old he won the VATC Caulfield Stakes and the VATC Caulfield Cup.

Amounis beat Phar Lap twice in weight-for-age races—a great achievement as Phar Lap was beaten only four times in 32 weight-for-age contests. Amounis beat him into third place in the 1930 VATC St George Stakes and into second place in the 1930 AJC Warwick Stakes.

Frank McGrath knew he had a colt of enormous promise the minute Peter Pan walked into his Doncaster Avenue stables in January 1932. He fell in love with the long-legged, two-year-old chestnut. It was this thoroughbred who was to respond to McGrath's handling and go on to win two Melbourne Cups. While McGrath would be the seventh trainer to complete the feat, the other six trainers had won their Cups in consecutive years, not in alternate years, as Peter Pan was to do.

Frank McGrath came close to having another Melbourne Cup winner when the champion New Zealand stayer, Beau Vite, was sent to his Kensington stables. Beau Vite was the best racehorse in Australia at the time. He had won the 1940 STC Hill Stakes, the AJC Colin Stephen Stakes, the AJC Metropolitan Handicap and the AJC Craven Plate. Taken to Melbourne he won the Moonee Valley W.S. Cox Plate as a lead-up to the Melbourne Cup.

As a result of gangster tactics of unknown gunmen, Beau Vite came close to missing his place in the 1940 Melbourne Cup field. On the Wednesday before the Cup, two intruders stalked the rear of the box stabling Beau Vite's stablemate, El Golea, and pushed a gun through a hole in the wall.

Both horses were of similar colour and both wore white bridles and rugs. The gunmen mistook El Golea for Beau Vite and shot him in a rear leg. The veterinarian called to assist both horses found that no real damage had been caused to El Golea and left the bullet in his leg. El Golea had two weeks before being the 9 to 2 favourite in the Caulfield Cup.

Beau Vite, the 7 to 4 favourite, finished fourth in the 1940 Melbourne Cup after carrying 9 st 7lb (60.5 kg). The following year El Golea, the 11 to 2 favourite, was unplaced in the race.

Beau Vite came back for the 1941 Melbourne Cup as 9 st 10 lb (62.5 kg) top-weight and ran a brave third to the winner, Skipton, who carried 7 st 6 lb (47 kg).

As well as training the winners of almost every major flat race in Australia, Frank McGrath excelled at training steeplechasers and hurdlers and won two VRC Grand National Hurdles, two VRC Grand National Steeplechases, two VATC Australian Steeplechases and the Moonee Valley Hurdle.

When he died in 1947, Frank McGrath had trained the winners of three Melbourne Cups, two Caulfield Cups, three AJC Doncaster Handicaps, four AJC Derbies, two VRC Derbies, three AJC Epsom Handicaps, three AJC St Leger Handicaps, two AJC Metropolitan Handicaps, two AJC Sires Produce Stakes, three L.K.S. Mackinnon Stakes, three VRC Cantala Stakes and three Moonee Valley W.S. Cox Plates.

Frank McGrath—a truly remarkable life in racing.

This story is compiled from excerpts from Bruce Montgomerie's book, Frank McGrath—A Champion's Life—*published 2015.*

JIM BENDRODT

DAVID HICKIE

While Bernborough's owner, Azzalin the Dazzlin' Romano, advertised his famous nightspot Romano's restaurant as the swishest eatery in Sydney during the 1930s and 1940s, his great competitor, the equally flash Jim Bendrodt, ran Prince's restaurant on the opposite corner at Martin Place.

James Charles 'Jim' Bendrodt—lumberjack, radio announcer, sailor, soldier, actor, champion athlete, professional dancer and restaurateur—was one of Sydney's most colourful entrepreneurs for 50 years, running dancing halls, skating rinks, nightspots and a string of racehorses.

Jim's father was a Danish sea captain who joined the Hudson Bay Company during its pioneering days around the remote coastal areas of Canada and ferried miners to the northern Arctic during the Yukon goldrushes.

Jim was born in 1896 and raised in the town of Victoria in British Columbia. As a teenager he learned to use his fists around the lumber camps of the Canadian backwoods, and boxed professionally. As a youngster he won titles at boxing, ice-skating and sculling, and played lacrosse at a high level as well as some semi-pro rugby.

Despite his obsession in later years to always appear among the best-dressed men in Sydney, with a red carnation in his buttonhole, he was also renowned for his ability to bounce even the toughest drunks from his nightspots.

In 1913, at age 17, Bendrodt had taken a job shovelling coal in the stokehold of a ship headed for Australia. He landed with a

£5 note, one suit, one hat and a pair of boots. Within a fortnight of his arrival he was earning £30 a week as a roller-skating champ. He and partner George Irving performed a duo act described as 'two daring young men with flying legs on roller-skates who entertained patrons of the Tivoli as they raced, tumbled and twisted to a climax like whirling dervishes'.

Bendrodt had held Canadian titles from 3-mile to 24-hour events and the roller-skating craze was just catching on in Sydney. Eventually he was matched against an imported US Champion named Echard in a 24-hour race billed as the 'world championship' at Sydney's Exhibition Building. Bendrodt bet all his savings on himself but lost by a mere 40 yards.

When war broke out in 1914 he was the 198th man to enlist in the initial 1500-man force, which was given eleven days' training and sent to annex German New Guinea. He was netting £200 a week from a dance hall, but within a fortnight he was a six-bob-a-day private on a troop ship in the Pacific.

A friend from those days later recalled:

> Jim was a dandy—always the best dressed man in town, with that red carnation in his buttonhole. All Jim's mob were shoddily dressed in woeful looking uniforms, made in a hurry for soldiers in a hurry. But not Jim; he'd had his uniform tailor-made, and was a picture of sartorial elegance as he sailed away.

When he returned to Australia in 1915 Bendrodt felt he hadn't yet done enough for the Allies' war effort. He sold everything to buy a first-class passenger ticket on the RMS *Makura*, bound for Vancouver, and sailed off to Canada to join the Royal Flying Corps.

On his return from military service he marched into J.C. Williamson's one day and said he could act. They believed him and he landed small parts in several plays starring Madge Fabian, Lou Kimball and Link Plummer. He later recalled that he was a lousy actor but discovered he was a terrific showman.

He used that showmanship running dance halls in Sydney in the 1920s and 1930s, became a professional dancer and married his partner Peggy Dawes. He also ran a dancing school in Pitt Street. Bendrodt's enterprises included the Palais Royal dance hall at the showground and the Trocadero in George Street. By the late 1930s he'd switched to ice-skating and transformed the Palais Royal into the Ice Palace. He told reporters he had learned to ice-skate on the frozen Canadian lakes in his youth.

He also became a noted campaigner against cruelty to animals, was a prominent and vociferous member of the RSPCA, and bred German Shepherd dogs.

Bendrodt wrote several books about horses and dogs and his short stories regularly featured in major American magazines. Two of his most famous stories concerned horses named Gay Romance, a filly that won him a fortune, and 'Irish Lad', which was in fact the story of his horse Spam who cost backers a fortune when he failed in the Melbourne Cup. Professor Walter Murdoch called Bendrodt 'the Poet Laureate of the horse and dog'.

During World War II Bendrodt began his famous campaign in the press and on radio deploring the slaughter of pet dogs, given up by their owners to be gassed during the days of meat rationing. His plea began: 'Why did you kill him, Mister? Why did you kill your friend?' The response was so amazing that newspapers and radio stations refused to charge him for the advertisements.

Bendrodt soon became a leading owner-trainer of racehorses, with stables at Kensington and a 150-acre model stud, Prince's Farm, at Castlereagh on the banks of the Nepean River, 40 miles west of Sydney.

In line with his obsession with kindness to animals, the facilities at the stud incorporated the ultimate in comfort for his horses, one visitor describing the stud as being 'run on the lines of a first-class hotel for horses'. Bendrodt objected to jockeys using whips on horses and other trainers often declared his kindness prevented him from working his horses hard enough to get them into racing condition. They were appalled by his habit of feeding them apples and chocolate.

Bendrodt was particularly criticised for the way he trained War Eagle, whom many experts considered would have been a champion under another trainer. War Eagle won the Lord Mayor's Cup at Rosehill in 1946, and ran placings in the AJC Sires Produce Stakes, Champagne Stakes, Hobartville Stakes and City Tattersall's Cup, but many considered he should have won numerous feature races.

Despite the supposedly easy training workouts, War Eagle held the 10-furlong record at Rosehill for many years. When he died Bendrodt erected a huge cage with eagles in it above the horse's grave at Prince's Farm.

The professionals also ridiculed Bendrodt for his handling of the preparation of War Eagle for the 1945 Melbourne Cup, when the horse finished 19th behind Rainbird. Bendrodt then imported the Irish St Leger winner Spam for the 1946 Cup and backed it to win more than £100,000. Ridden by Billy Cook, Spam finished 12th but Bendrodt always claimed the horse had been flattened by the Australian heat and the hard track.

Bendrodt's introduction to the turf was through a former jockey who worked as a waiter at his dance hall. In 1923 the waiter persuaded him to buy the pony Passella for £100. He kept the mare in a yard behind the dance hall and the waiter trained her in his spare time. The mare had her first start in Bendrodt's colours at Kensington and he bet £400 on her at 2 to 1 with bookie Jack Shaw. Passella, ridden by Bill Cook, dead-heated with another mare, Pretty Sweet, and in those days that meant the pair competed in a run-off an hour later.

Pretty Sweet just beat Passella in a jostling finish but the waiter urged Bendrodt to protest. The complaint was upheld and Passella won.

Bendrodt then bought books, studied breeding and horse care, and began training his own small string of horses.

In 1931, at the height of the Depression, he bought a horse called Firecracker for 60 guineas. Years later a commemorative plaque honouring jockey Bill Cook was unveiled at City Tattersall's Club. It featured three champions: Rainbird, on whom Cook won the 1945 Melbourne Cup; Amounis, on whom he took the 1930 Caulfield Cup; and Carioca, on whom he won eleven races including seven in succession. The plaque also featured the forgotten Firecracker. Below Firecracker were the words: 'the horse that saved the Palais Royal by winning at Menangle in 1931'.

In July 1931 Bendrodt had addressed his 150 employees at the Palais Royal. He had just sufficient cash to pay the £1200 he owed in wages. The Palais would have to close unless the staff adopted his daring plan to win enough to keep it going through the Depression.

Firecracker was entered for a race at Menangle, to be ridden by Bendrodt's friend Bill Cook. The plan was to bet the wages on the horse, with the employees to get double their money if it won and the rest of the winnings to be used to keep the Palais open. The employees agreed, and Bendrodt and eight of the Palais' bouncers drove to Menangle and backed Firecracker from 10 to 1 to 6 to 4, and the horse won by a length from the useful sprinter Gold-digger.

Bendrodt often recalled how he went to the 1937 yearling sales to buy a colt, but peered into a horse's box and fell for the small bay filly inside. He bought her for £450, named her Gay Romance, and later that year she won the Gimcrack Stakes at Randwick.

Bendrodt wagered everything he had on that race and collected a fortune in bets. The winnings helped finance Prince's restaurant, which he opened in Martin Place in 1938 and which soon became the showpiece of his empire.

Prince's was an instant success, but during the war it came in for a lot of criticism from over-patriotic 'blue-noses' who declared no one should enjoy themselves while the troops were away fighting. Bendrodt retorted that Prince's was a valuable recreation spot for troops on leave—they certainly spent a fortune there and made him rich—and the US forces recognised this by placing it at the top of their lists of recommended entertainment establishments.

Bendrodt often claimed that when Mrs Eleanor Roosevelt visited Australia he was the only civilian she sent for—to thank him for helping US troops in their brief spells of leave.

As a punter, Bendrodt often only bet in £5 notes, though every now and then he would 'have a go', but rarely on anyone else's horse. He used to say: 'Punting is one of those things there is no percentage in. I can go broke easier ways than that.'

Nevertheless, he collected £15,000 when Rimfire won the 1948 Melbourne Cup; he explained that he'd selected Rimfire on his breeding three weeks before the Cup and had backed it at 150 to 1.

Other good horses owned by Bendrodt included Snow Star, which won at Canterbury and Randwick in 1948, and Goshawk, one of the first horses to go to the United States from Australia.

One incident which highlighted Bendrodt's great love of horses concerned Tommy Smith's famous first winner, Bragger, a horse that campaigned through the 1940s for Smith and was still racing in top-class races, such as the Newcastle Cameron Handicap and Randwick Tramway Handicap, when he was ten years old.

Bragger was returning to Smith's stable after a spell when the float, carrying three horses, caught fire on Parramatta Road near Auburn. Driver Kevin Spain smelled smoke, jumped out and threw open the float doors. The straw was blazing and though he was easily able to lead out two horses, one of which was owned by Bendrodt, Bragger was straddled in fright across a partition and was very badly burned.

Smith fought for weeks to save Bragger and horse-lover Bendrodt enlisted the help of a doctor friend; all three men applied ointments and medicines for the best part of a month, often around the clock, before they finally gave up the hopeless cause and put an end to the horse's suffering.

In 1950, Bendrodt imported the sire Abbots Fell, acknowledged among breeders as the greatest living descendant of Carbine and, at that time, the highest-priced thoroughbred imported into Australia for stud. Bendrodt also imported numerous other horses from England, including the stallion Scarlet Emperor and the broodmare Tollgate.

Jim Bendrodt gave up racing during the 1950s because he said both training horses and selling his stud's produce to other racing men involved 'too much sadness and distress for an animal lover'. He publicly castigated racehorse owners for selling broken-down champions without thought or care as to what may become of them—he himself had refused to sell his beloved War Eagle at the end of his career, despite an offer for the then huge sum of £12,000.

For a time Bendrodt retreated to his old-world cottage in Eastbourne Avenue, Darling Point, where his collection of Royal Meissen porcelain and Bohemian crystal took pride of place. But in the late 1950s he opened a new haunt for the racing fraternity, Caprice Restaurant—opposite Royal Sydney Golf Club and beside the flying-boat base, on the water at Lyne Park, Rose Bay. The restaurant was fitted out at great expense and was described as 'a caravanserai for the connoisseurs of cuisine'.

Bendrodt sold Caprice in 1967. His wife, Peggy, later said, 'He was very upset at having to sell—but he knew his health was becoming worse and he could not continue with the special attention he always gave his patrons.' He took a trip back to Canada in 1968 and, upon his return to Australia, reappeared at the track as a small-time owner-trainer.

Jim Bendrodt died on a Saturday morning in February 1973. Later that afternoon his filly Tropic Star ran third at Randwick at 330 to 1.

THE ORACLE

A.B. 'BANJO' PATERSON

No tram ever goes to Randwick races without him; he is always fat, hairy, and assertive; he is generally one of a party, and takes the centre of the stage all the time—collects and hands over the fares, adjusts the change, chaffs the conductor, crushes the thin, apologetic stranger next him into a pulp, and talks to the whole compartment as if they had asked for his opinion.

He knows all the trainers and owners, or takes care to give the impression that he does. He slowly and pompously hauls out his race book, and one of his satellites opens the ball by saying, in a deferential way:

'What do you like for the 'urdles, Charley?'

The Oracle looks at the book and breathes heavily; no one else ventures to speak.

'Well,' he says, at last, 'of course there's only one in it—if he's wanted. But that's it—will they spin him? I don't think they will. They's only a lot o' cuddies, any'ow.'

No one likes to expose his own ignorance by asking which horse he refers to as the 'only one in it'; and the Oracle goes on to deal out some more wisdom in a loud voice.

'Billy K—— told me' (he probably hardly knows Billy K—— by sight) 'Billy K—— told me that that bay 'orse ran the best mile-an'-a-half ever done on Randwick yesterday; but I don't give him a chance, for all that; that's the worst of these trainers. They don't know when their horses are well—half of 'em.'

Then a voice comes from behind him. It is that of the thin man, who is crushed out of sight by the bulk of the Oracle.

'I think,' says the thin man, 'that that horse of Flannery's ought to run well in the Handicap.'

The Oracle can't stand this sort of thing at all. He gives a snort, wheels half-round and looks at the speaker. Then he turns back to the compartment full of people, and says: 'No 'ope.'

The thin man makes a last effort. 'Well, they backed him last night, anyhow.'

'Who backed 'im?' says the Oracle.

'In Tattersall's,' says the thin man.

'I'm sure,' says the Oracle; and the thin man collapses.

On arrival at the course, the Oracle is in great form. Attended by his string of satellites, he plods from stall to stall staring at the horses. Their names are printed in big letters on the stalls, but the Oracle doesn't let that stop his display of knowledge.

''Ere's Blue Fire,' he says, stopping at that animal's stall, and swinging his race book. 'Good old Blue Fire!' he goes on loudly, as a little court collects. 'Jimmy B——' (mentioning a popular jockey) 'told me he couldn't have lost on Saturday week if he had only been ridden different. I had a good stake on him, too, that day. Lor', the races that has been chucked away on this horse. They will not ride him right.'

A trainer who is standing by, civilly interposes. 'This isn't Blue Fire,' he says. 'Blue Fire's out walking about. This is a two-year-old filly that's in the stall —'

'Well, I can see that, can't I,' says the Oracle, crushingly. 'You don't suppose I thought Blue Fire was a mare, did you?' and he moves off hurriedly.

'Now, look here, you chaps,' he says to his followers at last. 'You wait here. I want to go and see a few of the talent, and it don't do to have a crowd with you. There's Jimmy M—— over there now' (pointing to a leading trainer). 'I'll get hold of him in a minute. He couldn't tell me anything with so many about. Just you wait here.'

He crushes into a crowd that has gathered round the favourite's stall, and overhears one hard-faced racing man say to another, 'What do you like?' to which the other answers, 'Well, either this or Royal Scot. I think I'll put a bit on Royal Scot.' This is enough for the Oracle. He doesn't know either of the men from Adam, or either of the horses from the great original pachyderm, but the information will do to go on with. He rejoins his followers, and looks very mysterious.

'Well, did you hear anything?' they say.

The Oracle talks low and confidentially.

'The crowd that have got the favourite tell me they're not afraid of anything but Royal Scot,' he says. 'I think we'd better put a bit on both.'

'What did the Royal Scot crowd say?' asks an admirer deferentially.

'Oh, they're going to try and win. I saw the stable commissioner, and he told me they were going to put a hundred on him. Of course, you needn't say I told you, 'cause I promised him I wouldn't tell.' And the satellites beam with admiration of the Oracle, and think what a privilege it is to go to the races with such a knowing man.

They contribute their mites to the general fund, some putting in a pound, others half a sovereign, and the Oracle takes it into the ring to invest, half on the favourite and half on Royal Scot. He finds that the favourite is at two to one, and Royal Scot at threes, eight to one being offered against anything else. As he ploughs through the ring, a Whisperer (one of those broken-down followers of the turf who get their living in various mysterious ways, but partly by giving 'tips' to backers) pulls his sleeve.

'What are you backing?' he says.

'Favourite and Royal Scot,' says the Oracle.

'Put a pound on Bendemeer,' says the tipster. 'It's a certainty. Meet me here if it comes off, and I'll tell you something for the next race. Don't miss it now. Get on quick!'

The Oracle is humble enough before the hanger-on of the turf. A bookmaker roars '10 to 1 Bendemeer;' he suddenly fishes out a sovereign of his own—and he hasn't money to spare, for all his knowingness—and puts it on Bendemeer. His friends' money he puts on the favourite and Royal Scot as arranged. Then they all go round to watch the race.

The horses are at the post; a distant cluster of crowded animals with little dots of colour on their backs. Green, blue, yellow, purple,

The late Bart Cummings shows Viewed the Melbourne Cup, Bart's 12th, after the horse's victory in the big race on 4 November 2008. (DAVID GERAGHTY/NEWSPIX)

Damien Oliver looks Heavenward after winning the 2002 Melbourne Cup on Media Puzzle. (RICHARD CISAR-WRIGHT/NEWSPIX)

Glen Boss celebrates Makybe Diva's first Melbourne Cup victory on 4 November 2003. (DARREN MCNAMARA/NEWSPIX)

Frank McGrath—the master trainer of great stayers such as Peter Pan, Prince Foote and Amounis. (NEWSPIX)

Azzalin Romano. (NATIONAL ARCHIVE)

A postcard showing Western Australian champion Eurythmic with F. Dempsey in the saddle. (ARM)

Phar Lap. (ARM)

Amounis wins the 1930 Caulfield Cup and sets up the biggest Cups double betting coup of all time. (ARM)

Phar Lap wins the 1930 Melbourne Cup. (ARM)

Mosstrooper. (PETER HARRIS)

Jim Bendrodt chats to his good mate, champion jockey Billy Cook. (ARM)

The Cent. (OAKBANK RACING CLUB)

RedRum (outside) defeats Crisp at the Grand National at Aintree in 1973. (EMPICS)

Roughneck wins the Great Eastern in 1978. (OAKBANK RACING CLUB)

Hallo Dandy at the Grand National in 1984. (EMPICS)

Trei Gnaree at the Grand National in 1990. (VRC)

Jim Haynes with Adam Lindsay Gordon. (R. MCMILLAN)

French grey, and old gold, they change about in a bewildering manner, and though the Oracle has a cheap pair of glasses, he can't make out where Bendemeer has got to. Royal Scot and the favourite he has lost interest in, and secretly hopes that they will be left at the post or break their necks; but he does not confide his sentiment to his companions.

They're off! The long line of colours across the track becomes a shapeless clump and then draws out into a long string. 'What's that in front?' yells someone at the rails. 'Oh, that thing of Hart's,' says someone else. But the Oracle hears them not; he is looking in the mass of colour for a purple cap and grey jacket, with black arm bands. He cannot see it anywhere, and the confused and confusing mass swings round the turn into the straight.

Then there is a babel of voices, and suddenly a shout of 'Bendemeer! Bendemeer!' and the Oracle, without knowing which is Bendemeer, takes up the cry feverishly. 'Bendemeer! Bendemeer!' he yells, waggling his glasses about, trying to see where the animal is.

'Where's Royal Scot, Charley? Where's Royal Scot?' screams one of his friends, in agony. ''Ow's he doin'?'

'No 'ope!' says the Oracle, with fiendish glee. 'Bendemeer! Bendemeer!'

The horses are at the Leger stand now, whips are out, and three horses seem to be nearly abreast; in fact, to the Oracle there seem to be a dozen nearly abreast. Then a big chestnut sticks his head in front of the others, and a small man at the Oracle's side emits a deafening series of yells right by the Oracle's ear: 'Go on, Jimmy! Rub it into him! Belt him! It's a cake-walk! A cake-walk!'

The big chestnut, in a dogged sort of way, seems to stick his body clear of his opponents, and passes the post a winner by a length. The Oracle doesn't know what has won, but fumbles with his book. The number on the saddle-cloth catches his eye—No. 7; he looks hurriedly down the page. No. 7—Royal Scot. Second is No. 24—Bendemeer. Favourite nowhere.

Hardly has he realised it, before his friends are cheering and clapping him on the back. 'By George, Charley, it takes you to pick 'em.' 'Come and 'ave a wet!' 'You 'ad a quid in, didn't you, Charley?' The Oracle feels very sick at having missed the winner, but he dies game. 'Yes, rather; I had a quid on,' he says. 'And' (here he nerves himself to smile) 'I had a saver on the second, too.'

His comrades gasp with astonishment. 'D'you hear that, eh? Charley backed first and second. That's pickin' 'em if you like.' They have a wet, and pour fulsome adulation on the Oracle when he collects their money.

After the Oracle has collected the winnings for his friends he meets the Whisperer again.

'It didn't win?' he says to the Whisperer in inquiring tones.

'Didn't win,' says the Whisperer, who has determined to brazen the matter out. 'How could he win? Did you see the way he was ridden? That horse was stiffened just after I seen you, and he never tried a yard. Did you see the way he was pulled and hauled about at the turn? It'd make a man sick. What was the stipendiary stewards doing, I wonder?'

This fills the Oracle with a new idea. All that he remembers of the race at the turn was a jumble of colours, a kaleidoscope of horses and of riders hanging on to the horses' necks. But it wouldn't do to admit that he didn't see everything, and didn't know everything; so he plunges in boldly.

'O' course I saw it,' he says. 'And a blind man could see it. They ought to rub him out.'

''Course they ought,' says the Whisperer. 'But, look here, put two quid on Tell-tale; you'll get it all back!'

The Oracle does put on 'two quid', and doesn't get it all back. Neither does he see any more of this race than he did of the last one—in fact, he cheers wildly when the wrong horse is coming in. But when the public begin to hoot he hoots as loudly as anybody—louder if anything; and all the way home in the tram he lays down the law about stiff running, and wants to know what the stipendiaries are doing.

If you go into any barber's shop, you can hear him at it, and he flourishes in suburban railway carriages; but he has a tremendous local reputation, having picked first and second in the handicap, and it would be a bold man who would venture to question the Oracle's knowledge of racing and of all matters relating to it.

BERT

C.J. DENNIS

Did you ever meet Bert? 'E's all over the town,
In offices, shops an' in various places,
Cocky an' all; an' you can't keep 'im down.
I never seen no one so lucky at races.
Backs all the winners or very near all;
Tells you nex' day when the races are over.
'E makes quite a pot, for 'is wagers ain't small;
An' by rights 'e 'ad ought to be livin' in clover.
But, some'ow or other—aw, well, I dunno.
You got to admit that some fellers is funny.
'E don't dress too well an' 'is spendin' is low.
I can't understand wot 'e does with 'is money.
'E ought to be sockin' a pretty fair share;
An' tho' 'e will own 'e's a big money-maker,
'E don't seem to save an' 'e don't seem to care
If 'e owes a big wad to 'is butcher an' baker.
'E don't tell you much if you meet on the course;
But after it's over 'e comes to you grinnin',
Shows you 'is card where 'e's marked the first 'orse,
An' spins you a wonderful tale of 'is winnin'.
Can't make 'im out, 'e's so lucky an' that.
Knows ev'ry owner an' trainer an' jockey;
But all of 'is wagerin's done on 'is pat.
Won't spill a thing, even tho' 'e's so cocky.
Oyster, that's Bert. 'E's as close as a book.
But sometimes I've come on 'im sudden an' saw 'im

Lip 'angin' down an' a reel 'aggard look,
Like all the woes in the world come to gnaw 'im.
But, soon as 'e sees you, 'e brightens right up.
'Picked it again, lad!' 'e sez to you, grinnin'.
'A fiver at sevens I 'ad in the Cup!
That's very near sixty odd quid that I'm winnin'.'
Mystery man—that's 'is style for a cert,
Picks the 'ole card, yet 'e's shabby and seedy;
'E must 'ave some sorrer in secrit, old Bert—
Some drain on 'is purse wot is keepin' 'im needy.
A terrible pity. Some woman, no doubt.
No wonder 'e worries in secrit an' souses.
If I 'ad 'is winnin's, year in an' year out,
Why I'd own a Rolls-Royce an' a terris of 'ouses.

AZZALIN THE DAZZLIN' ROMANO

DAVID HICKIE

Ask any old-time racegoer the ownership of the prominent silks 'orange, purple sleeves and black cap' and you'll find most would know them as the colours of Pioneer Concrete boss Sir Tristan Antico.

Ask about their history before that and a few will remember them as the colours carried to fame by the mid-1940s champion Bernborough. It is surprising, however, how few recall their ownership by one of the most colourful characters of Sydney in the 1930s, 40s and 50s—Azzalin Orlando Romano.

Romano, known around town as Azzalin the Dazzlin', was a leading figure in what passed for Sydney's smart set between the wars. His ritzy restaurant, Romano's, had a reputation as the swishest eatery in the city.

Romano's was *the* scene on New Year's Eve and, with the other upmarket restaurant Prince's—run by another horse owner, Jim Bendrodt, in Martin Place—Romano's prided itself as a rendezvous point where the young movers and shakers of the era dined to be seen and preferably photographed for the social pages.

Romano opened his original Romano's cafe at 105 York Street in 1927. In 1938 he acquired additional premises in Castlereagh Street, next to the Prince Edward Theatre and opposite the Hotel Australia, and began Romano's restaurant. He installed an air-conditioning plant, lighting and furnishings, which alone cost £40,000, a tremendous sum in those days.

Things moved slowly for a year or two, but then the war began, bringing a floating population and, of course, the Americans, who guaranteed boom times for restaurants. During the war years, when the restaurant-turned-nightclub became a favourite haunt of American servicemen, everyone stood to attention just before closing time for the playing of the *Star Spangled Banner* and *God Save the King.*

Romano's prospects looked decidedly dim at one point during the boom when the club was declared 'out of bounds' to American servicemen. An Australian publican-punter had flattened an American officer, who had made advances to his girlfriend, by smashing a champagne bottle over the officer's head. But the matter was quickly and discreetly resolved, and the ban lifted within a matter of weeks. In the interim Romano's waiters and doormen had merely advised inquiring GIs where to borrow civilian clothes and then ushered them in anyway.

Romano had invested in a farm at Baulkham Hills, northwest of Sydney, to supply his restaurant with vegetables, poultry and pig meat. He kept 6000 fowls on the property. Romano took particular delight in always reminding important visitors and the press, 'I am the pioneer of the first-class restaurant in Australia.'

A magazine of the era summed up:

> Romano's is the nightclub where Sydney's theatre and hotel crowds converge at all hours of the day or night. Romano's restaurant is as spectacular as its owner, a bewildering array of mirrors, blond wood furniture, upholstery in colour something between maroon and burnt orange, concealed lights and high-class dance bands. It is social and near social, expensive and extravagant, the venue of the great and the near great and the would-be great.

The Sydney Sun newspaper once noted, 'It became a kind of training ground for generations of Sydney's better-off youngsters.'

Romano also saw himself as a great patron of the theatre and the arts, particularly of the opera, and regularly played host to Toti Del Monte and other stars when they were in Australia. Romano hosted Monte's wedding reception in 1928 with 'thousands of people, champagne and diamonds, and a big gondola of orchids.'

Another celebrated guest was Gracie Fields. 'She came out to sing to the troops during the war,' Romano later recalled, 'and stayed at my house.'

Over the years many famous celebrities dined at Romano's, including Vivien Leigh, who was served by the same waiter who had attended her table in London years before, and knew exactly how she liked her chicken marinara. Maurice Chevalier went there every night with his pianist and his wife to drink chianti. 'He was in Sydney 26 days and didn't miss a single meal at my restaurant,' Romano boasted. 'That was the greatest honour anyone ever paid me. Frenchmen know their food.' Bob Hope, Katharine Hepburn and Frank Sinatra went there, too. Prince Philip, then a young naval lieutenant, dined at Romano's regularly during his service with the Royal Navy.

For those in the know, 'going down the mine' meant descending the wide, thickly carpeted staircase past a bust of Napoleon for a night at Romano's. Tony, the headwaiter, immaculate in tails, ushered patrons to their tables; another waiter would present the *carte de jour*; and a third would serve cocktails; a white-aproned attendant would then arrive with bread rolls.

Azzalin Romano was born Orlando Azzalin in Padua in northern Italy and spent his childhood in Verona, where his father was an official in the postal department. Young Orlando wanted to travel the world and, aged ten, he and a 14-year-old companion took a train to Vienna, where he found a job as a pageboy at Vienna's posh Hotel Bristol.

He was paid 15 shillings a week, barely enough to cover his education at the night school from which he eventually matriculated. Romano later summarised his own success story with the phrase, 'from pageboy to receptionist, to waiter, to cook, to wine butler, to head waiter, to manager, to managing director'.

From the Hotel Bristol he moved about the best hotels and restaurants in Nice, Monte Carlo, Paris and Berlin, and even travelled to the Czar's Russia to become a headwaiter at the Palace. 'I had the pleasure of attending every king of those days,' he later recalled.

His secret, he said, was that he always pursued what he termed 'the experience of the first class.' He explained, 'I wanted only to learn the highest standards in my business. In all my life I have refused to work in cheap places even if it meant taking less money.'

Young Romano had his wish to see the world and, along the way, became fluent in five languages—English, Italian, Spanish, German and French. He also worked on the big European railway trains before eventually heading for England, where his first job involved eighteen hours a day as a waiter at the Savoy Hotel, for 5 shillings a week.

Over the next fifteen years he climbed the grade, through boarding houses and private hotels, into positions of authority with the Ritz-Carlton Company, the Savoy Company and the Gordon Company. Among the leading hotel restaurants he managed were the Hyde Park Hotel and, in 1922, the Ritz. During those years Romano was also a crack amateur cyclist, winning three gold cups at London's Stamford Bridge track.

It was in England that Romano first learned about racing, but because his job kept him in hotels sixteen hours a day he became a punter by betting on the phone. His only ventures to the track were when he waited on the King and Queen during lunch in the Royal Enclosure at Ascot.

While he was headwaiter at the Ritz, Romano found it a major cause of irritation when customers would ask for his name but misunderstand it, mispronounce it or fail to catch it. Then an inspiration came one day as he walked past Romano's Restaurant in London. He immediately changed his name by deed poll. He later explained, 'Romano was so easy to remember. It's just like George in Italian. I have nothing against my original name, a first-class name in Italy, but you have to consider business.'

At an Ascot race meeting while he was in charge of a refreshment marquee for members of the Royal Automobile Club of England, Romano met a Sydney gent named David Stuart Dawson. Dawson persuaded Romano to come to Australia from London, in 1923, to work at a restaurant venture called Ambassadors, which, in its size, aims and expense, was indeed a pioneering step in the Sydney of that time. Several hundred thousand pounds were invested in the lavish establishment, but the response of Sydney's nightlife didn't meet the hopes of its promoters.

The flamboyant Romano quickly became a favourite of the social columns, which took delight in recording the details of his regular sojourns overseas.

For example, in 1934 it was exciting news that Romano, his wife and two children took a six-month trip and motored through England, Scotland, France, Italy and Switzerland. When he returned his opinions were extensively sought: that Vienna was no longer 'the fairyland of Fame', that London was now 'the brightest capital in Europe' and that Paris, in comparison, was 'a dead city'.

The social butterflies were especially interested in his news of 'the latest novelties in cafe entertainment' from the continent, notably that London cabarets were employing more and more American artists and were becoming brighter, and that the latest craze was to have small dancing floors.

Romano would sit in a corner of his club, with characteristic pipe or Havana cigar in hand and a glass of Scotch in front of him, and conduct proceedings. He later installed a portrait of his champion Bernborough in his special corner, and held court below it.

If he was throwing a party of his own, he would adjourn to a private dining room and sing for his guests. As a chorister in his youth, Romano had sung in the High Mass at St Mark's in Venice and at St Anthony's in Padua. During the 1914–18 war he sang at a charity performance in Covent Garden and later he sang at Ambassadors.

'My voice is baritone,' he would declare, 'but I don't know a note of music. My method is to buy a record by a first-class singer, then shut myself in a room and play it over and over again and try to imitate it.'

His favourite song was the prologue from Pagliacci.

During the Depression years Romano and his friends initiated the 'plonk club'. 'In those years,' he later explained, 'there were still a few of us who liked to eat good food and drink fine wines, but we just couldn't afford it. So we decided to keep up appearances, to keep the flag flying. We gave away the fine imported wines and bought plonk.' For 5 shillings a member of the 'plonk club' could have a good meal, half a bottle of plonk and an Australian cigar. Lunch lasted from midday until 4 p.m. and if you were late it meant you must have been doing some business and that meant you shouted for the club.

Romano's, like all nightspots of the era, did a roaring trade in sly grog. In 1935, on one of the rare occasions it encountered any official interference over this matter, a waiter and house manager were each fined £50 for selling sparkling hock at 12 shillings a bottle without a licence.

A police sergeant told the licensing court that the premises were frequented by people of high standing and liquor was sold extensively. He added that the place was run as a cabaret and was always open to the early hours in the morning.

Thereafter, Romano took the necessary precautions and, significantly, Police Commissioner Bill MacKay dined regularly at Romano's restaurant 'on the house'.

However, Romano was personally prosecuted in a Sydney court early in World War II and fined £500 for having presented a false statement of income. In his 1940 annual report, the Commonwealth Taxation Commissioner revealed that, between 1932 and 1938, Romano understated his income by £38,058, adding that this was a case of suspected fraud.

For the most part Romano was always scrupulously careful about his and his establishment's public image. When some influential citizens took a dim view of the high-spirited festivities within his site during the darkest years of World War II, Romano was quick to take on the image of, first and foremost, a man with the national interest at heart. Hence, in April 1943, he announced that his restaurant's famous afternoon tea dance was not to be held in future during working hours 'because of the manpower shortage and in the interests of the war effort'.

During the 1940s *The Adelaide News* said of him, 'This Romano is a personality, handsome, debonair, always immaculately dressed. He has an infectious smile, is a sparkling raconteur and is also a gifted after-dinner speaker. He sings well, and at parties is the life and soul of the company.'

The Sydney Daily Mirror tagged him, 'The man who went to Randwick in striped pants and frock coat, spats, grey topper and diamonds.'

Romano had amassed a small fortune from the illegal beer and spirits trade. When matters came to a head during the 1953 Liquor Royal Commission he admitted that he 'carried on for many years' at Romano's Restaurant selling liquor, which he bought on the black market without a permit. He revealed he was also a shareholder and director of the company which owned the notorious Colony Club sly grog den, in the southern suburbs on the Georges River.

Romano's two great passions were restaurants and racehorses and he pursued both with a flair which guaranteed him regular appearances in the headlines. He bought his first horse in 1943 but, within three years, became famous as the owner of Bernborough, 'the Toowoomba Tornado' who won fifteen races in succession in 1946 and, according to a newspaper of the time, 'captured the imagination of the racing public as no horse since the fabulous days of Phar Lap'.

Azzalin Romano raced many other top horses over the following seasons. At one point his string totalled 37 thoroughbreds.

In 1946 he paid the top price of 4300 guineas at the annual Easter Yearling Sales for a colt by French sire Le Grand Duc, from a mare called Vocal. The colt was a half-brother to the well-performed Modulation and, after what papers described as a 'brisk bidding duel with Mr A. Basser of Sydney', Romano bought the horse and named it Caruso. It won many good races.

The next year he again paid top price, 3500 guineas, for a bay colt by Midstream from Idle Woods, making it a full brother to Shannon. Romano named the colt Bernbrook and as a three-year-old it won the 1948 Chelmsford Stakes, beating Carbon Copy, Dark Marne and Columnist, and the 1949 Doncaster Handicap at Randwick.

During those years Romano also raced Lady Ajax, Bronze Gold, Grand Romance, Rimini and Haydock, and paid 3500 guineas for a half-brother to On Target and 2700 guineas for a brother of Flying Duke.

In 1950 Romano sold Bernbrook and Caruso to another US millionaire, William Goetz, Louis Meyer's son-in-law. It triggered a sudden announcement by Harry Plant that he had broken off his celebrated relationship with Romano because he had been 'unfairly treated'.

One newspaper of the time noted, 'Romano's zeal to rake in the dollars led to a bitter break with Plant, his trainer, friend and racing counsellor.' Horses trained by Plant for Romano had won a fortune—more than £50,000 in prizemoney, including more than £26,000 by Bernborough.

Plant, upset that Romano had sold Bernbrook and Caruso while on a trip to the USA, said he had no hint of the plan and declared, 'Romano and I are through for all time'. He also revealed that, after an exchange of letters, Romano, through his lawyer, had ordered Plant to quit the racing stables in Prince Street, Randwick, which Romano owned and Plant occupied and operated in.

Romano, who lived in a £40,000 Killara mansion and also ran a roadhouse near Liverpool on Sydney's western outskirts, continued to race many horses through the 1950s, but had wound down his interest in the sport by the end of the decade. His enthusiasm in culinary entrepreneurial opportunities led to frequent bursts of excitement. At one point in the 1950s he announced a grand plan to establish a chain of luxury restaurants around the capital cities in time for the 1956 Olympic Games in Melbourne; the scheme did not eventuate.

With the arrival of the 1960s the old Sydney nightlife scene was changing, and Romano sold his famous restaurant in 1964. *The Sunday Telegraph* summed it up thus:

> The salad days for the former Italian bellhop had been the 30s and 40s, when it was still profitable and desirable to run a grand restaurant. The mood survived into the early 1950s but was gone long before Romano sold out and retired. Napoleon's bust still casts a brave face in the foyer, but the grandeur had withered,

the menu that offered 350 splendid dishes had diminished and a swarm of captains and waiters who had smoothly served the tables had shrunk.

After he sold out, Romano's became a discotheque-style nightspot called 'Romano Au Go-Go'.

Romano then left Sydney on a world tour, but in early 1966 he suffered heart problems while travelling in East Africa, and a Ugandan surgeon administered what one newspaper described as 'frequent painkilling injections during a dramatic mercy flight' to the USA, where he underwent emergency surgery.

The three-hour operation, for the removal of an arterial aneurism, involved removal of several inches of weak, ballooning artery and its replacement by a synthetic section made of Dacron.

Romano's English wife, Alice, died in 1971. Their son Renzo had also been a restaurateur in Sydney in the late 1950s before heading for the USA in 1962, where he managed the airport restaurant in Honolulu; later he set out on the American mainland as a professional tennis coach. Romano also had one daughter.

Azzalin Romano lived out his latter years in a flat in exclusive Point Piper, overlooking Sydney Harbour, and died in St Vincent's Hospital in November 1972, aged 78.

SYDNEY CUP DAY

ANONYMOUS

It was on a Sydney Cup Day,
While strolling round the course,
Joe Thompson he comes up to me
And says, 'Do ya wanna back me horse?
Now if you want to back it
The odds are three to one,
Just give me thirty smackers
And I'll give you back a ton.'

Oh he may be very tricky,
And he may be very sly,
He can always find his match,
He only has to try,
And what he does is clever,
On that we all agree,
He may have got at one or two,
But he won't get at me.

Now Joe acts the injured party,
And bitterly complains.
Says he's offerin' me a certainty
If I only had the brains,
But if I didn't want it,
Well, he'd find some other bloke.
But in the meantime, while I'm thinkin'
Could I spare a chap a smoke?

Well I looked at Joe before me
And I lit his cigarette,
And gave him one for later on
And a fiver for a bet,
And he sauntered off towards the ring
His hat pushed on the side,
A man of means once again,
With a fiver's worth of pride.

Oh he may be very tricky,
And he may be very sly,
He can always find his match,
He only has to try,
And what he does is clever,
On that we all agree,
But an old tout who's down and out
Can always count on me!

THE WHISPERER

A.B. 'BANJO' PATERSON

A whisperer is a man who makes a living, often a very good living, by giving tips for races.

The well-dressed stranger or countryman who goes to a race meeting, as he leans over the rails and studies the horses, will find an affable stranger alongside him and they drift into conversation. The affable stranger says, 'That's a good sort of a horse,' and the ice is broken and before long the countryman is 'told the tale.'

Now, the tale has many versions, and it all depends on the listener which version is brought forward. The crudest plot that finds patrons is the old, old friend-of-the-owner story. In this drama the whisperer represents himself as a great friend of the owner of a certain horse, and if necessary he produces a confederate to represent the owner. The whisperer and confederate talk in a light-hearted way of putting a hundred each on, and they agree that they will do it if the price is good enough, but if they cannot get a fair price they will wait for another day.

The stranger thinks he ought not to miss such a chance as this, and carelessly suggests that he would like to be allowed to put a tenner on with their money. They demur and say that they have a good deal of other money to put on for friends and if they tried to put too much on, it might spoil the price. However, as being entreated to do so, they take the stranger's tenner as a great favour and that is the last he sees it.

This is a simple way to get money, but it has its drawbacks. If the stranger is an absolute novice, he may be persuaded to back a horse with no possible chance, and then the gang never lose sight of him and they try to get another tenner out of him for the next race.

If he looks like a man that knows anything at all, they have to suggest backing a horse with some sort of a chance, and if that horse happens to win, they have to leave the course hurriedly, because it is a very awkward thing to have an infuriated countryman looking for you with a racecourse detective when you depend on your wits for a living.

So the friend-of-the-owner story is only tried on novices and as a last resource, for it can only be worked on a very raw fool and raw fools as a rule have not enough money to be worth robbing. Also it is a breach of the law, and the true artist in whispering can 'find 'em' without that.

The higher-grade class of narrative depends for its success not on the tale but on the way it is told. The artistic practitioner goes to the races and picks out by some unerring instinct the right 'mark'. He may select a countryman or a sailor or a stuck-up—anyone that looks as if he had money and was ready for a gamble. The whisperer tells a tale suited to his more educated client.

This time the tale is that he has a friend in a racing stable (which is quite true), that White Cockade is favourite but has not been backed by its stable and will not try to win, and that he knows a horse that is on the whole 'an absolute cert if they spur it'. He can find out all about it from his friend in the racing stable. Will the client have £20 on it if he can find out that it is all right? The client, anxious to be up to date, says he will.

Off goes the whisperer and comes back very mysterious. 'Good thing! Paleface second favourite at 6 to 1. Better have twenty on it. The favourite is as dead as mutton!'

He hypnotises the client, who soon gets the suggestion that he must back Paleface, it would be absolutely chucking a chance away not to have a good punt on Paleface, 6 to 1 is a real gift about Paleface; after they have conversed for a while the client would eat a tallow candle and swear it was milk chocolate if the whisperer offered it to him.

It was once said of a really great whisperer that he could talk a punter off a battleship into a canvas dinghy in mid-ocean.

Like horse taming, it is all done with the eye and the voice. Having hooked his fish, the whisperer now pilots him up to a bookmaker and sees the money put on, and they go off to watch the race.

The favourite runs wide at the turn and loses his position and never quite gets into the fighting line, but Paleface hugs the rails and comes away in the straight and wins easily. The whisperer and his client go off together to draw £120 of the best and the whisperer, if he handles his client properly, should get at least £20 for himself out of it. More than that, the client will be good for more betting, certainly until the hundred is gone, and probably a bit more on the top of that.

Some of these whisperers do really well when money is plentiful and sportsmen generous, and they build up quite a connection with country punters. Some of them keep the same clients for years. No one has ever actually heard of a whisperer selling his business or floating it into a company, but that may come later on. They deserve all they make, too. Do you think, oh most astute reader, that you could make a living by going to the racecourse and finding out winners and then inducing perfect strangers to back them and give you a share of the proceeds?

Like most other professions, whispering tends to be overcrowded. Practically every ex-jockey or stable hand with the necessary brains has his little circle of punters, and some of the boys in the stables learn to 'whisper' winners before they can see over the half-door of the stable. It takes a really good judge of racing and of human nature to keep his clientele together for long; and sometimes even the masters of the art make mistakes, as the following absolutely true tale of the trainer and the whisperer will illustrate.

It was when things were dull in Melbourne but booming in Sydney that a crowd of Melbourne followers of racing came up to Sydney on the track of the money. One of the Melbourne visitors was an expert whisperer and he had not long been on the Sydney course before he saw a genuine bushman, bearded, cabbage-tree-hatted, sunburnt and silent.

Bearing down on the bushy, he told him the old tale, and said that he had a friend in Layton's stable and that one of Layton's horses was 'a certainty if they backed it'. Layton, it may be mentioned, was a leading Sydney trainer.

After the usual spellbinding oratory on the part of the whisperer, the bushie agreed to put £10 on the horse and went away to see some friends, arranging to meet the whisperer after the race. The horse won all right and the whisperer was at the meeting place bright and early.

He had not long to wait. Up came the bushman, smiling all over, and the whisperer expected a very substantial 'cut' out of the winnings. 'Did you back it?' he said. 'What price did you get?'

'I got fives—£50 to 10.'

'You won fifty, eh? Well, what about a tenner for me, for putting you on to it?'

'Oh, I don't know. Why should I give you a tenner? I'd have backed the horse whether I saw you or not.'

The whisperer tried persuasion and even pathetic appeal: he reduced his claim to 'two quid', but even at that the pastoral individual was adamant. At last the whisperer lost his temper.

'You'd have backed it without me telling you! You, you great yokel! What do you know about racehorses?'

'Well, I ought to know something. My name is Layton. I train that horse. I've just been away for a holiday in the bush. But I'll tell you what I'll do. I'll give you two pounds if you can point me out any man in my stable that told you to back it.'

As he finished speaking, as the novelist says, 'he looked up and found himself alone'.

THE COAT TUGGER

BETTY LANE HOLLAND

This is the story of a bloke you don't know
Now pushing up daisies in a place you don't go.
But, back in the thirties when racing was big
He'd tram it to Randwick to earn a few quid.
From last week's success he'd kept enough for the entry
Then into the Paddock to check out the gentry.
Dressed in good clobber, his collar well starched
Into the betting ring bustle he marched.

He was known as a tipster, coat tugger or tout,
A con man and trickster if cops weren't about.
'So sorry I knocked you. No please don't go yet,
I was rushing to find the best price I could get.
See, I have the good oil from the trainer, my friend
And all that he asks is a few quid to spend.
To show my remorse for what I just did
I'll pass you the info so you too get a quid.'

The story, the yarn, the tale or the patter,
Whatever you called it, did seem to matter,
With a wife and young children, it has to be said
His pride came in second to getting them fed.
No job did he have, yet every weekday
He'd front factory gates hoping foremen would say,
'Come on in, there's a job here for you,'
But he never got picked in the fortunate few.

And so to the races, each time was the same
New targets to try his nefarious game.
Plying his trade throughout the whole day,
Keeping well out of the wallopers' way.
Watching out for detectives whose job is to find
The thieves and pickpockets and all of that kind
The drunkard, the tipster, coat tugger and lout,
If they saw such behaviour—they'd just chuck 'em out!

So when he spotted a toff, who might get him a meal,
He'd bump him, say, 'Sorry,' then give him the spiel.
Once he'd given the tip he would follow and then,
If the tipped horse should win, he'd approach once again.
'Well done Sir, and also the odds were quite good,
It won as the trainer assured me it would.
As you would know, times are hard for him too,
So he'll tell us again, just a few quid will do.'

Next race, look around a new prospect to find,
It was really not easy to pick the right kind.
He'd find a new target, he'd give him a bump.
Bad luck. No more time, they're ready to jump.
So off on the tram, back home to his wife,
With just enough money to keep 'em from strife.
All next week again, he'd try for a job,
And again, turn to touting, to make a few bob.

PAM O'NEILL

PHIL PURSER

In 1963, when she was eighteen, Pam O'Neill was banned from walking through Eagle Farm's front gate with a horse.

Back then, long before Sky Channel was even dreamt of and long before you'd find a TAB in a pub (in the days when you were actually asked to move on from the TAB because you couldn't collect a winning ticket until 4 p.m. anyway), a girl called Pam O'Neill came along.

Constantly denied the right to have the rule changed to allow women jockeys to ride in races, Pam eventually had a small win when the powers-that-be thought they would silence her continual demands to get women licensed—and they allowed the occasional 'ladies' race to be run, where only women could ride. A quarter of a century later Pam said, 'They thought that would keep me quiet, but if you know me, it didn't, it just made me more keen.'

Pam rode a treble at the Gold Coast on her first day riding against males. It is probably a world record, no male or female in living memory has won three races on their first day of riding.

A month later she won her first feature race in the Booroolong Handicap on Samei Boy. She won eighteen races on her favourite horse Supersnack, or Winky as he was known in the stable, including the 1990 Rockhampton Cup.

In 1980, Pam achieved one of the highlights of her career when she won the first unisex race in Melbourne. On board the Geoff Murphy-trained Consular at Moonee Valley, she beat home the top male jockeys of the era including the great Roy Higgins. When Pam brought Consular back to the winner's stall, hundreds of women on the track moved towards her and gave her a loud round of applause.

She had backed herself to be successful against the men in a real 'ballsy' display that most men sniggered and laughed at. In the pre-Sky Channel days, pubs would have the radio playing Vince Curry's or Larry Pratt's Brisbane calls. The drinkers, come punters, would refer to Pam or her early contemporaries, if they were beaten on a favoured horse, as a 'hopeless (expletive) sheila'. If Pam won on Supersnack by leading all the way, the comment was, 'See, useless (expletive) sheilas can only ride front-runners.' The tirade of abuse continued for many years and, like any minority group in society, the women jockeys, such as Pam O'Neill and Linda Jones, soldiered on against seemingly insurmountable odds. The girls knew that they would not automatically get respect—and so they set about earning it.

Despite numerous setbacks and rejections, Pam finally got her permit to ride against men in 1979 but was not allowed to complete an apprenticeship. It meant she rode more than 400 winners without ever having the benefit of a claim.

It must fill her heart with pride to know that today, on racetracks throughout Australia, you will see plenty of female jockeys—from young hopeful girls to married women with children—all decked out in their riding silks. But I wonder if the girls riding today really know about the beginnings of their profession and I wonder what they would think about the 30-odd years of mockery that led to where we are now.

If I could take them back in time and walk with them into a public bar all those years ago and let them hear what was said about female jockeys, I'm sure many would turn and walk away—with tears in their eyes. That would, after all, be the normal human reaction. In fact, on reflection, they wouldn't even make it into the public bar—women were banned from them, too, back then—remember?

For female jockeys 'the good old days' are nothing but a figure of speech and a figment of the imagination. We listened to the races with a transistor radio up to our ears back in 'the good old days'. Now you can watch live on television and bet during the running of the race! In 'the good old days' they'd ask you to leave the TAB in Queensland, as it constituted a 'public gathering'. Now you can sit in air-conditioned comfort and enjoy food and a drink while you bet all day—if you so desire. In 'the good old days' the male jockeys were so poorly educated they were flat out putting a sentence together. Today's young jockeys, female and male, are so well-spoken when interviewed that it is a pleasure to see the exuberance of youth and hear the hope in their voices.

Yes, sir, the female jockey has certainly come a long way in 40-odd years, with Queensland women to the fore. In 1979 Cheryl Neale became the first Queensland female rider to win a metropolitan race interstate, when she won on Macluen at Moonee Valley. The Wehr sisters, Carlene, Ramona and Leonie, of Alice Springs, become the first sisters to fill all three placings in a registered race—at Alice Springs in July 1982. In March 1990 female jockeys rode all seven winners at the non-TAB Wondai meeting in Queensland. A kid called Melissa Seagren rode all six winners on the Queensland country track at Einasleigh in April 2001, and mother of two, apprentice Sheree Drake, won four races at Toowoomba on 12 November 2005. Rachel Mason rode four winners at Doomben one day in October 2005 to create a record for the number of wins by a female apprentice in Brisbane.

Elsewhere in the country, female jockeys were also making their mark. At Broome in Western Australia, in June 1990, Maria Hunter had eight consecutive winning rides over two meetings. In Victoria, Therese Payne rode four winners at Warracknabeal in July 1994; and Kim Arnold, Vanessa Hutchinson, Maree Payne and Christine Puls rode all the winners at a meeting at Murtoa in February 1995.

South Australian Clare Lindop became the first female jockey to ride in a Melbourne Cup in 2003. At 24 years of age, she finished unplaced on Debben. She won the Adelaide jockeys premiership in the 2004–05 racing season. Tracy and Kathy O'Hara created history by being the first sisters to ride in the same event in Sydney in December 2004.

It also would be wrong to recount this history without paying tribute to those who have lost their lives in race falls. The Queensland women I recall are Iris Neilsen, who died at Lismore track in 1988; Leanne Crook lost her life at Doomben in 1992; Heidi McNeish was killed in 1996; and Australia's first female Aboriginal jockey, Leigh Ann Goodwin—a mother—had her life support removed after a fall at Roma track in 1998. Other women such as Paula Lane have lost their lives as a result of trackwork falls.

I never met or spoke to any of those fallen female jockeys, but on the day before Leigh Ann Goodwin's funeral in Toowoomba, Radio TAB host Michael Maxworthy played the most beautiful tribute to her. He interviewed her mother about removing the life support and replayed her victory on her father's horse Getelion, which she rode to victory in Brisbane, at long odds, not long before her passing.

I taped that interview and carry it with me in the car everywhere I go throughout Queensland. Alone, on a remote road, I'll often listen to that tape; it helps me understand the brevity of life and the danger that jockeys live with every day in the game we all love. That tape is the reason you will only read positive stories about jockeys on my website—and many profiles on female riders. It's easy to condemn jockeys for bad rides and forget the safety element that is the main concern. We can all replace the twenty dollars that we lose when a runner gets 'slaughtered'; no one held a gun to our head and made us back it, anyway. But no amount of money can replace a lost life.

Female jockeys have certainly come a long way since a girl called Pam O'Neill backed herself all those years ago. During an interview at a 'legends' race at Melbourne Cup time a couple of years ago, Pam said, 'I think you are put on this earth to do something and my job was to get the rule changed so that women could ride against the men. And it was a very hard struggle. I remember when I was about eighteen I'd lead the horses up to the gate at Eagle Farm and hand them over to a male and I think that's what got me keen from an early age. I was a pony club rider and it just eventuated from there.'

Today the girls have earned respect. Out on the racetrack, they ask for no quarter—nor should they. They just wanted equality and they finally have that. In the main, the sniggering has stopped. But every time a female jockey dons the silks to ride in a race, she should remember the struggle of an eighteen-year-old kid called Pam O'Neill, who was stopped at the Eagle Farm gates and had to hand over her horse each day to a male.

Many men in racing officialdom should hang their heads in shame at the treatment Pam copped in those early days. If you ask me, they ought to build a statue to her—she should be in the Hall of Fame. If a bloke achieved what she did, they probably would have had the statue erected by now! May her memory live on every time a female rider flashes past the post to victory somewhere around Australia.

Phil wrote this article in 2005. In 2010 Pam O'Neill was inducted into the Racing Queensland Hall of Fame. Phil's informative website is <www.justracing.com.au>.

THE BEST TRAINER IN THE WORLD

BRUCE MONTGOMERIE

Australia almost lost legendary Melbourne Cup trainer Bart Cummings before he ever trained a horse. When he was 11, in 1939, Bart almost drowned while swimming off the jetty at Adelaide's famous Glenelg Beach.

He was going under for the third time when he was rescued by his 12-year-old schoolmate, Brendan O'Grady, the son of a local barber.

Brendan received a commendation from the Royal Humane Society of Australasia for his heroic action. If it hadn't been for his alertness and bravery, history would have been robbed of an iconic Aussie character—and arguably the greatest racehorse trainer this country has ever produced.

James Bartholomew Cummings became known to us all as 'Bart' because he shared his father's first name and the family used his middle name for convenience.

Bart's 'hands-on' involvement with the Melbourne Cup began when he was the strapper of 1950 winner Comic Court, trained by his father James. But the story begins long before that.

Bart Cummings came from hardy stock. His grandfather, Thomas Cummins, was a ploughman by profession. Born in 1828, Thomas migrated from Ireland to South Australia on the sailing ship *Empanadas* and arrived on Christmas Day 1853.

Thomas Cummins changed his surname to 'Cummings' on arrival and settled in the desolate South Australian hamlet of Eurelia, 280 kilometres north of Adelaide. At least he was now ploughing his own land, although it was rather barren land much of the time.

Bart's father, Jim, was one of six sons Thomas and his wife brought up on the drought-stricken pastoral land in the north of South Australia.

Following two bad years, which included a cyclone, dust storms and thunderstorms, young Jim had had enough of Eurelia and, leaving his parents' farm behind, he braved the unforgiving heat and trekked to Alice Springs to work for his bachelor uncle, James, who needed help running his large station, Granite Downs, at Ellery Creek.

Jim got precious little in return for all the hard work on his uncle's property, but he took to handling and riding horses naturally and was quick to make his name as a rider. Jim also worked as a relief driver on the famous Birdsville mail coach, driving the section between Bloods Creek and Alice Springs.

Jim's first major victory as a jockey came when he won the 1898 Alice Springs Cup on an aged mare named Myrtle, owned and trained by his uncle.

Fed up with conditions on his uncle's property, Jim took up his uncle's offer to take on Myrtle if he won the race. He took Myrtle, a gelding called Radamantos and an old stock horse, and headed south on the long and arduous 1720-kilometre ride back to Adelaide.

This was a truly amazing feat on its own, but two weeks after arriving at Jamestown he had Myrtle fit enough to win the local cup. It was the first official success for Jim Cummings as a trainer—and the beginning of the Cummings training dynasty.

Settling in Glenelg, Jim went on to set a record by training the winners of every classic race in South Australia and training winners in every state except Queensland.

By the time Bart Cummings was born on 4 November 1927 his father was established as South Australia's top trainer. Young Bart worked around the stables and had various jobs away from home while his father allowed him to find his own feet and make his own decisions about life.

As a child Bart fancied himself as a jockey and used to practise his riding skills on Cushla, a brilliant galloper who won nine races for Jim Cummings. She was a docile mare and helped teach the nine-year-old Bart Cummings to ride.

Bart was allergy-prone from childhood, and suffered from asthma all his life. When he was 16 an Adelaide specialist diagnosed him as being allergic to horses and chaff. The doctor's advice to stay away from both was advice Bart never heeded.

By 1947, at age 19, he was a registered strapper with the South Australian Jockey Club and worked for his father for £2 a week and his keep.

Jim's best racehorse, Comic Court, was to steer Bart Cummings on the path to becoming a trainer. Bart was Comic Court's usual strapper at race meetings and he often rode him at trackwork.

Comic Court had failed in his first two attempts in the Melbourne Cup, finishing fourth as a three-year-old in the 1948 Melbourne Cup and 20th as 7 to 4 second favourite in 1949.

Experts then considered Comic Court suspect at 2 miles, although he was bred to stay the distance, by Powerscourt out of Witty Maid, who was a granddaughter of Comedy King. He had multiple St Simon bloodlines on both sides of his pedigree, and the experts were proved wrong when Jim Cummings produced the five-year-old to win the 1950 Melbourne Cup.

Jim had owned Comic Court's sire and dam, Powerscourt and Witty Maid. However, when racing was banned in South Australia during the war, Jim Cummings took up temporary residence in Victoria and sold both of them to the Bowyer brothers, who bred four classic winning horses from them.

Comic Court was foaled in 1945 and given to Jim to train.

The 22-year-old Bart was the strapper for Comic Court's Melbourne Cup win and, as he led the horse back to the winner's stall, he daydreamed for the first time about training his own Melbourne Cup winner.

About this time Jim Cummings was spending more time in Melbourne than Adelaide, and young Bart was often left in charge of his father's home stables. Such responsibility was perfect grooming for the future champion trainer.

Still, Bart Cummings took no steps towards becoming a trainer until a decision by the South Australian Jockey Club forced him to take out a training licence. When his father went to Ireland for six months and wanted to leave Bart in charge of his team, the SAJC told Bart he would have to take out a training licence.

Bart took up training permanently in May 1953. He was given the bottom set of stables at his father's Glenelg complex and a couple of horses, one of which was the Port Adelaide Cup winner, Welloch.

Bart's first city winner was Wells, which won the SAJC Devon Transition Handicap (6 furlongs) at Morphettville on 12 February 1955. Three years later Stormy Passage gave Bart his first feature win in the city by taking out the 1958 South Australian Derby at Morphettville.

Bart's first weight-for-age winner came in the VATC Underwood Stakes (10 furlongs) at Caulfield when the unfancied Trellios beat the favourite, Lord, by half a length.

'J.B.' did it tough in his early days as a trainer and struggled to make a living for himself and his family. His perseverance, patience and uncanny knack of 'knowing good horses when he saw them' eventually made him a legend.

His first Melbourne Cup runner was Asian Court, who finished twelfth in 1958 at long odds. Success came with a blaze of glory in 1965, when one of Bart's four runners, Light Fingers, narrowly defeated another of his entries, Ziema. It was his fourth attempt at the Cup.

As early as 1962 one newspaper had stated, 'Not only is Cummings the man of the moment but also at least the racing man of the decade.'

His success was such, according to the report, 'as no other Australian horse trainer has known.'

Bart went on to win the next two Melbourne Cups, with Galilee and Light Fingers adding another quinella in the 1966 race and Red Handed winning in 1967. No trainer in history had achieved the feat of training three consecutive Cup winners. His eventual tally as a solo trainer would be a staggering twelve Melbourne Cups.

Bart set a Commonwealth training stakes-winning record in the 1966–67 season, by winning $358,918.

At that time Sydney's Tommy Smith was unsurpassed in Australian racing history as the most successful trainer ever, but Bart Cummings's record of successes in major races surpassed even that of the great T.J. Smith.

It was over a century since any trainer had prepared one horse to win the Caulfield, Melbourne and Sydney Cups, as Bart did with with Galilee.

Bart opened a permanent stable in Melbourne during 1968 with enough space for 60 boxes. Since 1965 he had been making two raids a year on Melbourne's rich purses, and the new set-up was his first step in his plan to become the first trainer to operate self-contained stables in three capital cities: Adelaide, Melbourne and Sydney.

At the close of the 1974–75 racing season, Bart Cummings had trained the winners of 20 Group 1 races with ten different horses, such as Leilani, Cap d'Antibes, Think Big, Leica Show and Lord Dudley winning in five different states. The races won include the Australian, Brisbane, Caulfield and Melbourne Cups, the Goodwood, Newmarket and Toorak Handicaps, WATC and QLD Derbies, the VRC Oaks, and Flight and Mackinnon Stakes. This is still a record for a trainer in any one season.

In 1975, Bart finally achieved his dream when he set up 'Leilani Lodge', at Randwick in Sydney.

In the late 1980s, Bart suffered a serious setback when he spent millions buying yearlings. Like many others he was hit hard in the recession of the early 1990s. Much of the money spent buying horses to syndicate was connected to a perfectly legal tax minimisation scheme and Bart was left holding the debt. His long-term friend Reg Inglis, through whom most of the yearlings had been purchased, helped Bart out with handlng the debt and the situation and through goodwill, and hard work, the great trainer avoided bankruptcy and continued training until the debt was cleared.

Bart was made a member of the Order of Australia in 1982 for his services to the racing industry. In May 2008 Racing NSW announced a new horseracing award to be known as The Bart Cummings Medal to be awarded for 'consistent, outstanding performances amongst jockeys and trainers' at New South Wales metropolitan race meetings through the racing season.

In recent times he was by far the most successful trainer at Group 1 level with 266 wins. Gai Waterhouse has 132 and Lee Freedman currently has 124. The only record better than Bart's currently is held by the late Tommy Smith, with 282. If we add Bart's two Group 1 wins while training in partnership with his grandson James, the tally is 268.

Bart was inducted into the Sport Australia Hall of Fame in 1991, was an inaugural inductee into the Australian Racing Hall of Fame and has since been elevated to the status of Legend—and the only other Legend is Phar Lap.

Bart had his face placed on a postage stamp in 2007 and shared the *Weekend Australian*'s 2008 'Australian of the Year' Honour with the 99-year-old Dame Elisabeth Murdoch. He was the only active racing trainer to be given life membership by the Victorian Racing Club.

From 2012 till his death in 2015, Bart trained in partnership with his grandson James, the eldest son of Bart's eldest son Anthony, a successful Sydney trainer himself who set up his own stables in the early 1990s after working with his famous dad for many years. Continuing the family tradition, Anthony has trained eighteen Group 1 winners since setting up his own stable.

Italian-born Luca Cumani, one of Britain's leading trainers, and the man whose horse, Bauer, was nosed out by Bart's horse Viewed in the Cup of 2009, paid his rival the ultimate compliment after the race: 'His record is amazing because I know how hard it is to win a Melbourne Cup. He is a special man . . . He is the greatest trainer in the world.'

Not bad for a bloke who was allergic to horses.

Bart Cummings died peacefully, surrounded by his family, on 30 August 2105. He was given a state funeral at Sydney's St Mary's Cathedral.

Part 8
JUMP RACES ARE DIFFERENT

INTRODUCTION—GALLANT HORSEMEN AND BRAVE STEEDS

Jumps racing has always been more popular in the cooler southern states of Australia. The winter weather there is more reminiscent of the cold climate in Britain, where riding over jumps is a winter activity.

The first Australian steeplechase was run in Sydney in 1832. It was conducted over almost 7 miles, from the Botany Road Bridge, adjacent to the 'old Randwick' track, to South Head Road via Coogee. I assume spectators had a choice of watching either the start or the finish, or riding along to observe.

Originally steeplechases were cross-country events and hurdles were conducted on normal racetracks. Tasmania's first hurdle race was held at Oatlands in 1833 and Victoria's first jumping race, a hurdle event at Batman's Hill, where Spencer Street Station now stands, occurred in 1839.

By 1841 Victoria's first steeplechase had been conducted near Flemington racecourse and, by the 1850s, jumps racing was well established in all the colonies.

Tasmania and Victoria led the way in the development of jumping as a sport. Provincial cities such as Warrnambool, Coleraine and Ballarat developed winter carnivals during the nineteenth century and, on 1 January 1866, the VRC Grand National Steeplechase over 3 miles was run for the first time on a program that featured the Derby and the Intercolonial Champion Stakes over 3 miles.

In 1868 the poet Adam Lindsay Gordon rode three steeplechase winners in one day at Flemington.

In South Australia hurdle racing developed in the 1840s and Oakbank's first race meeting was held in 1877.

The heyday of jumps racing in Australia was probably the latter half of the nineteenth century. All-comers were able to compete back then and, as late as 1927, an amateur rider, Mr J. Grice, was able to win the Grand National Steeple.

While enthusiasm for the sport continued to grow in the south, with new races being added to the calendar, like the A.V. Hiskens Steeple in 1936, other states were responding to changing public sentiment.

Reaction against the injuries and huge weights being carried—the entire field fell in the 1934 Grand Annual and, in 1935, Greensea won a Rosehill Hurdle carrying 13 st 12 lb (88 kg)—eventually led to steeplechasing, then hurdling, being phased out in New South Wales, Queensland and Western Australia.

Perth's last hurdle was run in 1941, and a horse named Anpapejo went down in history as the winner of the last hurdle race at Randwick, in 1942.

In recent times the new-style brush jumps, designed to improve safety for horses and riders, and innovations such as the Australian jockeys versus Irish jockeys series, have led to a revival of sorts. Annual hurdle races were even run again in Sydney for a few years from 1986.

You either love jumps racing or you don't, there's no in-between. I think there are few sports as exciting and exhilarating. I hope that we can persist in tolerating regional differences in this country so that great events like those at Ballarat, Oakbank and Warrnambool will continue to challenge horses and riders and thrill spectators for many years to come.

HERE'S LUCK—A TOAST

A.B. 'BANJO' PATERSON

It chanced one day I watched a steeplechase,
And one horse singled out and led them all
Across the fences at a rattling pace,
Until he hit a fence and took a fall
His rider laughed and muttered with a smile—
'Well, anyhow, I led 'em for a while.'

And this is the text for my theme tonight,
A moral that the wisest men have sung:
Our life is very short—and swift the flight
Of time—so, comrades, go at it while young.
And when old age comes on you'll find it good
To think you made the running while you could.

There's nothing now too solid or too high
For some of you to take and chance a spill;
But we must funk the fences bye and bye,
When limbs grow stiff and hands have lost their skill.
In wintry age we'll seek the hearthstone's blaze;
So, let us make the most of youth's bright days.

So now, my friends, good luck and may you keep
Stout hearts and true and honest kindly mirth,
When drawing nearer to the last great leap
That lands us on the other side of earth,
Where many a gallant horseman and brave steed
Has gone before to give us all a lead.

CRISP

JIM HAYNES

Ask racing men and historians in Australia to name the top ten Aussie horses of all time and I doubt that any lists would include the name Crisp. Ask any British racing fans to name an Aussie champion racehorse, before Choisir took Ascot by storm in 2003, and Crisp would be the only Australian name they'd be likely to know.

Crisp was a great Aussie battler who did what Aussies love doing—taking on the Poms at their own game. Australians take perverse delight in 'beating the Poms' at any sport originally devised in Britain. We have done it often at cricket, rugby and tennis, but we don't do it often in the Sport of Kings.

The great chestnut sprinter Choisir proved it could be done on the flat in 2003. He was followed by Takeover Target, Miss Andretti (the only horse in history to simultaneously hold a total of five track records in Australia and England) and, in one heart-stopping race in 2012, the mighty Black Caviar.

Those sprinters took on the English and won their races, but they didn't win their hearts the way a horse called Crisp did back in 1973.

Crisp probably had the biggest impact on the British racing scene of any Australian horses since Carbine sired an English Derby winner more than a hundred years ago. It took 32 years for Choisir and the sprinting brigade to come along and have anywhere near the same impact on racing in the Old Dart that Crisp had.

It's generally considered by racing pundits in Britain that Crisp was the best chaser to never win the Grand National. It's also generally thought that he deserved to win the great race in 1973.

Crisp was a first-generation Australian. He was foaled here in 1963, although he was by the English stallion Rose Argent from an English mare named Wheat Germ. His return to the 'Old Country' in 1972 was, therefore, the sort of journey made by many first-generation Aussies around that time.

Crisp was a big raw-boned gelding who raced over jumps in Australia with great success, winning the Cup Steeple in 1969 and the A.V. Hiskens Steeple at Moonee Valley in 1969 and 1970. On the second occasion he carried 73 kilograms.

Crisp was obviously something special. He was a naturally talented jumper and could carry weight easily. So, with opportunities for really gifted jumps horses very limited in Australia, it was decided to sell him to interests in Britain in 1971.

The original intention was to run Crisp in races up to 2 miles. It was thought that he would not 'get the journey' over the much longer, English classic steeplechase distances of 3 and 4 miles.

On arrival in Britain he was entered in a 2-mile handicap at Wincanton. Back then the National Hunt rules stated that any horse not having had three starts in the UK could not be properly handicapped and should be given top-weight.

Crisp was given top-weight of 12 st 7 lb (79 kg) in his first race. He swept to the lead after a mile and ran away from the field to win easily. He was then entered in the 2-mile Champion Chase, an international event of considerable stature, which he won impressively. Crisp was always able to carry weight and run time. He broke race records both in Australia and Britain.

Crisp was trained in England by ex–jumps jockey Fred Winter. Although he had been champion jockey four times, winning two Cheltenham Gold Cups, two Grand Nationals and riding a record 121 winners in the season 1952–53, Winter was about as close to being a 'battler' as an English trainer can be.

When Winter retired in 1964 he had no intention of applying for a training licence. In fact, he had applied for a job as a starter but the jockey club turned him down. So he set up the Uplands Stables in Lambourn and, in 1965, just three years after riding Kilmore to victory in the Grand National, he trained Jay Trump to win the event. The following year he did it again when 50 to 1 shot Anglo beat 46 starters.

Fred Winter was to go remarkably close to an Aintree hat trick in 1973 when Crisp produced one of the best jumping displays ever seen over the big fences, only to be caught in the final stride by a horse carrying 24 pounds (11 kg) less weight.

In spite of Crisp being a two-miler rather than a Grand National type, it was decided to have a crack at the world's most famous jumping race and connections entered Crisp for the Grand National of 1973.

Crisp was given top-weight of 12 stone (76 kg) and Fred Winter's riding plan for jockey Richard Pitman was not to hold him up at all, as he always liked to bowl along in his races, but to let him settle in front and try to slow the pace.

Crisp, however, had his own idea of how the race should be run; perhaps he didn't know he had 4½ miles to cover that day.

When the tape lifted he set off at a merry pace, jumping fence after fence as if he was out hunting. He took Becher's Brook in his stride the first time around and made ground consistently, jumping the enormous fences like an old pro. At the end of the first circuit he was 20 lengths in front.

At Becher's on the second circuit he was 25 lengths in front and still racing alone, but another horse had broken from the following pack and started to make up some ground on him. That horse was to go down in history as the greatest Grand National horse of all time. His name was Red Rum.

Crisp seemed safe; he appeared to be too far in front for anything to catch him if he just stayed on his feet. But, at the second last jump, Crisp ran out of steam and began to falter.

As he approached the last he began to roll sideways but his instinct took him over safely and he began the long 500-yard run in with his strength visibly failing.

Richard Pitman said later, 'It happened after the second last . . . just the way I had feared. It all fell apart . . . suddenly his legs were going sideways instead of forwards, grabbing instead of reaching. Those big lop ears went floppy. All of a sudden, his strength was gone. And on the firm ground I could hear hoofbeats, like thunder.'

With Red Rum coming up fast behind, Richard Pitman made what he later considered to be a dreadful error: the jockey gave Crisp a slap with the whip. Crisp was so tired that he shied when hit, staggered sideways away from the whip and lost all momentum. Pitman was forced to stop riding to get him round the Elbow.

Red Rum was finishing fast and, although Crisp was out on his feet, Pitman recalled, 'I could feel him tighten as he sensed the other horse approach. He was absolutely bottomed, but that racing instinct was in-built. Only he had nothing left to fight with.'

In the end the weight was too much and two strides before the finish Red Rum, carrying 24 pounds (11 kg) less, passed Crisp and went on to immortality by winning the first of a record three Grand Nationals. In the process he broke the record and ran the fastest time in the history of the race.

Red Rum won the race again in 1974 and 1977, and ran second in 1975 and 1976. He became the hero of Aintree and is buried there, near the winning post.

Crisp never ran in the Grand National again but he did run against Red Rum the following year, at level weights at Haydock Park, and defeated him convincingly.

After retiring from racing at the end of 1974, Crisp lived out his life as a hunter in the countryside around County Durham and North Yorkshire.

It is rare in sport for a second-placegetter to be remembered as well as the winner, but Crisp is revered in the annals of British racing and many, including commentator and television personality John Francome, list him as their favourite horse of all time.

When he died he was buried beneath a flowering cherry tree in the North English countryside. Richard Pitman, who still blames himself for Crisp losing the Grand National in 1973, was asked to write his obituary for *Horse & Hound* magazine. He ended the obituary by saying that every year, at Grand National time, the cherry blossoms would float down like tears onto Crisp's grave.

THE OPEN STEEPLECHASE

A.B. 'BANJO' PATERSON

I had ridden over hurdles up the country once or twice,
By the side of Snowy River with a horse they called 'The Ace'.
And we brought him down to Sydney, and our rider, Jimmy Rice,
Got a fall and broke his shoulder, so they nabbed me in a trice,
Me, that never wore the colours, for the open Steeplechase.

'Make the running,' said the trainer, 'it's your only chance whatever,
Make it hot from start to finish, for the old black horse can stay,
And just think of how they'll take it, when they hear on Snowy
  River
That the country boy was plucky, and the country horse was clever.
You must ride for old Monaro and the mountain boys today.'

'Are you ready?' said the starter, as we held the horses back.
All ablazing with impatience, with excitement all aglow;
Before us like a ribbon stretched the steeplechasing track,
And the sun-rays glistened brightly on the chestnut and the black
As the starter's words came slowly, 'Are, you, ready? Go!'

Well I scarcely knew we'd started, I was stupid-like with wonder
Till the field closed up beside me and a jump appeared ahead.
And we flew it like a hurdle, not a baulk and not a blunder,
As we charged it all together, and it fairly whistled under,
And then some were pulled behind me and a few shot out and led.

So we ran for half the distance, and I'm making no pretenses
When I tell you I was feeling very nervous-like and queer,
For those jockeys rode like demons; you would think they'd lost
their senses
If you saw them rush their horses at those rasping five-foot fences,
And in place of making running I was falling to the rear.

Till a chap came racing past me on a horse they called 'The Quiver',
And said he, 'My country joker, are you going to give it best?
Are you frightened of the fences? Does their stoutness make
you shiver?
Have they come to breeding cowards by the side of Snowy River?
Are there riders in Monaro?,' but I never heard the rest.

For I drove The Ace and sent him just as fast as he could pace it
At the big black line of timber stretching fair across the track,
And he shot beside The Quiver. 'Now,' said I, 'my boy, we'll race it.
You can come with Snowy River if you're only game to face it,
Let us mend the pace a little and we'll see who cries a crack.'

So we raced away together, and we left the others standing,
And the people cheered and shouted as we settled down to ride,
And we clung beside The Quiver. At his taking off and landing
I could see his scarlet nostril and his mighty ribs expanding,
And The Ace stretched out in earnest, and we held him stride
for stride.

But the pace was so terrific that they soon ran out their tether,
They were rolling in their gallop, they were fairly blown and beat,
But they both were game as pebbles, neither one would show the
feather.
And we rushed them at the fences, and they cleared them both
together,
Nearly every time they clouted, but they somehow kept their feet.

Then the last jump rose before us, and they faced it game as ever,
We were both at spur and whipcord, fetching blood at every bound,
And above the people's cheering and the cries of 'Ace' and 'Quiver',
I could hear the trainer shouting, 'One more run for Snowy River.'
Then we struck the jump together and came smashing to the
    ground.

Well, The Quiver ran to blazes, but The Ace stood still and waited,
Stood and waited like a statue while I scrambled on its back.
There was no one next or near me for the field was fairly slated,
So I cantered home a winner with my shoulder dislocated,
While the man who rode The Quiver followed limping down
    the track.

And he shook my hand and told me that in all his days he never
Met a man who rode more gamely, and our last set-to was prime.
Then we wired them on Monaro how we chanced to beat The
    Quiver,
And they sent us back an answer, 'Good old sort from Snowy River:
Send us word each race you start in and we'll back you every time.'

ROUGHNECK

JIM HAYNES

Oakbank, 1978.

It was a small field for the Great Eastern Steeplechase that year as the track was quite heavy and the weather was wet over Easter.

The atmosphere was a little dampened and the ground was soggy underfoot but it was still Oakbank, the great Easter Racing Carnival in the Adelaide Hills.

In 1978 most of the already small field either fell or retired. Oddly enough it was mostly the front-runners who fell or dropped out.

Of those left standing towards the end, three were way back in the field and one, a tough little chestnut gelding with the totally appropriate name of Roughneck, ridden by veteran jockey Peter Hely, was left way out in front.

What a fizzer of a race, you might think. How can four horses scattered over a mile of racetrack, with one horse half a mile in front, be of any interest?

You might think that.

You might also think these things demonstrate why jumps races hold little interest and are an anachronism.

You'd be wrong on both counts.

You might think, in a race like that, there's no real contest.

You'd be wrong again.

Unlike 1973, when The Cent and Mystic Moon went head to head, there was no cheering, no roaring of the crowd as Roughneck cleared the fallen log, came down the hill, entered the straight and approached the last two jumps.

There was just an uncanny quiet.

You see . . . Roughneck was just about out on his feet. He was visibly exhausted and laying in badly.

At the second last he clipped the jump and almost went down, just about touching his nose on the turf. He regained his footing but staggered sideways as the entire crowd caught its breath.

I'd never heard 50,000 people catch their breath before. It was a sound that filled the valley.

Hely somehow got him balanced again and approached the last jump.

In those few seconds I truly came to believe in something akin to Jung's theory of the collective subconscious or the power of prayer. I knew that everyone watching was willing that little chestnut gelding to get over that last fence. We all held our breath.

He steadied and approached the fence at a speed just fast enough to gain some momentum for a final jump.

Hely seemed to lift him by the reins and he rose to take the last fence . . . and landed safely.

Then the crowd breathed again.

And that's the loudest sigh of relief I've ever heard on a racetrack anywhere in the world and the clapping lasted until long after Roughneck had cantered slowly past the winning post.

No one had backed him. He was 40 to 1.

The nearest horse wasn't even in the straight when he cleared the last jump. He won by 40 lengths.

But that's the best battle down the straight that I ever saw.

THE GROG-AN'-GRUMBLE STEEPLECHASE

HENRY LAWSON

'Twixt the coastline and the border lay the town of Grog-an'-Grumble
In the days before the bushman was a dull 'n' heartless drudge,
An' they say the local meeting was a drunken rough-and-tumble,
Which was ended pretty often by an inquest on the judge.
An' 'tis said the city talent very often caught a tartar
In the Grog-an'-Grumble sportsman, 'n' returned with broken heads,
For the fortune, life and safety of the Grog-an'-Grumble starter
Mostly hung upon the finish of the local thoroughbreds.

Pat McDurmer was the owner of a horse they called the Screamer,
Which he called 'the quickest shtepper 'twixt the Darling and the sea,'
And I think it's very doubtful if the stomach-troubled dreamer
Ever saw a more outrageous piece of equine scenery;
For his points were most decided, from his end to his beginning,
He had eyes of different colour, and his legs they wasn't mates.
Pat McDurmer said he always came 'within a flip of winnin',
An' his sire had come from England, 'n' his dam was from the States.

Friends would argue with McDurmer, and they said he was in error
To put up his horse the Screamer, for he'd lose in any case,
And they said a city racer by the name of Holy Terror
Was regarded as the winner of the coming steeplechase;

But he said he had the knowledge to come in when it was raining,
And irreverently mentioned that he knew the time of day,
So he rose in their opinion. It was noticed that the training
Of the Screamer was conducted in a dark, mysterious way.

Well, the day arrived in glory; 'twas a day of jubilation
With careless-hearted bushmen for a hundred miles around,
An' the rum 'n' beer 'n' whisky came in wagons from the station,
An' the Holy Terror talent were the first upon the ground.
Judge McArd, with whose opinion it was scarcely safe to wrestle,
Took his dangerous position on the bark-and-sapling stand:
He was what the local Stiggins used to speak of as a 'vessel
Of wrath,' and he'd a bludgeon that he carried in his hand.

'Off ye go!' the starter shouted, as down fell a stupid jockey—
Off they started in disorder—left the jockey where he lay—
And they fell and rolled and galloped down the crooked course and rocky,
Till the pumping of the Screamer could be heard a mile away.
But he kept his legs and galloped; he was used to rugged courses,
And he lumbered down the gully till the ridge began to quake:
And he ploughed along the siding, raising earth till other horses
An' their riders, too, were blinded by the dust-cloud in his wake.

From the ruck he'd struggled slowly, they were much surprised to find him
Close abeam the Holy Terror as along the flat they tore.
Even higher still and denser rose the cloud of dust behind him,
While in more divided splinters flew the shattered rails before.
'Terror!' 'Dead heat!' they were shouting, 'Terror!' but the Screamer hung out
Nose-to-nose with Holy Terror as across the creek they swung,
An' McDurmer shouted loudly, 'Put yer tongue out! Put yer tongue out!'
An' the Screamer put his tongue out . . . and he won by half a tongue.

WEIGHT WAS RIGHT

A.B. 'BANJO' PATERSON

Banjo Paterson was well placed to gather great yarns. Well known and well connected in both Sydney and the bush, he was often told yarns by friends and acquaintances. He used the anecdotes on his regular radio broadcasts and in his newspaper articles. Here's an example.

***

Once, years ago, a son of the then Governor of NSW secured a ride in a picnic race. Intensely enthusiastic and a very lightweight, this young gentleman turned up, full of hope, to ride his first race.

He got on the scales with his saddle, and it turned out that he was two stone short of making the weight!

Not one of the amateurs had a lead bag to lend him, but no one would dream of leaving the Governor's son out. He was the main attraction of the meeting.

The officials had never been confronted with anything like this, but the caretaker was a man of resource. He shovelled a lot of sand into a sack and strapped it firmly on the pommel of a big saddle; weight was right, and away the field went.

It was an amateur hurdle race and, every time that the horse jumped, a puff of sand flew up, like the miniature spouts blown into the air by killer whales.

Simultaneously jumping and spouting, the vice-regal contender saw the race out, unsuccessfully, it is true; but he got more applause than the winner.

THE AMATEUR RIDER

A.B. 'BANJO' PATERSON

Him going to ride for us! *Him*—with the pants and the eyeglass and all.
Amateur! Don't he just look it—it's twenty to one on a fall.
Boss must be gone off his head to be sending our steeplechase crack
Out over fences like these with an object like that on his back.

Ride! Don't tell *me* he can ride. With his pants just as loose as
balloons,
How can he sit on his horse? And his spurs like a pair of harpoons;
Ought to be under the Dog Act, he ought, and be kept off the
course.
Fall! Why, he'd fall off a cart, let alone off a steeplechase horse.

***

Yessir! the 'orse is all ready—I wish you'd have rode him before;
Nothing like knowing your 'orse, sir, and this chap's a terror to bore;
Battleaxe always could pull, and he rushes his fences like fun—
Stands off his jump twenty feet, and then springs like a shot from
a gun.

Oh, he can jump 'em all right, sir, you make no mistake, 'e's a toff;
Clouts 'em in earnest, too, sometimes, you mind that he don't clout
you off—
Don't seem to mind how he hits 'em, his shins is as hard as a nail,
Sometimes you'll see the fence shake and the splinters fly up from
the rail.

All you can do is to hold him and just let him jump as he likes,
Give him his head at the fences, and hang on like death if he strikes;
Don't let him run himself out—you can lie third or fourth in the race—
Until you clear the stone wall, and from that you can put on the pace.

Fell at that wall once, he did, and it gave him a regular spread,
Ever since that time he flies it—he'll stop if you pull at his head,
Just let him race—you can trust him—he'll take first-class care he don't fall,
And I think that's the lot—but remember, he must have his head at the wall.

***

Well, he's down safe as far as the start, and he seems to sit on pretty neat,
Only his baggified breeches would ruinate anyone's seat—
They're away—here they come—the first fence, and he's head over heels for a crown!
Good for the new chum, he's over, and two of the others are down!

Now for the treble, my hearty—by Jove, he can ride, after all;
Whoop, that's your sort—let him fly them! He hasn't much fear of a fall.
Who in the world would have thought it? And aren't they just going a pace?
Little Recruit in the lead there will make it a stoutly run race.

Lord! But they're racing in earnest—and down goes Recruit on his head,
Rolling clean over his boy—it's a miracle if he ain't dead.
Battleaxe, Battleaxe, yet! By the Lord, he's got most of 'em beat—
Ho! did you see how he struck, and the swell never moved in his seat?

Second time round, and, by Jingo! He's holding his lead of 'em well;
Hark to him clouting the timber! It don't seem to trouble the swell.
Now for the wall—let him rush it. A thirty-foot leap, I declare—
Never a shift in his seat, and he's racing for home like a hare.

What's that that's chasing him—Rataplan—regular demon to stay!
Sit down and ride for your life now! Oh, good, that's the style—
come away!
Rataplan's certain to beat you, unless you can give him the slip;
Sit down and rub in the whalebone now—give him the spurs and
the whip!

Battleaxe, Battleaxe, yet—and it's Battleaxe wins for a crown;
Look at him rushing the fences, he wants to bring t'other chap
down.
Rataplan never will catch him if only he keeps on his pins;
Now! The last fence! And he's over it! Battleaxe, Battleaxe wins!

***

Well, sir, you rode him just perfect—I knew from the first you
could ride.
Some of the chaps said you couldn't, an' I says just like this a' one
side:
Mark me, I says, that's a tradesman—the saddle is where he was
bred.
Weight! You're all right, sir, and thank you; and them was the words
that I said.

MOSSTROOPER—THE BRADMAN OF THE TURF

PETER HARRIS

In 1929 and 1930 Mosstrooper burst on the scene very much like the young Don Bradman did in cricket. By the end of the 1929–30 cricket season in Australia, the 21-year-old Bradman had played 66 Test or first-class matches and had a batting average of 79.47 runs per innings. Soon after, in the first three tests against England from 13 June to 15 July 1930, Bradman scored 131, 254 and 334. In, before and just after this period, Mosstrooper reeled off wins like Bradman amassed runs, causing a newspaper cartoonist to dub the all-conquering jumper *Bradman of the Turf*.

When Mosstrooper returned to scale after winning the Australian Hurdle Race at Caulfield in 1930, his trainer and owner, Gus Powell, took off his hat and nodded in the horse's direction. 'Well, you're a battler all right,' he said, 'and you did just what I expected you to do to them'. That was all. Powell did not fall about in a paroxysm of celebration. He did not punch the air or fall to the ground, and he certainly did not hug anyone. Maybe he drew a bit more heavily on his pipe. But all around him some 40,000 racegoers were cheering themselves hoarse. They knew what Mosstrooper had achieved on that Saturday in August. Ploughing through the mud and jumping fifteen hurdles over 3¼ miles, Mosstrooper added yet another victory to an unrivalled sequence of performances.

It had begun almost thirteen months before, on 13 July 1929. As a novice jumper, Mosstrooper had finished a close and unlucky second in the Victoria Racing Club (VRC) Grand National Steeplechase at Flemington. Then, in the following month, he ran away with the Victoria Amateur Turf Club (VATC) Australian Hurdle and Steeplechase double. Come July 1930, he won with ease both the VRC Grand National Hurdle and Steeplechase in heavy going at Flemington. That was already more than any previous jumper had managed to achieve in so brief a period. When Mosstrooper romped home on a bog track for his second Australian Hurdle three weeks later, he was dubbed the 'Bradman of the Turf'.

In just over a year, by winning the four major jumping events in Australia, one of them twice, Mosstrooper raced himself into turf fame and the hearts of the racing public. 'All the superlatives have been used up in referring to Mosstrooper and his performances', declared a prominent racing journalist in *The Age*, writing under the pen name of 'Tasman'. For him, Mosstrooper was simply 'one of the greatest jumpers ever seen on Australian courses, probably the greatest.' The chestnut gelding's record could stand forever, Tasman speculated, because no other jumper would prove so superior to his opponents. Eighty-five years on, 'Tasman' has been proven a prophet: no jumper has come within cooee of emulating Mosstrooper's achievement in the jumping seasons of 1929 and 1930.

The 1930 Australian Hurdle was to be Mosstrooper's finest hour, the height of his fame. And so too for jockey Bob Harris. When Harris returned to the birdcage at Caulfield on Mosstrooper, Powell at once congratulated him. 'It was a great piece of riding', Powell told reporters. 'We have never seen better.' It was terse, but from one of Australia's greatest-ever horsemen it was eloquent praise—praise that continued back at the horse's race-day stall, as Powell told visitors just how well Harris had ridden.

Mosstrooper gave Harris the chance to show a wider public how skilful he was as a jockey. Harris had been riding in races, with moderate success, for 20 years when he teamed up with Mosstrooper. Over the years he had become a heavyweight jockey, and his engagements were few and far between. In fact, it was chiefly because Mosstrooper was being handicapped with high weights by 1930 that Powell turned to Harris. He wanted to minimise the dead weight that Mosstrooper would have to carry. What had been a drawback for Harris now gave him his greatest opportunity, and the jockey seized the reins held out to him. He rode Mosstrooper to three of his five major wins, earning accolades for each ride.

That Mosstrooper's victory in the 1930 Australian Hurdle was also Powell's finest hour is not so certain. At 62, he was a man of wide experience and outstanding accomplishment in the many ventures he had undertaken. All the same, he had never before committed himself to a task that had brought so much success, and with it such public affection and admiration. Through skill and hard work he had turned a former no-hoper into an undisputed champion. Although there were many great trainers in Powell's time, none might have made the time or found the determination to work what seemed a miracle: the re-making of Mosstrooper. Pre-Powell, Mosstrooper could not win a single race from 16 starts on the flat; for Powell, in 25 jumps races up to and including that wonderful Saturday at Caulfield, he won 10 and was placed four times. In just two racing seasons, Mosstrooper accumulated prizemoney of £12,591 (A$912,711), already the most ever earned by a jumps horse in Australia.

As the victorious owner-trainer, Powell should perhaps have been the most excited person at Caulfield Racecourse on 2 August 1930, but his reaction was typically low-key. Talking to reporters, he was keen to vindicate Mosstrooper's achievement.

I am glad my horse won, because by defeating Kentle and Swahili, he proved that his Grand National victories were not the flukes some people thought they were. Swahili fell in the Grand National Hurdle race and Kentle came down in the steeplechase. Both these horses stood up on Saturday, and Mosstrooper defeated them comfortably.

A month earlier, on the Monday after the 1930 VRC Grand National Steeplechase, handicapper Samuel Griffiths had issued his weights for the Australian Hurdle and Steeplechase, to be run on the first and second Saturday in August. Mosstrooper headed both lists, with 11 stone 12 pounds (11.12) and 12.10 respectively, up 19 pounds and 14 pounds on the weights he had carried to victory in the Flemington double. Bookmakers did not believe the increases would prevent him from winning, and they immediately installed him as favourite for the 'Caulfield Grand Nationals' (as the Australian Hurdle and Steeplechase were still informally called). When the mighty Redleap won the Australian Steeplechase, in 1892, he had lumped a record 13.12, and three other winners since had carried over 13 stone. On those figures, Mosstrooper was in with a genuine chance.

Unlike the bookies, many journalists were already prepared to say that Mosstrooper would *not* win the upcoming majors, still three weeks away. They thought that Swahili especially would beat him in the hurdle, and that Kentle, Mosstrooper's half-brother, would back up from the hurdle race to lead him home in the steeplechase. Not only would both horses be meeting Mosstrooper on better weight terms, they could be excused, supporters argued, for their performances at Flemington. However, turf columnist 'Flash of Steel' in the *Bendigo Advertiser* could not rate them above Mosstrooper. He questioned whether Kentle, injured in the Grand National Steeplechase, would be fit enough for the 3¼ miles of the Australian Hurdle, and he was not sure Swahili could stay that distance. Weight would not stop Mosstrooper, for 'Flash of Steel' he was 'the absolute winner'.

Mosstrooper's handicap, however, weighed on Powell's mind. Mosstrooper was not a big horse. The allotted 11.12 was the heaviest weight—by 15 pounds—of his hurdling career, and a sizeable increase on the 9.10 with which he had won the same race a year before. He had lumped 12.3 to win in September 1929, but that was in a steeplechase at Moonee Valley over just 2½ miles. In the Australian Hurdle he would have to race 6 furlongs further at a faster pace, and probably on a heavy track. So Powell settled on a different race strategy for Mosstrooper.

He decided that Bob Harris would ride him cold at the back of the field and only make a move late in the race. He would have to wait and wait, without letting the leaders gain a break that Mosstrooper could not overcome. Harris would have to bring him into the race gradually, but quickly enough to round up the leaders soon after entering the straight. Mosstrooper had come from well back before to win races. This time, however, his late surge might have to be longer and quicker overall. There should be no spurts, just a steady, sustained charge at the leaders. Harris would need all his patience and timing.

When rain bucketed down at Caulfield on the Thursday night before the Australian Hurdle, and showers continued the following day, Powell, who trained his horses at Caulfield, knew 'the heath' would be on the nasty side of heavy come Saturday.

On race day, in getting Mosstrooper ready for perhaps his greatest challenge, Powell had the horse's tail plaited and his legs greased. The mud would literally be flying, and Powell wanted as little as possible to stick. Then he carefully placed one thick blanket after another on Mosstrooper's back before easing a heavy saddle down on top of them. In the saddling enclosure, before Harris was legged up, Powell told his jockey not to take Mosstrooper down the track for a look at the first obstacle, but simply to wait at the starting barrier. It was the ploy of a trainer with a load on his mind—a man concerned, if not desperate, to alleviate the weight his charge had to carry in dangerous conditions.

Now it all depended on Harris and Mosstrooper, and luck in running. Going out of the straight the first time, Mosstrooper (the 3–1 favourite) was last, and for the first mile he would not stretch out. Harris had to niggle at him to remind him of the task at hand. The pace seemed too fast, too soon, and Mosstrooper was squeezed several times. Feeling claustrophobic, the gelding was unnerved by the crowding and by being closed in on the rail. But this was the cost of saving ground and conserving the horse's energy until he made his late surge. Meanwhile, lightly weighted Rossgole, the heavily backed horse from Sydney, had raced out to a lead of 12 lengths over the field. Trying to run his opponents off their legs, Rossgole had set a cracking pace in the bog-like conditions from barrier rise, but he could not keep it up and was passed by Swahili entering the railway stretch 6 furlongs from home.

The new leader was full of running, and many in the crowd doubted that Mosstrooper or any other rival could catch him.

In fact, at the 1-mile mark, when Mosstrooper began to sneak around the field, two or sometimes three horses out from the rail, Reonui, who had been prominent early, came again to pass him. Mosstrooper seemed to be gone. But even 5 furlongs out, Harris was sure he would win. Mosstrooper ran into third place as Polygonum took the lead at the 4 furlongs, and soon after, when Polygonum crashed into the second-last fence, Swahili was left in front again. But not for long. He was a sitting duck for the relentless Mosstrooper, who ran past him as they entered the straight. Once over the last hurdle, Gus Powell's champion cruised to the line 3 lengths clear of the resolute novice Lord Darnley (12–1). Kentle plugged home a further 4 lengths back in third place. Swahili (second favourite at 5–1) was a tiring fifth, and Rossgole (third favourite at 6–1) caved in to finish a distant last.

The applause began before Mosstrooper jumped the last hurdle and rose to a 'mighty roar'. At the St Leger and near the winning post on the flat the spectators were already standing, but in the stands they rose en masse to salute their champion. More cheering and clapping broke out when Mosstrooper returned to scale, and was kept up until the weight-right flag was raised and the hero led away to his stall. Experienced racing writers described the reception as extraordinary. 'Trentham' in *The Argus* wrote of the 'veritable tornado' of applause that greeted Mosstrooper as he passed the post. For 'Musket' of *The Sydney Mail*, the ovation eclipsed any ever given an 'equine hero' at Caulfield.

In *The Age*, 'Tasman' claimed there had never been a racecourse reception 'more enthusiastic or more prolonged than that so deservedly given to Mosstrooper, wonder horse, on Saturday'. A witness to well over 30 Australian Hurdle races, 'Flash of Steel' remarked in the *Bendigo Advertiser* that no running of the Caulfield classic had been 'more keenly enjoyed by the spectators'. The racegoers 'fully appreciated the tremendous nature of [Mosstrooper's] exploits', and the 1930 Australian Hurdle would be remembered 'long after the present generation has passed away'.

The crowd's deafening applause was also a tribute to Bob Harris, according to 'Khedive' in *The Sporting Globe*. He admired the way in which Harris, a past master in the art of jumps riding, had conserved Mosstrooper's energy and timed his finishing run to perfection. Comparing Harris to Tommy Corrigan, the nineteenth-century champion and the most successful Australian jumps rider ever, 'Khedive' judged that it would have been 'beyond the power of the idolised little Irishman to preserve a statue-like seat until flying leaders began to crack up and then commence to overhaul them with consummate measurement of his horse's powers'.

If he was not an 'iceman', Robert Neville Harris was definitely a cool customer. Only 32, he had been in the racing game for 20 years and around horses almost from the cradle. Apprenticed to his father just before his 12th birthday in 1910, he developed his riding skills mainly on the non-thoroughbred pony tracks in hectic, boots 'n' all sprints. It was the school of hard knocks—and not just from rival jockeys. By the age of 14, young Bob had been severely cautioned twice and eventually disqualified for 12 months by racing stewards. The times were tough, but even tougher were the authorities if you overstepped the mark in search of a quid. And plenty of jocks were doing just that out on the track. The boy was a fast learner, however, and his skills were soon recognised by leading trainers at Caulfield and Flemington. Young Harris became known as a rider 'who never loses his head, however exciting the finish may be', and by the end of the 1912–13 season he was the leading jockey in Victoria.

Harris' ingrained composure might explain why he came back to scale on Mosstrooper with a look of apparent indifference to the hullabaloo of the crowd and his triumph in the Australian Hurdle. Maybe after his Grand National victories on Mosstrooper a few weeks before, such a storm was nothing new, or he might have been simply too tired to raise an arm or a smile. He had just been through a gruelling day and a half. On the Friday out at Netherlea, Gus Powell's Lysterfield property near the Dandenongs, Harris had occupied himself breaking in three buckjumpers and, as 'Khedive' tells it, 'sat one of his mounts in sliding down a mountain side, with Mr. Powell using a stockwhip in his wake'.

Why take such risks on the eve of an important race? Had some sort of macho mania taken possession of the pair? Had Powell set Harris a challenge he could not as a man or a rider refuse? Surely Harris was already fit enough for his ride on Mosstrooper the next day. Anyway, there were plenty of other, safer, physical tasks at Netherlea for Harris, if his fitness was an issue. Perhaps Powell felt it was necessary to stir up or stimulate Harris. Perhaps it was no big deal for the jockey; he may have already done some rough riding for Powell at Netherlea. He had been coming up to Lysterfield before the big races for the past few months. Usually he was accompanied by Garnet Eaton, who rode Mosstrooper in routine trackwork and just about all his conditioning races on the flat. Powell liked to keep the jockeys active doing various chores, or send them out rabbit shooting across the rolling hills.

These stays at Powell's farm no doubt built a better understanding between trainer and jockey and helped Harris to keep fit, but their main purpose seems to have been to keep Harris out of the pubs. The story goes that he was often 'kidnapped' by friends on a Friday night to ensure he was capable of riding on the Saturday. The image of Powell cracking a whip behind Harris, as their mounts slid down a hill, may encapsulate a crucial aspect of their relationship: Powell felt he had to train his jockey as well as Mosstrooper.

By 1930, Mosstrooper was living proof of Powell's horsemanship, especially his skill as a conditioner. In the saddling enclosure before the Australian Hurdle, Mosstrooper was as 'perky and muscular' as ever, 'Trentham' noted in *The Argus*. Despite a long and demanding campaign (eight races in nine weeks, over a total of almost 15½ miles), Powell's 'battler' was still fit and keen. He naturally pulled up tired after the Australian Hurdle, but quickly recovered. Back in his race-day stall, he soon plunged his head into a bag of fresh grass brought from Lysterfield.

Stamina was Mosstrooper's forté.

For his success in the Australian Hurdle, Mosstrooper was penalised 9 pounds for the Australian Steeplechase. The gallant gelding would now have to carry 13.5 over 24 obstacles and 3½ miles. This time, Powell's cause for concern was so patent there was no point in keeping quiet about it. Adelaide's *Advertiser* called him the most worried man in Melbourne. 'He is only a little gelding', Powell told *The Advertiser*, 'and it means a lot to have to carry 13.5 over such a long journey. If I run him and he gets hurt people will blame me. If he does not run some people will say that I was not game enough'. Although Powell presented his problem as a dilemma about avoiding public condemnation, for him as a trainer the issue was essentially whether Mosstrooper could win, or even run well, lugging the top-weight of 13.5.

Nevertheless, early in the week of the Australian Steeplechase, Powell was not convinced that the weight was impossible. He had not made up his mind to scratch Mosstrooper. The gelding had bounced back from his taxing run in the Australian Hurdle, and on Tuesday morning worked solidly over 10 furlongs. *The Argus* trackman at Caulfield said he looked 'as fit as ever'. Later that day, Powell accepted for the steeplechase, to be run on the Saturday.

When acceptances were published, there was a 58-pound (26 kilograms) gap between Mosstrooper and bottom-weighted Good Whisky, who would carry only 9.3. Kentle was second top-weight with 12.3, 16 pounds less than Mosstrooper. On Wednesday morning, Mosstrooper took part in a school on the Caulfield steeplechase course with three other horses. He jumped three fences perfectly before being steered off the steeplechase track by Harris to do two circuits of the cinders track. On Thursday, with Eaton up, Mosstrooper was keen to go faster in a working gallop, again over 10 furlongs. He was obviously in good heart and good shape.

Powell was probably inclined to risk Mosstrooper under the big weight. His champion might never again be so well-primed to win a major race and make history, and there was a good deal of money riding on him to take out the Australian jumps double.

Melbourne's weather, and its effect on the track, was the most troublesome factor. If the rain that had been around for several days disappeared, the track might just firm up enough to give Mosstrooper a chance of running. Should Powell decide to run Mosstrooper, 'Flash of Steel' observed, 'not even the race for the Melbourne Cup will create a greater interest among racegoers than Mosstrooper's effort to record two double wins in successive years in the Australian Hurdle and the Australian Steeplechase'.

Although ambitious, Powell was a fair and selfless person, and he agonised over the decision. Unlike Hamlet, he did not lack advice. He received letters for and against. One man told Powell he had Mosstrooper going in doubles, and urged him to consider all those who would lose money if he scratched the horse. A woman who described herself as 'a lover of horseflesh' was concerned only for Mosstrooper's welfare.

> I would like to see you withdraw your wonderful horse Mosstrooper next Saturday, as with that awful weight something may happen which would be cruel, after his glorious victories. Let him stay as he is Glorious in Victory.

Nothing cruel did happen, unless it was cruel that Mosstrooper was to miss the opportunity to extend his already historic sequence of major victories. On Friday, Powell inspected the steeplechase course at Caulfield and made up his mind. On Saturday morning he went to the VATC office at the racecourse and withdrew Mosstrooper from the Australian Steeplechase. The rain had not eased off and the track was a quagmire. The stewards in fact almost postponed the meeting.

The result of the race confirmed Powell's good judgement in scratching Mosstrooper. In the small field of ten, four of the five starters weighted under 10.0 finished in the first four places. Kentle, top-weight in the absence of Mosstrooper, was pulled up 7 furlongs from home, and Namera, the second top-weight, finished a distant second-last. The race was won convincingly by the bottom-weight Good Whisky (12–1), with the two horses just above him in the weights—Orange Park (33–1) and Bang Bang (7–1)—finishing second and third. Given the awful condition of the track, it is surprising that only three previous winners of the Australian Steeplechase had run it in faster time than Good Whisky.

If Mosstrooper had run in the Australian Steeplechase, and won or finished close up in a place, it might have been his last race. The handicappers would have been obliged to give him huge weights in any future jumps race. So the persistent rain in early August 1930 did him and his owner-trainer a favour: Mosstrooper was to race for another three years under heavy weights, but, on firm tracks at least, these were not impossible burdens.

After missing the Australian Steeplechase, Powell could have sent Mosstrooper to Adelaide for its Nationals, or given him a brief let-up before taking on the rich Moonee Valley steeplechase in mid-September, but no matter which course he took, Mosstrooper would have been asked to carry 13 stone or more. He had been in work that jumps season for ten weeks and had covered just on 19 miles in nine races—an average of almost one 2-mile race each week. In six jumps races, Mosstrooper had won three majors in succession and been placed in the other three lead-up events. He had boosted his total stakes earnings to £12,751 (A$924,292), an Australasian record for a jumper. The durable campaigner was still fit and keen. But maybe enough was enough. Why tempt the gods?

Powell decided to tip his champion out for a spell. And so, for all its triumph, Mosstrooper's third campaign as a hurdler and chaser ended on a rather muted note. Had the rain not been so heavy and incessant, Australian jumps racing could have had its most memorable moment by far. Yet what a wonderful winter it had been. Make that two winters. For in 1929 and 1930, Mosstrooper put together two successive seasons of jumping that have never been matched in the history of Australian racing. No other jumper—not Redleap, Bribery or Roisel, not Redditch, Winterset or Crisp—was as durable, as versatile or as successful.

But what cared Mosstrooper for the milestones of history as he headed for the green, green grass of Lysterfield in the spring of 1930? Coming up at home were months of warm ease to amble and gambol in. What lay beyond, in what could be the hardest new campaign of all? Well, that was for Gus to worry about.

(This story is taken from Mosstrooper: Hack to Hero *by Peter Harris. It is available at <www.mosstrooperbook.com>).*

SHORT SHRIFT

HARRY 'THE BREAKER' MORANT

I can mind him at the start—
Easy seat and merry heart!
Said he, as he threw a glance
At the crawling ambulance,

'Some day I'll be on the ground
And the van will hurry round!
Doc will gravely wag his head,
"No use now, the poor chap's dead!"

'Every man must, soon or late
Turn up at the Golden Gate:
When we weigh in—you and I—
How can horsemen better die?'

On that sunlit steeple course
He lay prone beneath his horse,
Never more his pal may ride
By that gallant horseman's side.

'Reckless fool?' What matter, mate?
All his time he'd ridden straight—
Went (smashed 'gainst that wall of sod!)
Spurred and booted to his God.

Carve in stone, above his head,
Words that some old Christian said:
'Grace he sought, and grace he found,
'Twixt the saddle and the ground!'

DEATH IN THE AFTERNOON

LES CARLYON

Jumps racing is different. The Grand National had been robbed of its star, Sharp As, then its best supporting act, Derrydonnell. In the cold and the rain at Flemington, we stared at the bit players remaining, looking for a greatness we had assumed, until now, not to be there. Who, among these old warriors, could gallop for two laps and six minutes?

Tacloban looked the way a national horse should. He carried his head low and his hip bones stuck out to prove he had galloped hundreds of kilometres to harden up for this one day. But Andallah, the baby of the field at five, was the eye-catcher. Even in the grey light, his brown coat shone. And when Billy Londregan was legged up, the horse wanted to jig, to get on with it.

Here was the one doubt: national horses should never look too fresh. Long steeples are seldom about brilliance; they are always about cleverness. Jump racing is different. It is not so much about who is right but who is left.

John Craddock, a thirty-nine year old stock agent and trainer from Arthurs Creek on Melbourne's northern fringe, casually led Trei Gnaree around by the bit ring. He patted the old bay with the long back but looked at Andallah. Craddock had seen the horse who could beat him. With his hunting clip, Trei Gnaree looked right enough: big, strong, seasoned. Few fancied him, though. He had a problem you could not see. It was in his head. The racebook said Trei Gnaree had been 'pulled up' two starts back in a steeple in the Valley. The truth was Trei Gnaree had pulled himself up.

When the gates opened, the leggy Andallah jumped to the lead, ears pricked, no problems in *his* head. He stayed there for nearly two laps, going lightly for Londregan, who sat high, bridging his reins on the wither, and riding as if he knew he was on a good one. Andallah stayed there while the attrition, fall after fall, went on behind. He stayed there for around 4500 metres, for twenty-six of the twenty-eight jumps. Coming to the second last, in front of the cypresses just before the home turn, Andallah was about a length ahead of Bar the Shouting and Trei Gnaree. Andallah's ears were stilled pricked. He was still going sweetly.

Because of the angle, one cannot be sure what happened. Probably Andallah took off too soon. Certainly his forelegs struck the top of the jump. Andallah described a single awful somersault. His hindquarters hung in the air. He finished lying on his near side, his offside legs in the air and convulsing as if an electric current were charging through them, convulsing the way animals' legs do when the link between the brain and the extremities is lost. Andallah's head was facing the wrong way, back towards the fence that had killed him. The jumps are different. They do not forgive.

Brian Constable on Trei Gnaree glanced back at death, then ahead at life. Trei Gnaree, the horse they said wasn't putting in, the horse they said couldn't stay five thousand metres, fairly surged into the last jump, shook off Bar the Shouting, and strolled in by twelve lengths. John Craddock then gave his horse the finest reward an old chaser can hope for. He retired him.

The jumps are different, all right. They are an old sporting print come to life, a throwback to the world of Adam Lindsay Gordon and Tommy Corrigan, both of whom had to die to obtain idolatry. They are about a different sort of horse, too. Slow horses by flat standards, and older. Sound, tough horses with maybe not much blood, big and small, coarse and refined, united only by one quality—courage.

The rich sprints for two-year-olds are the new world. They are like rock videos: frantic and bug-eyed and reeking of money. You learn the colours, and all you see is a technicolour stampede. Sneeze on Slipper Day and you miss 'the incident'. The jumps are like epic novels: long, crowded with subplots and sidetracks, hard on their heroes. They do not flash by but grind on, not one chapter but many.

Eleven set out in the Grand National. Pal O'Mine fell at the third, sliding along spectacularly on his side. Then there were ten, Andallah gliding along in front, Trei Gnaree fifteen lengths back. Just after entering the straight at the end of the first lap, McMurphy bungled the thirteenth and tumbled over and over. Then there were nine.

At the last of the five jumps in the straight, Andallah stood off and took a breathtaking leap; it might be only his third start over the big fences, but he was starting to look special. Vim was inspired. He was a couple of lengths off the main bunch and decided to fly just like Andallah. He stood right off the jump—and planted his front legs right in it. Then there were eight, and Trei Gnaree was cruising up to second.

In this last lap, Oakleigh Jack was finally coming to terms with his limitations. A chestnut with a big blaze, Oakleigh Jack is the very horse who makes jumping different. A seven-year-old, bred in the beige rather than the purple, he had been to the races thirty-one times and had never run a place, earned not a cent. Still if everything fell . . .

At the second on the river side, old Oakleigh landed awkwardly and suddenly looked tired. He seemed to run half-heartedly to the next jump, blundered through, then fell down quietly. He is a modest horse with a lot to be modest about, and he had the grace not to make a spectacle of himself. Then there were seven. Trei Gnaree had dropped back to fourth. Maybe they were right; maybe he couldn't stay.

Coming to the final turn, Trei Gnaree had come with another surge. He, Andallah and Bar the Shouting, last year's winner, could all win. A tight finish was possible. The other two were more seasoned but Andallah was going the easiest. Until he fell. And then there were six, and the plot changed again.

Instead of a tight finish, it was a procession. Commission Red ran past Tacloban near the line for third. King Dollar was half a furlong back imitating Cliff Young. Somewhere behind him was Waldara, last but not dishonoured. He was still on his feet—sort of.

Jump races are different. After the major flat races, the ritual is for the trainer to go for a drink in the committee bar, as though he, rather than the horse, had done all the work. After Saturday's presentation, Craddock went to head off with Trei Gnaree. He was called back. Didn't he want a drink?

'No,' he said. 'No, I'm going with the horse. He's my horse.'

Note: Trei Gnaree won the VRC Grand National at Flemington on 14 July 1990.

CASTLEBAR

A.B. 'BANJO' PATERSON

Bidding good morrow to all our cares,
Riding along with a joyful heart.
Little we reckon of world affairs,
All that we ask is a decent start,
Thought the jumps are big and the distance far
We will get to the finish on Castlebar.

Little Blue Peter goes sailing by,
Little Blue Peter may stand or fall,
For his rider reckons no man can die
Till his day comes round—so he chances all!
And away to the front where the good ones are
Go Little Blue Peter and Castlebar.

Bay and chestnut and brown and black,
I hear in the timber their hoof beats drum,
As I clear the fence on the Prospect track
I turn in the saddle and watch them come
But the chestnut horse with the big white star,
Why isn't he following Castlebar?

Dear little woman with eyes of blue,
With lissom figure and easy grace,
I turn in the saddle and long for you
As the field sweeps on at a rattling pace.
But I know that away on the heights afar
Your heart is following Castlebar.

ADAM LINDSAY GORDON

JIM HAYNES

The Australian love affair with rhymed verse goes hand in hand with our love of racing. It all began with an ex-patriot Briton who wanted to be taken seriously as a poet, but ended up being remembered for his galloping rhymes and his riding ability.

His disappointment at not having his 'serious' poetry taken seriously, along with financial troubles and injuries sustained while steeplechasing, eventually led to his suicide. Yet the very same factors made him the inspiration for our most famous writers and are the reason he is revered today as the father of Australian rhymed verse.

Adam Lindsay Gordon was born in the Azores in 1833 while his parents were staying on his grandfather's plantation, probably for the sake of his mother's health. His father was a retired Bengal Cavalry captain who had married his first cousin. The family was an old and famous Scottish one, which had produced many distinguished men.

On their return to England young Gordon was sent to Cheltenham College. He had constant trouble at school and was there for only a year before he was sent to a church school in Gloucestershire.

At the age of fifteen he was sent to the Royal Military Academy, Woolwich, where he was good at sports but undisciplined and not inclined to study. In 1851 his father was asked to withdraw him and, after another spell at Cheltenham College, where, rumour has it, he was finally expelled, he finished his education as a private pupil of the headmaster of the Worcester Royal Grammar School.

Gordon lived with an uncle in Worcester but began to lead a wild and aimless life, contracted debts, and was a great anxiety to his father. He also fell in love with, and proposed to, a young woman at this time, but she refused him. Finally it was decided that he should go to Australia and make a fresh start.

This was a common procedure at the time with 'respectable' families. Sons who got into trouble with debt or women were often shipped off to the colonies and sent money at regular intervals to keep them there. Breaker Morant was another of these 'remittance men'.

Gordon was just over twenty when he arrived at Adelaide in 1853. He immediately obtained a position in the South Australian mounted police and was stationed at Mount Gambier. He was a tall man and handsome in the saddle, but out of the saddle his posture was bad and his eyesight very poor. He was shy, sensitive, and inclined to be moody.

In 1855 he resigned his position and took up horse-breaking in the south-eastern districts of South Australia. An interest in horseracing, which he had developed as a youth in England, continued in Australia. He had developed a reputation for being 'a good steady lad and a splendid horseman'.

His father died in 1857 and his mother about two years later. He received the then massive amount of £7000 from his mother's estate towards the end of 1861. In 1862 he married seventeen-year-old Margaret Park and bought a cottage at Port MacDonnell, near Mount Gambier, where they lived for two years. This cottage, which the poet gave the rather twee and poetic name of 'Dingley Dell', is preserved to this day.

In 1864 Gordon had his first poetry published and also came third in the Border Watch Handicap Steeplechase, the most famous Mount Gambier horse race. The day after, he made his famous leap on his horse, Red Lancer, over a high fence between Leg of Mutton Lake and the Blue Lake. He landed on a small 1.8-metre ledge with a 60-metre drop into the Blue Lake below. An obelisk, erected in 1887, now marks the spot.

In 1865 he was asked to stand for parliament and was elected by three votes to the South Australian House of Assembly. He spoke several times but had no talent for speaking in public and made a poor politician. He resigned his seat in November 1866.

He was earning himself a reputation as a rider over jumps and often won or was placed in local hurdle races and steeplechases. He was also contributing verse to various magazines. Around this time, he bought several properties, including one in Western Australia which he visited in 1867. But he lost money on all his land purchases.

Next he moved to Ballarat in Victoria, where he rented livery stables and set up a general horse business as a dealer and breaker. However, Gordon had no head for business and the venture was a failure. In March 1868 he had a serious accident when a horse smashed his head against a gatepost.

Later that same year he was bankrupted by a fire in his livery stable and, to add to his misery, his infant daughter died just short of her first birthday, and his wife also left him for some time.

In spite of being short-sighted he was becoming very well known as a gentleman rider, and on 10 October 1868 actually won three steeplechase races in one day at the Melbourne Hunt Club meeting at Flemington. He began riding for money but was not fortunate and had more than one serious fall. He sold his business in 1868 and moved to Brighton, in Melbourne.

In Melbourne Gordon succeeded in straightening his financial affairs, made a little money from race riding and became friendly with literary figures of the day such as Marcus Clarke and Henry Kendall.

In March 1870 Gordon again injured his head in a bad fall while riding in a steeplechase at Flemington and he never completely recovered from the accident.

In June 1870 he learnt that his claim to his family's ancestral land in Scotland had been rejected on a legal technicality.

His last book, *Bush Ballads and Galloping Rhymes*, was published on 23 June 1870. Gordon had just asked his publishers what he owed them for printing the book, and had realised that he had no money to pay them and no prospects.

That day he bought a package of cartridges for his rifle and went home to his cottage at Brighton. Next morning he rose early, walked into the scrub at Brighton Beach and shot himself.

Gordon wrote volumes and volumes of 'serious' poetry. All through his short adult life he wrote poetry in the very ornate literary style of the old ballads and the romantic poets. Most of his verse seems tedious and old-fashioned today, but then so does most of Tennyson's poetry.

He was finally recognised as a literary figure of some standing and, in 1934, his bust was placed in Westminster Abbey. He is the only Australian writer to receive that honour, although he was, of course, actually British.

When he is remembered by the Australian public these days it is generally not for his serious poetry or his place in the literary world. Firstly, he is remembered as the poet who originally wrote galloping rhymes, like 'How We Beat the Favourite', and sentimental verses like 'The Sick Stockrider', and who inspired Paterson, Lawson, Morant, Ogilvie and a host of other verse writers. All four poets mentioned said Gordon was their favourite poet and their inspiration, so it is fair to say that Adam Lindsay Gordon is the father of Australian 'bush' verse.

Secondly, many Australians over the years have used a couplet of Gordon's when writing in their friends' autograph and remembrance books, without even knowing it was Adam Lindsay Gordon they were citing. The lines so often quoted are a fragment of a very long poem titled *Ye Weary Wayfarer*:

Life is mostly froth and bubble, two things stand like stone.
Kindness in another's trouble, courage in your own.

Gordon is also remembered for his daring deeds as a horseman and steeplechase jockey and for his rather romantic and tragic life.

HOW WE BEAT THE FAVOURITE

ADAM LINDSAY GORDON

'Aye, squire,' said Stevens, 'they back him at evens;
The race is all over, bar shouting, they say;
The Clown ought to beat her; Dick Neville is sweeter
Than ever—he swears he can win all the way.

'But none can outlast her, and few travel faster,
She strides in her work clean away from *The Drag*;
You hold her and sit her, she couldn't be fitter,
Whenever you hit her she'll spring like a stag.

'And p'rhaps the green jacket, at odds though they back it,
May fall, or there's no telling what may turn up.
The mare is quite ready, sit still and ride steady,
Keep cool; and I think you may just win the Cup.'

Dark brown and tan muzzle, just stripped for the tussle,
Stood *Iseult*, arching her neck to the curb,
A lean head and fiery, strong quarters and wiry,
A loin rather light, but a shoulder superb.

'Keep back on the yellow! Come up on *Othello*!
Hold hard on the chestnut! Turn round on *The Drag*!
Keep back there on *Spartan*! Back you, sir, in tartan!
So, steady there, easy!' And down went the flag.

We started, and Kerr made a strong run on *Mermaid*,
Through furrows that led to the first stake-and-bound,
The Crack, half extended, looked bloodlike and splendid,
Held wide on the right where the headland was sound.

I pulled hard to baffle her rush with the snaffle,
Before her two-thirds of the field got away;
All through the wet pasture where floods of the last year
Still loitered, they clotted my crimson with clay.

The fourth fence, a wattle, floored *Monk* and *Bluebottle*;
The Drag came to grief at the blackthorn and ditch,
The rails toppled over *Redoubt* and *Red Rover*,
The lane stopped *Lycurgus* and *Leicestershire Witch*.

She passed like an arrow *Kildare* and *Cock Sparrow*
And *Mantrap* and *Mermaid* refused the stone wall;
And Giles on *The Greyling* came down at the paling,
And I was left sailing in front of them all.

I took them a burster, nor eased her nor nursed her,
Her dark chest all dappled with flakes of white foam,
Her flanks mud bespattered, a weak rail she shattered,
We landed on turf with our heads turned for home.

We crashed a low binder, and then, close behind her,
The ground to the hoofs of the favourite shook,
His rush roused her mettle, yet ever so little,
She shortened her stride as we raced at the brook.

She rose when I hit her, I saw the stream glitter,
A wide scarlet nostril flashed close to my knee,
Between sky and water *The Clown* came and caught her,
The space that he cleared was a caution to see.

And forcing the running, discarding all cunning,
A length to the front went the rider in green;
A long strip of stubble, and then the quick double,
Two stiff flights of rails with a quickset between.

She came to his quarter, and on still I brought her,
And up to his girth, to his breastplate she drew,
A short prayer from Neville just reached me, 'The Devil!'
He muttered . . . locked level the hurdles we flew.

A hum of hoarse cheering, a dense crowd careering,
All sights seen obscurely, all shouts vaguely heard;
'The green wins!' 'The crimson!' The multitude swims on,
And figures are blended and features are blurred.

'*The Clown* is her master!' 'The green forges past her!'
'*The Clown* will outlast her!' '*The Clown* wins!' '*The Clown*!'
The white railing races with all the white faces,
The chestnut outpaces, outstretches the brown.

On still past the gateway she strains in the straightway,
Still struggles, '*The Clown* by a short neck at most!'
He swerves, the green scourges, the stand rocks and surges,
And flashes, and verges, and flits the white post.

Aye! So ends the tussle, I knew the tan muzzle
Was first, though the ring men were yelling, 'Dead heat!'
A nose I could swear by, but Clarke said, 'The mare by
A short head.' And that's how the favourite was beat.

AINTREE

JIM HAYNES

I was at Aintree in 1984 for the Grand National.

It was my only first-hand experience of the famous English Grand National, a race I'd watched every year from childhood on the newsreels and television, ever since I saw Elizabeth Taylor ride the winner in the movie *National Velvet*, at the old Empire Picture Palace.

Being there is always worth the trip, and the crowd and the excitement of the day itself make such experiences worthwhile, even though you don't see much in a huge crowd at an event like the Grand National or the Melbourne Cup. But at least you can say you've been there.

Here's a strange quirk of memory: I remember the winner of the first steeplechase on the program that day, because I backed it due to its name, Little Bay. It was probably a simple descriptive name, but to me it was the name of a Sydney beach I knew well, and it was my only winner all day.

I watched the Grand National from a position at the top of the straight, just down from the elbow, which really marks the start of the run in, and opposite The Chair. The Chair is the fifteenth of 30 jumps and the tallest and broadest fence on the course, at 5 feet 2 inches. It also has a 6-foot-wide ditch on the take-off side.

You get good value watching a Grand National at Aintree. You actually get to see two very different 'battles down the straight'.

On the first circuit of the 2¼-mile course the horses jump The Chair and the Water Jump in the straight. On the second circuit these two fences are not jumped and the horses take the last fence just before the elbow and then face an almost 500-yard run to the line.

You can't really understand the incredible rush that comes from seeing and hearing a field of 40 horses take a jump like The Chair unless you have experienced it. The sound of the horses landing and galloping on from the fence is unforgettable.

The sense of impending chaos and the absolute craziness of what is being attempted, and the courage of the men and horses attempting it, brings a lump to the throat and an adrenalin rush to the spectator that verges on the primeval.

On the second circuit a bunch of some half-a-dozen horses were still in it as they passed my vantage point. It was a relatively incident-free race in 1984 so there were still many chances on the run in, and that bunch of brave jumpers, still going hard down the straight after 4 miles, was a stirring sight.

The leading bunch fighting it out down the straight included the previous year's winner, Corbiere, and the runner-up from the previous year, and favourite at 9 to 1, Greasepaint.

Greasepaint tired on the run in and was eventually beaten by 4 lengths that day by Hallo Dandy, ridden by Neale Doughty and trained by the great Gordon Richards. Corbiere was third.

Greasepaint was to be unlucky in the Grand National. He started favourite the following year also, and finished a brave fourth behind Last Suspect, Mr Snugfit and Corbiere, who added another third to his win in 1983 and his third in 1984.

Greasepaint was owned by an Irishman named Michael Smurfit and trained by another Irishman named Dermot Weld. I'd never heard of either of them until 1984, and most Aussies hadn't heard of either of them until nine years later, when Vintage Crop, owned and trained by the same two men, won the Melbourne Cup carrying the same colours that Greasepaint carried that winter day at Aintree.

There's really nothing like Aintree on Grand National Day. It's one of those special sporting events like the FA Cup, or the Melbourne Cup, or the Kentucky Derby, or Wimbledon, or the AFL Grand Final: unique events where the actual experience is more important than the result.

OUT OF SIGHT

A.B. 'BANJO' PATERSON

They held a polo meeting at a little country town,
And all the local sportsmen came to win themselves renown.
There came two strangers with a horse, and I am much afraid
They both belonged to what is called the 'take-you-down brigade'.

They said their horse could jump like fun, and asked an amateur
To ride him in the steeplechase, and told him they were sure
The last time round he'd sail away with such a swallow's flight
The rest would never see him go—he'd finish out of sight.

So out he went; and, when folk saw the amateur was up,
Some local genius called the race 'the Dude-in-Danger Cup'.
The horse was known as 'Who's Afraid', by Panic from The Fright
But still his owners told the jock he'd finish out of sight.

And so he did; for Who's Afraid, without the least pretence,
Disposed of him by rushing through the very second fence;
And when they ran the last time round the prophecy was right,
For he was in the ambulance, and safely 'out of sight'.

STEEPLECHASING

A.B. 'BANJO' PATERSON

Of all the ways in which men get a living there is none so hard and so precarious as that of steeplechase riding in Australia. It is bad enough in England, where steeplechases only take place in winter, when the ground is soft, where the horses are properly schooled before being raced, and where most of the obstacles will yield a little if struck and give the horse a chance to blunder over safely.

In Australia the men have to go at racing-speed, on very hard ground, over the most rigid and uncompromising obstacles, ironbark rails clamped into solid posts with bands of iron. No wonder they are always coming to grief, and are always in and out of hospital in splints and bandages. Sometimes one reads that a horse has fallen and the rider has 'escaped with a severe shaking'.

That 'shaking', gentle reader, would lay you or me up for weeks, with a doctor to look after us and a crowd of sympathetic friends calling to know how our poor back was. But the steeplechase rider has to be out and about again, 'riding exercise' every morning, and 'schooling' all sorts of cantankerous brutes over the fences. These men take their lives in their hands and look at grim death between their horses' ears every time they race or 'school'.

The death record among Australian cross-country jockeys and horses is very great; it is a curious instance of how custom sanctifies all things, that such horse-and-man slaughter is accepted in such a callous way. If any theatre gave a show at which men and horses were habitually crippled or killed in full sight of the audience, the manager would be put on his trial for manslaughter.

Our racetracks use up their yearly average of horses and men without attracting remark. One would suppose that the risk being so great the profits were enormous; but they are not. In 'the game' as played on our racecourses there is just a bare living for a good capable horseman while he lasts, with the certainty of an ugly smash if he keeps at it long enough.

And they don't need to keep at it very long. After a few good 'shakings' they begin to take a nip or two to put heart into them before they go out, and after a while they have to increase the dose. At last they cannot ride at all without a regular cargo of alcohol on board, and are either 'half muzzy' or shaky according as they have taken too much or too little.

Then the game becomes suicidal; it is an axiom that as soon as a man begins to funk he begins to fall. The reason is that a rider who has lost his nerve is afraid of his horse making a mistake, and takes a pull, or urges him onward, just at the crucial moment when the horse is rattling up to his fence and judging his distance. That little, nervous pull at his head or that little touch of the spur, takes his attention from the fence, with the result that he makes his spring a foot too far off or a foot too close in, and . . . smash!

The loafers who hang about the big fences rush up to see if the jockey is killed or stunned; if he is, they dispose of any jewellery he may have about him; they have been known almost to tear a finger off in their endeavours to secure a ring. The ambulance clatters up at a canter, the poor rider is pushed in out of sight, and the ladies in the stand say how unlucky they are, that brute of a horse falling after they backed him.

A wolfish-eyed man in the Leger stand shouts to a wolfish-eyed pal, 'Bill, I believe that jock was killed when the chestnut fell,' and Bill replies, 'Yes, damn him, I had five bob on him.' And the rider, gasping like a crushed chicken, is carried into the casualty room and laid on a little stretcher, while outside the window the bookmakers are roaring 'Four to one bar one,' and the racing is going on merrily as ever.

TOMMY CORRIGAN

A.B. 'BANJO' PATERSON

Tommy Corrigan died of his injuries several hours after falling while riding a horse called Waiter in the Caulfield Grand National Steeple on 11 August 1894. He had a remarkable record of 235 wins from 794 rides, including the 1881 Grand National Hurdle, the 1881, 1885 and 1886 Grand National Steeple, the 1882 and 1889 Caulfield Grand National Steeple, and the 1875, 1876, 1879 and 1882 Grand Annual Steeple.

***

You talk of riders on the flat, of nerve and pluck and pace,
Not one in fifty has the nerve to ride a steeplechase.
It's right enough, while horses pull and take their fences strong,
To rush a flier to the front and bring the field along;
But what about the last half-mile, with horses blown and beat,
When every jump means all you know to keep him on his feet.

When any slip means sudden death, with wife and child to keep,
It needs some nerve to draw the whip and flog him at the leap,
But Corrigan would ride them out, by danger undismayed,
He never flinched at fence or wall, he never was afraid;
With easy seat and nerve of steel, light hand and smiling face,
He held the rushing horses back, and made the sluggards race.

He gave the shirkers extra heart, he steadied down the rash,
He rode great clumsy boring brutes, and chanced a fatal smash;
He got the rushing Wymlet home that never jumped at all,
But clambered over every fence and clouted every wall.
You should have heard the cheers, my boys, that shook the members' stand
Whenever Tommy Corrigan weighed out to ride Lone Hand.

They were, indeed, a glorious pair, the great upstanding horse,
The gamest jockey on his back that ever faced a course.
Though weight was big and pace was hot and fences stiff and tall,
'You follow Tommy Corrigan' was passed to one and all.
And every man on Ballarat raised all he could command
To put on Tommy Corrigan when riding old Lone Hand.

But now we'll keep his memory green while horsemen come and go;
We may not see his like again where silks and satins glow.
We'll drink to him in silence, boys, he's followed down the track
Where many a good man went before, but never one came back.
And, let us hope, in that far land where the shades of brave men reign,
The gallant Tommy Corrigan will ride Lone Hand again.

OAKBANK

JIM HAYNES

If it's unique atmosphere you're after, an event where the experience outweighs the result, may I suggest an Easter visit to Oakbank, in the Adelaide Hills, for the Great Eastern Steeplechase.

You won't be lonely if you visit Oakbank at Easter; about 50,000 others usually do the same thing.

Many camp for the entire weekend or longer at various vantage points around the track. Others make the day trip to the track and fill the lovely old stands and lawns of the picturesque course.

This event combines the elements of a rural show, fairground, picnic race day and family camping trip into one glorious weekend of fun. Oh yes, and there are horse races too. In fact, there are several horse races that are a real blast from the past. At Oakbank you get a glimpse of a bygone age when real horses raced over proper fences in the type of races that Adam Lindsay Gordon wrote about and rode in.

Australian steeplechasers are not as valued and followed and well known to the racing public as their English and Irish counterparts, who have the whole winter racing season to themselves. Still, you can't doubt the courage and character of horses that run in a race like the Great Eastern. These are horses to be admired and remembered.

Australian steeplechasers are often tough old stayers, failures and rejects from flat racing with more endurance in their legs than speed. After a few often less-than-memorable seasons racing on the flat, some have the strength, disposition and character to train on for a jumping career. Without this option, these horses would not have a future. Other horses just love to jump and are born to hurdle and steeplechase.

In those states that still stage jumps races in Australia (the southern states of Victoria, Tasmania and South Australia), hurdles and steeplechases are seen by many as a winter sideshow to each race day, with one or two jumping races on each program through the colder, wetter months.

The Great Eastern is no sideshow to a race day, although the centre of the course is itself a sideshow alley with rides, carnival attractions and fairy floss for kids of all ages. The Great Eastern is the centrepiece of the whole weekend, the reason we're all there.

The Von Doussa Steeple on Easter Saturday and the Great Eastern on Easter Monday are classic races of a kind now almost gone from the calendar. The course at Oakbank is so long and undulating that two race-callers are required to view the whole racetrack and call the races using a tag-team system.

Here is a memory of the 1973 event, in which the local hero was a black horse called The Cent and the Victorian interloper was a tough grey horse, almost white in fact, called Mystic Moon. He was trained by Yarra Glen trainer Stan Craddock, whose son John trained Trei Gnaree to win the VRC Grand National seventeen years later.

For most of the crowd it really was a case of black and white that year. South Australians don't take kindly to Victorian 'raiders' and The Cent was favourite both in the ring and in the hearts of the majority.

Mystic Moon had won important races in Victoria and, according to many locals, should have stayed there and won some more instead of spoiling a good weekend for South Australian horses.

Now, the Great Eastern, like the Grand National, is not for the faint-hearted.

Horses in the Great Eastern actually pass the winning post three times in their 5-kilometre trip. So imagine the exhilaration and excitement that gripped the crowd that day in 1973 when the black horse and the grey horse came neck-and-neck down the straight the third time.

The horses jump a fallen log on a rise above the grandstand area and then race down a long sweeping hill to the straight and the winning post.

Over the fallen log they came, the brave grey and the big local jet-black horse.

Down the hill and along the straight they fought side by side. The roar of the crowd was deafening in the shallow valley where the grandstands, lawn and finish are situated. The tiring horses bumped and fought all the way to the post. The roar of the crowd told you The Cent had won before the judge's cursory glance at the photo confirmed the decision, a short neck.

The local horse was welcomed back with rapturous applause and rousing cheers, but the protest flag was soon flying and it took stewards a long time to dismiss the Victorian protest.

As a New South Welshman and a man who has never managed to back a horse that finished a Great Eastern, let alone won one, I was a truly neutral observer. And I must admit I felt rather sorry for the gallant grey that tried so hard so far from home with so few friends.

South Australians are a loyal lot, and they never forgot the big black horse that defeated the Victorian champ. When The Cent died years later they buried him near the winning post at Oakbank, and 50,000 people visit his grave every Easter.

RIO GRANDE

A.B. 'BANJO' PATERSON

Now this was what Macpherson told
While waiting in the stand;
A reckless rider, over-bold,
The only man with hands to hold
The rushing Rio Grande.

He said, 'This day I bid goodbye
To bit and bridle rein,
To ditches deep and fences high,
For I have dreamed a dream, and I
Shall never ride again.

'I dreamed last night I rode this race
That I today must ride,
And cantering down to take my place
I saw full many an old friend's face
Come stealing to my side.

'Dead men on horses long since dead,
They clustered on the track;
The champions of the days long fled,
They moved around with noiseless tread—
Bay, chestnut, brown, and black.

'And one man on a big grey steed
Rode up and waved his hand;
Said he, "We help a friend in need,
And we have come to give a lead
To you and Rio Grande.

'"For you must give the field the slip;
So never draw the rein,
But keep him moving with the whip,
And, if he falter, set your lip
And rouse him up again.

'"But when you reach the big stone wall
Put down your bridle-hand
And let him sail—he cannot fall,
But don't you interfere at all;
You trust old Rio Grande."'

'We started, and in front we showed,
The big horse running free:
Right fearlessly and game he strode,
And by my side those dead men rode
Whom no one else could see.

'As silently as flies a bird,
They rode on either hand;
At every fence I plainly heard
The phantom leader give the word,
"Make room for Rio Grande!"

'I spurred him on to get the lead,
And I chanced full many a fall;
But swifter still each phantom steed
Kept with me, and at racing-speed
We reached the big stone wall.

'And there the phantoms on each side
Drew in and blocked his leap;
"Make room! Make room!" I loudly cried,
But right in front they seemed to ride—
I cursed them in my sleep.

'He never flinched, he faced it game,
He struck it with his chest,
And every stone burst out in flame—
And Rio Grande and I became
Phantoms among the rest.

'And then I woke, and for a space
All nerveless did I seem;
For I have ridden many a race
But never one at such a pace
As in that fearful dream.

'And I am sure as man can be
That out upon the track
Those phantoms that men cannot see
Are waiting now to ride with me;
And I shall not come back.

'For I must ride the dead men's race,
And follow their command;
'Twere worse than death, the foul disgrace
If I should fear to take my place
Today on Rio Grande.'

He mounted, and a jest he threw,
With never sign of gloom;
But all who heard the story knew
That Jack Macpherson, brave and true,
Was going to his doom.

They started, and the big black steed
Came flashing past the stand;
All single-handed in the lead
He strode along at racing-speed,
The mighty Rio Grande.

But on his ribs the whalebone stung—
A madness, sure, it seemed—
And soon it rose on every tongue
That Jack Macpherson rode among
The creatures he had dreamed.

He looked to left, and looked to right,
As though men rode beside;
And Rio Grande, with foam-flecks white,
Raced at his jumps in headlong flight
And cleared them in his stride.

But when they reached the big stone wall,
Down went the bridle-hand,
And loud we heard Macpherson call
'Make room, or half the field will fall!
Make room for Rio Grande!'

'He's down! He's down!' And horse and man
Lay quiet side by side!
No need the pallid face to scan,
We knew with Rio Grande he ran
The race the dead men ride.

Part 9
THE GOLDEN AGE

INTRODUCTION—THE AGE OF GREAT STAYERS

If Australian racing has a 'golden age' most people would say it was either the 1920s, or the 1950s and 1960s. Though some would argue that colonial days were the great age of racing, with horses like The Barb and Carbine and trainers such as John Tait and Etienne de Mestre around.

However, because we all tend to fall into the trap of thinking our time is the best, I have decided to resist the temptation to say that my lifetime was the best era in Aussie racing history. Instead, I will try to remind readers that there were great horses and great times for racing before we were born, in other words, beyond living memory.

The period covered here is really the dawn of what we might call 'modern racing'. If today's racegoers were transported back to Flemington, Doomben, Morphettville or Randwick in 1920, we would find it old-fashioned, sure, but very familiar. A hundred years ago, racing was pretty much as we know it now: the saddlecloths and silks, racing styles and distances, rules and regulations, tote and bookmakers, etc., remain more or less unchanged.

True, in the early days races were started with the horses lined up behind a wire barrier that lifted (starting stalls came in the 1950s), and there were four enclosures for the spectators—the Members, Paddock, Leger and Flat—and every one of them was packed because there was no off-course legal betting. All the same, racing was pretty much as it is today, generally, and it was an age of mighty champions.

So here is the story of that era in our racing history, the age of great stayers that ended with the horse many believe was the greatest of them all.

CHAMPIONS 1901-1921

JIM HAYNES

In the two decades between 1901 and 1921, Australia enjoyed a period of growth and prosperity. The Depression years of the 1890s were merely a memory, we had Federation, the economy was booming and so was racing, and the public had some outstanding horses to follow and admire.

This was a golden age for stayers and the first of the bunch was perhaps the greatest three-year-old in our racing history, a son of Positano foaled in 1903, named Poseidon.

In 1904 the Moses family, from the famous Arrowfield Stud in the Hunter Valley, purchased the Martini-Henry mare Jacinth, with a colt foal at foot, at the dispersal of Neotsfield Stud, also in the Hunter. They paid 400 guineas and decided to sell the colt at the Sydney Easter Yearling Sales of 1905.

The colt, Poseidon, was sold to Sir Hugh Denison for 500 guineas, which looked like a very good result for the Moses family when he managed to win only one race from six starts as a two-year-old. Poseidon's amazing three-year-old season, however, made the 500 guineas look like petty cash.

Poseidon started fourteen times as a three-year-old for eleven wins and three seconds. The wins included the VRC and AJC Derbies and St Legers, the Eclipse Stakes, and the Caulfield and Melbourne Cups. He remains the only horse to ever achieve that sequence of wins.

He returned as a four-year-old to win seven from twelve starts. His weight-for-age victories that year included the AJC Spring Stakes, Cumberland Stakes and AJC Plate, as well as the Eclipse Stakes for a second time, the Melbourne Stakes and the Rawson Stakes.

He carried the 9 st 3 lb (58.5 kg) to become the first horse to ever win consecutive Caulfield Cups; and he finished eleventh, carrying a massive 10 st 3 lb (65 kg), behind Apologue in the Melbourne Cup of 1907.

Poseidon lived to the age of 26 and stood at stud at Eumerella, in Gulgong, New South Wales. He was a moderately successful sire; his son Rascasse won the Queensland Derby and another son, Telecles, won the Moonee Valley Cup.

Following the retirement of Poseidon, great stayers continued to dominate the racing scene as far as public popularity was concerned. Three of the greatest stayers ever bred to race in Australia dominated this era, and they were three very different horses—Trafalgar, Prince Foote and Comedy King.

Of the three, Trafalgar was undoubtedly the most popular, although the other two were more brilliant, more versatile and better-performed overall. Prince Foote was probably the best of the three in terms of sheer talent.

A small bay horse, foaled in 1906 and trained by the master trainer of stayers, Frank McGrath, Prince Foote was the product of all English bloodlines, being by the imported stallion Sir Foote from the imported mare Petrushka, and so had the great 1875 Epsom Derby winner Galopin on both sides of his pedigree. Galopin started eleven times for ten wins and a second, and was the leading sire in Britain in 1888, 1889 and 1898.

As a two-year-old Prince Foote won the AJC Sires' Produce Stakes in what was a moral victory for non-colonially bred horses, but he was considered by many to be too small to be a good stayer. Frank McGrath proved the doubters wrong when the horse took out the AJC and VRC Derbies, both St Legers, the Champion Stakes and the Melbourne Cup as a three-year-old. In that year Prince Foote started eleven times for nine wins.

His greatest victories were in the AJC Derby where he was badly checked twice, fell back through the field, was forced to race wide and went around every other horse to win by a length and a half; and the Melbourne Cup, where he came late and flew past Trafalgar and Alawa to win by 3 lengths.

Owned by the Newcastle coal baron and shipowner, John Brown, Prince Foote was a great success at stud, being the sire of dual Derby winner Richmond Main, Craven Plate winner Prince Viridis, and 1922 Sydney Cup winner Prince Charles. He was also a good sire of broodmares and his daughter, Princess Berry, was the dam of Rosehill Guineas winner, Balloon King.

Trafalgar, foaled the year before Prince Foote, was a son of Wallace, which made him a grandson of the great Carbine. He was a light chestnut with a flaxen mane and tail, so his colouring was identical to the great stayer Peter Pan, who was to grace the racetracks of Australia three decades later.

Trafalgar was a more solid horse than the later champion, and his popularity with the racing public was based as much upon his courage and dour staying ability as it was on his good looks. He started 59 times for 24 wins, eleven seconds and six thirds. His best wins were in the Sydney Cup, the AJC Plate and the Melbourne Stakes. His greatest run came in the Melbourne Cup of 1910, when, carrying 9 st 2 lb (58 kg), he unwound a mighty finish to come from near last and just failed to catch Comedy King, carrying 7 st 8 lb (48 kg). The margin was half a head.

Trafalgar was one of the most loved horses to ever race in Australia. He ran in three consecutive Melbourne Cups carrying huge weights—more than 9 st (57 kg) each time—and finished fourth, second and eleventh, but he was always the crowd favourite. Some idea of his popularity can be gained by looking at the events surrounding the running of the Melbourne Stakes of 1911, three days before Trafalgar's final Melbourne Cup run.

Most punters considered the 10 furlongs of this race far too short for a dour stayer like Trafalgar. His old nemesis, Comedy King, was red-hot favourite at 5 to 4 on, while Trafalgar was unwanted in the ring at 15 to 1. The great stayer was to finish behind Comedy King eight times in his career but that day, when he produced another of his great finishing runs to defeat the imported champion, the Flemington crowd cheered him all the way back to scale—a show of affection rarely seen for a horse that had just defeated an odds-on favourite.

Comedy King went on to win the Melbourne Cup of 1910 and was the first imported horse ever to do so. He was bred at King Edward's stud in 1907 and purchased and imported by the popular Melbourne bookmaker Sol Green as a foal at foot with his dam, Tragedy Queen. His sire, Persimmon, a son of St Simon, started only nine times for seven wins, a second and a third, but those wins included the Epsom Derby, the St Leger, the Eclipse Stakes and the Ascot Gold Cup twice.

Sol Green was born into a poor Jewish family in London and was apprenticed to the royal upholsterer as a lad. When he discovered how little his master made, he decided there had to be more to aim for in life and he set off for Australia at fifteen, travelling fourth class to Melbourne with sixpence in his pocket. He slept in old boilers on the docks and bought and sold anything he could get his hands on. Eventually he became the biggest bookmaker in Victoria and one of Australia's wealthiest men, with massive real estate holdings in Melbourne and rural areas.

Sol Green never forgot his humble origins. He gave enormous amounts of money to charities, established a housing estate for ex-servicemen and a children's playground in South Melbourne, and constantly donated large sums to Melbourne's public hospitals.

Green's popularity was one reason for the public support of his imported champion, Comedy King. The handsome black galloper won the Caulfield Futurity as a three-year-old before going on to win six times from twelve starts at four, including the AJC Spring Stakes and Autumn Stakes in Sydney, and the St George Stakes, Essendon Stakes, All-Aged Stakes and Melbourne Cup in his hometown. He returned at five to win the Eclipse Stakes before finishing a gallant fifth in his second Melbourne Cup, lumping a massive 9 st 7 lb (60.5 kg).

At stud Comedy King continued to make his mark in Australian racing history. He sired two Melbourne Cup winners, King Ingoda and Artilleryman, and many other useful stayers, like the immortal Shadow King who started in six Melbourne Cups for two seconds, two thirds, a fourth and a sixth. His granddaughter Witty Maid was the mother of Comic Court, who won the Melbourne Cup for

Jim Cummings in 1950, and his son Artilleryman was perhaps the best racehorse ever foaled in Australia.

Bred by Sol Green at Shipley Stud in Victoria in 1916, Artilleryman was purchased for 1000 guineas at the stud dispersal sale by well-known grazier and businessman Sir Samuel Horden.

His dam was the well-bred New Zealand mare Cross Battery, who had Carbine's sire Musket and the great imported sire Fisherman on her sire's side and was a great-granddaughter of the unbeaten Melbourne Cup winner Grand Flaneur on her dam side.

Reputed to be the best-looking horse ever to race in Australia, the headstrong brown colt's wins at three years old included the 1919 AJC Derby, Caulfield Guineas, Memsie Stakes, C.B. Fisher Stakes and Melbourne Cup. He dead-heated in the AJC Derby with Richmond Main, a son of his sire's contemporary Prince Foote, and ran second to that colt in the VRC Derby after pulling fiercely throughout the race. In the Melbourne Cup, however, Artilleryman settled the matter of who was the superior racehorse by defeating Richmond Main by 6 lengths at equal weights. He then completed his three-year-old season by taking out the 1920 St George Stakes, Governors' Stakes, King's Plate and St Leger Stakes in Melbourne and the Rawson Stakes in Sydney.

While being spelled, Artilleryman developed a growth on a hind leg and thickening of his veins, but he was still sent out as a 12 to 1 on favourite for the St Leger in Sydney. In a boil-over he ran second to Millieme and then failed in the Sydney Cup and the All-Aged Stakes. It was obvious to vets that the horse had an enormous growth or cancer internally, and this proved to be true when he suddenly haemorrhaged and died in January 1921.

The year after Artilleryman's Melbourne Cup win the great race was won by another popular champion in Poitrel, carrying 10 st (63.5 kg), which places him behind Carbine and Archer as the third-greatest Cup-winning weight carrier. Poitrel was bred and owned by the Moses brothers of Arrowfield Stud, who had sold Poseidon to Sir Hugh Denison. Luckily for the brothers Poitrel failed to reach his reserve at the 1916 Easter Sales and the brothers reluctantly decided to race him themselves. He went on to win seventeen of 37 starts, although his career was blighted by brittle hooves.

Poitrel, foaled in 1914, was sired by St Alwyne, a son of the English champion performer and sire, St Frusquin, who was by St Simon. St Alwyne was imported by the Moses brothers and brought more of the wonderful St Simon blood into Australia.

Poitrel failed in three races as a two-year-old but managed three wins from just five starts at three. It was as a four- and five-year-old that he claimed a unique record in Australasian racing history—when he beat the great New Zealand mare Desert Gold in record time in the Spring Stakes and, in winning the same race again at five, he defeated Gloaming, who jointly held the Australasian record of nineteen consecutive wins with Desert Gold. Poitrel also won the Cumberland Stakes and AJC Plate at four, real staying races.

Poitrel then won a string of weight-for-age races and ran a close second to Kennaquhair in the Sydney Cup with 9 st 9 lb (61 kg) in an Australasian record time for 2 miles of 3 minutes 22.75 seconds. The two horses dead-heated in the AJC Spring Stakes that year, giving Poitrel his third win in that race, and he also won the AJC Plate again before heading for Melbourne for the first time, as a six-year-old, to take on the great Western Australian champion Eurythmic in the Melbourne Stakes and Melbourne Cup.

Eurythmic had arrived in Melbourne from Western Australia and won the Memsie Stakes, October Stakes, Caulfield Stakes and Caulfield Cup, all in a row! He made it five in a row in Victoria, and nine straight wins, in the Melbourne Stakes, with Poitrel finishing third behind Greenstead. Poitrel also finished behind Eurythmic again later, running second to him in the C.B. Fisher Plate. Between the two defeats, however, Poitrel won the one that mattered, outstaying Erasmus, Comedy Queen and Eurythmic to win the Melbourne Cup with 10 st (63.5 kg).

Poitrel's last start was another dead heat for first, this time with John Brown's good stayer Richmond Main, in the Rawson Stakes at Rosehill. At stud Poitrel was a moderate success, the best of his sons being Belgamba, who won three St Legers.

Apart from his great record as a dour stayer, Poitrel is remembered as being the conqueror of three absolute champions of his era—Desert Gold, Gloaming and Eurythmic.

DESERT GOLD—THE KIWI RAIDER

JIM HAYNES

The Melbourne and Sydney spring and autumn racing carnivals had been attracting 'raiders' from New Zealand, as well as the neighbouring colonies or states of Tasmania and Queensland, for decades.

In the 1880s the amazingly versatile Malua had arrived from Tasmania to win not only the Melbourne Cup at 2 miles, but also the Newmarket Handicap at 6 furlongs and the Grand National Hurdle over 3 miles! The great Queenslander Le Grand, winner of thirteen races from 21 starts, raced successfully in Sydney and Melbourne, winning the AJC Derby in 1883 and the VRC Champion Stakes in 1884.

New Zealand horses had been making the trip across the Tasman for many decades, and prizemoney was much better in Australia. New Zealand's rich limestone soil and cooler climate produced great horses, notably stayers. We need look no further than the two greatest of all time, Carbine and Phar Lap, to prove the point. But one of the first Kiwi raiders to storm our shores was a flying filly who won hearts wherever she went.

Desert Gold, the first horse to string together a remarkable nineteen victories in Australasia, was New Zealand bred, owned and trained.

At two she won at her first four starts, in the Great Northern Foal Stakes, Royal Stakes, Manawatu Sires Produce Stakes and the North Island Challenge Stakes, but ran second in the Great Northern Champagne Stakes.

It was her last start as a two-year-old, the Hawke's Bay Stakes of May 1915, which began her amazing sequence of nineteen successive wins. As a three-year-old, Desert Gold won fourteen races and she remained unbeaten until age four, when she came up against a two-year-old named Kilflinn in the North Island Challenge Stakes of April 1917. At three she won the Hawke's Bay Guineas, New Zealand Derby and Oaks, Great Northern Derby, Oaks and St Leger.

When she came to Australia at five she defeated the best Australian horses at weight-for-age. She suffered her first defeat in Australia at the hands of Poitrel in the Spring Stakes over a mile and a half. She won the All-Aged Stakes in Sydney and the St George Stakes in Melbourne and carried top-weight of 9 st 6 lb (60 kg) in the 1918 Melbourne Cup, finishing eighth behind Wakeful's son Night Watch, carrying 6 st 9 lb (42 kg).

Back in New Zealand, when she was a six-year-old, she defeated the three-year-old Gloaming—who was later to equal her record of nineteen straight wins—when he missed the start in the Taranaki Stakes in 1919. However, the two later met four times and each time Gloaming won.

Desert Gold retired to the Okawa Stud, where she had been bred, and her daughters and granddaughters produced many winners, among them the brilliant Gold Rod, a champion sprinter-miler in New Zealand in the 1930s, who also won the Epsom and Doncaster Miles at Randwick in Sydney.

Desert Gold raced through the dark days of World War I and brought some joy into the gloomy war years for New Zealanders and Australians. Her amazing sequence of wins was followed eagerly in the press by two nations for whom anything but war news was a blessed relief.

With an overall record of 36 wins, thirteen seconds and four thirds from 59 starts, Desert Gold's win rate stands at 61 per cent, and her amazing place rate at 90 per cent. Both of these strike rates are very close to those of another legendary New Zealand mare of a later era, Sunline.

While Desert Gold was New Zealand bred, her sire, All Black, was imported from Britain, and her dam, Aurarius, was

Australian bred, being a daughter of the great sire Maltster and a granddaughter of Wallace. This meant that Desert Gold had both Carbine and St Simon on her dam side and Galopin on both sides of her pedigree.

ROAMING WITH GLOAMING

JIM HAYNES

Gloaming took over Desert Gold's mantle as New Zealand's favourite horse, but Australia can claim the honour of having at least bred the champion. He was owned and trained in New Zealand, however, and returned to plunder the rich races in the land of his birth.

Gloaming was bred at the Melton Stud in Victoria in 1915, but his bloodlines were all British—both sire, The Welkin, and dam, Light, were imported. His pedigree is interesting as he was inbred, to the great Galopin, on his sire side, and to no less than three good horses—Sterling, Rosebery and Bend Or—on the dam side.

He was purchased for a mere 230 guineas by New Zealander George Greenwood and shipped over to New Zealand to be trained by Dick Mason. He became shin-sore at two, so he was gelded and turned out. At three he showed enough promise to be shipped back across the Tasman to begin his racing career in the Chelmsford Stakes in Sydney. He won the race by 8 lengths in record time and then won the AJC Derby at his second start.

In a truly remarkable career, Gloaming raced from age three until he was nine—even today that would be outstanding but in the 1920s it was unheard of. He started 67 times, won 57 times and ran second nine times. His only unplaced result came in the North Island Challenge Stakes at three, when he managed to get his head tangled in the starting wires and fell, taking no part in the race. So, it is true to say that Gloaming ran first or second in every race he ever contested.

The accident probably occurred in an attempt to anticipate the rise of the barrier wires. The horse had done the same thing several starts previously in the Taranaki Stakes over 6 furlongs, but had untangled himself and chased down the field to run second. Unfortunately for Gloaming's connections two factors stopped him winning a remarkable victory that day. Firstly the race was over the short sprint distance of 6 furlongs, giving Gloaming little time to catch the field, and secondly he was racing against the great mare Desert Gold, in the twilight of her career, and she held on to win by a neck. Gloaming defeated the great mare on four subsequent occasions.

Gloaming returned to Sydney every year (he reputedly crossed the Tasman fifteen times!) but bled as a five-year-old, became too sick to train at six, and suffered a minor injury in training at eight, so he only raced in Australia at three, four, seven and nine. His record on this side of the Tasman was fourteen starts for nine wins and five seconds, and it took great horses like Poitrel, Heroic and Beauford to deny him more victories. On the occasions when he was fit enough to race in Sydney, he not only won the AJC Derby, Chelmsford Stakes and Hill Stakes, he also won the Craven Stakes three times, defeating his old rival Beauford on the last occasion. He started once only in his birthplace state of Victoria, winning the 1924 Melbourne Stakes, at the age of nine, at his last start in Australia, but he did an exhibition gallop before the Cox Plate and was paraded before the 1924 Melbourne Cup.

The gallant bay gelding began his amazing run of nineteen straight victories with the first of his three Craven Stakes wins in Sydney at age four; the other eighteen wins were all in New Zealand, and the sequence ended when he ran second at his attempt to win a fourth successive Islington Plate at age six. Gloaming was defeated that day by the good young miler Thespian, who broke the race record in winning and was beaten out of a place behind Gloaming at his next start. The nineteen wins were over distances ranging from 4 furlongs to 12 furlongs. Distance didn't mean a lot to Gloaming: he was as effective over a mile and a half as he was over half a mile.

In what would be considered a completely 'upside down' racing career today, he had begun racing at three by winning over 9 furlongs and then at 12 furlongs, and then won twice over 4 furlongs at age five!

It is easy to disparage Gloaming's record by saying that New Zealand racing provided easy pickings for the talented galloper. Perhaps the depth of racing was not great on the 'Shaky Isles' during his career, but the truth is that he had to race against two of the greatest New Zealand gallopers of all time in Desert Gold and The Hawk, as well as good younger horses like Thespian, and great Australian champions like Poitrel and Eurythmic, in what was a golden age of racing.

The Hawk, another legendary New Zealand galloper, started 136 times for a record of 32 wins, eighteen seconds and twenty thirds. He was by the locally bred New Zealand sire Martian from an imported mare, Sparrow Hawk. Ironically, however, Martian carried all-English bloodlines while Sparrow Hawk was a great-granddaughter of New Zealand bred Carbine, as well as the great St Simon.

The Hawk raced until he was thirteen years old and successfully 'raided' the lucrative Australian carnivals as a five- and six-year-old, winning the Hill Stakes, All-Aged Stakes, Futurity Stakes, Lloyd Stakes, Caulfield Stakes, Challenge Stakes and Rawson Stakes, and the St George and Essendon Stakes twice each.

It was in a memorable clash with The Hawk, aged six, in the Ormonde Gold Cup over a mile at Hastings in May 1925, that Gloaming ended his career at the age of nine. The only two other acceptors were scratched, so the two champions were involved in a match race at equal weights, both carrying 9 st 10 lb (62.5 kg).

The Hawk led to the halfway mark and then the two raced head to head until Gloaming pulled away to win by a length. It was his eighth win in succession as a nine-year-old.

Gloaming lived out his days on his owner's property near Canterbury, New Zealand, and was buried there—at a place now called Gloaming's Hill—when he died in 1932. In one of those 'spooky coincidences' his trainer Dick Mason died the following week, and his owner, George Greenwood, several weeks later.

EURYTHMIC—THE BEST FROM THE WEST

JIM HAYNES

While Desert Gold and Gloaming had 'attacked' the rich racing carnivals of Sydney and Melbourne from the east, the great champion Eurythmic made his attack from the west. Many old-timers still believe he is the best horse to ever be trained and owned in Western Australia, although Fred Kearsley, trainer of the great Northerly, would probably disagree.

Eurythmic was bred at the Camyr Allyn Stud at Scone in New South Wales, and purchased as a yearling by Mr Lee-Steere, chairman of the West Australian Turf Club (WATC). His sire was the imported stallion Eudorus, a great-grandson of St Simon, and his dam was the Australian-bred mare Bob Cherry. Bob Cherry was a daughter of Bobadil, the champion three-year-old of his day and a grandson of St Simon. The mare was also a granddaughter of Wallace on her dam side, and had Musket on both sides of her pedigree.

No doubt the presence of St Simon, Musket and Carbine in Eurythmic's pedigree was a big factor in Mr Lee-Steere's decision not only to purchase the horse to race in Western Australia, but also to leave him ungelded. Eurythmic was to prove a remarkable champion, winning 31 of his 47 starts and being placed a further ten times. He also became the first horse to pass the stakes-winning record set by his great-great-grandfather, Carbine.

Sadly, Eurythmic failed to pass on his ability or that of his ancestors when retired to stud. On the racetrack, however, he was a champion of the highest order, being unplaced only six times, two of which were in the Melbourne Cup when he finished a gallant fourth at his first attempt and broke down at his second.

In an odd way Mr Lee-Steere's plan backfired. He purchased the colt to race in his home state of Western Australia. Eurythmic was so good, however, that he ran out of competition in the west and had to be brought back east to fulfil his potential.

Trained by John Kelly, Eurythmic won ten of his fourteen starts in Western Australia, including the WATC Derby, St Leger, Perth Cup and Osborne Stakes. He was then sent back east, to be trained by Jack Holt in Melbourne.

Little attention was paid to the horse at first by Melbourne racing men, who considered Western Australian racing well below par. Eurythmic slipped under the radar and won the Memsie Stakes at 20 to 1. By the time he had easily won the October Stakes and Caulfield Stakes, however, it was a different matter and he was sent out as the shortest-priced favourite ever, at 6 to 4, to win the Caulfield Cup. He then won the Melbourne Stakes before finishing fourth in the Melbourne Cup, behind Poitrel.

Eurythmic then won eight races in a row, starting with the C.B. Fisher Plate, in which he defeated Melbourne Cup winner Poitrel. His wins in Sydney included the Autumn Stakes, Cumberland Stakes and Sydney Cup, carrying a massive 9 st 8 lb (61 kg), and his champion status was confirmed when the VRC handicapper gave him 10 st 5 lb (66.5 kg) for the 1921 Melbourne Cup. This was the same weight carried to victory in 1890 by his illustrious forebear, the mighty Carbine.

Eurythmic's victories since coming east had been so emphatic and impressive that he was sent out as 5 to 1 favourite for the Cup, despite having to equal a weight-carrying record to win the big race.

In racing there are days when your luck simply runs out, and it is doubly unfortunate if that day happens to be Melbourne Cup Day, as it was for the horse many called 'the best from the West'.

Eurythmic's troubles began at the start when a strand of wire from the starting barrier caught his mouth, causing him to miss the start. Even so, he was galloping well and cruising into the race at the half-mile mark when he suffered severe interference, causing him to pull a muscle in his pastern. The champion limped home in last place as the three-year-old filly, Sister Olive, whose only other win had been as a two-year-old, led the field home to become only the fourth of her sex to win the mighty race in its 60-year history.

Eurythmic's jockey, W. McLachlan, always swore the horse would have won that day. When the interference occurred McLachlan said that Eurythmic was 'only cantering, and could have gone to the front at any time'.

While this claim can be dismissed as mere speculation, there is no doubting Eurythmic's ability to carry weight and to stay. His win in the Sydney Cup is regarded as his greatest ever achievement, and he returned to racing in the autumn of 1922 and carried a massive 10 st 7 lb (67 kg) to victory in the Futurity Stakes. So who is to say that he might not have equalled Carbine's record that Melbourne Cup day, had his luck not run out?

Eurythmic's record speaks for itself. He won quality races against great horses, including the Caulfield Stakes three years in a row, before retiring to stud aged six. He was, indeed, 'the best from the west'.

HEROIC—THE EQUINE HEADLINE

JIM HAYNES

The mid-1920s was an age of champions. Great horses like Gloaming, Windbag, Spearfelt, The Hawk and Manfred racing over distance, as well as good horses like Lilypond, Pilliewinkle, Purser and the tough old stayer David.

These last two horses were part of the supporting cast in the curtain-raiser to this great era. It began at the Sydney Autumn Carnival, Easter 1923, the day that David won the Sydney Cup.

The final race that day was the Highweight Handicap and one of the runners was the Melbourne horse Purser. The well-named gelding, by Sea Prince out of Paper Money, had won the Moonee Valley Cup and the Warrnambool Cup and had twice been placed in the Caulfield Cup. His chances at Randwick that day, however, seemed rather forlorn. In a field of 29 runners he had to carry the huge top-weight of 11 st 3 lb (71 kg), his best days appeared to be behind him and he had not won a race for more than six months.

His trainer, Cecil Godby, and his big-betting owner, Jack Corteen, knew better and the betting ring was hammered in a well-planned coup as Purser was backed in from 20 to 1 to 5 to 1 within seconds of betting opening on the race. He won by a length and a half.

The Easter Yearling Sales began the following day at Inglis Saleyards and the money won by Corteen the previous day was used to purchase a chestnut colt from the second crop of the imported stallion Valais, out of imported mare Chersonese.

Valais raced only seven times for a win in the Windsor Stakes and two placings in top-class races in England, but he carried the blood of Bend Or on both sides of his pedigree. The Bend Or bloodline was the most popular and successful in the world at that time, producing stallions which topped the sires lists in Britain, France, the USA and Australia. In fact, there was so much of the bloodline available in Britain that the Moses brothers, of Arrowfield Stud, had been able to purchase Valais for 2000 guineas after he had stood for one season in England. They also purchased Chersonese, who had the Bend Or bloodline through her grandsire Cyllene, who was also the grandsire of Valais.

This close in-breeding to Bend Or produced the colt that Corteen and Godby were so keen to purchase. They were cashed up and kept bidding until the colt was knocked down to them for 1800 guineas, the highest price paid at the sale. They named him Heroic.

Few horses in turf history have had a more sensational career than Heroic. The powerful chestnut was rarely out of the headlines for all the wrong reasons.

A docile animal at home, he was a barrier rogue with shocking manners on the racetrack. At two years of age he overcame a nasty eye infection which almost ended his career before it began by threatening to permanently blind him. The problem was solved by veterinary persistence and he won the Breeder's Plate easily at his first start and, in spite of his shocking performances at the barrier, won six of ten starts to establish a new stakes-winning record for a two-year-old in Australia. In doing so Heroic humped weights that are unimaginable for a two-year-old today. In carrying 10 st 2 lb (64.5 kg) to victory in the Alma Stakes at Caulfield, he set a weight-carrying record for a two-year-old, which was not broken until 1954. He finished off 1924—his first season—by winning the AJC Champagne Stakes carrying 9 st 6 lb (60 kg).

Heroic began his three-year-old season in Sydney in typical fashion by putting on a shocking display at the barrier and pulling throughout the race to run ninth, as favourite, in the Warwick Stakes.

As a Melbourne horse he was soundly booed and jeered that day by Sydney punters. A week later, however, many of those same racegoers happily cheered him, as the 'local horse', when he defeated the New Zealand champion Gloaming over 9 furlongs in the Chelmsford Stakes at Randwick.

Gloaming had been beating Australia's best for years and the parochial Aussie racegoers took Heroic to their hearts immediately when he broke the race record in defeating the New Zealand owned and trained champion.

Heroic's finest moment and one of his worst displays of bad manners occurred in the same race, the AJC Derby of 1924. The Derby was then run in the spring and Heroic started raging favourite at 10 to 9. The only two others considered to have any hope were the great stayer Spearfelt and the Rosehill Guineas winner with the delightfully politically incorrect name of Nigger Minstrel.

As Sydney racegoers know, the Derby starts in the straight at Randwick, where the Leger enclosure, now long gone, was once filled with massive, noisy crowds. In 1924 the crowd was huge and it upset Heroic, who bucked and kicked as his long-suffering jockey, Hughie Cairns, attempted to get him into line behind the barrier wires.

When the barrier went up Heroic buckjumped and headed to the outside fence. Cairns attempted to straighten him and take him to the inside rail, but the strong-willed chestnut kept running out. The result was that the field raced away around the first turn as the Derby favourite zigzagged down the famous Randwick straight in a display more reminiscent of a Keystone Cops comedy sequence than a classic thoroughbred race.

In an oddly run race the field travelled at snail's pace behind a runaway leader, Sir Dighlock. Heroic, many lengths last at the mile, was able to sustain a huge run into second place at the half-mile, 20 lengths behind the tearaway leader.

The famous rise at the top of the Randwick straight took care of Sir Dighlock, who quickly compounded when Heroic raced past him. The two other fancied runners then attacked the champion chestnut, who gallantly held them off to win by a head from Nigger Minstrel, with Spearfelt another head away in third place.

Heroic was then rushed home to Melbourne for a crack at the VRC Derby and, only a week after his truly heroic victory in the AJC Derby, started favourite at 6 to 4 on a bog track in the Caulfield Guineas.

Once again the barrier rogue put on a display of bad manners, digging in his hooves and refusing to go into line until the clerk of the course cracked a stockwhip at his rump. He dwelt at the start when the barrier went up, but raced around the field to win the mile race by 3 lengths being eased up.

Heroic once again made the headlines when he was barred from running in the VRC Derby of 1924.

His owner, Jack Corteen, raced all his other horses in partnership with another owner George Tye. The two owners had combined their resources and stables and had all their horses trained by Cecil Godby at his private training establishment at Alandale, out of Melbourne.

After the great betting plunge that enabled Corteen to buy Heroic at a record price, the old stayer Purser had revitalised his career to win the AJC Winter Stakes in 1923 and the All-Aged Stakes in 1924. He then returned to Melbourne and was entered for the Caulfield Cup, along with another very good horse owned by Corteen–Tye, named The Monk.

It was given out that The Monk would run in the Caulfield Cup and Purser, an eight-year-old who had been given 9 st 5 lb (59.5 kg) for the race, would not. Purser ran very poorly in the Coongy Handicap. Although Hughie Cairns claimed he had been hit in the face by a clod, the horse only plodded in to finish eleventh, and he would have to set a weight-carrying record to win the Caulfield Cup.

Both horses were accepted for the Caulfield Cup, however, and it wasn't until after 2 p.m. on race day that The Monk was a late scratching and Purser, to be ridden by Gloaming's regular jockey George Young, was sensationally backed in from 50 to 1 to 15 to 1. The old horse, who carried St Simon blood close up on both sides of his pedigree, was up to the task and won easily, setting a new weight-carrying record for the famous 1½-mile race.

A hostile demonstration after the race was followed by an inquiry the following week and the shock announcement that owners Tye and Corteen, trainer Godby and jockey Cairns, who had ridden Purser in the Coongy but not in the Caulfield Cup, were all banned from racing for a year.

This meant that all horses owned by Tye and Corteen were also banned. Heroic, the VRC Derby favourite, was thus unable to start in the Derby or the Melbourne Cup and bookmakers pocketed many, many thousands of pounds.

More sensations were to follow. Appeals were heard and dismissed, Heroic was spelled, and then sold to Corteen's good friend Martin Wenke for 14,000 guineas. The VRC questioned both men and refused to accept that the sale was legitimate, and Heroic was then sold at a public auction and knocked down for the record price of 16,000 guineas.

Heroic was purchased by a colourful character in Charles Kellow, a well-known former champion cyclist who had made his fortune selling those new-fangled motorcars in the first two decades of the century and performing entrepreneurial stunts such as delivering newspapers to country towns by motorcar during the rail strike of 1903, and setting a record in 1908 for driving from Melbourne to Sydney (25 hours and 40 minutes!).

No horse in Australian history made as many headlines as Heroic—at least headlines that didn't concern racing results—and every move in the saga was reported in the press and devoured eagerly by his adoring public.

Kellow sent Heroic to Jack Holt to be trained and the task must have aged the great trainer considerably. The horse won only three of his first fifteen starts for Holt and his barrier manners became even worse than before. At the Randwick Autumn Carnival of 1925 he won the Autumn Stakes, and four days later was entered in two classic races on the same day, the All-Aged Stakes over a mile and the Cumberland Stakes over 14 furlongs. The record books show him as 'unplaced' in both races, but the truth is that he simply refused to start both times and took no part in either race!

Heroic won the Memsie Stakes and Caulfield Stakes in 1925 but was as erratic as ever, placing and finishing unplaced all through the spring. At wit's end with the erratic champion, Jack

Holt proposed a daring plan to Kellow. He would train Heroic to sprint and attempt to win the 1926 Newmarket Handicap with the wayward champion.

Holt's friend, rival trainer James Scobie, had the good New Zealand stayer Pilliewinkle, and the two men wanted to try for the Newmarket–Australian Cup double with their two horses.

Kellow agreed—he needed to recoup many thousands lost on Heroic through the spring—and the plan was put into action. Holt's stable jockey, Billy Duncan, had had enough and was happy to step aside and allow Heroic's former jockey, Hughie Cairns, who had served out his one-year riding ban, to take charge of the horse again.

For once Heroic jumped away with the field and charged home to win the classic sprint, his only win in eleven starts between October 1925 and April 1926. Pilliewinkle fulfilled his part of the deal by winning the Australian Cup, and Kellow recouped huge amounts to restore his bank balance.

Back in Sydney, for the autumn of 1926, Heroic decided he would start in the Cumberland Stakes that year and duly won the race, but failed carrying 9 st 7 lb (60.5 kg) in the Sydney Cup, as he did the following year carrying even more, a hefty 10 st (63.5 kg).

Heroic showed his true class when he went on a winning spree at the Victorian Spring Carnival of 1926, taking out six races in a row: the Underwood and Memsie Stakes, the Cox Plate, and the William Reid, C.F. Orr and St George Stakes.

Two weeks after his St George Stakes win he was unplaced attempting to win the Newmarket sprint for a second time, carrying a whopping 10 st 2 lb (64.5 kg).

Heroic's final victory saw him win at 2 miles for the first time in his career, in the Governor's Plate at Flemington in March 1927. After four unplaced runs at the Sydney Autumn Carnival he was retired, aged five, to start his career at stud in the spring of 1927.

More sensations were to follow as Heroic went on to be the nation's leading sire for four consecutive seasons. From nine crops he sired 184 winners of 964 races. Among his progeny were the mighty Ajax and Melbourne Cup winner Hall Mark.

Another sensation followed when the champion sire suddenly became impotent after nine seasons of great results at stud. Nothing could solve the problem and Heroic lived on for another six years until his wayward behaviour finally took its toll. A bolt of lightning in a sudden storm caused the old horse to gallop wildly across the paddock and slip over on the wet grass in December 1939. He broke a leg and was put down at the age of eighteen. His record of 21 wins, eleven seconds and four thirds is no real indication of the erratic champion's true ability.

THE GOLDEN AGE: 1924-1926

JIM HAYNES

In the history of Australian racing there has probably never been such a golden age as that which occurred in the mid-1920s.

Heroic, The Hawk and Gloaming were all racing and winning major races, and four other great champions in Spearfelt, Windbag, Manfred and Amounis joined them during this time.

Spearfelt was a small horse who was bred in the Goulburn Valley in Victoria in 1921 but raised at Widden Stud in New South Wales after his mother died while being transported there with her foal at foot. He may well be the only bottle-raised horse to win the Melbourne Cup, and the little champ-to-be was purchased cheaply, for a mere 120 guineas, by Mr D.C. Grant, who was looking for a cheap colt with Carbine bloodlines to be trained by his friend, Melbourne trainer Vin O'Neill.

Spearfelt was a grandson of Spearmint, an Epsom Derby winner and son of Carbine. He won five races at two, then took the VRC Derby before starting favourite in the Melbourne Cup of 1924. The little colt ran into interference and finished an unlucky third behind Backwood.

The following year he won the VRC St Leger and the King's Plate, but fell heavily in the Sydney Cup and then contracted pneumonia. He was still not fully recovered and was racing below his best when he ran mid-field in the Melbourne Cup that year behind Windbag.

He was fully recovered by the spring of 1926 and won the AJC Spring Stakes before finishing third behind Manfred in the Melbourne Stakes.

Trainer Vin O'Neill thought Spearfelt was poorly ridden in the Melbourne Stakes and replaced jockey George Young with Hughie Grant for the Melbourne Cup three days later. Manfred pulled up sore after his Melbourne Stakes victory and was scratched from the Cup, which Spearfelt won, equalling Windbag's record time of the year before, 3 minutes 22.75 seconds.

The record crowd of 118,877 at the Cup that year remained an Australian record for a sporting event for 43 years, until broken by the Carlton–Essendon Grand Final crowd in 1968.

Spearfelt's career was blighted by sickness and injury and he won only nine races, but he was a brilliant champion. He was also a success at stud, counting many good horses among his progeny, including the 1943 Melbourne Cup winner Dark Felt.

***

Windbag was bred at the famous Kia Ora Stud in New South Wales in 1921 by Percy Miller and was by the imported English stallion Magpie, who would go on to be Australian Champion Sire in 1928–29. His dam was the New Zealand mare Charleville, a granddaughter of St Simon, which meant that St Simon was on both sides of Windbag's family, as Magpie was St Simon's great-grandson.

Windbag was a 'bad walker' and was famously knocked down at the Inglis Yearling Sales to agent Ian Duncan for 160 guineas. Duncan then decided he couldn't take the horse due to his poor gait and Clive Inglis graciously cancelled the sale and convinced the breeder's brother, Robert Miller, to race him.

From this embarrassing start Windbag became the Sydney champion horse of his day, winning eighteen races in his career and a Melbourne Cup.

In fact, he had a very unusual Melbourne Cup preparation. He started racing in July 1925, winning over 6 furlongs at Randwick, and stayed in training right through the winter and spring, taking the Spring Stakes, Craven Plate and Randwick Plate at the Sydney Spring Carnival before heading to Melbourne, where he ran third behind Pilliewinkle in the Melbourne Stakes before winning the Melbourne Cup.

The 1925 Melbourne Cup was history-making as it was the first to be broadcast on radio, by the ABC. Manfred led for most of the race and the pace was hot, but Windbag outstayed his younger rival to win by half a length in record time with Pilliewinkle, the Australian Cup and Melbourne Stakes winner, a close third. Spearfelt also raced in the Cup that year, but was not well and finished well back.

Windbag didn't sire a Melbourne Cup winner, but he did sire many good horses including Chatham, the outstanding miler who won two W.S. Cox Plates in the 1930s.

Although Windbag, the older, tougher stayer, beat the three-year-old Manfred in the 1925 Cup, the younger horse was a strong-minded individual whose effort to win the AJC Derby in 1925 eclipsed Heroic's effort of the previous year.

Manfred shared a few things in common with Heroic. Both were sired by Valais, both were notorious barrier rogues, and both put up unbelievable efforts to win the AJC Derby.

In the AJC Derby of 1925 Manfred, who had won the Champagne Stakes at two, refused to start until the clerk of the course rode at him with his whip. He finally set off, seven seconds after the barrier had risen, and trailed the field by a good half furlong before settling for jockey Billy Duncan, who did not attempt to fight the horse but allowed him to settle at his own pace. He caught the field at the mile and raced level with Frank McGrath's champion Amounis before racing clear at the top of the straight to win easily.

Manfred also counted the Cox Plate, VRC Derby, Caulfield Cup, Caulfield Stakes, Melbourne Stakes and October Stakes in his tally of eleven career wins—an impressive resume.

Manfred had Bend Or on both sides of his bloodline, and his dam was a great-granddaughter of St Simon via his brilliant son Persimmon. He was a great success at stud and sired many winning horses, including The Trump, who completed the Caulfield Cup–Melbourne Cup double in 1937.

***

Amounis was an unlucky horse in some ways; he ran into Manfred at his best and later Nightmarch and then the mighty Phar Lap. Yet Amounis had the distinction of beating Phar Lap in the VATC St George Stakes of 1930, when Phar Lap was three and Amounis was seven. He also stopped Phar Lap's great winning streak of 24 victories by defeating the 'Red Terror' by a head in the Warwick Stakes of 1930. He was the only horse to beat Phar Lap twice.

Like Windbag, Amounis was bred by Percy Miller at Kia Ora and was by Magpie. His dam, Loved One, was a great-granddaughter of St Simon, giving Amounis the familiar champion's bloodlines of 'St Simon on both sides'.

In Sydney Amounis won two Epsom Handicaps, a Rosehill Guineas, Chipping Norton Stakes, All-Aged Stakes, Craven Plate and Warwick Stakes and, in Melbourne, three Linlithgow Stakes, two Essendon Stakes and two Cantala Stakes, as well as a Cox Plate, and the Futurity and St George Stakes. He then won the Caulfield Stakes and the Caulfield Cup at eight. In fact, Amounis has the distinction of having won at least one race that would today be a Group 1 event in every year of his career from age three to age eight.

With a record of 33 wins, eleven seconds and eight thirds from 79 starts, Amounis was the 'iron gelding' of his era.

AUSTRALIA'S FAVOURITE HORSE

JIM HAYNES

Phar Lap's spectacular career has been continually documented and mythologised in books and films for 80 years, and his tragic end has been analysed and debated again and again.

In spite of his iconic status, it would be hard to imagine any champion whose career had less auspicious beginnings than the 'Red Terror'.

Both his sire and dam were failures on the track and, in breeding terms, both were outcasts, unwanted even by breeders of mediocre racehorses at the poorer end of the racing game.

In researching the breeding history of Phar Lap's sire Night Raid, his dam Entreaty and granddam Prayer Wheel, the phrase I came across most frequently was 'got rid of'.

Night Raid was bred in England but was not a well-conformed horse when young and, although he was well bred, his breeder 'got rid of' him for a mere 100 guineas as a yearling. He was trained by a good trainer named Tom Hogg but only ever ran third in a poor-class 'selling' race, so Hogg 'got rid of' him to Australia, where he was trained in Sydney by Peter Keith and managed one win in a restricted race at Randwick, and even that was a dead heat.

Keith then 'got rid of' him to breeder Paddy Wade, who stood him at stud in Wagga Wagga, New South Wales, but the horse could not even attract mares from local owners, so Wade decided to 'get rid of' him to New Zealand breeder A.F. Roberts and sold him for half what he had paid for him.

Phar Lap's dam, Entreaty, had an even worse history. Her dam Prayer Wheel was a failure on the track and a failure at stud and was culled from the breeding stock of Trelawney Park, aged fifteen, and sold for 20 guineas. It was not even known if she was in foal at the time, but she was, to the imported stallion Winkie.

Prayer Wheel was sold again before giving birth to a black filly. Named Entreaty, the filly was put into training but damaged a shoulder and raced once only, at five, and performed poorly. She was left in the paddock and forgotten by her owners until they heard that Roberts was looking for second-rate mares to be served by outcast stallion Night Raid, so they promptly 'got rid of' her to Roberts for 60 guineas. Phar Lap, born in 1926, was her first foal, from Night Raid's second crop.

More than anything, Phar Lap's success demonstrates the importance of being able to see potential in bloodlines and ignore racetrack results and preconceptions.

Harry Telford had the ability to do just that—and he didn't have the budget to do much else!

If we ignore results and look at breeding we see, as Telford did, that Night Raid was a grandson of both Bend Or and Spearmint and had Galopin blood on both sides and St Simon and Carbine (and thus Musket) blood. Prayer Wheel had Musket blood on her dam side and Entreaty had St Simon and Galopin blood via her sire. It was a potent mix.

Telford was a battler, a Sydney trainer who was born in Ballarat but grew up in New Zealand. He was obsessed by bloodlines and spotted the chestnut colt—lot 41 in the catalogue for the 1928 Trentham Sales—and implored his brother in New Zealand to buy the colt 'if he was sound'. His 'limit' was a paltry 200 guineas.

Telford's main problem was that he didn't even have the 200 guineas to back his judgement and had to convince one of the owners he worked for to pay for the horse.

The owner Telford decided to 'convince' was David Davis, who ran a successful import business in Sydney. Davis was born in Russia into a Jewish family who emigrated to the USA and was a US citizen, which partly explains the decision to race Phar Lap in the States five years later.

Davis agreed to fund the purchase and Telford's brother Hugh was in the sale ring at Trentham when the last lot of the day, lot 41, was led in. Hugh was not quite alone; one other bidder was present, but he was acting as agent for a buyer who had gone home and was unsure about his limit, so the colt was knocked down to Hugh Telford for 160 guineas on a day when 2300 guineas had been paid for a previous lot and prices on average were between 1000 and 2000 guineas.

Not only were Phar Lap's immediate family poorly performed, the colt himself was gangly and ungainly, well over 16 hands as a yearling (big even by today's standards) and a slow developer.

On the journey across to Sydney on board the *Wanganella*, Phar Lap became seasick and did not eat; he also broke out in pimples, which covered his face. He arrived looking more like a cartoon horse than a racehorse.

David Davis was so unimpressed on seeing the horse he had been cajoled into buying that he refused to pay for his training. Once again Harry Telford backed his own judgement and arranged to lease the horse for three years, cover all costs and pay Davis one-third of all prizemoney. An Asian friend of Telford's evidently suggested the Thai word 'farlap' meaning lightning flash, perhaps a reference to the colt's glossy deep chestnut coat when he had recovered his health. The superstitious Telford, with November glory in his mind even then, wanted a seven-letter, two-word name as these had a good Melbourne Cup-winning record. So, the horse became Phar Lap.

Phar Lap was disinterested and lazy on the track and kept growing until he stood at 17 hands, so Telford had him gelded. Even so he ran poorly at eight of his first nine starts as a late two-year-old and early three-year-old. He did show a glimpse of what was to come by winning a Juvenile Maiden at Rosehill at his fifth start, after finishing last at his previous.

He then finished second in the Chelmsford Stakes and went on the first of his great winning jaunts, taking the Rosehill Guineas, AJC Derby, Craven Plate and VRC Derby before being sent out at even money favourite for the Melbourne Cup.

Phar Lap had run the same time for both Derbies and broke Manfred's record by a quarter of a second. In the Cup, with only 7 st 6 lb (47 kg), he had to be ridden by lightweight jockey Bobby Lewis.

It is often mistakenly stated that Lewis took the mount from Phar Lap's 'regular jockey' Jim Pike, who could not make the weight. The truth is that the colt had been ridden in his first fourteen races by eight different jockeys, although Pike had ridden him in both Derbies and would become his regular jockey, riding him at every one of his sixteen starts as a four-year-old—for fourteen wins. Pike rode the great chestnut 30 times in total, for 27 wins and two seconds.

The 'Red Terror' could really be a terror to ride and he refused to settle for Lewis in the 1929 Cup. The jockey said later he just could not get the horse's head down or stop him reefing and pulling and so reluctantly he let him lead, only to be run down and finish third behind Nightmarch and Pacquito.

Nightmarch, the first good horse to be sired by Phar Lap's sire, was from the 'outcast' stallion's first crop and was a year older than Phar Lap.

The Phar Lap bubble had burst: the 'wonder horse' seemed to be just another 'good 'un', especially when he was beaten into third again, behind Amounis, on his return to racing in the St George Stakes in the autumn.

The spring of his three-year-old season would prove to be a mere aperitif to Phar Lap's career on the racetrack. In the eighteen-month period starting from March 1930, and ending with his eighth placing, carrying 10 st 10 lb (68 kg), in the Melbourne Cup of 1931, the 'wonder horse' started 32 times for 30 wins and two seconds, winning every major race in Sydney and Melbourne from a mile to 2 miles.

Those wins included the W.S. Cox Plate twice, two more Craven Plates to add to the one he won at three, the Melbourne Cup with ridiculous ease, carrying 9 st 12 lb (62.5 kg), and all the other classic races of the spring and autumn carnivals in both cities.

The great horse won weight-for-age races by 20 lengths and broke the existing records for all distances between 1½ miles and 2 miles.

He started at prices like 14 to 1 on, and it is common knowledge that he remains the shortest-priced horse to win the Melbourne Cup, and the only ever odds-on winner. What some racegoers may not know is that he actually shut down the betting ring on no less than twelve occasions, when no bookmakers would take bets on the races he won. He also travelled to Adelaide and won two classic races there.

Jim Pike always said his greatest victory was when he took on the sprinters and beat them in the Futurity Stakes at Caulfield. On a bog track carrying 10 st 2 lb (64.5 kg), the big-hearted champion missed the start and then took off around the entire field to run down the good sprinter Mystic Peak.

Drama and sensation were part of Phar Lap's career. He was shot at before winning the 1930 Melbourne Stakes and then hidden away at St Albans Stud near Geelong before winning the Cup three days later. He almost emulated the greats of former eras, like his ancestor Carbine, by winning four major races over eight days, three major races in a week and four major races in a month several times.

Phar Lap could probably have also won the Caulfield Cup of 1930, and the fact that he was left in the field and scratched quite late was controversial at the time. It was, indeed, part of a cunning plan.

Nothing outside the rules of racing took place, but some consider the actions of Telford and fellow Sydney trainer Frank McGrath rather sneaky, while other racing men say it was a stroke of genius.

The plot revolved around three great horses: Phar Lap, Amounis and Nightmarch.

Nightmarch had defeated Phar Lap in the Melbourne Cup of 1929 but, the following spring, Nightmarch was defeated four times in a row by Phar Lap. Nightmarch's owner, Mr A. Louisson, had been heard to say that he would take the horse back to New Zealand for the New Zealand Cup if Phar Lap contested the Caulfield Cup.

In a conversation with Telford, Frank McGrath suggested that his great stayer Amounis, the only horse to defeat Phar Lap twice, would win the Caulfield Cup if Nightmarch and Phar Lap didn't start. He suggested that Telford leave Phar Lap in the Caulfield Cup field until Louisson took his horse home. In that time they could get very lucrative odds about their two horses winning the Caulfield–Melbourne Cups double.

The plan worked perfectly. Seeing that Phar Lap was set to contest the Caulfield Cup, Louisson took Nightmarch home and he duly won the New Zealand Cup. Then Telford scratched Phar Lap, stating that he didn't want to over-race the horse, and Amounis won the Caulfield Cup. Phar Lap, of course, famously and easily won the second leg and the two trainers sent a battalion of bookies near bankrupt.

Both Davis and Telford have been accused of over-racing their champion and Davis has been criticised for starting Phar Lap, against Telford's wishes, in the Melbourne Cup of 1931, with the cruel weight of 10 st 10 lb (68 kg), and for taking the horse to America.

Davis, however, seems in retrospect to have been a fair-minded man. He was grateful to Telford for finding the horse and allowed him to remain as part-owner for a modest £4000 when the lease expired. It was also Davis who had Phar Lap's skin, heart and skeleton returned to Australasia after his tragic death.

It is also worth remembering that Telford had already won a Melbourne Cup with Phar Lap carrying his colours while under lease, while Davis had not had that honour.

Myths develop quickly in racing as in other fields of dreams and the truth is often forgotten when fiction and films are created from fact. Telford has been criticised for leaving young Tommy Woodcock in charge of the valuable champion in the USA, but the fact is that Telford's daughter had just died and he was organising her funeral. It is also true that a team of four, which included jockey Bill Elliott and vet Bill Nielsen, travelled to the USA with Woodcock and Phar Lap. David Davis was also in the USA managing the campaign. So the horse's assault on the US was meticulously planned.

It is a mark of Phar Lap's ability that the VRC changed the weight-for-age rules in 1931 to include allowances and penalties, in an attempt to bring the extraordinary horse 'back to the field'. They also gave him a massive 22 pounds (10 kg) over weight-for-age in the 1931 Cup.

Further testament to Phar Lap's greatness are the sensation he caused in the USA and the ease of his win in the invitational Agua Caliente Handicap, in Tijuana Mexico, at his first start on dirt after a long sea journey and an 800-mile road trip. He was also recovering from a bad stone bruise to a heel and raced in bar plates for the first time—and broke the track record. That win, his only start outside the relatively minor racing arena of Australia, made him the third-greatest stakes-winning racehorse of all time, in the world.

Phar Lap's tragic death and the theories surrounding it have been well documented, as well as becoming entrenched in racing folklore. The nation mourned and the autopsy showed a severe gastric inflammation from duodenitis-proximal jejunitis, a condition exacerbated by stress.

Later studies, as recently as 2008, showed the presence of arsenic in large quantities, which has led to all sorts of theories, ranging from Percy Sykes's statement that all horses at that time had arsenic in their systems, to theories of deliberate poisoning. Phar Lap had evidently been fed foliage cut down after being sprayed with arsenic-based insecticide.

Two things seem certain: the well-documented symptoms the horse suffered are totally consistent with duodenitis-proximal jejunitis, and there was a lot of arsenic in his system. The rest is conjecture.

Phar Lap was such a towering figure that the history of thoroughbred racing in Australia is divided into 'before' and 'after' Phar Lap. All champions since him have only ever been 'the best since Phar Lap'. So it's entirely appropriate that this summary of our early champions and crowd favourites ends with him.

Comparing horses of different eras is silly, but people keep doing it. The exercise was described as 'folly' by the US *Blood-Horse Magazine*, which nevertheless, in 1999, ranked the top 100 horses ever to race in America. The panel placed Phar Lap, on the strength of one start in Mexico, 22nd.

When the findings were published, one of the panel recalled a conversation with Francis Dunne, who had been a placings judge at Agua Caliente and later a senior racing administrator in New York State. Dunne was asked, after Secretariat's Triple Crown win in 1973, whether he thought Man O' War or Secretariat was the greatest horse of them all. He replied, 'Neither: I saw Phar Lap.'

PHAR LAP

ANONYMOUS

How you thrilled the racing public with your matchless strength
and grace;
With your peerless staying power and your dazzling burst of pace.
You toyed with your opponents with a confidence so rare,
Flashing past the winning post with lengths and lengths to spare.
No distance ever proved too great, no horse or handicap,
Could stop you winning races like a champion, Phar Lap.

With a minimum of effort you would simply bowl along,
With a stride so devastating and an action smooth and strong.
And you vied with the immortals when, on Flemington's
green track,
You won the Melbourne Cup with nine stone twelve upon
your back.
How the hearts of thousands quickened as you cantered back
old chap,
With your grand head proudly nodding to the crowd that yelled,
'Phar Lap.'

Who that saw it could forget it—how you won the Craven Plate?
When a mighty son of Rosedale, whom we'd justly labelled 'great',
Clapped the pace on from the start in a middle-distance race,
Just to test you to the limit of endurance, grit and pace.
He was galloping so strongly that the stands began to clap,
For it seemed as though your lustre would be dimmed at last,
Phar Lap.

But you trailed him like a bloodhound till your nostrils touched
his rump
Then your jockey asked the question and, with one tremendous
jump,
Something like a chestnut meteor hurtled past a blur of black
And, before the crowd stopped gasping, you were halfway down
the track,
And, the further that you travelled, ever wider grew the gap,
And you broke another record—one you'd set yourself, Phar Lap.

The hopes of all Australians travelled with you overseas,
Wishing to inspire you to further victories.
And at Agua Caliente you proved you were the best,
Then your great heart stopped beating—so they brought it home
to rest.
And Australians won't forget you while the roots of life hold sap,
For the greatest racehorse that was ever foaled was you, Phar Lap.

GLOSSARY

ALLOWANCES The weight a horse must carry can be reduced because an apprentice is riding the horse—this allowance starts at 4 kilograms and reduces in stages as the apprentice rides a certain number of winners, until he or she may have 'outridden their allowance'.

APPRENTICE An apprentice is a future jockey. He or she must be at least sixteen years of age. In less important races, apprentices receive weight allowances.

BETTING RING A betting ring is the group of bookmakers taking bets on the race day on the course.

BIRDCAGE A birdcage is an enclosure where horses parade and are unsaddled after a race. Only authorised people are permitted in this area.

BLEED Horses occasionally bleed at the nose due to rupturing blood vessels. These horses have to be excluded from racing for a time, and horses that bleed twice are banned from racing again.

BLINKERS Blinkers are side pieces attached to a horse's head to prevent sideways vision. They are used to keep horses focused.

BOG TRACK If the turf is extremely wet, it is described as a bog track. In Australia track conditions are listed as fast (close to perfect), good, dead, slow and heavy (very wet).

BOOKMAKER The bookmaker is the person who sets the odds for a race and takes the bets on it. Skilled bookmakers set their 'book' to win most races.

BROODMARE A broodmare is a female horse used for breeding.

COLT A colt is a male horse that has not been gelded and is less than four years old.

CRACK In horse circles 'crack' means the best. It can refer to the horse or the jockey.

CUP The Melbourne Cup is the only true cup race, although many cups can be won in racing. It originated in 1861 and was run over 2 miles, now 3200 metres. The Melbourne Cup is a handicap race for all horses and is held on the first Tuesday in November.

DAM A horse's female parent; a granddam is the female grand-parent. A horse is said to be 'out of' its dam.

DEAD HEAT The term dead heat is used when two horses cross the finish line together. When races were run over three heats, any dead heats were re-run.

DERBY The Derby originated in England in 1780, with the first Derby held in Surrey at Epsom Downs. The race was named after the winner of the toss of a coin between the 12th Earl of Derby and Sir Charles Bunbury. Diomed, owned by the steward of the jockey club, Sir Charles Bunbury, won the first Derby. Traditionally the Derby is the classic race of the turf, restricted to three-year-old horses and run over 1½ miles (2400 metres).

DISTANCE A large pole situated on each racecourse in earlier times, sometimes about a furlong from the winning post or near the turn, was known as 'the distance' and horses that did not 'make the distance' in a heat were 'out of the running' and could not compete in the subsequent heats.

FILLY A filly is a female horse less than four years old. When a filly becomes a four-year-old, she is called a mare. Once a mare gets to stud, she becomes a broodmare.

FIRST-UP A horse returning to the races from a spell is said to be first-up. If that horse wins its first race, it is referred to as a first-up victory. Some horses are 'first-up' specialists and race well 'fresh'.

FLAT The public enclosure in the centre of the track with a restricted view of the races. A very cheap or free enclosure, now defunct in Australia except at Oakbank.

FLAT RACING Racing without jumping.

FURLONG A furlong is one-eighth of a mile, or 201.168 metres after metric measurements were introduced in Australia on 1 August 1972.

GELDING A gelding is a male horse whose testicles have been surgically removed. In general, geldings are easier to train.

HANDICAP A handicap is a race where the horses are given advantages or disadvantages in weight to give each entrant an equal chance of winning.

HANDS The height of a horse is measured in hands; 1 hand equals 4 inches or 11.6 centimetres. Most thoroughbred horses stand at 15 to 17 hands. A horse is generally taller than 14.3 hands or 59 inches (150 centimetres). Under that it is a 'pony'.

LAYING IN/LAYING OUT Under pressure or when fatigued, some horses tend to shift ground to one side or the other.

LEGER The second best, and less expensive, public enclosure at racetracks, a furlong from the winning post—now defunct.

LENGTH In racing, place and winning margins are measured in lengths. A length is the distance from the nose of a winning horse to its hindquarters. As horses vary in size, so does the length; however, the variation is very small. On average a length is slightly greater than 2 metres. Margins of less than a length are a neck, a half-neck, a half-head, a short half-head and a nose.

MAIDEN A horse that has never won a race; or a race for such horses.

MEMBERS 'The Members' is the enclosure reserved for the members of that club and their guests. It has the best view of the course and the winning post.

OAKS The Oaks race day originated in England in 1779 and is the female equivalent of the Derby, restricted to three-year-old fillies. It was named after the Surrey residence of the Earl of Derby.

ODDS The bookmaker sets the odds or probability of a horse winning the race. As the amount of money bet on a horse increases, the odds are reduced as the horse's chances of winning seem to increase.

PADDOCK The main public enclosure on a racetrack, these days often called the Public Enclosure (as opposed to the Members). Originally it was a paddock where horses were paraded, saddled and mounted before each race.

PLUNGE A large amount of money suddenly invested on one horse—often in a planned 'coup' in an attempt to get as much money on as possible before the odds are lowered.

ST LEGER A classic long-distance race.

SECOND UP The second race after a 'spell'. Horses are generally thought to perform poorly 'second up'.

SHIFT OUT A horse that 'shifts out' moves away from the fence to a firmer, faster part of the track or to get a clear run. If forced to do so, a horse may also shift towards the fence. Horses often drift in or out when tired or whipped, this is referred to as 'shifting under pressure'.

SIRE A sire is a horse's male parent; a grandsire is a horse's male grandparent. A horse is said be 'by' the sire.

SPELL A spell is a break from training and racing where a horse can rest and put on weight in a paddock.

SPRINTER A sprinter is a horse that races short distances, from 800 to 1400 metres.

STAKES Stakes are racing events offering large amounts of money for the winner and the placegetters.

STAYER A stayer is a horse that races long distances of 2000 metres or more. A good stayer is not only able to run the distance but is also fast enough to win.

STEEPLECHASE A steeplechase is a race over many different and difficult obstacles. Originally it was a cross-country race with a church tower serving as a landmark to guide the riders.

STRAIGHT-OUT BET A straight-out bet is a bet for a win only. If a field is small or has a short-priced favourite horse, the bookmaker takes win bets only. If a horse completely dominates the race, the bookmaker will not take any bets.

STRAPPER A strapper is a stablehand caring for one or several horses on raceday.

STUD A property specifically set up for breeding horses.

TOUT Also called 'coat-tugger', 'urger' or 'whisperer', a tout is a person who makes a living selling tips on a racetrack by various methods, often nefarious and unprincipled—a con man.

WASTE Most jockeys struggle to keep their weight low. They use exercise, fasting and sweating to reduce their weight and these methods are called wasting.

WEIGHT-FOR-AGE Weight-for-age (or wfa) is a method of weight allocation for horses, allowing horses of different ages and gender to compete in the same race under the most equal conditions. Top races use a weight-for-age scale, allowing the best horse to win. The scale was introduced in England in the eighteenth century and has been modified slightly over the years.

YEARLING A yearling is a one-year-old horse. To standardise horses' ages, every racehorse in Australia turns one year older on 1 August.

ACKNOWLEDGEMENTS

I would like to thank Rebecca Kaiser and Michelle Swainson at Allen & Unwin and copyeditor Susin Chow, who was the best person we could have found for the job. Thanks to Les Carlyon, David Hickie, Bruce Montgomerie, Wayne Peake, Peter Harris, Tony Kneebone, Penny Hand, Phil Purser, and Betty Lane Holland for their willingness to be part of this collection.

For the photos—thanks to the old AJC Library and the Victorian Racing Museum, and those two great racing photographers, Steve Hart and Ern McQuillan.